THE AUTHOR

E. Hudson Long, Chairman of the Department of English and Co-Chairman of the Department of American Civilization at Baylor University, has long been recognized as one of the leading authorities on Mark Twain. The present book, for which he was aided by Carnegie research grants during the summers of 1948 and 1949, is the result of many years of reading and collecting Mark Twain's works and Twain scholarship.

He has also contributed articles on Mark Twain, and other American authors, to literary magazines and scholarly journals and is the author of *O. Henry, The Man and His Work* and co-editor of *The American Tradition in Literature*.

A native of Texas, Dr. Long attended public schools in Dallas and Baylor University in Waco, receiving from the latter the degrees of bachelor of arts and master of arts. He did graduate work at the University of Virginia, was an extra-mural student at Oxford University, and received his doctorate from the University of Pennsylvania. He has taught at Vanderbilt University, Ohio State University, University of Pennsylvania, University of Delaware, and Alabama Polytechnic Institute. During the Second World War he was Assistant Historian of the Combined Chiefs of Staff, in Washington.

DBOOK

MARK TWAIN HANDBOOK

By

E. Hudson Long

Baylor University

HENDRICKS HOUSE • NEW YORK

Manufactured in the United States of America

To Martha and Crawford

CONTENTS

PREFACE

THROUGH THE YEARS a great deal of Mark Twain scholarship has accumulated. From 1940 through 1950 more items of research were published about Samuel Clemens than any other American author, his work is beginning to receive more serious attention abroad, and at the same time his general popularity remains secure with the reading public. But as with most major authors we find a diversity of opinion about his life and writings. My purpose has been not only to summarize Twain scholarship but to evaluate the various contributions; another objective has been to indicate what still needs to be done. For instance, there is no definitive edition of Twain's complete works; many fugitive pieces are undiscovered; full collections of his letters and speeches are yet to be made; and periods of his life, such as the years on the Mississippi and those spent abroad, await fuller investigation.

Even now important scholarship is in progress. Dr. Henry Nash Smith, literary executor of the Mark Twain Estate, is engaged upon a definitive biography; and recently a large collection of family letters, scrapbooks, and miscellany has been added to the Twain collection at the University of California, from which Dr. Smith will add to our knowledge of Mark Twain.

My research was supported in part by funds made available jointly by the Carnegie Foundation and Vanderbilt University, and I wish to thank Dr. Walter Clyde Curry for his kindness in securing this assistance for me. I am deeply grateful to the late Dixon Wecter for his many acts of friendship and his generosity in granting me access to the unpublished materials of the Mark Twain Literary Estate. It was a privilege while at the Huntington Library to discuss Mark Twain with Dr. Franklin Walker and Dr. Norman Holmes Pearson. I am indebted to a number of other friends and scholars: Dr. Richmond Croom Beatty generously gave his time to read my entire manuscript; Dr. Sculley Bradley offered valuable suggestions and encouragement; Miss Edna Haney assisted me in reading proof.

For their assistance I wish to express my appreciation to the librarians and staffs of the Henry E. Huntington Library and Art Gallery, the Joint University Library at Nashville, Tennessee, the Library of the University of Texas, and the Baylor University Library.

I am grateful to Dr. Gay W. Allen, general editor of the "Handbooks of American Literature," for his consideration and helpfulness. Dr. Walter Hendricks, the publisher, gave his time and interest to make this a better book. And to my wife I am especially indebted for help and encouragement.

E. H. L.

Waco, Texas

ACKNOWLEDGMENTS

I WISH TO express my appreciation to Harper & Brothers, Publishers, for permission to quote from the following copyrighted books by Mark Twain: *What Is Man? and Other Essays, The Mysterious Stranger and Other Stories, Europe and Elsewhere, Mark Twain's Letters, Mark Twain's Autobiography, Mark Twain's Notebook, Mark Twain in Eruption,* and *The Love Letters of Mark Twain*; and I thank Harper & Brothers for permission to quote from *Mark Twain: A Biography* by Albert Bigelow Paine, and from *A Bibliography of the Works of Mark Twain* by Merle Johnson.

Grateful acknowledgment is made also to the authors and publishers for permission to quote from the following copyrighted publications:

Mark Twain's Travels with Mr. Brown, copyright 1940 by Alfred A. Knopf, Inc.

The Curious Republic of Gondour by Samuel L. Clemens, copyright 1919 by Boni and Liveright. Used by permission of Liveright Publishing Corporation.

The Adventures of Thomas Jefferson Snodgrass by Mark Twain, copyright 1928 by Pascal Covici. Used by permission of Crown Publishers, Inc.

The Letters of Quintus Curtius Snodgrass by Mark Twain, copyright 1946 by Southern Methodist University Press.

Mark Twain, Business Man by Samuel C. Webster, copyright 1946 by the author.

Mark Twain at Work by Bernard DeVoto, copyright 1942 by Harvard University Press.

Mark Twain's America by Bernard DeVoto, copyright 1932 by the author.

Lionel Trilling's Introduction to *Adventures of Huckleberry Finn,* copyright 1948 by Rinehart & Company, Inc.

Mark Twain, Son of Missouri by Minnie M. Brashear, copyright 1934 by University of North Carolina Press.

Mark Twain: The Man and His Work by Edward Wagenknecht, copyright 1935 by Yale University Press.

Sam Clemens of Hannibal by Dixon Wecter, copyright 1952 by Houghton Mifflin Company.

The Ordeal of Mark Twain by Van Wyck Brooks, copyright 1933 by E. P. Dutton & Company, Inc.

Mark Twain in Nevada by Effie Mona Mack, copyright 1947 by Charles Scribner's Sons.

Mark Twain by Stephen Leacock, copyright 1933 by Appleton-Century-Crofts, Inc.

Life of Bret Harte by Thomas E. Pemberton, copyright 1903 by Dodd, Mead & Company, Inc.

Mark Twain: Man and Legend by DeLancey Ferguson, copyright 1943 by Bobbs-Merrill Company, Inc.

The League of Frightened Philistines by James T. Farrell, copyright 1937 by Vanguard Press, Inc.

American Literature: A Journal of Literary History, Criticism, and Bibliography, published by Duke University Press.

Michigan Alumnus, published by the Alumni Association of the University of Michigan.

CHRONOLOGICAL TABLE

Significant Events in Mark Twain's Life, and Publication Dates.

1835	Born at Florida, Missouri, November 30.
1839	The Clemens family moved to Hannibal, Missouri.
1847	John Marshall Clemens died in March.
1847	Worked as a printer on either the Hannibal *Journal* or *Gazette*, following his father's death.
1848–50	Probably worked for Joseph P. Ament as a printer on the Hannibal *Courier*. Worked perhaps until 1851.
1850–52	Orion Clemens started the *Western Union* in September, 1850. In the spring of 1851 he combined it with the Hannibal *Weekly Dollar Journal* under the name Hannibal *Journal and Western Union*, which became the *Journal* in February, 1852. Sam helped his brother.
1852	"The Dandy Frightening the Squatter" appeared in the *Carpet-Bag* for May.
1853	Left Hannibal in June to go to St. Louis.
1853	August, in New York. Visited Philadelphia during the winter and corresponded for the Muscatine (Iowa) *Journal*.
1854	February, visited Washington, D. C.
1854	Summer, in Muscatine, Iowa with his mother and Orion. Probably worked on Muscantine *Journal*.
1855	Winter and spring, in St. Louis. Joined Orion in Keokuk during the summer.
1856	Worked for his brother, in Keokuk until fall. Left again for St. Louis.
1856	October 18, began the Thomas Jefferson Snodgrass letters for Keokuk (Iowa) *Daily Post*. Moved from St. Louis to Cincinnati.
1857	Lived in Cincinnati during the winter and met the Scotchman named Macfarlane.

1857 April, boarded the *Paul Jones* for New Orleans, intending to go to South America, but met Horace Bixby, who agreed to teach him the river.

1858 Learned the river as a "cub" and piloted freighters.

1858 June, brother Henry killed in steamboat explosion. Sam reproached himself because of quarrel with the pilot which had caused him to be left behind instead of Henry.

1859 April 9, Samuel Clemens' pilot license granted.

1859 Wrote "Sergeant Fathom" burlesque of Isaiah Sellers, New Orleans (daily) *Crescent,* May 17.

1861 Outbreak of the Civil War put an end to piloting. January 21, first "Quintus Curtius Snodgrass" letter in New Orleans (daily) *Crescent,* the last appearing on March 30.

1861 June, "campaign that failed" service in Missouri.

1861 Twenty-one day journey by stagecoach to Carson City, Nevada, during late July and early August.

1862 The "Josh" letters for the *Virginia City Territorial Enterprise,* written between mid-February and the last of July.

1862 August, joined the staff of the *Enterprise,* to remain there until May, 1864.

1862 "The Petrified Man" hoax published in *Territorial Enterprise,* probably October 5; reprinted by *San Francisco Daily Evening Bulletin,* October 15.

1862 During November and December, reported the Second Territorial Legislature of Nevada from Carson City for the *Enterprise.*

1863 February 2, in a dispatch to the *Enterprise* from Carson City, first signed himself "Mark Twain."

1863 Early summer, first visit to San Francisco, in company with friendly-rival newspaperman, Clement T. Rice (The Unreliable).

1863 "The Empire City Massacre" hoax printed in *Territorial Enterprise,* October 28.

1863 December, met Artemus Ward, at Virginia City.

1864 January, elected "Governor" of the Third House by fellow newspapermen at Carson City.

1864 February 21, New York *Sunday Mercury* published "Those Blasted Children," Twain's first known Eastern publication. Reprinted by the San Francisco *Golden Era,* March 27.

1864 May, became involved in a controversy with a rival editor, leading to a proposed duel, in violation of Nevada law, which caused Mark's exit to San Francisco.

1864 Summer and fall, worked for the San Francisco *Morning Call,* the *Golden Era,* and the *Californian.*

1864 Exposure of municipal corruption led to departure from San Francisco to the Tuolumne Hills in the Mother Lode Country in December.

1865 January, pocket-mining at Angel's Camp.

February, returned to San Francisco; wrote "Jim Smiley and His Jumping Frog" which reached Artemus Ward too late for inclusion in his book.

1865 November 18, the "Jumping Frog" story printed in the New York *Saturday Press.*

Supported himself in San Francisco by writing potboilers for the press.

1866 March 7, sailed for the Sandwich Islands to write a series of travel letters for the Sacramento *Union;* in Hawaii four months and a day.

1866 June 25, special dispatch on the burning of the clipper ship *Hornet* at sea.

1866 October 2, embarked on the lecture platform, talking on the Sandwich Islands at the San Francisco Academy of Music. Popularity of this lecture brought a tour of California and Nevada, resulting in great popularity.

1866 December, sailed for New York, crossed the isthmus.

1867 January, arrived in New York.

1867 March and April, visited St. Louis, Hannibal, and Keokuk.

1867 May, *The Celebrated Jumping Frog of Calaveras*

County, and Other Sketches published by C. H. Webb in New York.

1867 May 6, lectured successfully at Cooper Union in New York.

1867 June 8, sailed on the *Quaker City* for the Holy Land excursion as correspondent for the San Francisco *Alta California.*

1867 November 19, returned to New York.

1867 November, served briefly as private secretary to Senator William M. Stewart of Nevada.

1867 December 27, first meeting with Olivia Langdon.

1868 January 2 or 3, first date with Olivia, to hear Charles Dickens read.

1868 March, journeyed to California to secure publishing rights to his *Alta* correspondence. Lectured there during the spring and summer. July 6, sailed for New York.

1868 August, first visit with the Langdon family in Elmira.

1868 November and December, conducted strenuous lecture tour.

1869 February 4, became engaged to marry Olivia.

1869 July, *The Innocents Abroad* published.

1869 August, purchased a partnership in the Buffalo *Express* through loan of $25,000 from Jervis Langdon.

1869 November and December, lectured under James Redpath's management.

1870 January, continued lecture tour.

1870 February 2, married Olivia Langdon.

1870 March, wrote for the New York *Galaxy,* until April, 1871.

1870 July 5, hasty trip to Washington, photographed by Matthew Brady, and met General Grant.

1870 August 6, Jervis Langdon died.

1870 November 7, Langdon Clemens prematurely born in Buffalo.

1871 February, *Mark Twain's (Burlesque) Autobiography and First Romance* published in New York.

1871 Spring and summer, the Clemens family vacationed at

Quarry Farm, Elmira, New York, henceforth to be their favorite summer retreat.

1871 October, moved to Hartford, Connecticut, renting a house at Nook Farm.

1871 Fall lecture tour to finish paying debts caused by sacrifice of Buffalo interests.

1872 Lecture tour continued through early February.

1872 February, *Roughing It* published by the American Publishing Company.

1872 March 19, Olivia Susan (Susy) Clemens born.

1872 June 2, Langdon Clemens died (Twain's only son).

1872 August, sailed for England.

1872 November 9, honored at Lord Mayor's dinner in London.

1873 Summer spent in Britain and on the Continent with family.

1873 November–December, lectured in England.

1873 December, *The Gilded Age* in collaboration with Charles Dudley Warner, published by the American Publishing Company.

1874 January, sailed home from England.

1874 June, Clara Clemens born.

1874 September, dramatized version of *The Gilded Age* opened in New York.

1875 *Old Times on the Mississippi* appeared in the *Atlantic Monthly,* January–June and August.

1875 July 21, *Sketches, New and Old,* published by the American Publishing Company.

1876 December, *The Adventures of Tom Sawyer* published by the American Publishing Company.

1877 April, production of a play *Ah Sin* in collaboration with Bret Harte, which opened in Washington, May 7.

1877 May 16, visited Bermuda with Rev. Joseph Twichell.

1877 September, *A True Story and the Recent Carnival of Crime* published by James R. Osgood.

1877 December 17, made Whittier birthday speech in Boston.

1878 March, *Punch, Brothers, Punch! and Other Sketches* published by Slote, Woodman and Company.

1878 August, walking tour with Twichell through the Black Forest.

1878–79 Lived abroad in Germany and Italy.

1880 March, *A Tramp Abroad* published by the American Publishing Company.

1880 June, the so-called "Cleveland Edition" of *1601, or Conversation as It Was by the Fireside in the Time of the Tudors.* The "West Point" edition seems to have been 1882.

1880 July 26, Jean Clemens born.

1881 November, visited Canada for a fortnight.

1882 January, *The Prince and the Pauper* published by James R. Osgood.

1882 April–May, trip down the Mississippi to New Orleans, and a return journey with Horace Bixby.

1882 June, *The Stolen White Elephant* published by James R. Osgood.

1883 May, *Life on the Mississippi* published by James R. Osgood.

1883 May, again visited Canada briefly.

1884 Summer, campaigned for Grover Cleveland.

1884 November–December, lecture tours with Cable.

1885 January, *Adventures of Huckleberry Finn* published by Charles L. Webster and Company.

1885 January–February, continued lecture tour with Cable.

1885 Fall, published General Grant's *Memoirs.*

1888 Master of Arts degree from Yale.

1889 December, *A Connecticut Yankee in King Arthur's Court* published by Charles L. Webster and Company.

1890 Summer, engrossed in the Paige typesetting machine.

1890 Autumn, Susy entered Bryn Mawr.

1891 June, family closed Hartford home and went to Europe.

1891–92 Winter in Berlin.

1892 March, *Merry Tales* published by Charles L. Webster and Company.

1892	May, *The American Claimant* published by Charles L. Webster and Company.
1893	February 25, The *£1,000,000 Bank-Note* published by Charles L. Webster and Company.
1893	Spring, family in Italy; Twain made trips to America to stave off failure of the Paige machine.
1894	Spring, *Tom Sawyer Abroad* published by Charles L. Webster and Company.
1894	April 18, Charles L. Webster and Company executed assignment papers, carrying Samuel Clemens into bankruptcy with it.
1894	Summer, Clemens' family remained in France. Twain visited the United States in July and August.
1894	November, *The Tragedy of Pudd'nhead Wilson and the Comedy Those Extraordinary Twins* published by the American Publishing Company.
1894	Winter in Paris.
1895	May, returned home, spent early summer at Quarry Farm.
1895	Mid-July, commenced the lecture trip which produced *Following the Equator.*
1896	May, *Personal Recollections of Joan of Arc* published by Harper.
1896	August 18, Susy, favorite child, died.
1896	November 17, *Tom Sawyer Abroad, Tom Sawyer, Detective, and Other Stories* published by Harper.
1896	Winter in London.
1897	March, *How to Tell a Story and Other Essays* published by Harper.
1897	November, *Following the Equator* published by the American Publishing Company.
1898	Last debts paid during the winter.
1900	May, *How to Tell a Story and Other Essays,* with new material added, published by the American Publishing Company.
1900	June, *The Man That Corrupted Hadleyburg and Other Stories and Essays* published by Harper.

1900 October, *English as She Is Taught*, published by the Mutual Book Company of Boston.

1900 Autumn, returned to America, where he received a national welcome; took house at 14 West Tenth Street, New York.

1901 February, *To the Person Sitting in Darkness*, published by the Anti-Imperialist League of New York.

1901 Summer on Saranac Lake; fall cruise to Nova Scotia on Henry Rogers' yacht.

1901 October 20, Yale conferred the Litt. D. degree on Clemens.

1902 April, *A Double Barrelled Detective Story*, published by Harper.

1902 June, University of Missouri conferred LL. D. degree on Clemens.

1903 April, *My Debut as a Literary Person with Other Essays and Stories*.

1903 October, Clemens family settled in Italy for Livy's health.

1904 April, *Extracts from Adam's Diary*, published by Harper.

1904 June 5, Olivia Langdon Clemens died.

1904 September, *A Dog's Tale*, published by Harper.

1905 September, *King Leopold's Soliloquy* published by the R. P. Warren Company of Boston.

1906 *Eve's Diary; The $30,000 Bequest and Other Stories*, both published by Harper.

1907 February, *Christian Science* published by Harper.

1907 Oxford honored Clemens with the Litt. D. degree.

1907 October, *A Horse's Tale* published by Harper.

1909 April, *Is Shakespeare Dead?* published by Harper.

1909 *Extract from Captain Stormfield's Visit to Heaven* published by Harper.

1909 December 23, death of Jean.

1910 Mark Twain died April 21, buried at Elmira, New York.

1910 July, *Mark Twain's Speeches* published by Harper; a second edition issued in 1923.

1916 *The Mysterious Stranger* published by Harper.

1917 *What Is Man? and Other Essays* published by Harper. First published anonymously, August 20, 1906, at the De Vinne Press.

1917 *Mark Twain's Letters* published by Harper.

1919 *The Curious Republic of Gondour and Other Whimsical Sketches*, published by Boni and Liveright.

1923 *Europe and Elsewhere* published by Harper.

1924 *Mark Twain's Autobiography*, published by Harper.

1926 *Sketches of the Sixties* by Bret Harte and Mark Twain, published by John Howell, San Francisco.

1928 *The Adventures of Thomas Jefferson Snodgrass*, published by Pascal Covici, Chicago.

1935 *Mark Twain's Notebook*, published by Harper.

1935 *Slovenly Peter* (Der Struwwelpeter) translated by Mark Twain, published by the Limited Editions Club, later by Harper.

1938 *The Washoe Giant in San Francisco* (Sketches for the Golden Era) published by George Fields, San Francisco.

1938 *Mark Twain's Letters from the Sandwich Islands*, published by Stanford University Press.

1940 *Mark Twain's Travels with Mr. Brown*, published by Knopf.

1940 *Mark Twain in Eruption* (Autobiographical material), published by Harper.

1941 *Mark Twain's Letters to Will Bowen*, published by the University of Texas, Austin.

1942 *Mark Twain's Letters in the Muscatine Journal*, published by the Mark Twain Association of America, Chicago.

1946 *The Letters of Quintus Curtius Snodgrass*, published by Southern Methodist University Press in Dallas.

1949 *Mark Twain to Mrs. Fairbanks*, letters published by the Huntington Library.

1949 *The Love Letters of Mark Twain*, published by Harper.

1952 *Report from Paradise*, published by Harper.

MARK TWAIN HANDBOOK

CHAPTER I

THE GROWTH OF MARK TWAIN BIOGRAPHY

Introduction

More than any other classic American writer, Mark Twain assumes the proportions of a folk myth. He appeals to his readers not only as an author but also as a personality, for Samuel Clemens the man is often present in his books. Aside from his fame as a novelist, Twain's position in letters rests also upon works which are perhaps best described as fictionized autobiography. To his contemporaries, he was a personage—at his death, known and honored throughout the world; yet with the exception of a few discerning critics, Twain's age regarded him primarily as a humorist and a striking personality. The affection given Mark Twain was even more to the man, popular and beloved, than to a literary artist. Indeed, his writings were so much a part of his life that it becomes difficult to separate the two. So completely has Clemens been identified with his work that it remains the fashion—as with Poe—to read reflections of biography into his books. No other American author seems to have left so complete (if perplexing) an account of his own life, and some investigators have so often searched for subtle or devious meanings where probably none exist that the biography has sometimes suffered distortion.

Although at the time of Twain's death the number of critical studies devoted to him was not formidable, there has been a steady growth of interest until today the bibliographical material appearing annually rivals that concerning Poe, Melville, and Whitman. Mark Twain's emergence in the minds of our own day as a major figure in American literature, together with appreciation of his genius abroad, has produced a corresponding growth of biographical and critical writing. More than 200 articles and a dozen books have appeared since 1920, and two journals are devoted chiefly to him.[1]

At the same time that Samuel Clemens made the personality of Mark Twain interesting to the world, he also represented something distinctly American, for Twain was of the continental United States, a product of the same section which produced Abraham Lincoln.[2] The first major writer to emerge west of the Mississippi, he captured the American past, the idyll of the small town before the machine age, and the enduring romance of the great river. Besides, he was a born storyteller and a successful entertainer, and with these qualities he endeared himself to a vast, uncritical audience. As Clemens' position in our literature continues to rise, it becomes increasingly clear that Mark Twain possessed a profound knowledge of human beings in many and varied phases of life. Samuel Clemens the artist transmuted this into literature, and with an increasing appreciation of his literary creations there has come an equal interest in the mind of the man. Certain aspects of his life present a "problem" to psycho-analytical biographers; and critics, both friendly and unfriendly, have searched for the secrets of his innermost thoughts. Thus arises the question: was Mark Twain, in his own mind, afraid and a failure, or was he courageous and secure, as adult as Melville or Hawthorne in his realization of evil?

1 *The Twainian* and *Mark Twain Quarterly*.

2 The affinities between Twain and Lincoln are discussed by Bernard DeVoto, *The Portable Mark Twain* (New York: Viking Press, 1946), p. 5, and by Dixon Wecter, "One Word More," introduction to *The Adventures of Huckleberry Finn* (New York: Harpers, 1948), pp. xx–xxi.

Fortunately the major facts of Mark Twain's life are well known (a summary is given in this *Handbook* in a "Chronological Table," p. xiii). Of course, there are some obscure periods, such as the years immediately following the death of his father, which even the latest biographers have not revealed completely, but factual information has been gradually added by persistent scholarly activity. Samuel Clemens enjoyed the role assigned him by his own generation; because he liked acting a part, he dramatized his own life history by mingling actuality with fiction. Not the way it was, but as it should have been, was generally the way he told it; for Mark Twain, the creative artist, never let mere fact interfere with the narrative. Consequently biographers, although possessing a vast bulk of autobiographical material, have faced the difficult task of disentangling fact from fancy. Furthermore, with the paradox of Mark Twain the exuberant fun maker, on one hand, in contrast to the utterer of bitter pessimism on the other, the critics have explored the details of his intimate life for an explanation. In brief, Twain presents the fascination of questions to be answered; and as a result, criticism of his work has been invariably bound with a search into biographical fact.

Mark Twain biography has grown, then, with our interest in his work; and as his literary standing has risen, we have sought explanations through a greater knowledge of his life. By a process of simple accumulation of newly discovered facts, accurate knowledge of his backgrounds, and clearer insight into his motives, the story unfolds more reliably. Mark Twain the legend, the national figure, the great personality remains, but Mark Twain the man as he was and the author of international scope comes into focus. Whether Mark Twain stands at the apex of the first cycle of our American literature, taking his place with Whitman, Melville, and Hawthorne, or whether he marks the beginning of a new age in fiction, he remains a pivotal figure.

The change in attitude from that which dismissed Twain as a "phunny phellow" to Dixon Wecter's solemn declaration that *Huckleberry Finn* is "probably the greatest novel written in this hemisphere,"[3] tells much of the growth of modern literature and thought. What critics and biographers have thought of Mark Twain, how their theories evolved, and what they have concluded become interesting in evaluating the actual facts of his life. Yet to sift the chaff of legend from the grains of truth, we must first know why the different interpretations have arisen. Since each generation must solve its specific problems, the writings of Samuel Langhorne Clemens take on a new significance for the future, as they have increased our knowledge in the past. Whatever the trend in scholarship, however, whether Mark Twain's value should appear greatest as realist, satirist, or humanitarian, it was as a humorist that he looked upon this life.

Beginnings of Biography

John Camden Hotten's account of Twain's life appeared in 1873. Prefixed to the *Choice Humorous Works of Mark Twain,* it was republished in subsequent editions in London and helped to introduce the American humorist to the British public.[4] Hotten quoted liberally from Mark's own account of his activities, especially from *Roughing It,* to outline the career of a popular humorist and successful entertainer. This bare sketch, padded with anecdotes and with appreciations of Mark's humor taken from current journals, is the first glimpse that the reading public received of a life then seeming to hold no complexities.

The first separate biography of Samuel Clemens was *Mark Twain: The Story of His Life and Work* (1892) by

3 *Mark Twain* (San Marino, California: Huntington Library, 1947), p. 6.

4 *Choice Humorous Works of Mark Twain* (London: Chatto and Windus, 1873 revised 1888). Twain arranged with Chatto and Windus for a near-duplicate book of Hotten's edition of 1873, having the same title.

Will M. Clemens.[5] Despite three brief notes from Mark printed in the preface, he neither liked the book nor approved of its author, especially as many people mistook the man for a relative. For the facts of Twain biography this story holds little value, but as a source of materials that became part of the legend it is interesting. The American success story of the wild, reckless boy who starts as a poor printer and becomes "a man of family and a millionaire" unfolds.[6] Anecdotes are related, some obviously fictitious, a few genuine. The figure finally created is that of an entertainer who is also a serious thinker, and above all practical; in money matters, "He is a literary Midas."[7] With a ready wit he extricates himself from embarrassing situations, entertains people for hours with his conversation, and always enjoys a prank. Here are the legends and typical anecdotes such as have obscured Twain biography and made the facts difficult to ascertain.

In 1898 Robert Barr contributed a brief, unimportant character sketch to *McClure's Magazine*.[8] The following year, however, *McClure's* published an excellent short biographical appraisal by Mark's nephew, Samuel E. Moffett.[9] Though written by a relative, it is objective and not a family memoir. Twain himself liked this account of his life, which he considered accurate and appropriate.

5 This narration of Mark Twain's life is antedated only by the brief account from Hotten in his pirated *Choice Humorous Works* (London, 1873) and by a 16-page pamphlet, circa 1886, by an unknown author, and distributed free to the purchasers of Duke's Mixture Smoking Tobacco.

6 *Mark Twain: The Story of His Life and Work* (San Francisco: Clemens Publishing Co., 1892), p. 10.

7 *Ibid.,* p. 194.

8 Robert Barr, "Samuel L. Clemens, 'Mark Twain': A Character Sketch," *McClure's Magazine,* X, 246–251 (Jan., 1898).

9 "Mark Twain as Interpreter of American Character," *McClure's* XIII, 523–29 (Oct., 1899). This later appeared as "Mark Twain: A Biographical Sketch" in *The $30,000 Bequest,* and in recent editions of Twain is available in *In Defense of Harriet Shelley.* The author was a favorite nephew of Mark's, and the subject of the essay "Samuel Erasmus Moffett" in *Europe and Elsewhere.*

Testimony of Friends and Relatives

In September, 1910, William Dean Howells paid personal tribute to his friend. Although not a complete biography, *My Mark Twain* (1910) is an interesting record of intimate friendship between two leading literary figures. For its account of Samuel Clemens during the final years, *My Mark Twain* remains an important book, the best of the writings produced by his friends and associates. Howells does not minimize Twain's eccentricities, but he is far more concerned with the fundamental values of the man. What some might term vanity, Howells concedes to be love of the dramatic, feeling for costume, and a keen sense of pleasure in harmlessly shocking others. "He had," says Howells, "the Southwestern, the Lincolnian, the Elizabethan breadth of parlance, which I suppose one ought not to call coarse without calling one's self prudish."[10] There are intimate recollections; once Mark, wearing "white cowskin slippers, with the hair out," did an imitation of a "crippled colored uncle to the joy of all beholders." To Howells it seemed that Mark possessed "the heart of a boy with the head of a sage."[11]

None was in a better position to observe the home life of the Clemens family than Howells, who declared, "I should say that this marriage was one of the most perfect."[12] Livy always impressed him as an intelligent woman, kindly, and with the sense of humor necessary to appreciate Clemens' genius. Frequently a visitor in the home, Howells speaks from experience, and those who know Howells cannot doubt his veracity. Had he not approved of Mrs. Clemens, he might have maintained a gentlemanly silence, but he would never have falsified with praise.

Often during walks, he and Mark Twain admired na-

[10] William Dean Howells, *My Mark Twain* (New York: Harpers, 1910), p. 4.

[11] *Ibid.*, p. 5.

[12] *Ibid.*, p. 13.

ture, talked about books, and discussed their beliefs. Twain thought there must be a conscious source of things, but "he never went back to anything like faith in the Christian theology, or the notion of life after death, or in a conscious divinity."[13] Howells records Mark Twain's views on racial equality, his sympathy for the colored race, and his desire to ameliorate their condition; but Howell's statement that Mark had a colored butler "because he could not bear to order a white man about" implies a distinct awareness of racial differences.[14] The same abhorrence that caused him to detest slavery made him praise labor unions as the working-man's only hope of "standing up like a man against money and the power of it."[15] From these conversations, recalled by Howells, we gain a first-hand knowledge of many private attitudes and deep convictions. Memories of social visits reveal the lighter, though no less intimate, nature of Clemens. In the parlor, at the dinner table, or in the billiard room, many amusing or enlightening incidents occurred, which Howells charmingly preserved.

Howells' Mark Twain is a gay, entertaining, youthful man, kind, generous, wise, and filled with compassion. He admits that Mark's humor might sometimes shock or offend the uninitiated, and that one who did not know him might dislike his fiery outbursts; yet the reminiscences close:

> Emerson, Longfellow, Lowell, Holmes—I knew them all and all the rest of our sages, poets, seers, critics, humorists; they were like one another and like other literary men; but Clemens was sole, incomparable, the Lincoln of our literature.[16]

To this memoir of Samuel Clemens, Howells appended eighty pages of his own critical reviews of Mark Twain's books. Not only is *My Mark Twain* a primary source book for the later stages of Twain's life, but it is of interest as the

13 *Ibid.*, p. 32.
14 *Ibid.*, p. 34.
15 *Ibid.*, p. 43.
16 *Ibid.*, p.101.

opinion of a contemporary who valued his work and presented a critical appraisal that remains fresh. Here may be found the answers to many of the so-called "problems" magnified by subsequent critics of Clemens' life and work.

As I Remember Them (1913), based on the days when Joe Goodman, R. M. Daggett, Dan DeQuille, and Mark Twain were colleagues, preserves the personal recollections of a Virginia City journalist, C. C. Goodwin. A frontier newspaper man who became a judge, Goodwin vigorously recalled the fellowship and excitement enjoyed by Mark on the Comstock when Western journalism first schooled him for a career. Interesting in its portraits of Mark's associates—men from whom he learned much—the book provides a vivid narrative of hearty times. Not a biography of Clemens in any sense, *As I Remember Them* preserves the associations and friendships contributing to the development of Mark Twain—all told by one who knew them.[17]

While vacationing in Bermuda, Elizabeth Wallace, a school teacher, met Mark Twain during his final years; she later visited at Stormfield and corresponded with him. Her recollections in *Mark Twain and the Happy Island* (1913), reveal chiefly the tender, considerate side of his nature. Miss Wallace remembered his attachment to children, particularly little girls, and his entertaining conversations, occasionally enlivened by tirades against the "general asininity of us all."[18] She recalled, also, that Clemens nourished a "particularly tender spot in his heart for all things English."[19] To her he was "the King," courteous, considerate, generous, and lovable, which the letters included in this idyllic presentation seem to confirm.

Of Mark Twain's readers, none was more enthusiastic

17 C. C. Goodwin, *As I Remember Them* (Salt Lake City: Salt Lake Commercial Club, 1913).

18 Elizabeth Wallace, *Mark Twain and the Happy Island* (Chicago: A. C. McClurg, 1913), p. 15.

19 *Ibid.*, p. 58.

than Brander Matthews, Columbia University English professor, literary historian, and critic. From the *Jumping Frog* in its original edition, Matthews followed each succeeding volume, his conviction growing that Twain was a native humorist worthy to stand beside the great figures of literature. This ardent interest, stimulated by a personal meeting in 1883, matured into friendship. Matthews knew Twain's faults, and he has told them in "Memories of Mark Twain" in *The Tocsin of Revolt* (1922). As a member of the American Copyright League, Matthews found that even a great humorist can sometimes take himself too seriously. Other times he observed Mark's hair-trigger temper, which could smolder steadily into hatred. But their friendship, despite a few upsets, continued through years of banqueting, speeches, and vacations filled with games—happy times when Mark acted like a boy.

These memories are interesting also because Twain confided to Matthews how his books wrote themselves, stopping when the tank of inspiration ran dry, and refusing to commence until it filled again. Of equal interest is the account of Mark's speeches, a few of which astonishingly failed because of an unfortunate choice of subject. To Matthews, it seemed that Samuel L. Clemens the man and Mark Twain the writer ever remained separate personalities, one the embodiment of ethical integrity, the other the droll humorist. Both met only when Clemens' natural dignity appeared through his fun making. Through these friendly pages we see a great storyteller, a witty speaker, a man who retained the impulsiveness of boyhood. Matthews, in fact, saw youth in the white suit and Oxford gown: "When he robed himself thus in burning red or in snowy white, he was a boy again, he was Tom Sawyer. . . ."[20] This was Mark Twain; then Samuel L. Clemens appears in the portrait of

20 "Memories of Mark Twain," *The Tocsin of Revolt* (New York: Scribners, 1922), p. 292.

a devoted husband, kind father, honorable business man, and finally the disenchanted, serious observer of the human scene. Matthews readily admits, however, that with so complex a subject as Twain there could be many interpretations.

A Lifetime with Mark Twain (1925) is the story of Katy Leary, faithful and devoted servant for more than thirty years in the Clemens household. Katy recalled the family before the fireplace after dinner, with Mark reading aloud from Browning or Dickens; then about nine o'clock when the children had gone to bed, the butler brought in "a pitcher of hot water and a bottle of the best Scotch whiskey" for Mark, while Mrs. Clemens took tea. "After they'd had the tea and the toddy, they would set [sic] and talk and laugh—happy and contented; and then they'd go to bed about ten o'clock, and that would finish the day."[21]

Through these intimate recollections we see the family entertaining with dinner parties, play productions for the children, or Mark Twain spinning stories. Henry Irving once told Katy that Mark had "the makings of a very great actor in him."[22] Mrs. Clemens was beloved by her servant; if Mark was ever "henpecked" by Livy, it escaped the eyes of Katy Leary. Katy knew the Clemens family intimately through their economic depression and their journeys abroad. As death took Susy, Jean, Mrs. Clemens, and finally Mark Twain, she continued to serve, remaining with Clara when all the rest were gone. To her simple mind, Mark was a great man, kind, generous, and admirable, despite his eccentricities and outbursts of temper. For her the Clemens family remained as perfect as Katy could have wished.

Unfortunately better known than Goodwin's book, *Gold*

21 Mary Lawton, *A Lifetime with Mark Twain* (New York: Harcourt, Brace, 1925), p. 9.

22 *Ibid.*, p. 36.

Rush Days with Mark Twain (1930) is less reliable. And although at publication the reviewers generally accepted it at face value, the book actually is neither biography nor criticism. Originally published in pamphlet form as *Memories of Mark Twain and Steve Gillis,* it is full of contradictions and inaccuracies, for "Bill" Gillis as an old man remembered not only much that never happened, but incorrectly nearly everything that did.[23] It has no biographical value, and its only interest for the reader of Mark Twain is that "Bill" Gillis was among those who once had seen him.

Clara Clemens' *My Father, Mark Twain* (1931) is informal biography, making no pretense at being a full-length study, but it presents her father as his family knew him. It is an important supplement to our biographical material, fresh, revealing, a picture of private life that could come from no other source. Through the eyes of his daughter we see a more intimate side of Twain's personality than was revealed by Howells. Here is the private life of a father with his children, told by a daughter, who was often a close comrade. The book, well illustrated from family photographs, makes available, also, a number of hitherto unpublished letters. Mark appears first as the father of three little girls, whom he always had time to entertain, and for whom he always showed love and consideration. Like Howells, Clara Clemens remembers his solicitation for anyone in distress. In fact, the general picture of the home, while more intimate, is essentially the same as that given by Howells. And the love story of Mark and Livy remains as Howells described it, and as Mark himself declared it, from the time before his wedding when he wrote, ". . . I am so happy I hardly know what to do with myself—and I bless

23 William R. Gillis, *Goldrush Days with Mark Twain* (New York: Boni, 1930). The original pamphlet was published by the Sonora, California, *Banner* in 1924.

you, and give honest gratitude to God that it is so,"[24] until in remorse he referred to her as "she that was the life of my life."[25]

The Clemens temper is not neglected, but revealed through anecdotes and letters. To a supplicant for favor, Mark exploded: "I have long wanted to meet you, get acquainted with you and kill you. . . . What do you want with a consulship? What you want is a rope. . . . The thing for you is a burial permit. You have only to speak, I will see that you get it."[26] When some people whom he disliked called, he said: "All the old cats in Christendom seem to have chosen this particular day to visit here. It never rains disagreeable people but it pours them. . . . When I get a sight of either of these women I am 'done' for that day. When they both come in one evening I degenerate into pure lunacy."[27] The youthful delight in shocking people (already noted by Howells) is further revealed by his daughter. Once when Livy read to him about a very devout minister, Mark began to dance a hornpipe while he sang irreverent nonsense.[28] And Livy, as her daughter recalled, torn between "mirth and horror," shrieked with dismay. Clara Clemens remembered her own embarrassment when Mark said to their clergyman, his intimate friend, Joseph Twichell, "Joe, that's a clever trick of yours to pound the pulpit extra hard when you haven't anything to say." To which Twichell laughingly replied, "Mark, it was clever of you to discover it."[29]

My Father, Mark Twain gives an account of Clemens' financial failure and his efforts to pay his debts that parallels the ones by Howells and Albert Bigelow Paine. The

24 Clara Clemens, *My Father, Mark Twain* (New York: Harpers, 1931), p. 13.

25 *Ibid.*, p. 253.

26 *Ibid.*, p. 69–70.

27 *Ibid.*, p. 84.

28 *Ibid.*, p. 26.

29 *Idem.*

relationship of the author with his family, remembered by Clara Clemens, shows Twain delighting in his home and enjoying his friends. He exhibits a sensitive nature, upset by annoyances, frequently giving way to temper—essentially the same type of character that appeared to William Dean Howells.

There are more personal touches, such as the reference to his "favorite 'dishes' cooked in the old Southern way."[30] The white clothes and the Oxford robe also have their place in the story, for to his daughter Mark Twain's desire to attract attention is no more psychologically confusing than it was to Howells. He enjoyed it with a boyish delight that Tom Sawyer would have understood. And Clara Clemens reveals Twain's profound gratitude to Henry H. Rogers, the Standard Oil Company official, who aided Clemens to recoup his fortune. Indeed, the entire family acclaimed Rogers their most generous friend.[31]

The chief value of Clara Clemens' book is its picture of Mark Twain with his family, and the letters that are included intimately reveal Mark's devotion to Olivia. Though nothing more than a story of the Clemens home as it centered around Twain, this book is necessary to anyone seeking to deal with the problems created by Brooks and his followers.

Mark Twain, Business Man (1946) was written by Samuel Charles Webster as a vindication of his father Charles L. Webster, to whom Clemens seemed at times impossible in business dealings. More interesting to the student of Twain, however, is the new information contributed about the Clemens family at the beginning of the Civil War. Webster gives the most complete portrait that we have of Mark Twain's mother, remembered at first hand by members of the family. Here, too, are letters more intimate than any published since Clara Clemens' book. Not only Jane Clem-

30 *Ibid.*, p. 78.

31 *Ibid.*, p. 83.

ens, but Annie Moffett Webster, Pamela, Orion, and his wife, Mollie Stotts Clemens, receive their fullest treatment to that date. Webster traces the ancestry and background of Mark Twain's immediate family from its origins on both sides in Virginia through the migrations which ended in Hannibal.

Samuel Clemens the young man appears, who buys good clothes as soon as he can afford them, and whose keen interest in attractive dress was increased, no doubt, because earlier he had had to wear "hand-me-downs, not from the shelves but from the boss."[32] And the young man even studies French. The youthful delight in innocently shocking people continued, and his niece, Annie Moffett Webster, was sometimes a victim. This same niece has preserved a vivid memory of Jane Clemens:

> She was a great beauty, a fine dancer, and very witty. She kept her beauty to the last, as well as her love of color and dancing. I have known her to dance when she was seventy-five. She was very straight and dignified. When she went back to Keokuk in her last years to live with Uncle Orion he said that when she went to the theater dressed in her black velvet with white lace, her lavender kid gloves and ostrich-tip bonnet, she always created a stir. At eighty-five she looked the duchess.[33]

Jane's love of color was as great as Mark's; not only did she decorate with red, she would also have liked to wear it. She enjoyed embroidery and knitting. She loved to meet people, but her dislikes were strong. She never tired of telling stories of her early days, speaking in a soft, drawling voice, much like her son's. John Marshall Clemens, as described by his widow to her niece, was "a man of great dignity, a keen sense of honor, and the highest degree of neatness and fastidiousness."[34] One sees that Twain inherited qualities from both parents.

[32] Samuel C. Webster, *Mark Twain, Business Man* (Boston: Little, Brown & Co., 1946), p. 25.

[33] *Ibid.*, p. 40.

[34] *Ibid.*, p. 43.

The effects of border state confusion, and Sam Clemens' changing attitudes and wavering allegiances at the beginning of the Civil War are more clearly explained by Webster than by anyone else. If Sam suffered from an emotional strain of divided loyalty, so did his brother-in-law, with whom he was living, and so did many other Missourians. We find Clemens first shouting "Hurrah for Jeff Davis" at a group carrying the Confederate flag, but later he was infuriated because some boys tried to burn a Union flag. When Sam left military service to join his brother Orion on his journey to Nevada, no member of the family apparently objected, or felt that he should do otherwise.

Mark Twain, Business Man contains new letters from Twain in Nevada, some in a more gloomy mood than is generally associated with him at that period, because as Webster explains, the optimistic letters had already been published. Olivia Langdon later appears as her "in-laws" saw her. The Langdon family, so Mark's relatives recall, were not "conventional wealthy Victorians," but socially progressive with liberal ideas about relief for the indigent and racial problems.[35] If there was anything about Olivia Langdon that the Clemens family disapproved of, there is no record of it here. Generous and broad-minded, she appears the wife Mark thought her to be.

Though Webster's chief interest was the affairs of the publishing house, of which he has given us our fullest account, his main contributions concern family life; and his book corrects some of the previous statements made on that subject. He reveals Mark's impulsive and difficult nature, recording how Charles L. Webster even had to run personal errands for Mark and his family. Webster corrects some statements by Paine and the conclusions drawn from them by later writers. The evidence of Jane Clemens' senility

[35] *Ibid.*, p. 113.

casts doubt on Paine's romantic story of blighted young love; for when Jane Clemens was telling about that in her old age she was also narrating how Pamela had been stolen by the Indians and carried away never to be seen again.[36] The mystery of how Madame Caprell, the fortune teller, knew so much about Clemens is cleared by Webster, who reveals that she actually learned it all from a talkative Hannibal neighbor.[37]

Horace Bixby, who once said Mark was not a good pilot, borrowed money from Clemens, which as Webster shows, he not only refused to repay, but became quarrelsome and angry when pressed for payment.[38] Webster throws further doubt on the factual values of Orion Clemens' autobiography, which has furnished much interesting conjecture; and the chapters dealing with Mark Twain's own autobiography, substantiate what is already known—that as a recorder of his own life, Twain was unreliable. Where Paine left the impression that there was no sweetheart in Twain's entire life before his wife, Webster tells us of an early romance, when for a brief period during his river days Sam Clemens was attracted by Laura Dake.[39]

Mark Twain, Business Man is a source book for the student of Twain biography; there is material from memoirs and personal letters of the Clemens family not available elsewhere. It is by far the fullest picture of Twain's relatives, especially Jane Clemens. The problems of the Civil War episode are made clearer and the relationship between Twain and his business associates, though generally unfavorable to Mark, is informative.

Mark Twain and I (1940) by Opie Read is a series of anecdotes of old-fashioned joke-book variety. Since Read knew Clemens, some of the stories may be authentic, but

36 *Ibid.*, p. 224.
37 *Ibid.*, pp. 52–59.
38 *Ibid.*, p. 73.
39 *Ibid.*, pp. 51–59.

one suspects the touch of the storyteller in them all, and the book has no biographical value.

Nearly everybody who knew Mark Twain has set down something about him. Charles Warren Stoddard, onetime secretary, relates his experiences on a lecture tour abroad with Mark.[40] Henry Watterson, good Kentuckian, recalls pleasant times enlivened by bourbon.[41] From the Western years, we have accounts by friends like Dan DeQuille,[42] and comments of Bret Harte, whose conduct later caused a breach of association.[43] Interesting is Harte's description of Clemens at their first meeting:

> His head was striking. He had the curly hair, the aquiline nose, and even the aquiline eye—an eye so eagle-like that a second lid would not have surprised me—of an unusual and dominant nature. His eyebrows were very thick and bushy. His dress was careless, and his general manner one of supreme indifference to surroundings and circumstances.[44]

Hostile in tone were the statements of Senator William M. Stewart, who related a number of unpleasant incidents, objected strongly to his own characterization in *Roughing It,* and made accusations against Mark which at this distance scarcely seem to hold water.[45] In another vein, S. J. Woolf described the celebrity who sat for his portrait.[46] And the indefatigable seeker after reminiscences will find no lack of contributors, but a wealth of material, most of it

40 Charles Warren Stoddard, *Exits and Entrances* (Boston: Lothrop, 1903).

41 Henry Watterson, *Marse Henry: An Autobiography* (New York: George H. Doran, 1919).

42 "Reporting with Mark Twain," *Californian Illustrated Magazine,* IV (1893), pp. 170–178.

43 See references in Henry C. Merwin, *Life of Bret Harte* (Boston: Houghton Mifflin, 1911).

44 Thomas E. Pemberton, *Life of Bret Harte* (New York: Dodd, Mead & Co., 1903), p. 73.

45 *Reminiscences of Senator William M. Stewart of Nevada,* ed. by George R. Brown (New York: Neale Publishing Co., 1908).

46 S. J. Woolf, "Painting the Portrait of Mark Twain," *Colliers,* XLV (May 14, 1910), pp. 42–44.

useful, as for instance, the account by Professor William Lyon Phelps.[47]

Authorized Biography

Albert Bigelow Paine's *Mark Twain: A Biography* (1912) contains too much information—whatever its faults—ever to be entirely neglected. As secretary and companion during the final years, authorized biographer, and Clemens' literary executor, Paine had the advantage of intimate association and first access to extensive materials. Undertaking to tell everything, he narrated the only full-length life yet written. No student can afford to dispense with Paine, but one should have at hand supplements and corrections from more scholarly—if at times less entertaining—sources. Our chief quarrel with Paine arises not alone from his Victorian manner of altering for propriety, but more for his acceptance of unreliable sources and his failure at times to investigate primary materials. Yet he erected a monumental biography to the man he honestly admired, who always remained for him—as for other intimates—"the King."

In the preface to the twelfth edition of his book, in 1935, Paine defended himself against attack, chiefly from Bernard DeVoto. To the charge of inventing either incident or dialogue, Paine replied that an abundance of both made such methods unnecessary. Admitting the need for certain revisions in his original edition, Paine explained the corrections, based upon the investigations of the Rev. C. J. Armstrong of Hannibal.[48] But these were his only emendations. How young Sam stood by his father's coffin and made

47 William Lyon Phelps, *Autobiography With Letters* (New York: Oxford University Press, 1939), pp. 62–72.

48 Briefly these were: Mark Twain's father was not elected clerk of the Surrogate Court, but died before the election; Sam was not apprenticed to Ament right after his father's death, the apprenticeship starting a year or so later; the title of "To Mary in H——l" is amended "To Miss Katie of H——l."

the promise so perturbing in the imagination of Van Wyck Brooks, Paine defended, saying he took the story from a record by Orion, who was present.[49] And from inconclusive evidence a plea is even made for the coonskin story and the "pocket mining incident." Paine, it appears, never realized that he had ever failed in accuracy or insight. For the writing of a life such favorable conditions have rarely existed, and the book does entertain, since Paine constructed a straightforward account, wherever possible permitting Twain to speak for himself. Thus Mark, like David Crockett before him, told stories that never happened. Tall tales, of course, divert the general reader, but scholars have inherited the problem of sifting the fictional passages from the real biography. As more corrections are made, *Mark Twain: A Biography* naturally diminishes as a source book.

Paine's desire to tell everything caused him to subordinate Twain's literary career to the narrative of other activities. The biographer, in brief, neither critic nor literary historian, was unable to relate Mark's books to the tradition of native American humor. He accepted anecdotes too readily, especially for the California and Nevada periods, for which he principally relied on the *Autobiography*. Finally, there is the Victorian "window-dressing," the bowdlerization that put propriety above virility. But despite the errors in Paine's book, most of it is true to the character and personality of Mark Twain. He left a good account of Sam's boyhood, and until someone makes a more detailed study of the final years, we shall depend upon Paine for that period also. Though not to be read without the corrections and additions of subsequent investigators, *Mark Twain: A Biography* is a full and entertaining narrative of much that

49 *Mark Twain: A Biography,* Centenary Edition, 2 vols. (New York and London: Harpers, 1935), vol. I, p. xviii. Originally published in 3 vols. in 1912, then issued in 4 vols. The Centenary Edition contains 4 vols. in 2; page numbers are the same in all editions.

Samuel L. Clemens did, and it will probably remain the foundation for all future studies. In addition, Paine includes a valuable list of Mark Twain's works in the order of publication, a few samples of unpublished material, and such interesting items as the Whittier birthday dinner speech. Whatever his defects, until someone completes a definitive biography, we shall have to consult Paine on matters not available elsewhere.

Autobiography, Notebooks, Letters, and Speeches

The *Autobiography* (1924) was dictated at intervals over a period of years; Mark, who intended it should not be published for a century, tried to be utterly frank and unconventional.[50] The latter quality, however, appears chiefly in the unorthodox manner of composition. As Twain dictated he chose whatever subject happened momentarily to strike his fancy, regardless of chronology or unity. Such method allows a wide variety of subjects and furnishes entertaining table-talk, anecdotes, and reminiscences, but it does not produce a life-story, artistically constructed. When Mark talks about his uncle's farm, his boyhood, and his early surroundings, he forms graphic descriptions, heightened by sense perceptions as fine as Spenser's. These vivid memories of past experiences, give the *Autobiography* its touches of poetic quality, but as a *tour de force* it is unsustained. With the stipulation to withhold publication until long after his death, Mark declared: "I am writing from the grave. On these terms only can a man be approximately frank. He cannot be straitly & unqualifiedly frank

[50] Mark himself passed certain portions of the Autobiography for appearance during his life; see "Chapters from My Autobiography," *North American Review,* September, 1906—December, 1907. A. B. Paine left about one-fifth of this material uncollected, and he frequently revised that which he arranged for publication. See DeLancey Ferguson, "The Uncollected Portions of Mark Twain's Autobiography," *American Literature,* VIII, 37–46 (March, 1936).

either in the grave or out of it."[51] The two volumes selected for publication in 1924 by Albert Bigelow Paine reveal the rambling method of composition, but show, too, the vitality of a mind occupied with a variety of interests. And there is Mark's disinclination to separate creative imagination from biographical fact, for as he put it,

> When I was younger I could remember anything, whether it had happened or not; but my faculties are decaying now, and soon I shall be so I cannot remember any but the things that never happened.[52]

Mark Twain the selective artist never let fact spoil a good story, while the humorist never let an incident pass uncolored by his wit. If he were in the mood to create fiction, biography went by the boards. Yet, Mark's intentions were to make his autobiography a combination of daily diary and memories from the past, a contrast he believed would add interest.

Thus, pieces written during the '80's or '70's were included with items taken from the day's news—now of interest, if at all, only because Mark preserved them. Though he fully intended to write the true story of his inner life, actually it was not his nature to do so; for the actor in him crowded the diarist from the stage. In the passages about Livy and Susy, he came closest to self-revelation. But Mark's version of the publication of General Grant's memoirs, the fiasco of the type-setting machine, and his travels on the lecture platform are not unadorned narrative; Twain re-

[51] It should be remembered that the *Autobiography* as edited by Paine was carefully selected to prevent anything shocking or too frank from appearing. More of the material which Mark at first thought should remain unpublished for a hundred years was later issued by DeVoto as *Mark Twain in Eruption,* and still more unpublished autobiography is in the possession of the Mark Twain Estate.

[52] *Mark Twain's Autobiography,* introduction by Albert Bigelow Paine (New York: Harper, 1924), I, 96. For instance: Mark was at fault in his memory of his father's reading *Hiawatha* (an old tale on the frontier), and other biographical happenings, such as how he took his pen name, the Comstock duel, and his youthful apprenticeship.

membered he was entertaining an audience. What actually gives the book its place among important autobiographies is the charm and insight with which Mark recounts the story of young Sam Clemens: first the little boy, then the youth, and finally the young man from Hannibal emerging into the literary artist. In these passages the *Autobiography* has poetic perception, humor, and vivid descriptions, such rare stuff as Mark's best fiction is made of.[53]

For biographical purposes, as Paine soon discovered, Mark's autobiographical dictations were not trustworthy. Only careful checking could make them accurate. As DeLancey Ferguson has stated:

> In fact, after one has spent months in seeking the skeleton of truth behind some of Mark's more picturesque draperies, it is a relief to come to a tale like that of Livy's effort to cure her husband of swearing. No witnesses were present then, and the biographer can relish a good story, well told, without having to ask if it really happened that way.[54]

And one can relish Mark's recollections of Livy, the children, their devoted servants, and the many friends who visited the Clemens home. It is often inaccurate, yet the subject matter from memory passed through the alembic of Twain's art to become not the facts bare of imagination, but each dressed to play its part, adroitly and humorously transforming all into the storyteller's version of the way it should have been.

Bernard DeVoto edited *Mark Twain in Eruption* (1940) to rectify the omissions of Albert Bigelow Paine. From the unpublished papers of the Clemens literary estate, to which he had succeeded Paine as executor, DeVoto selected anec-

[53] The passages about Hannibal and Sam's visits to his uncle's farm are among the most delightful descriptions of a past era, while the stories of Jim Wolfe, Sam's playing bear, the incorrigible Wales, and Rev. Alexander Campbell are some of Mark's best humor.

[54] DeLancey Ferguson, *Mark Twain: Man and Legend* (Indianapolis: Bobbs-Merrill, 1943), p. 329.

dotes, opinions, and reminiscences, most of them too personal for previous publication, some too virulent. Like the *Autobiography,* this sequel is a rambling discourse upon people Twain knew, events catching his interest, and occasionally himself. For the sake of unity, DeVoto selected what he considered relevant, also what he considered interesting. Only slight changes were necessary, mostly of punctuation, a few of grammar, and here and there the breaking up of an interminable sentence.

The attack upon Theodore Roosevelt, begun in the *Autobiography,* continues here more strongly, showing greater apprehension for the future of the nation. To Mark, there was little good in the popular Teddy, whose elevation to the presidency foreboded the end of the Republic and the inevitability of "monarchy"—the only autocratic or dictatorial form of government Mark knew, hence his stock term for all absolute rule. One section concerns Andrew Carnegie, whose conceit Mark heartily disliked, and Carnegie's fellow plutocrats with their hired politicians, although sometimes escaping, frequently receive the cutting lash of Mark's wrathful tongue.[55]

In nostalgic mood, "Hannibal Days" recalls similar *Autobiography* passages as Mark depicts his school days, the old-time minstrel show, and tells of an amusing experience with a mesmerist that is worthy of Tom Sawyer. The antics of Jim Wolfe, once plagued with the cats, are here continued in two anecdotes of that extremely bashful boy, this time afflicted with wasps.[56] Mark's comments on the writing of his own books and his experiences with publishers, some of whom he thought dishonest, add little to the record. But in telling of his own unfortunate business failures, Mark unburdens himself: "It always made me sick

55 "An A B C Lesson" shows that Mark was aware of how Standard Oil Company was protected by the tariff at the expense of the nation. *Mark Twain in Eruption* (New York and London: Harpers, 1940), pp. 105–106.

56 *Ibid.*, pp. 136–142.

before I got halfway to the middle of it," he says, "but this time I have held my grip and walked the floor and emptied it all out of my system, and I hope never to hear of it again."[57] Mark happily recalls the history of some of his books; pausing over the less important *1601* and the *Snodgrass Letters,* he also tells the story of the *Yankee* and *Old Times on the Mississippi*.

Mark Twain in Eruption contains scathing comments on his contemporaries, wisely withheld by Paine, but printable today. Of Bret Harte, Mark said, "He hadn't a sincere fiber in him. I think he was incapable of emotion, for I think he had nothing to feel with."[58] Mrs. Thomas Bailey Aldrich is dismissed with: "I do not believe I could ever learn to like her except on a raft at sea with no other provisions in sight."[59] Her husband fared better, though Mark disliked his vanity, as he did that of Edmund Clarence Stedman, who ". . . believed that the sun merely rose to admire his poetry. . . ."[60] Others, namely Bayard Taylor and Rudyard Kipling, Mark liked, and a visit from Eleanor Glyn left him pleased:

> I talked with her with daring frankness, frequently calling a spade a spade instead of coldly symbolizing it as a snow shovel; and on her side she was equally frank. It was one of the damnedest conversations I have ever had with a beautiful stranger of her sex, if I do say it myself that shouldn't. She wanted my opinion of her book and I furnished it. I said its literary workmanship was excellent, and that I quite agreed with her view that in the matter of the sexual relation man's statutory regulations of it were a distinct interference with a higher law, the law of Nature.[61]

Various facets of Twain's mind appear: he praises Grover Cleveland, denounces Anglo-Saxon imperialism, recalls the admirable, narrative art of Jim Gillis in Jackass Gulch, and

57 *Ibid.,* p. 195.
58 *Ibid.,* p. 265.
59 *Ibid.,* p. 293.
60 *Ibid.,* p. 294.
61 *Ibid.,* p. 315.

delights over his pastor's predicament with a profane hostler. Finally, Mark returns to his customary indictment of the human race in general, and restates his philosophy of inevitable events, linked to a primal cause.

When A. B. Paine edited *Mark Twain's Notebook* (1935), he left the impression that it was intimate autobiography with nothing modified, nothing changed. "The entries," announced Paine, "whatever their interest, or lack of it—are as he left them, and they bring us about as near as we shall ever get to this remarkable man, easily the most remarkable of his time."[62] Paine is probably right in saying that Mark was never deliberately salacious or indecent, only occasionally frank and rough. The excerpts Paine published are random jottings about whatever Mark found momentarily of interest. Twain talked to himself—freeing his mind by "blowing off steam" in his notebook—and many subjects are denounced more strongly in private than in print. Yet Paine has kept the safety valve in place; and although here and there some steam escapes, the full blast remains to be published.[63] Mark never did keep a consistent or orderly diary, for he claimed that he was discouraged by a youthful attempt which ended daily: "Got up, washed, went to bed."[64] His journal is neither formal nor regular, because Mark was always jotting down sudden thoughts and occasional feelings. Beginning with some very brief notes on the Mississippi River, written when Clemens was learning piloting, Paine next prints a few entries made by Twain in the West, mostly such complaints as: "Rain, beans, and dish-water—beefsteak for a change—no

62 *Mark Twain's Notebook,* ed. by A. B. Paine, (New York: Harpers, 1935), p. xi. But Paine did not print all of the Notebooks, for DeVoto later drew upon them for *Mark Twain in Eruption,* and the Twain Estate has several volumes that have not been printed.

63 The manuscripts in the papers of the Mark Twain Estate show that what Paine selected for publication is indication of what Mark confided to his journal, but not the culmination.

64 *Notebook,* p. 1.

use, couldn't bite it."[65] During his trip to the Sandwich Islands Mark began making humorous maxims: "Never refuse to do a kindness unless the act would work great injury to yourself, and never refuse to take a drink—under any circumstances."[66] Once in Honolulu, Twain is delighted with the islands, but notes: "More missionaries and more row made about saving these 60000 people than would take to convert hell itself."[67] On his way back to San Francisco and during the subsequent voyage to New York, Captain Ned Wakeman began taking shape in his mind as literary material. And comments appear characteristic of the later Twain: a certain "Mrs. Grundy" is termed a "damned old meddling, moralizing fool,"[68] and a passenger who from fear of cholera allowed his courageous wife to wait upon him is dismissed as a "whining puppy." Once in New York and finally embarked on his excursion to the Holy Land, a "wide-mouthed horse-laughing young fellow" irritates Mark into saying, "I wish he would fall in the harbor."[69]

During his travels Twain pauses with notebook to free his mind. Endor with its caked camel dung is dismissed, "Endor is a fit place for a witch."[70] Sleepless from lying on the ground before an Arab house, Mark exploded, "Lice, fleas, horses, jackasses, chickens and, worse than all, Arabs for company all night."[71] A visit to ancient Jericho convinces him, "No Second Advent—Christ been here once, will never come again."[72] From a survey of the country he observed, "The ravens could hardly make their own living, let alone board Elijah."[73] Returning through Egypt he crisply jotted: "Shepheard's infamous hotel."[74] Aboard ship, Mark turned again to trenchant comments on human na-

65 *Ibid.*, p. 6.
66 *Ibid.*, p. 12.
67 *Ibid.*, p. 21.
68 *Ibid.*, p. 40.
69 *Ibid.*, p. 57.
70 *Ibid.*, p. 94.
71 *Ibid.*, p. 97.
72 *Ibid.*, p. 99.
73 *Ibid.*, p. 100.
74 *Ibid.*, p. 111.

ture: "Terrible death to be talked to death."[75] Back in the States, Twain paused in New York before journeying to Washington, where he devoted a section of his notebook, mostly uncomplimentary, to the Senators, and Congressmen, but Paine hastens the reader to San Francisco and whisks him next to Bermuda. This running glance at the travel notes stops only for inclusion of some delightful passages on Mark's difficulties with the impossibility of the German language.[76]

Creative ideas appear sporadically. Notes made in 1883 suggest possible plots: "Write the Second Advent, with full details—lots of Irish disciples—Paddy Ryan for Judas and other disciples. Star in the East. People want to know how wise men could see it move while sober. John interviewed."[77] While writing the *Connecticut Yankee* Mark filled his diary with invectives against monarchy and established church, equalled only by his privately expressed contempt for Paige of the typesetting machine. Then across the continent, through Europe, and over India, the journal moves toward the final years. The maxims, as Mark ages, become more frequent and scathing: "The man who is a pessimist before 48 knows too much; if he is an optimist after it, he knows too little."[78] And Mark concludes, "Man was made at the end of the week's work, when God was tired."[79] To Paine, who in an afterword declared that Mark Twain was now disclosed at his best and at his worst, there appeared nothing to add. But the published excerpts in Mark Twain's *Notebook* do not disclose the emphasis of

[75] *Ibid.*, p. 112.

[76] Mark wrote, "Told 2 German gentlemen the way to the Wolfsbrunen, in elaborate German—one put up his hands and solemnly said, 'Gott im Himmel.' " *Ibid.*, p. 138.

[77] *Ibid.*, p. 167. Mark did write the Second Advent with the scene in Arkansas, but it remains at this date among his unpublished manuscripts.

[78] *Ibid.*, p. 380.

[79] *Ibid.*, p. 381.

thought, the savage attack, or the frankness revealed by his diaries and journals in their original state.[80]

Mark Twain was a good talker. Sought as an after-dinner speaker, welcomed around the world as a lecturer, he made all kinds of addresses on innumerable occasions.[81] In 1910 Mark Twain's selected speeches were published with an introduction by William Dean Howells; later Albert Bigelow Paine added to and re-arranged them.[82] This second collection, *Mark Twain's Speeches* (1923), is separated into three periods, the first beginning with San Francisco covers his early career; the second the middle years; and the final period presents the national figure, sought for advice and applauded for his humor. Mark Twain's speech-making career remains to be told, but investigators are steadily adding speeches to those already collected. Once, at least, in the Whittier birthday dinner speech, an interesting fiasco occurred. Yet even then, Howells, who was present, later wrote, "I never heard Clemens speak when I thought he had quite failed."[83] Those fortunate enough actually to hear Mark Twain declare that his printed speeches can never produce the same effect. A great actor, Mark held his audience through dramatic art and personal magnetism. Something of that colorful personality shows in the speeches; otherwise they add little to biographical interpretation.

Albert Bigelow Paine's edition of *Mark Twain's Letters* (1917), like all his work on Twain, is carefully selected and

[80] It will no doubt be many years before we have Twain's notebooks and journals as he wrote them.

[81] The list of Twain speeches is necessarily incomplete, and may be enlarged by research through the files of newspapers, both at home and abroad.

[82] *Mark Twain's Speeches,* with an introduction by A. B. Paine and an appreciation by W. D. Howells (New York: Harpers, 1923); although some omissions from the previous volume occur, there are about eighty additions.

[83] *Ibid.,* p. ix. Today's readers seem to find this speech funny, as did the unidentified guest, who laughed and shrieked through the silence which prevailed.

bowdlerized. But it is a necessary addition, being—as Paine regarded it—a supplement to the personal side of Mark Twain. Unaware of other writing existing from Clemens' youth, Paine began his collection with the fragment of a letter, written when Sam was seventeen.[84] The letters continue in chronological order until a few days before Twain's death. Whenever it seemed necessary, Paine added a word of explanation. The early letters show the Pepysian art that enabled Mark to preserve such bits of social history as the customs on the Philadelphia "bus."[85] His concern over the well-being of his relatives appears early, too, and we find him taking his mother on a visit to New Orleans. Though Paine generally deleted words and changed phrases for propriety, he did include, "Ma was delighted with her trip, but she was disgusted with the girls for allowing me to embrace and kiss them. . . ."[86]

Paine omits the Civil War interlude to take Sam directly out West from the Mississippi River. Desire for sudden wealth made young Clemens first a miner; then as frontier journalist, he describes his associates, literary and otherwise.[87] These letters further reveal Clemens' ability to portray people and depict places;[88] as biography they document Mark's whereabouts, activities, and friends.

Letters written before the *Quaker City* sailed reveal Mark wrestling with his conscience,[89] but soon he is enjoy-

84 *Mark Twain's Letters,* arranged with comment by Albert Bigelow Paine (New York and London: Harpers, 1917), I. 21.

85 *Ibid.,* p. 28.

86 *Ibid.,* p. 46.

87 Paine prints Artemus Ward's letters of advice to Clemens, but unfortunately he does not have Sam's replies. *Ibid.,* pp. 94–96.

88 The violence of the frontier appears in such a passage: "P.S. I have just heard five pistol shots down street—as such things are in my line, I will go and see about it." Then he adds a second postscript that the pistol shots killed two policemen whom he knew. *Ibid.,* p. 89.

89 To his relatives in St. Louis he wrote: "My mind is stored full of unworthy conduct toward Orion and towards you all, and an accusing conscience gives me peace only in excitement and restless moving from place to place." *Ibid.,* p. 128.

ing the excursion and writing home about such exciting incidents as meeting the Czar of Russia.[90] On Mark's return to the States, the letters tell of his success as a lecturer, and the excitement following his decision to write the *Innocents Abroad.*[91] Though saving money for his approaching marriage, Sam continued to contribute to his mother's support. And only a week before the wedding ceremony he found time to correspond with Jim Gillis, an old crony in a cabin on Jackass Hill.[92] The letters reveal a loyal interest in his friends and a feeling of loving obligation to his relations; later, after his marriage and the birth of little Langdon, they show the equally devoted husband and father.[93]

As Mark progressed in the literary world, the letters tell of his friendship for Howells, whom he selected as mentor. Correspondence with Howells, Twichell, and Aldrich increased, while he wrote to other authors on both sides of the Atlantic. To Andrew Lang, Twain confided that he had never sought to "help cultivate the cultivated classes," but had always written for the "masses," not to instruct but always to entertain them.[94] The letters literally circle the earth, for the Clemens family was on the move as Mark's fortunes varied, with a return to the lecture platform the only ready solution. Happiness and success, sorrow and disaster, follow each other, but they are not here so intimately revealed as in later sources. Paine intended *Mark Twain's Letters* as a supplement to his biography, and so they remain.

A letter from Clemens to Mary Hallock Foote in 1887

[90] One letter tells something of his visit to Spain. *Ibid.,* pp. 137–138.

[91] *Ibid.,* p. 156.

[92] *Ibid.,* p. 170.

[93] Mark Twain must have felt the responsibility for Langdon's death too keenly to mention it, for the letters to Twichell show his devotion to his baby son, and he again mentions Langdon with sorrow on the day of Jean's death. Letters to Twichell, *Ibid.,* pp. 177–180. Mention of Langdon, inscribed in Guest Book, Twain Estate Papers.

[94] *Letters,* II, 527. Mark explained: "It is not that little minority who are already saved that are best worth trying to uplift, I should think, but the mighty mass of the uncultivated who are underneath." *Idem.*

was published in facsimile by Benjamin DeCasseres as *When Huck Finn Went Highbrow* (1934). For forty-two weeks Twain read the poetry of Robert Browning to a Browning class composed of women; Mark declared, "All you need in this life is ignorance and confidence; then success is sure."[95] In addition to revealing Twain's enthusiasm for Browning, DeCasseres records a pleasant memory of seeing Clemens in 1908 leading a group of delighted youngsters into a children's matinee at the Empire Theatre to see Maude Adams in *Peter Pan*.

Mark Twain's Letter to Will Bowen (1938), written from Buffalo, February 6, 1870, addresses his old friend from Hannibal in a nostalgic mood. Mark remembered schoolday incidents, some about people and places later utilized in *Tom Sawyer*. Like a happy boy, Clemens confided his good fortune in his new home and recent bride, saying, "She is the very most perfect gem of womankind that ever I saw in my life—& I will stand by that remark till I die."[96] This letter was reprinted in *Mark Twain's Letters to Will Bowen* (1941), a collection of sixteen letters to "My First, & Oldest & Dearest Friend," written intermittently from 1866 to 1900.[97] A member of Tom Sawyer's gang, Will Bowen was one of three boys whose combined characteristics furnished Mark the material for Tom himself.[98] The origin of *The Adventures of Tom Sawyer* appears first in these letters.[99] They reveal, also, the friendship of Sam Clemens for a boyhood chum, from whom he was not sepa-

95 Benjamin DeCasseres, *When Huck Finn Went Highbrow* (New York: Thomas F. Madigan, 1934).

96 *Mark Twain's Letter to Will Bowen* (San Francisco: Book Club of California, 1938), p. 10.

97 The final letter is addressed to Mrs. Bowen after Will's death.

98 *Mark Twain's Letters to Will Bowen*, ed., Theodore Hornberger (Austin: University of Texas, 1941), p. 3. Albert Bigelow Paine thought that the other two were John Briggs and Sam Clemens. *Biography*, I, 54.

99 Particularly, the letters of January 25, 1868, and February 6, 1870, which contain some material later used in the "Boy's Manuscript" of 1870 or 1871. *Ibid.*, pp. 16–21; the latter is most easily procured in DeVoto's *Mark Twain at Work*.

rated, despite distance, time, or circumstance.[100] Twain fondly reminisced over school days, boyhood pranks, and old places, yet in a subsequent letter bluntly stated his aversion for maudlin sentiment over the past, disparaging the sentimental as unworthy of a man.

An interesting volume of Clemens' correspondence *Mark Twain to Mrs. Fairbanks* (1949), edited by Dixon Wecter, shows young Sam Clemens seeking advice from Mary Mason Fairbanks, discussing his literary ambitions, and confiding details of his none-too-easy courtship of Livy. These letters tell much of Samuel Clemens' change from the wild humorist, out of the West, into the author, settled with his family in Hartford in 1871. Since Mrs. Fairbanks, who served as mentor during the *Quaker City* excursion, remained a valued friend until the end, they are an important biographical link. Dixon Wecter identifies a number of the "Innocents," who are named for us.[101] Biographical errors, also, are corrected; for instance in the chronology of Mark's courtship of Livy.[102] Wecter also cites Twain's awareness of social abuses, in Mark's "Open Letter to Commodore Vanderbilt," where that old millionaire is advised to "go and surprise the whole country by doing something right."[103] There is more about the financial aid and sound business guidance given Clemens by Jervis Langdon, and it was he (so we learn) who suggested Buffalo rather than Cleveland as the place to start in journalism, while he concretely backed Mark with $25,000, half of it advanced in cash.[104] There is also more Twain humor, of course: when the coachman, Patrick McAleer, came dressed in a more expensive coat than Mark's, he wrote, "It did not seem to

[100] The previously discussed "Letter to Will Bowen" is included with slight changes, pp. 18–21.

[101] *Mark Twain to Mrs. Fairbanks,* ed., Dixon Wecter (San Marino, California: Huntington Library, 1949), pp. xiii–xiv, xvii–xviii, 84.

[102] *Ibid.,* p. 36.

[103] *Ibid.,* p. 81.

[104] *Ibid.,* p. 102.

me that a man's coachman ought to wear a finer coat than himself, & so, under way, I swapped coats with Patrick and—"[105]

Mark's pessimism, early in evidence, is expressed on the death of a Mr. Benedict, revealing that the death of his own little son, five years before, was still a source of grief. Clemens says, "Grand result of a hard-fought, successful career & a blameless life. Piles of money, tottering age, & a broken heart."[106]

Mark suggested a publishing procedure as democratic at it is unorthodox: "If I were a publisher would I submit a MS to my one poor solitary 'reader?' No—I would pass it around to fifty people of different ranks & circumstances, & abide by the verdict of the majority."[107] Finally there is the unfortunate story of Mark's complete separation from his old friend, Dan Slote, with whom he fell out over a business deal.[108]

The Love Letters of Mark Twain (1949), also edited by Dixon Wecter, is one of the most revealing biographical items to appear since the Paine biography. Here is the intimate record of a noble love story, a perfect marriage equaled only by the life of Robert and Elizabeth Browning. *The Love Letters of Mark Twain* proves useful, too, in setting the biographical facts straight. Mark's first "date" with Livy is here verified as January 2 or 3, 1868.[109] The character of the Langdon household—actually somewhere between the "stagnant fresh-water aristocracy" of Van Wyck Brooks and the "progressive, even iconoclastic" society of Max Eastman—seems distinctly liberal in some of its social sympathies, yet at the same time "pious-provincial" in cer-

105 *Ibid.*, p. 124.

106 *Ibid.*, p. 200.

107 *Ibid.*, p. 212.

108 *Ibid.*, p. 247. See also Samuel Webster, *Mark Twain, Business Man*, pp. 151–64.

109 *The Love Letters of Mark Twain*, ed. by Dixon Wecter (New York: Harpers, 1949), p. 6.

tain standards of daily life.[110] The difficulties of getting permission for marriage, either from Livy or her father, appear first in flat rejection, followed by indecision, before final acceptance. Even then Mark confided to Twichell, "they capitulated & marched out with their side-arms."[111]

Mark's frank happiness over his success on the lecture platform, contrasts with the opposite statements from George W. Cable.[112] "We've had an immense time here with these three big audiences in this noble Central Music Hall,"[113] Mark exulted to Livy, leaving one to conjecture whether Cable, who never enjoyed Mark's great popularity, may not have allowed envy to tinge his memory.

The intimate story of Twain's financial losses and settlements is now fully revealed for the first time.[114] And here, also, the first detailed account of Susy's horrible illness and tragic death makes clearer the feelings of her parents and the deepening of Twain's pessimism.[115] And the illness of Jean, generally glossed over by biographers,[116] is explained in more detail.

This book permits a more penetrating insight into Mark Twain's personal sorrows than before. Susy's illness and Jean's epilepsy were of course known, but never so clearly; *The Love Letters of Mark Twain* is important for emphasis as well as for new materials.

The full story of the "prowler" in the Clemens' home is told, Mark playing the part of detective Simon Wheeler in his own household.[117] We learn, too, the circumstances under which Clemens met President Grant, unlike those re-

110 *Ibid.*, p. 8.
111 *Ibid.*, p. 23.
112 Paine, II, 785–6.
113 *Love Letters*, p. 230.
114 *Ibid.*, pp. 306–7.
115 *Ibid.*, pp. 319–20. Susy suffered a raging fever and a brain infection which blinded her before death.
116 *Ibid.*, pp. 331–2. Jean died from an epileptic fit, after having the disease for years.
117 *Ibid.*, p. 197–201.

lated by his authorized biographer.[118] The miniature of Livy, the sight of which began their romance, is now accurately described in Wecter's introduction.[119]

Above all, these letters present the love story of Samuel Clemens and Olivia Langdon, ideally based upon mutual devotion and enduring in complete physical and spiritual compatibility. Furthermore, these letters should help to destroy the myth of the feminine-tyrant invented by Van Wyck Brooks—if anything is left of that mythical creation, following the refutations of DeVoto, Wagenknecht, and Ferguson.

Formal Biography

Although Archibald Henderson knew Mark Twain, his contribution to biographical material is not a personal memoir or reminiscence, but more an attempt to summarize the man and his work. *Mark Twain* by Henderson, a professor in the University of North Carolina, therefore, begins the formal biography of Clemens.[120] Henderson attempted a biographical appraisal and critical interpretation, which it has been the fashion to dismiss as curiously devoted to the thesis that Mark Twain was a Southern gentleman. Obviously, Henderson does emphasize the Southern influence, but it is also true that many students of Twain, intent upon his denunciations of slavery and false sentimentality and thinking only of the middle border and the far West, have forgotten, as DeLancey Ferguson reminds us, that Mark came of Kentucky and Virginia ancestry.[121]

Henderson's critical appraisals are sometimes penetrating. Convinced that "Mark Twain was a great American

118 *Ibid.*, p. 154. 119 *Ibid.*, p. 2.

120 Archibald Henderson, *Mark Twain* (New York: Frederick A. Stokes, 1911). A London edition appeared in 1911, and the American edition was printed in Edinburgh.

121 DeLancey Ferguson, *Mark Twain: Man and Legend* (Indianapolis: Bobbs-Merrill, 1943), p. 15.

who comprehensively incorporated and realized his own country and his own age as no American has so completely done before him," Henderson called him, "a philosopher and sociologist who intuitively understood the secret springs of human motive and impulse. . . ."[122] He saw Twain as neither sectional nor national; indeed, Henderson's ultimate praise is that Mark Twain's writings "crossed frontiers, survived translation, and went straight to the human, beneath the disguise of the racial."[123] It is to Mark Twain the world author—not the native American humorist—that this professor paid his respects. In separate chapters, Henderson treated the man, the humorist, the world-famed genius, and the philosopher-moralist-sociologist. Although not a full-length biography, or a complete critical analysis, this book does point in the direction taken by such later scholars as Ferguson and Wagenknecht.

Henderson appended a bibliography of articles on Twain's life and work, one of the first, and still useful to the student of Mark Twain's reputation abroad. But investigators of today will take strong issue with Henderson, however, in his interpretation of Mark Twain's outlook during the final years. To say that he was not a pessimist,[124] but one who accepted fatalism as a supreme truth, does not square with the recent findings of scholarship.

Mark Twain, Son of Missouri (1934) by Minnie M. Brashear is an important work on Mark Twain's boyhood and the influences that went into his development until he became a pilot. A specialized study, it added factual information about Clemens' youth and his earliest writings. The description of Hannibal, its citizens and environment, is the fullest prior to Dixon Wecter's *Sam Clemens of Hannibal.* Miss Brashear emphasizes, too, the influence exerted on little Sam by Uncle John Quarles and his farm. Pointing

122 Henderson, *op. cit.*, p. xi. 123 *Ibid.*, p. xii.
124 *Ibid.*, p. 211.

out that Clemens grew up in a democratic western atmosphere, which prevented his being entirely a Southerner, she states, nevertheless, that the Southern tradition, which was present, affected his temperament and personality. Actually the slavery system brought to Missouri was of the earlier colonial type before the invention of the cotton gin, and she reminds us:

The horror of being "sold down the river," which forms the leading motif of *Pudd'nhead Wilson,* and the description in the novel of the cruel methods of the overseer on an Arkansas plantation, make the contrast between the Missouri system and that of the large cotton plantation apparent.[125]

In the fullest record to that date of Mark Twain's pre-Hannibal background, Miss Brashear explains that a miniature Civil War had indeed been enacted in Marion County between abolitionists and slavery advocates before the national conflict occurred:

He came of proud stock at a time when it was putting its impress upon a new land—clumsily, to be sure, as is the way of all pioneering. He made his way socially and professionally with the help of his wit, as many another genius has done. If Dean Swift had had a bigger and better heart, their cases would be comparable in this respect. His sensitiveness to social distinctions was a source of his strength because he was robust enough for it to give edge to his humor. He belonged from the first among the important people of his community.[126]

The epic quality which appears in Twain's writings Miss Brashear believes to derive in part from his early environment when the frontier was pushing onward to California. Clemens drew sources from original elements because "He knew both what was good and what was bad in a western town of heroic aspiration . . .,"[127] one for which he became the spokesman.

125 Minnie M. Brashear, *Mark Twain, Son of Missouri* (Chapel Hill: University of North Carolina Press, 1934), pp. 58–9.

126 *Ibid.,* pp. 73–4.

127 *Ibid.,* p. 75.

Miss Brashear has added new facts to our knowledge of Twain's early writing. She discloses that the editorial controversy involving young Sam was not caused by poking fun at a rival editor for being jilted in love (as generally supposed) but resulted instead from an editorial about mad dogs. Miss Brashear utilizes Hannibal papers, published from 1839 to 1853, to divide the Hannibal *Journal* writings which can be assigned with certainty to Twain into four groups. The first is a series of editorials on the mad dog controversy.[128] The second, a more ambitious experiment with feature-story writing, for which Sam used the pseudonym, W. Epaminondas Adrastus Blab, may also be identified by reference to "My First Literary Venture," Mark's own account of his "week" as editor of the Hannibal *Journal,*[129] an experience which actually began his newspaper career. It is the last of the four "feature stories" comprising this second group, "Blabbing Government Secrets," that Miss Brashear finds suggestive of the later Mark Twain. A third group of early writings centers around the poem, "To Miss Katie of H——l"; the fourth group comprises three columns of miscellaneous squibs.

Miss Brashear studied the formative elements in Sam Clemens' early life, especially the first twenty-five years, and through a careful and complete investigation into the Hannibal of that day gave us a new interpretation of its general culture. Especially valuable is the chapter "The Shadow of Europe"; equally important is "Sam Clemens' Reading," which establishes that he had access to Shakespeare, Milton, Cervantes, Goldsmith, and the Bible. By destroying unreliable concepts of Twain's early environment Miss Brashear directed attention to a neglected aspect of Twain scholarship, one later to be treated even more fully by Dixon

128 *Ibid.,* p. 107.
129 *Sketches New and Old,* pp. 95–98.

Wecter. In brief, *Mark Twain, Son of Missouri* is a valuable book on this period of Twain's life.

The best general, comprehensive evaluation of Mark Twain appearing up to the centenary of his birth is Edward Wagenknecht's *Mark Twain: The Man and His Work* (1935); this volume sums up succinctly all that was then known. Wagenknecht did not attempt to write a detailed biography, his purpose being an appraisal through careful examination of all the evidence. The book appeared too early in 1935 to make use of the *Notebook* edited by Paine or the revised edition of Merle Johnson's *Bibliography,* but these would not have altered any conclusions. To Wagenknecht, "Mark Twain was an actor who appeared beneath the proscenium arch of the heavens in many different rôles."[130] Appearing as Tom Sawyer, he preserved through memory the idyll of his youth, as Colonel Sellers he experienced many dreams and hopes, as the Connecticut Yankee he spoke his Americanism with humor and with satire, and as Joan of Arc he championed chivalry and idealism. Wagenknecht clearly shows that while Mark Twain was a realist on the one hand, he was, also, equally the idealist on the other.

Wagenknecht sketches the outlines of Mark Twain's youth and early manhood; when the facts are inadequate or missing, he makes no pretense, but admits it. He emphasizes the importance of the wide variety of experiences in Twain's life, and explains that Mark was unusually close to his materials, so much so that his life and his work may be one.[131] From boyhood came the descriptions later found in the poetic passages of his works, of which Wagenknecht says, "Not even 'The Eve of St. Agnes' is richer in sense-impressions than those descriptions."[132] From the findings of

130 Edward Wagenknecht, *Mark Twain: The Man and His Work* (New Haven: Yale University Press, 1935), p. 3.

131 *Ibid.*, p. 5.

132 *Ibid.*, p. 7.

Miss Brashear and the Reverend C. J. Armstrong, Wagenknecht gives a brief but accurate description of Hannibal and the Clemens family. He rejects the theory that Mark was happiest as a pilot, pointing out that Clemens did not return to the river when he had the opportunity, and he quotes from Mark himself to bolster his position.[133]

Twain's development as a man of letters is traced from the newspaper offices of the West to the "world of eastern respectability." We see the home, built in Hartford in 1874, where he lived with his family for "seventeen happy years," and Quarry Farm near Elmira, where during the summer "much of Mark Twain's best writing was done."[134]

Wagenknecht, however, agrees with Brooks that Mark Twain sought to attract attention as a character, rather than as an artist, and that "he did not take himself very seriously as a man of letters."[135] But his interpretations differ from those of Brooks, though he does agree that Clemens, reacting as he did to the world, lived inwardly rather than outwardly, and concludes: "If we would understand Mark Twain, as man and as artist, it is time, then, to turn to the world within as he built it up through the various agencies that became available for his use."[136]

In this world within, the emotions went deep. As an example of ecstasy, Wagenknecht cites the picture of the ice storm in *Following the Equator*.[137] In the face of nature Twain reacted with natural rapture, but in the arts, where a more special or technical appreciation is required, he was indifferent to esthetic problems and often simply "smart." In spite of Clemens' reading, Wagenknecht claims that "Mark Twain pays comparatively little attention to the recognized classics, to the giants of letters."[138] It is from the

133 Ibid., p. 11.

134 *Ibid.,* p. 14.

135 *Ibid.,* p. 17.

136 *Ibid.,* p. 19.

137 *Following the Equator,* II, Chapter XXIII.

138 Wagenknecht, *op. cit.,* p. 34.

literature of the frontier that he developed, for the "frontier itself existed as literature," and Twain appears here as the inheritor and the fulfillment of this tradition, not as the creator of something new.

Indeed, the "frontier" is credited with setting Mark apart from other literary men of his day, such as Howells and James. His imagination was stimulated by the forest and the river; through the Negro slaves he felt the imagination of a primitive race, absorbing a distinct folklore element into his nature. "Yet he never copies blindly," says Wagenknecht; "whatever he used was transformed, recharactered, transmuted into art."[139] An overabundance of creative energy appears his undoing, for Twain liked to improvise, drawing largely upon memories of youth. This damaged the plot structure, but it did not spoil his art in evoking character. Although he frequently deprecated his own work, and was always modest about his literary achievements, eventually he did come to have faith in the value of his best efforts, as Wagenknecht proves by Mark's statements about the interest of posterity in his *Autobiography*.[140]

In the section of the book given to "Mr. Samuel L. Clemens" we see a man interested in clothes, who despite his slouchy appearance in Nevada, had been "the glass of fashion in his pilot days." As for food, he ate whatever he liked and as much as he cared to. And he enjoyed his liquor; his greatest pleasure, however, was smoking. Always young in mind, Clemens retained the youthful desire to shock people. Wagenknecht explains:

> The first time Mrs. Aldrich saw him, she thought he was drunk, and if you think Mrs. Aldrich was merely a prim, fussy New England woman, I give you Calvin H. Higbie, Mark's partner in Western mining activities, who was nothing of the sort. Higbie mistook him for a lunatic![141]

[139] *Ibid.*, p. 53.
[140] *Ibid.*, p. 67.
[141] *Ibid.*, p. 96.

From Clemens' restlessness in travel, his love of pageantry, and delight in color, Wagenknecht concludes that he was forever youthful. Another aspect of youth appears unfortunately in his inability to stand alone: "The same tendency appears all through his life. Without it, Mrs. Clemens would never have obtained the supremacy she established over his literary work."[142] Of this last, Wagenknecht says:

> I am not inclined to feel that, so far as his actual choice of themes was concerned, or the general bent and balance of his work, her influence was really determinative. After all, he did attack the missionaries, he did write *Huckleberry Finn,* he did formulate his philosophy of determinism. There was too much virility in him to permit himself to be pushed very far from his native bent; his qualities and his limitations were alike such that he could never have been the conventional man of letters under any circumstances.[143]

Wagenknecht attributes the pessimism of Twain's last years to his tenderness, his idealism, his hopes and dreams for the human race, which led him to expect mankind to be less cruel, mean, and degraded than it actually was. During his boyhood in Hannibal Sam Clemens encountered horrible incidents, he saw all shades of life on the river boats, he observed the human animal in the mining camps; and what he knew of the more civilized aspects of life did not alter his convictions that while there are noble human individuals the race as a whole is despicable. Wagenknecht states it:

> The griefs and sorrows of Mark Twain's personal life pass over then, as by a natural transition, into his sympathy for humanity, impelling him powerfully in the direction of pessimism as he contemplates the wrongs that humanity has to bear.[144]

Mark Twain emerges from this volume a generous, kind man, intelligent but undisciplined. An artist with poetic

142 *Ibid.,* p. 97.
143 *Ibid.,* p. 185.
144 *Ibid.,* p. 229.

qualities, Twain appears something of a seer, sceptical of the future from his observation of the present and his study of the past, finally more sad than hopeful. This sound evaluation of both the man and his work has not yet been entirely superseded by any subsequent volume. Wagenknecht has documented his material, if not minutely, at least adequately. Appended to the text is a comprehensive bibliography of primary and secondary sources, which is invaluable to the student.

Mark Twain's Western Years (1938) by Ivan Benson is the standard work on that period of Clemens' biography. Benson has examined material previously unavailable, including a number of writings not reprinted, and his study shows the important influence of Samuel Clemens' life in Nevada and California upon his literary career. On the *Enterprise* Clemens first took up writing as a sole means of support; it was then that he adopted his later-famed pseudonym; and there, too, he first began to address anything beyond a local audience. From Nevada Sam Clemens, writing as Mark Twain, developed into a personality, and through the medium of the newspapers gave vent to his natural inclinations to amuse, shock, and satirize. Sam had written humorous sketches like the Snodgrass correspondence, and travel letters for the Muscatine *Journal,* and he had engaged in editorial controversy and personal satire—all before leaving for Nevada. But in the West he abandoned entirely the misspellings and conventionalities of his earlier pieces.

Benson traces Mark's career as a silver miner, motivated by the same desire to strike it rich that actuated the others. Pseudo-scientific conjectures and interpretations receive no sympathy in this book, which presents Sam Clemens as a normal young man, enjoying the freedom of the West, and the excitement of possible wealth. The duality of roughness and tenderness, noted by other Twain biographers, appears, Benson saying, "Samuel Clemens, in Virginia City and throughout his whole life, could withstand a remarkable amount of roughness without wincing; there are those who say that he even enjoyed it."[145] As a reporter on the *Territorial Enterprise* of Virginia City, Twain was influenced by his associates: Joe Goodman, editor of the paper, "whose kindly guidance, skillful tutorship, and understanding friendship followed Mark Twain beyond the Comstock into later years;"[146] William Wright (Dan De Quille), Sam's boon companion, who then showed greater promise than Clemens; Rollin M. Daggett, a courageous man, never hesitating to express honest convictions in print; Steve Gillis, "king jokester of a tribe of Comstock joking giants," who was a printer on the paper; and Denis McCarthy, part owner of the *Enterprise,* later to be Mark Twain's business manager on the 1866 lecture tour. Sam Clemens adjusted himself pleasantly into this group because it suited him and he liked it. Benson, in a word, believes that "Clemens developed those qualities which were inherent in him."[147]

After successively trying his hand as printer, pilot, and miner, explains Benson, Sam Clemens finally in the West settled upon writing as a career. The West, alone, allowed him the free expression to develop the personality since associated with his pen name throughout the world. Benson has carefully examined the facts of Samuel Clemens' adoption of "Mark Twain" as a pseudonym with the conclusion that the story remembered by Mark actually never happened.[148] *Mark Twain's Western Years* shows how Clemens' associates in Virginia City aided him to become a journalist;

145 Ivan Benson, *Mark Twain's Western Years* (Stanford University, California: Stanford University Press, 1938), p. 63.

146 *Ibid.,* p. 68.

147 *Ibid.,* p. 71.

148 *Ibid.,* p. 81.

there, too, Artemus Ward advised him to get his writings printed in the East if possible. From California Twain went as correspondent to the Sandwich Islands, an assignment leading to his career as writer of travel letters and lecturer; for when Mark Twain left the West to start upon the journey leading to the *Innocents Abroad,* it was as both author and lecturer. Previously, however, he had written scathing social satires, perpetrated hoaxes, and composed "The Jumping Frog."

Showing Twain's development into a professional writer, Benson invalidates several stories printed by Paine, such, for instance, as the Comstock duel.[149] This volume includes a valuable bibliography of Mark Twain's writings in the newspapers and magazines of Nevada and California, from 1861 through 1866, and a number of early items are reprinted in the appendix, some of them not available elsewhere. For the student of Mark Twain in the West this careful study checks the undocumented material in Paine against the facts.

Although Franklin Walker's *San Francisco's Literary Frontier* (1939) is a history of the literature produced in San Francisco and its vicinity from the Gold Rush of 1849 to the opening of the railroad in 1869, the pattern of the book is biographical. Walker traces Twain's career as a pilot, the military interlude, which resulted in his coming West, Mark's journalistic career in Washoe, his mining experience, and finally the story of his San Francisco days. Not only do Artemus Ward, Bret Harte, and Mark's newspaper cronies appear, but Adah Menken in *Mazeppa,* the literary "Bohemians" and much that went with them. Walker, moreover, reveals the taste of Twain's audience through a discussion of the San Francisco publications. A significant "moralistic strain" now emerged in Twain's features written for the *Territorial Enterprise* and sent as daily letters

[149] *Ibid.,* p. 112.

from San Francisco.[150] Mark became a satirist and a reformer.

Though succumbing to a fad for spiritualism, Twain managed to escape a literary rage, designated by Walker as "A Rash of Poetry." Mark was genuinely popular; he was one of the boys. When he finally left California for his Old World excursion, it was as the "Wild Humorist of the Pacific Slope," who reported on Europe for the readers of the *Alta California,* affirming their convictions and sharing their irreverence. "San Francisco," says Walker, "had given Mark Twain the most valuable aid that could be offered to a writer during his apprentice days: it had provided financial support and an appreciative audience long enough for him to gain sufficient repute to stand on his own legs."[151] As an exposition of Twain's literary progress, *San Francisco's Literary Frontier* is a valuable chapter in the story of Mark Twain's Western years.

In no sense a scholarly contribution, Cyril Clemens' anecdotal narrative, *Young Sam Clemens* (1942), is an unpretentious study of the years until 1866. Because the author visited places where Twain once lived and where people who knew young Sam were happy to remember him, the story is fresh and often amusing. But instead of biography, the book is a perpetuation of legendary matter.[152]

DeLancey Ferguson's *Mark Twain: Man and Legend* (1943) is a sane and scholarly treatment of all that was then known or conjectured about Mark Twain as a man and writer; it is the best book in its field. In the eight years following the publication of Wagenknecht's book much was added to the Twain canon, which Ferguson has evaluated and augmented through his own research. The only fault

150 Franklin Walker, *San Francisco's Literary Frontier* (New York: Knopf, 1939), p. 196.

151 *Ibid.,* p. 324.

152 Cyril Clemens, *Young Sam Clemens* (Portland, Maine: Leon Tebbetts Editions, 1942).

of this volume for the student is that it omits footnotes. Though designed for the general reader, Ferguson's work is so sound in a scholarly sense and his conclusions so sane that we must regret the loss of adequate annotation. The chief original contribution is a description of the manuscript of *Huckleberry Finn,* which the author has examined carefully.[153] But the book's greatest value is that DeLancey Ferguson has carefully read Mark Twain's writings and all the research produced upon them; he has minutely studied the problems of Twain biography to make a judicious presentation. Passing lightly over Mark's non-literary activities, Ferguson treats him principally as a man of letters, telling how Twain wrote his books and why he wrote them as he did. Ferguson prefers to deal with facts instead of theories; thus the problems of influences on Sam Clemens from his boyhood, the effect of the West on his literary style, whether or not Livy and Howells exerted a good influence on his art, the final pessimism—all are carefully considered. For the first time since 1935 Twain is again in the hands of a critic competent to evaluate his writings against the background of English and American literature to which they belong. This study presents an accurate portrait of Samuel Clemens the man, a summary of biographical scholarship weighed on judicial scales, and as a criticism of the total writings of Mark Twain it equals any that we have.

Ferguson views Mark Twain as a product of traditional frontier humor, but he doubts, for instance, if Artemus Ward influenced him, except as a lecturer. Mark is revealed as essentially Victorian in many ways, yet he had learned the "facts of life" on the frontier and on the river. His innate sense of conduct demanded by good breeding kept Clemens from the grosser indulgences of his environ-

153 DeLancey Ferguson, *Mark Twain: Man and Legend* (Indianapolis: Bobbs-Merrill, 1943), pp. 217–230. Based on the same author's "Huck Finn A-Borning," *Colophon,* n.s. III, 171–180 (Spring, 1938).

ment. Though believing that Mark was really a good pilot, Ferguson remains unconvinced that he ever wished to return to the river. Other problems are discussed, and the account of Twain's early writings is of value to the student. Ferguson, who has considered the revisions in Twain's work more thoroughly than anyone else, is at his best with *Innocents Abroad* and *Huck Finn,* throwing light on their artistry.

Although *The Big Bonanza* was first issued in the fall of 1876, its reappearance with an informative introduction by Oscar Lewis (1947) makes available a storehouse of information on the country that turned Sam Clemens into Mark Twain. Mark's associate on the Virginia City *Territorial Enterprise,* his roommate and intimate friend, Dan De-Quille (whose true name was William Wright), knew Nevada. In *The Big Bonanza,* written years later with Twain's encouragement, Dan retold the anecdotes and reminiscenses of the discovery and history of the Comstock Lode. Here are the delightful stories of "Old Virginia," "Pancake" Comstock, and his wife who wouldn't stay bought, the polite Frenchman who escaped roasting, and a host of other characters and their escapades. Unlike the writing which he and Mark did in their youth, *The Big Bonanza* distinguishes between imagination and fact. With all of the humor and burlesque, there is the actual history of the Lode and how it was worked. Although the book sold well only in the West, its worth has long since been recognized by historians for its fresh and vivid atmosphere of the fabulous mines. Published for the first time in the introduction are several letters by Mark Twain, chiefly of interest in showing his loyalty to old pals from Washoe. Though not Twain biography this is a book rich in background materials of Mark's life in Nevada.

A very specialized study of the same period, Effie Mona Mack's *Mark Twain in Nevada* (1947) is a full account of

Mark's three years there, which emphasizes the conclusions already formed by Ivan Benson. Dr. Mack adds the social background to *Roughing It* in minute details. She states in her preface, "Never before or since in any part of the world, not even in the Gold Rush to California, was there such an extravaganza put on as in the Rush to Washoe. And there never has been a writer before or since Mark Twain who has left such a vivid picture of it."[154] Her study shows that *Roughing It* faithfully presents in fact and spirit the character and customs of the early days of Nevada. While there is nothing new, for instance, in telling how Joseph Thompson Goodman was the discoverer of Mark Twain, and how Dan DeQuille served as mentor, Dr. Mack's purpose is to show that Sam Clemens owed more to Virginia City than to San Francisco. More completely than anyone else, she has gone through the available records and newspapers, and she traces in detail these formative years. But there is more of Nevada than of Mark Twain, and excellent as the book remains as a guide and supplement to *Roughing It,* its primary value is social history. Dr. Mack unfortunately relied too much on Paine's "official life" and on Mark's own mingling of fancy and reality, but she has given proper emphasis to the Comstock Lode and Washoe in the making of the essential Twain.

Even more specialized is *Mark Twain and Hawaii* (1947) by Walter Francis Frear, whose long residence in the islands fitted him admirably for this exhaustive study of Mark Twain's four months and a day there. Frear demonstrates that the importance of the visit was out of all proportion to its length, for it was the interstice between Clemens' years of preparation and the following years of success. Always an "oasis" or happy memory to Twain, the islands exerted an influence greater than mere pleasant retrospective value,

154 Effie Mona Mack, *Mark Twain in Nevada* (New York: Scribner's, 1947), p. viii.

for his writings there show a style in transition from the crude, briefer compositions of frontier journalism to the more formal manner of the future. And Hawaii brought Mark to a new profession, later to prove financial salvation —lecturing. Frear has not merely treated the visit to Hawaii, the journey and return, but in a lengthy volume explores all its influences, together with Mark's continuing references throughout a lifetime.

On the islands occurred the fortuitous meeting with the United States Minister to China, Anson Burlingame, who gave Twain a new sense of importance as an individual, and thus encouraged him. Frear reveals that Burlingame's advice to seek improvement through superior associations—so often impugned as snobbery—was in reality sorely needed. Though unfortunately phrased, it proved helpful, for Mark by occupation and association had dropped into habits he needed to discard. Then it was Burlingame, after raising Twain's self-esteem, who also made it possible to produce the scoop on the burning of the *Hornet*. Yet it was more immediately as lecture material, rather than through associations or in his writings, that Hawaii paid dividends. Frear says, "The Sandwich Islands lecture was practically his sole dependence on the platform for a year and a half and a chief standby for over seven years—in the West, Middle-West, East and in England."[155] When Mark Twain left California for the East, he was established not only as a Western humorist, but thanks to his Hawaiian visit—the importance of which Frear narrates fully—he was a successful lecturer and writer of travel letters.

Though not a biography *The Literary Apprenticeship of Mark Twain* (1950) by Edgar M. Branch presents a chronological interpretation of Samuel Clemens' development as a writer. The early Hannibal sketches, while possessing no

155 Walter Francis Frear, *Mark Twain and Hawaii* (Chicago: Lakeside Press, 1947), p. 167.

true literary value, are important nevertheless for their "comic disposition," which Branch credits with placing "Sam Clemens squarely in the stream of American realism."[156] The colloquial nature of these apprentice pieces naturally required character portrayal through ordinary, everyday language, as well as the presentation of native subjects. And in fact the "speech rhythms of the vernacular" continued through the travel letters written by the printer and pilot, despite the intrusion of occasional bits of "elegance."[157] With the Thomas Jefferson Snodgrass letters, both crude and imitative, we find young Sam "more consciously in the tradition of American humor," merging numerous features of Sut Lovingood, Simon Suggs, and Jack Downing; interesting indeed is the continuity pointed out by Branch between the "unlettered, first person speech" of Snodgrass in 1856 and the "masterful language" of Huck Finn in 1884.[158] The earlier Snodgrass' successor, Quintus Curtius, who discarded the misspellings and bad grammar of his predecessor, reveals (if nothing more) sound comments on "the militaristic reversal of human values."[159]

It is as reporter in Washoe that Branch finds Twain "highly personal, exaggerated, and comic," working to cause guffaws, perpetrating hoaxes, indulging in burlesque, and ridiculing with satire. "He picked subjects," Branch says, "for their potential fun and laughter, and delighted in a slapstick style and a fluid form."[160] The importance of all this, as well as the influence of Dan DeQuille, is evaluated, until we find Sam Clemens, thirteen years after "The Dandy Frightening the Squatter" producing "Jim Smiley and His Jumping Frog," part of that literary treasure-trove discovered on Jackass Hill. Moreover, it was in 1865 that a sense

156 Edgar M. Branch, *The Literary Apprenticeship of Mark Twain* (Urbana: University of Illinois Press, 1950), p. 21.

157 *Ibid.*, p. 26.

158 *Ibid.*, p. 43.

159 *Ibid.*, p. 55.

160 *Ibid.*, p. 95.

of his past began to appear in Clemens' writings; then, too, Washoe comedy was utilized, not alone for laughter, but in the interest of truth, for if Twain the Nevadian had produced laughter, the Californian became, also, the "Moralist of the Main." Observing that the Sandwich Island letters had value as preliminary training for the *Innocents,* Branch (unlike Frear) does not regard them as anything more. But with the sailing of the *Quaker City* Mark's apprenticeship was over: "He was launched on a long voyage and a long career."[161]

Mark Twain as a Literary Artist (1950) by Gladys Carmen Bellamy demonstrates that Twain was much more the conscious craftsman than is generally believed. While admitting that Mark was never a "self-conscious" artist in the sense that Henry James was, Miss Bellamy follows Walter Blair and Lionel Trilling in claiming that he was more "conscious" in his literary activity than frequently admitted. The book employs something of the Van Wyck Brooks thesis that Twain failed to achieve complete artistic success, but the reason advanced is that Mark failed to secure "a comprehensive grasp of writing discipline"; indeed, the "importance of form in writing" and "concern with technique" were fully realized by Clemens, who unfortunately nearly always failed to reach them.[162]

Miss Bellamy categorizes Clemens' fundamental ideas into four "primary bases" of thought: "moralism, determinism, pessimism, and patheticism,"[163] which she then discusses. "The burlesque satire of the early Mark Twain touched not only the fashions, the manners, and the ideals of the Western Gilded Age, but its ethics as well,"[164] Miss Bellamy tells us, for she does not follow Brooks in believ-

161 *Ibid.,* p. 194. *The Literary Apprenticeship of Mark Twain* concludes with a chapter on the fulfillment of the artist in *Huckleberry Finn.*

162 Gladys Carmen Bellamy, *Mark Twain as a Literary Artist* (Norman: University of Oklahoma Press, 1950), p. 34.

163 *Ibid.,* p. 64.

164 *Ibid.,* p. 85.

ing that Clemens surrendered his integrity to the frontier. Yet she finds the moralist at cross purposes with the determinist, frequently with the artist, for she states, "In other words, life cannot be prized unless its content is valuable. And here the moralist in Mark Twain suffers a defeat; he tries to save mankind to a life which he often paints as despicable and futile."[165] It is in burlesque that Miss Bellamy finds Mark an artist, for she disagrees with Brooks that the artist was undone by the humorist. Instead, she reaches the conclusion that "most of his early writings are not true humor but satire," and she declares, "It was unfortunate for Mark Twain as an artist that his attention was centered on the limitations of mankind rather than on the possibilities."[166]

Miss Bellamy advances the theory that Clemens regarded reality as ugliness and beauty as a dream, and she makes a detailed examination of the travel books (the fullest thus far in print) to demonstrate that Clemens could not bring the two aspects of life together harmoniously in artistic form. In short, Twain lacked control, and it was only through detachment, says Miss Bellamy, that he created his best work, a detachment secured: (1) by telling a story through some simple character, such as Huck, Jim, or Captain Stormfield, (2) by placing the story far removed in time and space as in *The Mysterious Stranger,* (3) by viewing the human race with detachment, (4) by reducing life to the unreality of a dream.[167] Thus while admitting *Huckleberry Finn* to the permanent realm of art, Miss Bellamy thinks that Mark did not fully succeed generally, because he was unable to discipline himself. She values Twain's extensive portrait gallery, his magnificent imagination, and his profound insight into the ways of human beings.

[165] *Ibid.,* p. 118. [166] *Ibid.,* p. 154.
[167] *Ibid.,* pp. 371–4.

Kenneth R. Andrews' *Nook Farm: Mark Twain's Hartford Circle* (1950) considers the social and intellectual *milieu* of the two happiest decades of Samuel Clemens' married life. Andrews has made the most complete study thus far of the friends and neighbors comprising a close-knit group in Hartford's choice residential district. Here at Nook Farm Clemens lived lavishly, enjoyed the devotion of his family, the respect of his friends, and the admiration of his widely-increasing reading public. Surrounded by a cultural environment he definitely aspired to, Samuel Clemens soon became one of its leaders. Even religion proved no deterrence, for the genial congregationalism of Horace Bushnell, which had replaced dour Calvinism, permeated the community. The religion of love preached by Beecher was soon followed by the message of ethics and wide humanity voiced by his successors. "Through the years, then," says Andrews, "Burton, Parker, and Twichell presided more and more over a 'religious' activity turned secular as memory of the old theology grew dim."[168] It is a pleasant life, as retold by Andrews' detailed study. Joseph Twichell, Charles Dudley Warner, and their neighbors are considered in relation to each other and for the influence they exerted on Twain's thought.

In contrast to Miss Bellamy's thesis, Andrews believes that Twain's best works were the products of instinct rather than conscious art. It is nostalgia—something which Andrews finds also in Warner and Mrs. Stowe—which gave rise to Twain's greatest books. He says of *Huckleberry Finn,* "Its greatness cannot be attributed to conscious skill and its success testifies not to art but to instinct."[169] Though Mark was more the conscious artist than the "series of improvisatory spurts" here discussed indicate, *Nook Farm* is useful

168 *Nook Farm: Mark Twain's Hartford Circle* (Cambridge, Massachusetts: Harvard University Press, 1950), p. 50.

169 *Ibid.,* p. 214.

in evaluating Clemens as a writer. Its chief contribution, however, is that it gives us greater knowledge of how the life led in Hartford during the 1870's and 1880's affected Mark Twain.

Henry Seidel Canby's *Turn West, Turn East* (1951) presents Mark Twain and Henry James in terms of the two great, opposing forces in American culture—the ties binding us to Europe and the contrasting pull of frontier expansion. Yet in many ways Canby shows Twain and James to be opposite sides of the same coin, possessing the same basic values in their concern for the integrity of the individual confronted with a moral problem, whether it be a Huck Finn or an Isabel Archer. Fundamentally Twain and James dealt with the existence of good and evil, and each in his own way was a humorist. Dissimilar as their methods seem, Canby says, "Yet Mark, like Henry, might have got his formula from the great Russian Turgenev, who was contemporary with both. All three selected the situations most likely to express the central figure of a story—which is more valuable in the kind of stories all three wrote than plot."[170] While adding no new material, this sensible study reveals the similar qualities, so often typically American, which the two authors contributed to world literature through their respective art.

Dixon Wecter's *Sam Clemens of Hannibal* (1952) was begun as part of what surely would have been the definitive biography of Mark Twain, a project cut short by Wecter's sudden death while serving as literary executor of the Clemens estate. Based on a full examination of Twain's unpublished manuscripts, plus a careful investigation of family papers, court records, census reports, and newspapers, Wecter's fragmentary study gives more information about Samuel Clemens to the age of eighteen than any other source;

170 Henry Seidel Canby, *Turn West, Turn East: Mark Twain and Henry James* (Boston: Houghton Mifflin Company, 1951), p. 159.

for he has re-created Hannibal street by street and house by house. Here is the most complete account of Clemens' ancestry, the fullest narrative of his father and mother, and the most detailed description of their daily home life and community activities. And certain matters are illuminated. The autopsy performed on his father, which the boy witnessed through a keyhole, left Sam Clemens with one of the shocking memories of his life, too carefully guarded ever to be mentioned, except to Orion. Even in his notebook, years later, Twain veiled the facts by saying it was his uncle's post-mortem.[171] This shock, no doubt, contributed to Sam's sleepwalking on the night of his father's funeral.

Sam Clemens of Hannibal, also, adds richly to our knowledge of young Sam's schooling, religious training, and the folkways which guided his later conduct, as well as revealing more of the autobiographical element in Twain's fiction. For instance, Wecter finds that the source of Mark Twain's high ethical standards was the "integrity and dignity" of John Marshall Clemens. And he has discovered that the incident of Colonel Sherburn's shooting of Boggs in Chapter XXI of *Huckleberry Finn* was taken directly from Judge Clemens' record of the depositions in the shooting of Sam Smarr by William Owsley in Hannibal.[172] Wecter gives more details of Tom Sawyer's gang than did Paine; he shows that Jimmy Finn, pauper and town drunkard, furnished the name and general characteristics for Pap in *Huckleberry Finn.* Interesting, too, is the use Wecter makes of the uncompleted forms of *The Mysterious Stranger* and tales of Tom and Huck to show that as the dream of boyhood faded the disillusioned Mark Twain was unable to finish them. Though there are few revisions in this story of

171 Dixon Wecter, *Sam Clemens of Hannibal* (Boston: Houghton Mifflin Co., 1952), p. 116.

172 *Ibid.,* pp. 106–8.

Twain's youth, there are numerous important matters of emphasis given, and Wecter concludes:

> No major artist ever made more of his boyhood than did Samuel Clemens. He found himself better adapted to Hannibal than to any other environment he ever met. As adult life with its casuistries and introspections grew more complex, he worshipped this golden age all the more—achieving in *Tom Sawyer* and *Huckleberry Finn* the universal Hannibal, the home town of boys everywhere.[173]

In *Twins of Genius* (1953) Guy A. Cardwell has written a complete account of Mark Twain's association with George W. Cable, especially during the winter of 1884–85, when they toured the country, giving readings from their books. Cardwell has collected the press notices, and he includes all the available letters, exchanged by Twain and Cable from July, 1881, through October, 1906, except those already printed. It seems that each influenced the other, though perhaps Twain at the time derived more from the tour through their discussions of social justice and problems of human relationships then existing in the South.

The most recent biography is *The Adventures of Mark Twain* (1954) by Jerry Allen, which is partly narrative and partly Mark's own autobiography and fiction. Miss Allen has brought a great deal together from many scattered sources to make one of the most readable books about Twain, but like Mark she has embroidered biographical facts with his fiction. The whitewashing of the fence in *Tom Sawyer* appears as part of the biography, and certain facts now discredited by scholarship, such as the story of Isaiah Sellers and Clemens' pen name, are retained. But the book, especially the last half, is rich in background material, and Miss Allen devotes considerable space to Twain's social criticisms of these later years. Her studies of the sociological import of *Huckleberry Finn* and *A Connecticut*

[173] *Ibid.*, p. 264.

Yankee are a useful contribution. The student, however, will regret the lack of any documentation.

Van Wyck Brooks and the Psychological Approach

When Van Wyck Brooks wrote *The Ordeal of Mark Twain* (1920) he raised questions, some still unanswered, and started a dispute, which soon became bitter. Indeed, much since written about Twain has been mainly an attack upon Brooks' theories, or even upon Brooks himself for having advanced them. *The Ordeal of Mark Twain* divided Twain biographers into rival camps, yet it is really not a biography in the strict sense of being a "life"; actually it is a psychological study. Other authors were being examined in the same manner, for it was then the fashion. Brooks starts out with a set of theories, and as usual with theorists, he uses what will fill his needs and ignores what does not. Despite this, he has reached certain conclusions that still appear valid. In addition, he shows at times a penetrating insight into Mark's character. The book is by no means as valueless as some critics would have us believe. DeVoto and Benson have both attacked Brooks with so much vigor that the attack becomes almost personal, while Ferguson, appealing to common sense, simply rejects the theories. Whether or not one agrees with Brooks, one cannot accept Paine's advice to DeVoto to ignore him; for he has raised too many issues about Mark Twain and the America that produced him, despite the obvious limitations of his approach, to be ignored.

Much of the book is pseudo-science, an attempt to substitute psychological theorizing for common sense, and a tendency to make something mysterious out of the obvious. The purpose is to explain the bitter pessimism that developed in Twain's mind, the despair which made him regard man as the meanest of animals and life as a tragic mistake. How could one who had achieved such popularity and success, the affection of his countrymen, and the acclaim of the world, have felt as Mark Twain did about life? Not content with an objective explanation, Brook insists upon "some far more personal root . . . some far more intimate chagrin."[174] Searching for a "deep malady of the soul" Brooks even convinces himself that Mark's delight in billiards, which led him to beg for one more game at four o'clock in the morning, is really not enthusiastic playing, but actually a fear of being alone. "Why do so many of his jokes turn upon an affectation, let us say, of moral cowardice in himself?"[175] asks Brooks. Mark could not face himself because "he had transgressed some inalienable life demand," becoming a frustrated personality, a victim of arrested development, of which he was not entirely conscious, but which crushed the spirit of the artist in him. Declaring that Twain lives today in only two or three books, Brooks further asserts that his appeal is largely to rudimentary minds. It is not so much the accomplishment that interests Brooks as the conjecture of what might have been, for this failure as an artist had "signs of an endowment, as one cannot but think, more extraordinary than that of any other American writer."[176] Brooks then accurately points out many of Twain's traits, but misunderstands the reason for their being. Mark had a nature alike barbaric and sweet; he had a passion for the limelight; he possessed an inner humility; there was a great deal of comic impudence in him; he lacked an inner control over his own boundless energy in creative efforts; during his final years he developed a mechanistic philosophy. From this, Brooks condemns Twain as a "frustrated spirit, a victim of arrested development," saying, "the poet, the artist in him, conse-

174 Van Wyck Brooks, *The Ordeal of Mark Twain* (New York: E. P. Dutton, Revised Edition, 1933), p. 20.

175 *Ibid.*, p. 24.

176 *Ibid.*, p. 29.

quently had withered into the cynic and the whole man had become a spiritual valetudinarian."[177]

The theory then elaborated is that the only period of life in which Sam Clemens was really happy was during his four years as pilot on the Mississippi. As evidence we are told, "the earlier pages of *Life on the Mississippi,* in which he pictures it, are the most poetic, the most perfectly fused and expressive that he ever wrote."[178] Having found himself in a pilot's career, Clemens is supposed to have lost himself when he left it. Brooks calls the world into which Mark was born "drab," and "tragic." The entire social setting of life in Hannibal is made to appear close to the backwoods underprivileged found in Erskine Caldwell. Hannibal is denounced: "A desert of human sand!—the barrenest spot in all Christendom, surely for the seed of genius to fall in."[179] And the Clemens family itself becomes a "loveless household"; all of them, "like so many rusty machines, without enough oil, without enough power, grating on their own metal."[180] Without giving proof enough to satisfy most Twain investigators, Brooks declares that little Sam was born a predestined artist. First, his environment is declared to be ugly and soul-destroying; next, his mother is charged with warping him beyond hope. Because Sam Clemens, standing beside his father's coffin, promised his mother that if she would not send him back to school, he would be a better boy, Brooks believes he thereby forsook the artist inherent within. From then on he must follow the mirage of wealth. Only as a pilot could Sam reconcile concurrently his opposing wishes: to be an artist and to win his mother's approval, an approbation which was the same as that of the pioneer society to which she belonged. In condemning Jane Clemens' influence upon her son, *The Ordeal of Mark Twain* denounces pioneer society in general. As a pilot Sam

177 *Ibid.,* pp. 40–41.
178 *Ibid.,* p. 43.
179 *Ibid.,* p. 46.
180 *Ibid,* p. 47.

was successful financially, winning the praise of his family and neighbors, while at the same time he was an individual. "It is an outburst of pure aesthetic feeling, produced by a supreme exercise of personal craftsmanship," says Brooks.[181] Moreover, here is a fertile field for observation and schooling. "He will not always be a pilot; he is an artist born; some day he is going to be a writer."[182] But this is all shattered by the Civil War, when Sam Clemens, after four years as a pilot devoted to the ideal of craftsmanship, is suddenly thrown into a world obsessed with exploitation. There was one standard for success: the accumulation of wealth.

The West fares no better in this narrative than the Mid-West. There Mark encountered the "promoter's instinct," which Brooks illustrates with the story of Jim Gillis, who refused to admit that California plums were too acid to eat. Unable to stand apart from his Washoe associates, Clemens capitulated to his environment. Since it was impossible for him to secure wealth and prestige, while remaining at the same time an artist with creative instinct, he abandoned his own aspirations, descending to the level of his associates. Brooks theorizes that Mark failed as a miner because he could not really bring himself to pursue wealth alone; then concludes:

> So here he was faced with a dilemma. His unconscious desire was to be an artist, but this implied an assertion of individuality that was a sin in the eyes of his mother and a shame in the eyes of society. On the other hand, society and his mother wanted him to be a business man, and for this he could not summon up the necessary powers in himself. How often this dilemma has occurred in the lives of American writers! It was the dilemma which, as we shall see in the end, Mark Twain solved by becoming a humorist.[183]

But not until he fought an inner battle, according to Brooks, who reads something of chagrin into Mark's man-

181 *Ibid.*, p. 68. 182 *Ibid*, p. 73.
183 *Ibid.*, p. 106.

ner of entering the *Enterprise* office to join the staff. For in becoming a humorist, Twain felt that he was "compromising rather than fulfilling his own soul."[184] From then on Mark thought of his writing as only a product, another way to earn money; it was never an artistic creation. Taking no pride in his work, Mark could never be happy as he had been while a pilot. That his creative instinct was still in rebellion, Brooks deduces from his deprecatory remarks about the "Jumping Frog," yet Mark capitulated nevertheless to the "gregarious, acquisitive instinct of the success-loving pioneer."[185]

With Clemens' marriage to Olivia Langdon, the wife supersedes the mother for Brooks as the blight upon his art, and Elmira is pictured as a place without moral freedom or intellectual culture: "A provincial fresh-water aristocracy, resting on a basis of angular sectarianism, imposed its own type upon all the rest of society, forcing all to submit to it or to imitate it."[186] Just as he had surrendered in Hannibal and in the West, Twain submitted here, producing not the literature he wished to write, but only the kind of books accepted by his wife and Elmira. So long as he was popular with the masses, and earned enough money, everything was all right. Adopting the values and ideals of the society for which he wrote, Mark Twain kept his eye on the demand, and supplied it. Brooks feels that he never wrote as he really longed to, but always, instead, turned out what he thought would sell. It was this failure, deep within, which he realized, that led to the development of his pessimistic philosophy in his old age: "Mark Twain's attack upon the failure of human life was merely a rationalization of the failure in himself."[187] This then, was the ordeal, an artist who wished to create beauty through the truthful expression of his in-

184 *Ibid.*, p. 111.
185 *Ibid.*, p. 117.
186 *Ibid.*, p. 139.
187 *Ibid.*, p. 313.

dividuality, selling his birthright to earn wealth and popularity.

The defects inherent in such a study readily become apparent; Brooks has attempted to psychoanalyze a dead man, which at best can produce only conjectural results. It is not surprising, then, that Brooks' method is often inadequate. And there are other defects in this study: there is no basic knowledge of either the Mississippi Valley or the Far West; there is a general disparagement of all humor, and finally there are a good many conclusions based on evidence spun from imagination.

Although he does not continue Brooks' attack on Twain, Stephen Leacock was influenced by it. His *Mark Twain* (1933), in partial acceptance, deplores the influence first of the mother and later the wife. While stating that the East exerted a bad influence on Twain, he ignores Brooks to commend the environment of Hannibal and the West. Indeed for Leacock, "The West made Mark Twain."[188] With a gusto that could not be dampened, Mark continued to write *for* the East, but not *of* it. Leacock admits that Mark was held to those bounds considered respectable by Livy, Joe Twichell, and Howells, that after all it was the Victorian age, but finally concludes, "They did their loving best to ruin his work—and failed; that's all."[189] As a humorist, Twain became a national figure and a legend; to Leacock, a successful humorist himself, Mark's desire to be taken as a serious writer is simply a natural trait of human nature. In the stories of Tom and Huck Leacock feels Mark was at his best; after pointing out the faults in both books, he says of the latter:

> But the bulk of the book is marvellous. The vision of American institutions—above all, of slavery—as seen through the unsullied mind of little Huck; the pathos and charm of the Negro

[188] Stephen Leacock, *Mark Twain* (New York: D. Appleton & Co., 1933), p. 21.

[189] *Ibid.*, p. 64.

race shining through the soul of Nigger Jim—the western scene, the frontier people—it is the epic of a vanished America.[190]

In short, Leacock agrees with Brooks that Mark Twain was hindered, but unlike Brooks, he believes that Twain rose above these obstacles. There is an appreciation of the best of Mark's work, especially his humor, although Leacock fails as critic when he turns to the writings of the latter years and to the historical narratives. As biography this book is not important; as a comment by a fellow humorist it is interesting.

Edgar Lee Masters, under the influence of the Brooks thesis, continued the negative approach to Mark Twain.[191] The man emerging from Masters' study is not admirable. Although he took his biographical material from Paine, adding nothing of his own, and ignoring subsequent contributions, Masters nevertheless presents a radically different figure. To the Paine material he added Brooks' frustration theory, but this time with a Mid-Western accent. Agreeing that Mark was thwarted, Masters seeks the explanation in cultural uprooting. The implication is that Mark should have stayed in Missouri. But chiefly he finds fault with his subject for not having entered into the class struggle. Perhaps Masters himself had come under the influence of the dialectical materialists, so popular in the thirties, and he infers that Mark's career was blighted because political and economic ideas were relegated to the background in his fiction. If Mark Twain had always written with a social, political, or economic purpose, then Masters would have felt that he was living up to his full stature as an artist. While agreeing with Brooks that Twain failed as a satirist, he blames the failure on Mark's having neither the mind nor the character for the task. The Brooks pos-

190 *Ibid.*, p. 86.

191 *Mark Twain: A Portrait* (New York: Charles Scribner's Sons, 1938).

tulate of a loveless household, and the baleful influence of Jane Clemens and Calvinism, causes Masters to accept the episode of contracting measles as a turning point in life, an attempt "to be done with the suspense and the terror."[192]

Masters briefly traces Twain's career in the West and repeats Brooks' charge that Mark sought success in money, not literature. His marriage is disparaged as "luxurious living, and no thinking at all."[193] Once in the toils of Olivia, Clemens was emasculated, while Howells and Twichell also contributed to his failure. To Masters he was a coward: "Twain did nothing and said nothing to make enemies of the ruling powers, the bosses of the hour. . . . He always sailed in safe water."[194]

Masters reveals his own ideas about the obligation of the artist to enter the class struggle—an example of the obsession of the period with economics—but this book, a continuation of the frustration theory, adds nothing of any value to the student of Mark Twain.

In *The Times of Melville and Whitman* (1947) Brooks continued his assertion that the "frontier was generally stagnant in its formal culture."[195] His treatment of the far West, however, shows a modified attitude; no longer is it a place of artistic frustration, for Brooks must now admit, "Mark Twain was the serio-comic Homer of this old primitive Western World, its first pathfinder in letters, its historian and poet."[196] Yet Brooks persists in saying that Clemens had little pride in literature, preferring piloting,[197] that he was primarily interested in making money,[198] and that he suppressed honest opinion to secure public approbation.[199] Notwithstanding, *The Times of Melville and*

192 *Ibid.*, p. 18.
193 *Ibid.*, p. 83.
194 *Ibid.*, p. 101.
195 Van Wyck Brooks, *The Times of Melville and Whitman* (New York: E. P. Dutton & Co., 1947), p. 78.
196 *Ibid.*, p. 300.
197 *Ibid.*, p. 453.
198 *Ibid.*, p. 459.
199 *Ibid.*, p. 462

Whitman evidences an appreciation of Twain's folk art and Brooks no longer condemns humor. To understand the changed attitudes, one needs to know the attack waged on Brooks' theories by Bernard DeVoto.

DeVoto and the Rebuttal

Before the controversy developed which was to turn Mark Twain biographers into divergent factions, John Macy—who later would reaffirm his views—wrote a sensible essay in *The Spirit of American Literature* (1913). Anticipating, as it were, the pseudo-scientific insistence upon Mark's limitations through environmental influence, Macy affirmed that he was a humorist, naturally and by preference, a writer who must be approached as such.[200] Mark, neither a victim of censorship, nor a sufferer from frustration, meditated like Swift on human folly, seeing life with breadth and penetration. Then seriously intent upon truth, he humorously approached mankind, generally tolerant, sometimes affectionate, but with true chivalry scorning the false, mean, and cruel. Macy interprets the final pessimism as ethical and materialistic determinism, in a word explaining it: "Character is fate."[201]

Mark Twain had universal proportions and an interest in most of the vital problems of our race, says Macy, who admitting the unimportance of his philosophy as such reaffirms his wide range, depth of insight, and his knowledge of good and evil. For Twain's work, taken in total, constitutes of Mankind, ". . . the greatest canvas that any American has painted."[202] Later in *The Story of the World's Literature* (1925) Macy, with the theories of Van Wyck Brooks before him, denies them, stating that Mark's wings were never clipped, either by personal associates, or anything

200 *The Spirit of American Literature* (New York: Doubleday, Page, 1913), p. 250.

201 *Ibid.*, p. 275.

202 *Idem.*

inherent in American life. Indeed Macy declares, "He said all he had to say, he knew how to say it, and circumstances fostered his genius."[203]

In a succinct account of Mark Twain, C. Hartley Grattan also took issue with the pseudo-scientific appraisals. He admitted that the humorist had a volatile temperament and possessed a wide range of feeling; Mark was "an idealist of a most uncompromising sort," who was swept to the heights by the noble and sublime, but plunged into despair by the horrors mankind committed.[204] Though primarily a critical essay, this piece is one of the most valid summations of Mark Twain's characteristics. Mark, an improviser in both life and literature, lacked the discipline which made Henry James a great structurist, but he had on the other hand an accumulation of deep and varied experiences. "So volatile a temperament and so comprehensive an experience have rarely been housed in one man,"[205] concludes Grattan, who finds this the logical explanation for the unevenness of Twain's work. Of Brooks' theory Grattan observes, "No civilization can be so arranged that it will detect and coddle genius from the cradle to the grave."[206] He admits that Mark often gave himself up to the money-making of the Gilded Age, but nevertheless contends that "he was strong enough to reject it insofar as it violated his ideals of decency and honor."[207]

Bernard DeVoto wrote *Mark Twain's America* to refute the charges of Van Wyck Brooks against Clemens and his environment. It is not a biography, but as the author in-

203 *The Story of the World's Literature* (New York: Horace Liveright. Inc., 1925), p. 532.

204 C. Hartley Grattan, "Mark Twain" in *American Writers on American Literature,* edited by John Macy (New York: Horace Liveright, Inc., 1931), p. 276.

205 *Ibid.,* p. 275.

206 *Ibid.,* p. 277.

207 *Idem.* DeVoto called Grattan's essay on Mark "the finest treatment of him in print," *Mark Twain's America,* p. 218.

tended, a preface to Twain's writings. For the student, it is the most important book since Paine's official life. DeVoto examines historically the country into which young Sam Clemens was born and the influences which went into his development. Himself a product of the West, a student of the frontier and its literature, DeVoto presents Clemens as the natural heir of frontier culture: the folk stories of the pioneer, Negro lore, together with the formative influence of the native humorists. DeVoto demonstrates the presence of beauty in frontier life and shows the poetic quality imparted to Mark Twain's prose by the forest and the prairie. There is the epic sweep, the length and breadth of the great river, which also afforded opportunity to watch an entire civilization passing in review. Mark's debt to the earlier humorists of the old Southwest is discussed and for the first time brought clearly into focus.

But DeVoto's account of the frontier is not all poetry; there is violence with the horrors of gang warfare, the "Butcher-knife boys," the Murrells, who murdered, plundered, and terrorized. Vice in all forms flourished in the river towns and on the steam boats; the world's oldest profession ranged from the parlor houses to the "cribs"—everything from plumes and silk to rags and filth. There was gambling, accompanied by all degrees of card sharks and confidence men. These phases of life were a part of Mark Twain's America, part of the influences that made Mark Twain. As a corrective to Brooks, DeVoto wastes no time on what Mark Twain might have said: "I have no interest beyond his books. My effort has been to perceive where and how they issue from American life."[208] The purpose is to bring discussion back to what Mark Twain actually wrote, away from suppositions and theories. As the book is not a complete biography, its chief concern is the

208 *Mark Twain's America* (Boston: Little, Brown and Co., Revised Edition, 1935), p. xi.

Mid-Western and Far Western phases, by which time DeVoto believes Mark Twain was fully developed; thus there is brief treatment of the final years. To DeVoto, Samuel Clemens was a normal boy, who grew up naturally with no desire to be anything other than he was. A flaw in the permanent value of the book is that so much space is consumed in refutation of the psychopathic theories about Twain, arguments which needed demolishing, but now no longer seem worthy of the importance given them.

DeVoto affirms the freedom of the frontier from Puritanism with its destructive inhibitions; he emphasizes the richness of its folk art, masculine in tone and therefore often humorously coarse and uproarious. "Samuel Clemens," says DeVoto, "was born to this humor, realism, and philosophy. All his life he was a story-teller, in the manner and idiom of the frontier."[209] The realistic backwoods humor of Longstreet, the robust fun of "Sut Lovingood," the legendary anecdotes attributed to Davy Crockett—all, explains DeVoto, preceded and helped produce Mark Twain. Clemens' work on Western newspapers, which contained the embryo of his more mature satire and irony, completed the development. DeVoto says:

> Washoe and California had finished what the mid-western frontier and the Mississippi had begun. These casual pieces outline the future: the humorist, the social satirist, the pessimist, the novelist of American character, Mark Twain exhilarated, sentimental, cynical, angry, and depressed, are all here. The rest is only development.[210]

Concerning the question of Eastern influence on Twain's art, DeVoto adds, "He came East and he accepted tuition."[211] But this tuition is not seriously regarded, since the excisions of Mrs. Clemens and Howells were of the kind that editors of that day would have insisted upon anyway.

209 *Ibid.*, p. 94.
210 *Ibid.*, p. 166.
211 *Ibid.*, p. 207.

Mark's literary vocabulary, it is noted, changed little after he left California. Thus it was more the genteel tradition which held Mark Twain in bounds, even as it held Robert Browning. Mrs. Clemens and Howells are freed of the charges that they robbed America of a great artist. Instead, the humor of the frontier, sometimes deviating into bad taste, was turned in a more refined direction, yet it still found adequate expression through the medium of Twain's genius. As the climax of frontier literature, he remains for DeVoto the humorist and storyteller, whose work best depicts our civilization because only he in this tradition possessed the powers. DeVoto states:

> No other writer of his time touched the life of America at so many places. His mind was encyclopaedic, restless, inquisitive, untiring. Criticism has said that he directed no humor against the abuses of his time: the fact is that research can find few elements of the age that Mark Twain did not burlesque, satirize, or deride.[212]

Mark Twain, then, fulfilled his promise as an artist, being neither betrayed by his times nor untruthful to himself. Not only did he widen the range of our fiction and create vivid characters, but he transformed it all into art through the glow of imagination. DeVoto in depicting Mark Twain's America has explained the sources and analyzed the elements constituting his art. He believes that Mark wrote about what interested him, and that most of his restrictions resulted in conformations to good taste, rather than weakening of his material.

Specifically DeVoto has corrected certain biographical errors, such as the story of selling the coonskin, the Comstock duel, and the origin of the "Jumping Frog"; the inaccuracies concerning the apprenticeship to Ament and Mark's premature grayness; and he has called attention to purely theoretical interpretations of such incidents as

[212] *Ibid.*, p. 267.

Twain's walk to Virginia City, and the promise at his father's death. Important, too, is the critical material, which remains the fullest analysis of Twain's more important books. For DeVoto, "There is more of America in Mark Twain's books than in any others. . . . He wrote books that have in them something eternally true to the core of his nation's life."[213] And they were written, says DeVoto, with "splendor . . . imagination . . . greatness."

Fred Lewis Pattee, even as John Macy, seemed to anticipate something of the approaching Brooks-DeVoto controversy in his *A History of American Literature Since 1870* (1915). He valued highly the Hannibal background, and states, "His books nowhere rise into the pure serene of literature unless touched at some point by this magic stream that flowed so marvelously through his boyhood. The two discoverers of the Mississippi were De Soto and Mark Twain."[214] After his education on the river, Mark then entered upon what Pattee—rejecting any thought of corrupting influence—regarded as the graduate course of the Western years. For him there are three Mark Twains: "the droll comedian . . . indignant protester . . . romancer"—and it is the third, who caught the "sunset glow" of a vanished phase of America, the age of Mississippi steamboats and Western gold rush days, who lives as a great artist.[215]

In a later study for the American Writers Series, *Mark Twain: Representative Selections* (1935), Pattee did not reverse his opinions, but gave them fuller expression. Aware of the vogue enjoyed by Brooks, he rejected all the theories expounded as Mark's ordeal; the charges against Jane Clemens and Olivia, Pattee dismissed by terming their exponents "theory-riding Freudists." He repudiates, too, the

213 *Ibid.*, p. 321.

214 *A History of American Literature Since 1870* (New York: Century Co., 1915), p. 48.

215 *Ibid.*, p. 58.

deprecation of Hannibal and Washoe, for Pattee insisted that here Mark found inspiration for his finest work. That the East prevented his complete realization of that early inspiration Pattee dismissed as "Nonsense! Twaddle!"[216] Indicating the proper approach to Mark's work to be through his humor, Pattee affirms that Clemens' sensitive conscience and complex emotional attitude do not necessarily make a frustrated Shelley. Of Mark's position in literature Pattee is not so enthusiastic, but regardless of critical estimate, he insists upon Mark Twain as the product of an environment fortunate for his talents, and his greatest talent was the gift of making people laugh.

A sound informative volume, *Mark Twain at Work* (1942), is a limited but important study of Twain's methods of writing. Bernard DeVoto has explained something of Mark's habits of composition and solutions of difficulties. Clemens' episodic methods are apparent in his attempts to use the materials of *Tom Sawyer,* the first of these being the "Boy's Manuscript" in which Tom's adventures are performed by Billy Rogers.[217] Indeed the seed from which the central action of *Tom Sawyer* developed—"random and clumsy scenes"—began first as burlesque, and with little attention to "minutiae."[218] It was not until Mark turned to memories of youth, picturing the idyll of boyhood, preserving the nostalgic dream, that he hit upon the key to greatness. As DeVoto says:

> Time has stopped short; the frontier has passed by and the industrial revolution is not yet born. Life is confident and untroubled, moves serenely at an unhurried pace, fulfills itself in peace. Islanded in security, in natural beauty, St. Petersburg is an idyll of what we once were, of what it is now more than ever

216 *Mark Twain: Representative Selections,* ed. with introduction, F. L. Pattee (New York: American Book Co., 1935), p. xxvii.

217 DeVoto dates this manuscript about 1870, *Mark Twain at Work* (Cambridge: Harvard University Press, 1942), p. 5.

218 "Boy's Manuscript" is here printed, *Ibid.,* pp. 25–44.

necessary to remember we once were. Here also the book captures and will keep secure forever a part of America . . . of America over the hills and far away.[219]

Yet *Tom Sawyer* developed only after several false starts, and after some of the same materials—the description of the society amid which Sam Clemens matured—had been utilized in *The Gilded Age*. DeVoto's discussion of *Huckleberry Finn* shows how Mark undervalued the effort, even pigeonholed it, as the momentum of initial enthusiasm slowed to a halt. Elsewhere Clemens explained a similar break in writing *Tom Sawyer:* "—my tank had run dry; it was empty; the stock of materials in it was exhausted; the story could not go on without materials; it could not be wrought out of nothing."[220] Thus Mark worked, declaring that whenever he struck a snag, he had merely to wait, even if for two or three years, until the tank of inspiration again filled.

DeVoto believes that Twain laid *Huckleberry Finn* aside during the summer of 1876, because in his original idea to continue *Tom Sawyer* there was no "dynamic purpose." Though achieving some great passages, Clemens lost interest, letting *Huck* fall by the wayside while he regaled Joe Twichell with *1601* and collaborated with Bret Harte on *Ah Sin*. For six years *Huck* remained on the shelf; meanwhile Clemens busied himself with *A Tramp Abroad* and *The Prince and the Pauper*. Not until Mark revisited the river to collect materials for *Life on the Mississippi* did he again turn to *Huck;* in fact the river book was partly a rehearsal of materials. DeVoto says, "His trip down the river had refilled the tank; he was ready to work again."[221] Twain's unpublished Notebooks reveal how he selected certain subjects, discarded some, altered others, or used them intact—all resulting in a masterpiece.

219 *Ibid.,* p. 24.
220 *Mark Twain in Eruption,* p. 197.
221 *Mark Twain at Work,* p. 63.

The final essay entitled "The Symbols of Despair" DeVoto calls "a chapter, hitherto unwritten, in the biography of Mark Twain," one "agonizing as personal history."[222] DeVoto believes Twain was so deeply hurt by his personal disasters that the wound affected the artist as much as the man. Hence came the urge to write, not alone to alleviate his grief but "to vindicate himself as a writer, to restore the image [of himself] that had been impaired."[223] Frustration, however, ensued as projects were abandoned or came to naught:

> The force that was impelling him to write was, clearly, both desperate and remorseless. Only a man who was hellridden could write so much. Think of the inner desperation this indicates—and think how that desperation must have grown and spread when time after time he was forced to realize that he could not finish what he had begun.[224]

The desperation arising from this sense of failure led Mark in exculpation to write *What Is Man?,* in which the philosophy of determinism eventuates into a defense. At the same time, another manuscript was started, broken off occasionally, finally to remain truncated, but valuable in revealing Twain's inner feelings. The theme is that of a person of integrity, struck down by catastrophes, disgraced before the world, yet not through faults of his own. Still more was required to bring the artist peace of mind, for it was not even enough to escape blame or view disaster as a bad dream from which one awakes. DeVoto indeed suspects another answer:

> If nothing existed but a homeless thought wandering forlorn among the empty eternities, then his smaller agony and his personal guilt were also a dream. If everything was dream, then clearly the accused prisoner might be discharged. The accusa-

222 *Ibid.,* p. 105.
223 *Ibid.,* p. 110.
224 *Ibid.,* p. 112.

tion begotten by his experience could be stilled by destroying all experience.[225]

Thus came *The Mysterious Stranger,* which concludes with Satan's statement: "It is all a dream—a grotesque and foolish dream."[226]

Summary and Conclusion

The growth of Mark Twain biography and the critical evaluation of Clemens' published autobiographical writings has been, for the most part, a continuous evolution. Although split, for a time at least, into the separate and disparate channels of Brooks and DeVoto, it has shown no diminution, until only a few important phases of Mark Twain's life remain to be detailed. A glance at the many books written about Samuel Clemens, beginning with John Camden Hotten's sketch in 1873, shows the steady progress leading to the scholarly methods and understanding of Wagenknecht, Ferguson, Trilling, and Wecter. First naturally came Will M. Clemens' "potboiler," now interesting only for collectors, to be followed by the eulogistic tributes of friends and associates, finally culminating in Paine's monumental biography.

To reach a critical evaluation and understanding of the contributions made thus far to Twain biography we may best follow, not the order of their publication, but rather the chronology of Mark Twain's life. At present there are five books which treat this life as a whole.[227] The first, Archibald Henderson's *Mark Twain* (1911), though now unimportant as biography, made two distinct contributions to the interpretation of Twain's work. Henderson revealed the international citizen—the world-humorist, at home and abroad—bestowing his praise or venting his censure regard-

225 *Ibid.,* pp. 129–30.

226 *The Mysterious Stranger,* p. 140.

227 Lionel Trilling is now writing a critical biography.

less of race or place. Approaching Mark as a humorist, he emphasized at the same time, the serious thinker, moral and sociological. Paine's *Mark Twain: A Biography* (1912) we may reacclaim as a valuable storehouse of source material, at times both inaccurate and inadequate, frequently lacking in perception, but containing too much information to be totally discarded. Finally, the scholarly studies of Wagenknecht and Ferguson, while penetrating, were not intended as full-scale, detailed narratives. Though providing an accurate portrait, both need supplement from other sources. Nevertheless, DeLancey Ferguson's *Mark Twain: Man and Legend* (1943) remains to this moment our best single volume, taking preference over Wagenknecht's *Mark Twain: The Man and His Work* (1935); written later, it contains material unavailable to Wagenknecht, who produced an equally valuable book when it was published. The latest biography, *The Adventures of Mark Twain* (1954), by Jerry Allen is entertaining and brings a great deal of material together, but it makes no advance in scholarship.

Minnie M. Brashear's *Mark Twain, Son of Missouri* (1934) inaugurated a new era of restricted, concentrated research in Twain biography. Miss Brashear shows, largely through contemporary newspapers and her intimate knowledge of the scene, that the cultural resources of the region have been underestimated, and this carefully limited study traces young Sam's reactions to his actual environment. More intimate in knowledge of the Clemens family, Samuel C. Webster's *Mark Twain, Business Man* (1946) adds, also, new information about Hannibal—especially the Clemens family, their customs, attitudes, and habits prior to the Civil War. Brashear presents the outside influences from a region; Webster adds the particular nature of the family matrix. Dixon Wecter's *Sam Clemens of Hannibal* (1952) is a definitive presentation of both, in which the facts are summarized judiciously and fresh discoveries are introduced to further emphasize the influence of Hannibal upon Mark Twain's entire career.

As yet no intensive study of Mark Twain on the Mississippi has appeared; thus one of the most colorful, romantic, and important aspects of his biography awaits definitive treatment. But the rich field of the Western years has been explored. Ivan Benson has supplied new data, disclosed misconceptions, and corrected old errors through a study of Mark's contributions to Western periodicals. As a biographical account *Mark Twain's Western Years* (1938) is a reliable guide to what he did, how he wrote, and the people who influenced him. More restricted in scope, Effie Mona Mack's *Mark Twain in Nevada* (1947) emphasizes the influence of Comstock journalism in Mark's development. Although not a special study of Twain, Franklin Walker's *San Francisco's Literary Frontier* (1939) integrates Mark accurately into the rapid development of a definite literary culture which left its impress upon his personality.

Walter Francis Frear's account of the Sandwich Islands visit, *Mark Twain and Hawaii* (1947), treats fully every phase of that sojourn of four months and one day, its subsequent influence on Twain as a lecturer and writer, and his persisting memories of it. This book may be said to bring down the curtain on the prologue to Samuel L. Clemens' career; having adopted a pseudonym in the West, he appeared upon the Eastern stage as Mark Twain.

For general treatment of these preceding backgrounds *Mark Twain's America* (1932) is invaluable. Bernard DeVoto developed a panoramic picture of the times and customs amid which Mark grew up, the American life from which his books emerged. Written as a corrective to the interpretations of Van Wyck Brooks in the *Ordeal of Mark Twain* (1920), this study of the frontier, while stressing its violence and hardship, attested also the folk-art, the idyll of Hannibal's non-competitive society, the magic attraction of the river boats, and the glorious adventure in the West. An affirmation of frontier society, graced with its component of Southern gentility in Hannibal, uproariously masculine in the barrooms of Washoe, cosmopolitan in its world of Mississippi steamboats and California gold coast, *Mark Twain's America* reveals a curriculum unequalled for nourishment of genius.

The Eastern years in Mark Twain's life have not been so carefully investigated. But Albert Bigelow Paine's *Mark Twain: A Biography* (1912) is indispensable; indeed, here is a Boswellian account of the final four years made possible only through daily association. William Dean Howells' *My Mark Twain* (1910) is the best of our memorabilia from his friends, while Clara Clemens' *My Father, Mark Twain* (1931), containing a selection of love letters and personal documents, gives an intimate picture of the family. Kenneth R. Andrews' *Nook Farm* (1950) is a comprehensive study of Clemens' Hartford environment. Until somebody creates similar studies for the Eastern days spent in Buffalo, Elmira, and New York, together with an account of Mark Twain abroad, we must content ourselves with the above, thankful for such rich source materials.

The figure of Samuel Clemens which emerges from all these biographical studies is that of a sensitive, intelligent child who grew into a young man, self-reliant, industrious, and honest, then became a loving father adored by wife and children, and finally stood admired, honored, and respected by his reading public and his host of friends. The young boy who left Hannibal to make his way alone in the cities of the East possessed courage and fortitude, as did the young man who set out alone for the Amazon—hardly the actions of one unable to rely upon himself or face the world. It took industry to learn piloting, even as it did to succeed in journalism on the Pacific coast. And the same industry and courage appeared when Twain, ill in health and impoverished through business failure, set out to lecture his way round the world in order to pay his debts and rebuild a fortune.

That Mark enjoyed worldly success is apparent; he liked to live well, but he had no inclination toward exploitation. In *The Gilded Age* and *A Connecticut Yankee* he emphatically announced his dislike of imperialism and all forms of human subjugation, whether arising from monarchy, capitalism, or whatsoever form of privilege; for Clemens had no use for any form of dictatorship, whether coming from oligarchy or proletariat. Whatever oppressed the individual, denying him equal rights, Mark fought; he was a democrat, and democracy like Christianity values the individual, whose worth, regardless of color, race, creed, or wealth, depends upon character, honor, and integrity.

It is true that during his later years, following catastrophes of death, illness, and bankruptcy, Twain became for a time frustrated and bitter, but with the gradual working out of his final philosophy of life he became again the successful man and writer. And if in his final outlook he viewed the future with pessimism, he may have felt the imminence of world conflicts, depressions, and upheavals. One whose sensitive nature had always been keenly aware of human suffering—even as a lad in Hannibal, or as a young man in the West—was not likely to be insensitive to world trends then beginning to take shape.

We have the life story of a man, forced from early necessity to make his way in the world, who accomplished that task, who never shirked his duties to his family or community, who made many lifelong friends whom he never forsook or forgot, no matter how separated by distance or time. In short, it is the American success story of a noble character, colorful personality, beloved man, and creative genius.

SELECTED BIBLIOGRAPHY

Branch, Edgar M. "A Chronological Bibliography of the Writings of Samuel Clemens to June 8, 1867," *American Literature,* XVIII, 109–59 (May, 1946).

[The most complete bibliography of this period. Invaluable.]

Brownell, George H. "About Twain in Periodicals," *Twainian,* I, No. 7, 4–5 (1939).

[Additions to Merle Johnson's *Bibliography*.]

Henderson, Archibald. *Mark Twain.* New York: Frederick A. Stokes, 1911.

[Contains excellent bibliography covering 1869 to 1910; especially useful for foreign criticism.]

Johnson, Merle. *A Bibliography of the Works of Mark Twain,* revised edition. New York: Harper & Brothers, 1935.

[Indispensable; the most thorough book at the present, containing descriptions of first editions.]

Leary, Lewis, ed. *Articles on American Literature Appearing in Current Periodicals, 1920–1945*. Durham, N. C.: Duke University Press, 1947.

[Pp. 127–138 list articles on Clemens. Very helpful to the student.]

Paine, Albert Bigelow. *Mark Twain: A Biography*. New York: Harper & Brothers, 1912. IV, 1674–1684.

[Appendix X to the final volume gives a useful chronological list of Clemens' writing from 1851 to 1910.]

Rinaker, Clarissa. Bibliography of Mark Twain in *Cambridge History of American Literature.* New York: Macmillan, 1921. III, 635–639.

[Best to 1921.]

Spiller, Robert E., *et al.*, eds. *Literary History of the United States.* New York: Macmillan Company, 1948. III, 442–450.

[The bibliography of this history is good for both primary and secondary sources.]

Wagenknecht, Edward, *Mark Twain: The Man and His Work.* New Haven: Yale University Press, 1935.

[Contains a full working bibliography to 1935. Good secondary material.]

AUTOBIOGRAPHICAL SOURCES

The Love Letters of Mark Twain, edited by Dixon Wecter. New York: Harper & Brothers, 1949.

[A valuable addition to the facts of Twain biography, as well as picturing an ideal love story.]

Mark Twain's Autobiography, with an Introduction by Albert Bigelow Paine. New York: Harper & Brothers, 1924.

[A two-volume selection from Twain's autobiographical papers.]

Mark Twain in Eruption, edited by Bernard DeVoto. New York: Harper & Brothers, 1940.

[Autobiographical papers from the Clemens Literary Estate, a valuable contribution to our knowledge of Twain's mind and thought.]

Mark Twain's Letters, arranged with comment by Albert Bigelow Paine. New York: Harper & Brothers, 1917.

[A two-volume collection of letters, but by no means complete.]

Mark Twain's Letters to Will Bowen, edited by Theodore Hornberger. Austin: University of Texas, 1941.

[Sixteen letters from Twain to "My First & Oldest & Dearest Friend," interesting for reminiscences about Hannibal.]

Mark Twain to Mrs. Fairbanks, edited by Dixon Wecter. San Marino, California: Huntington Library, 1949.

[Interesting, intimate correspondence.]

Mark Twain to Uncle Remus, 1881–1885, edited by Thomas H. English. Atlanta, Georgia: Emory University Library, 1953.

[Letters from Twain to Joel Chandler Harris.]

Mark Twain's Notebook, prepared for publication by Albert Bigelow Paine. New York: Harper & Brothers, 1935.

[Selections from Twain's journals, brief and sketchy.]

Mark Twain's Speeches, with an Introduction by Albert Bigelow Paine, and an Appreciation by William Dean Howells. New York: Harper & Brothers, 1923.

[A selection of Twain's speeches, not complete.]

BIOGRAPHY

Allen, Jerry. *The Adventures of Mark Twain.* Boston: Little, Brown and Co., 1954.

[The most recent biography, based partly on Twain's fiction.]

Andrews, Kenneth R. *Nook Farm: Mark Twain's Hartford Circle.* Cambridge, Massachusetts: Harvard University Press, 1950.

[A full treatment of Clemens' friends and associations during the Hartford years.]

Bellamy, Gladys Carmen. *Mark Twain as a Literary Artist.* Norman: University of Oklahoma Press, 1950.

[Useful and provocative; mainly critical rather than biographical.]

Benson, Ivan. *Mark Twain's Western Years.* Stanford University, California: Stanford University Press, 1938.

[The standard work on Twain's life and writings in the West. Contains material not printed before.]

Branch, Edgar Marquess. *The Literary Apprenticeship of Mark Twain.* Urbana: University of Illinois Press, 1950.

[More critical than biographical; a highly useful addition to Twain scholarship.]

Brashear, Minnie M. *Mark Twain, Son of Missiouri.* Chapel Hill: University of North Carolina Press, 1934.

[Invaluable for the period covered; takes Clemens up to his departure for the river. Prints new material.]

Brooks, Van Wyck. *The Ordeal of Mark Twain.* New York: E. P. Dutton & Company, revised edition, 1933.

[Revised edition varies slightly from 1920 version. A book often penetrating in revealing Twain's sensitivity and artistic nature, but lacking in understanding of frontier environment. Of no value as conclusion, but helpful of suggestion.]

——. *The Times of Melville and Whitman.* New York: E. P. Dutton & Company, 1947.

[Contains much about Twain; interesting mostly for Brooks' enlightened revisions of his former attitude toward the frontier.]

Canby, Henry Seidel. *Turn West, Turn East: Mark Twain and Henry James.* Boston: Houghton Mifflin Co., 1951.

[Contrasts Twain and James to show the basic Americanism of both.]

Cardwell, Guy A. *Twins of Genius.* Michigan State College Press, 1953.

[A detailed study of the relationship between Twain and George W. Cable, containing a number of unpublished letters.)

Clemens, Clara. *My Father, Mark Twain.* New York: Harper & Brothers, 1931.

[A valuable, intimate picture by Clemens' daughter.]

Clemens, Cyril. *Young Sam Clemens.* Portland, Maine: Leon Tebbetts Editions, 1942.

[Adds nothing to our knowledge of Clemens.]

Clemens, Will M. *Mark Twain: The Story of His Life and Work.* San Francisco: Clemens Publishing Company, 1892.

[Of no value, but of interest as the first book of Twain biography.]

DeCasseres, Benjamin. *When Huck Finn Went Highbrow.* New York: Thomas F. Madigan, 1934.

[Tells of Twain's admiration for Browning's poetry.]

DeQuille, Dan (William Wright). *The Big Bonanza.* New York: Alfred A. Knopf, 1947.

[An important book on Virginia City and the Comstock Lode, written by Mark's old friend on the *Territorial Enterprise.* Splendid for the Western background.]

DeVoto, Bernard. *Mark Twain's America.* Boston: Little, Brown, and Company, 1935.

[Reprint of the 1932 edition. The best book on the backgrounds that produced Clemens. Indispensable.]

——. *Mark Twain at Work.* Cambridge, Massachusetts: Harvard University Press, 1942.

[Not biography, but an important account of how Clemens wrote, and a penetrating analysis of his pessimism.]

Ferguson, DeLancey. *Mark Twain: Man and Legend.* Indianapolis: Bobbs-Merrill Company, 1943.

[The best single volume on Twain at present.]

Frear, Walter Francis. *Mark Twain and Hawaii.* Chicago: The Lakeside Press, 1947.

[A definitive treatment of Twain's visit to the Sandwich Islands and its influence.]

Gillis, William R. *Goldrush Days with Mark Twain.* New York: Albert and Charles Boni, 1930.

[Inaccurate, of no biographical value.]

Grattan, C. Hartley. "Mark Twain" in *American Writers on American Literature.* New York: Horace Liveright, Inc., 1931.

[The best essay on Twain in print, until superseded by Dixon Wecter's in the *Literary History of the United States.* Still of value.]

Henderson, Archibald. *Mark Twain.* New York: Frederick A. Stokes, 1911.

[A perceptive study; still of interest.]

Hotten, John Camden. Biographical Introduction to *Choice Humorous Works of Mark Twain.* London: Chatto and Windus, 1873, revised 1888.

[The first sketch of Twain's life, anecdotal and full of inaccuracies.]

Howells, William Dean. *My Mark Twain.* New York: Harper & Brothers, 1910.

[Clemens as seen by a friend and fellow writer; an important contribution to Twain biography.]

Lawton, Mary. *A Lifetime with Mark Twain.* New York: Harcourt, Brace & Company, 1925.

[The memories of Katy Leary, for thirty years a servant in the Clemens household; an interesting contribution.]

Leacock, Stephen. *Mark Twain.* New York: D. Appleton & Co., 1933.

[Not important, but interesting as an account of Twain by another fine humorist.]

Lemonnier, Léon. *Mark Twain: L'Homme et Son Oeuvre.* Paris: Librairie Arthème Fayard, 1946.

[Interesting French appraisal, sound in values.]

Mack, Effie Mona. *Mark Twain in Nevada.* New York: Charles Scribner's Sons, 1947.

[A full account of Clemens during the days of the Comstock Lode, though containing more about Nevada than about Twain.]

Masters, Edgar Lee. *Mark Twain: A Portrait.* New York: Charles Scribner's Sons, 1938.

[Repeats all the fallacies of the Brooks theory; of no value to the student of Twain.]

Matthews, Brander. "Memories of Mark Twain," *The Tocsin of Revolt.* New York: Charles Scribner's Sons, 1922, pp. 253–94.

[Interesting biographical contribution.]

Paine, Albert Bigelow. *Mark Twain: A Biography,* 3 vols, New York: Harper & Brothers, 1912; reissued in 4 vols.; then in 2 vols. in 1935.

[The authorized life; still a storehouse of information and indispensable, despite the need for corrections of many passages.]

Wagenknecht, Edward. *Mark Twain: The Man and His Work.* New Haven, Connecticut: Yale University Press, 1935.

[Best single book to 1935 on Twain's life and work.]

Walker, Franklin. *San Francisco's Literary Frontier.* New York: Alfred Knopf, 1939.

[Sheds light on Twain's activities in California.]

Wallace, Elizabeth. *Mark Twain and the Happy Island.* Chicago: A. C. McClurg & Company, 1913.

[A charming picture of Clemens' visits to Bermuda.]

Webster, Samuel Charles. *Mark Twain, Business Man.* Boston: Little, Brown and Company, 1946.

[Adds biographical information about the early years of Twain, as well as the business transactions. An important contribution.]

Wecter, Dixon. "Mark Twain" in *Literary History of the United States.* New York: Macmillan & Company, 1948. II, 917–939.

[The best single essay on Mark Twain in print.]

——. *Sam Clemens of Hannibal.* Boston: Houghton Mifflin Co., 1952.

[Definitive study of Clemens' youth; invaluable for the Hannibal influence on Twain's mature art.]

ARTICLES OF BIOGRAPHICAL VALUE

Booth, Bradford A. "Mark Twain's Friendship with Emeline Beach," *American Literature,* XIX, 219–30 (November, 1947).

[Letters covering forty years of friendship.]

Brashear, Minnie M. "Mark Twain Juvenilia," *American Literature,* II, 25–53 (March, 1930).

[Describes earliest journalism of Clemens and shows the cultural importance of Hannibal as a town.]

Clemens, Clara. "Recollections of Mark Twain," *North American Review,* CCXXX, 522–529, 654–659; CCXXXI, 50–57 (November, December, 1930; January, 1931).

[Intimate family memoirs and letters.]

Eastman, Max. "Mark Twain's Elmira," *Harper's Magazine,* CLXVI, 620–32 (May, 1938).

[Important article on the social and religious attitudes of the Langdons and their friends.]

Lorch, Fred W. "Lecture Trips and Visits of Mark Twain in Iowa," *The Iowa Journal of History and Politics,* XXVII, 507–547 (October, 1929).

[Details of Twain's Iowa visits from 1867 to 1890.]

——. "Mark Twain in Iowa," *The Iowa Journal of History and Politics,* XXVII, 409–56, 507–47 (July, 1929).

[New facts of biography on Muscatine and Keokuk periods, 1853–55. First printing of two letters to Annie Taylor and three "Snodgrass" letters.]

——. "Mark Twain and the 'Campaign that Failed,'" *American Literature,* XII, 454–70 (January, 1941).

[A comprehensive examination of the facts and a sound evaluation.]

Roberts, Harold. "Sam Clemens: Florida Days," *Twainian,* I, 4–6 (March, 1942).

[The influence of John A. Quarles and his farm.]

Webster, Samuel Charles. "Mark Twain: Business Man—Letters and Memoirs," *Atlantic Monthly,* CLXXIV, 37–46 (June, 1944); 72–80 (July, 1944); 71–77 (August, 1944); 90–96 (September, 1944); 74–80 (October, 1944); 100–106 (November, 1944).

[New materials of biographical import, later used in the same author's book on this subject.]

Wecter, Dixon. "The Love Letters of Mark Twain," *Atlantic Monthly,* CLXXX, 33–9 (November, 1947).

[Printed later in book form.]

——. "Mark Twain and the West," *Huntington Library Quarterly,* VIII, 359–77 (August, 1945).

[The best single article on Clemens in Nevada and California.]

CHAPTER II

BACKGROUNDS

HANNIBAL

"MY PARENTS," wrote Mark Twain, "removed to Missouri in the early 'thirties; I do not remember just when, for I was not born then and cared nothing for such things."[1] Located at the forks of Salt River (since become proverbial) Florida was a mere village in Monroe County, scarcely two hundred miles away from Indian territory. Here on November 30, 1835, the impartial bestower of genius, that once touched a farmer's cot in Alloway, selected the small home on one of Florida's two black muddy streets. Until the age of four the boy, christened Samuel Langhorne Clemens, lived amid the rude houses, mostly of logs, backed against the cornfields with rail fences on either side. A log church, puncheon-floored, beneath which hogs slept until disturbed by the dogs, served on week days as a schoolhouse. The village boasted two stores, one owned by Sam's uncle, John A. Quarles, where a man who made a purchase was entitled to draw a drink of whisky from the barrel, or a boy was given half a handful of sugar. Existence was primitive and purchases came cheap.[2] Business, however, was expected to expand with the community, but unfortunately Florida refused to grow, despite the aid of young Sam, who claimed:

[1] *Autobiography,* I, 94.

[2] Mark lists chickens at ten cents apiece, butter at six cents a pound, and whisky at ten cents a gallon. Pipe-smoking cost nothing with an abundance of tobacco growing. See the interesting list given by Twain. *Ibid.,* I, 9–10.

The village contained a hundred people and I increased the population by 1 per cent. It is more than many of the best men in history could have done for a town. It may not be modest of me to refer to this, but it is true. There is no record of a person doing as much—not even Shakespeare. But I did it for Florida, and it shows that I could have done it for any place—even London, I suppose.[3]

Surely memories before removal to Hannibal are nil, though Mark tells us, "For many years I believed that I remembered helping my grandfather drink his whisky toddy when I was six weeks old, but I do not tell about that any more, now; I am grown old and my memory is not as active as it used to be."[4] Soon the Clemens family moved again, pushed onward by financial necessity and the hope of better conditions. They were not movers by nature, but Hannibal offered promise of improved fortunes for the family. Here John Marshall Clemens became a leading citizen, serving on committees for municipal improvement, while he dreamed of riches to accrue someday from the Tennessee land.[5]

Hannibal, somnolent on the West bank of the Mississippi, actually held no opportunities for wealth. Yet around it rushed the tides of Western expansion as the continent opened before the optimistic pioneers courageously pushing forward, intent upon their fortunes. At its very door the great Mississippi presented a never-ending spectacle, continuously varied. While viewing the drama, however, the little town was not a participant; actually Hannibal was a market place for nearby farmers. Thus Sam Clemens'

[3] *Ibid.*, I, 95.

[4] *Ibid.*, I, 96.

[5] This tract of land in Fentress County, East Tennessee, never brought the Clemens family anything, but John Clemens regarded it as a potential source of wealth. At the time of purchase he said, "Whatever befalls me, my heirs are secure; I shall not live to see these acres turn to silver and gold, but my children will." *Ibid.*, I, 3. This Tennessee Land figured importantly in Twain's contributions to *The Gilded Age*.

youth began in idyllic, ante-bellum days, amid a pre-industrial society, for the industrial revolution and the sectional conflicts leading to civil war were yet to intrude upon Hannibal in the days of Tom Sawyer.[6]

By inheritance Sam was a Southerner. John Marshall Clemens came from Virginia, bringing with him the ideals of gentlefolk.[7] Not wealthy himself, he belonged to the class of small planter or professional man, in which tradition he fitted himself for the law. The Clemenses, though not important in Virginia, were minor slaveholders, part of John Clemens' inheritance being three slaves. Forced by his father's death to assume male-headship of the family when only seven years old, he became self-supporting. Circumstances then took the family into Kentucky—the first move calculated to relieve financial pressure. There young Clemens fell in love with and married Jane Lampton, whose family, also from Virginia, claimed kinship with the Earls of Durham. Upon moving to Kentucky the Lamptons intermarried with the Montgomery and Casey families. Soon they were faced with fighting Indians; Kentucky annals record how the sister of Mark's great grandmother narrowly escaped being captured by Indians.[8]

From his father Sam Clemens inherited his intellect and his integrity. Never a financial success, the elder Clemens was instead a valued citizen of each community into which he moved.[9] Although visions of wealth never materialized,

6 In Marion County, however, something of a miniature Civil War had been rehearsed between abolitionists and slave owners with victory for the latter. Brashear, p. 73. See Twain's "A Scrap of Curious History," *What is Man? and Other Sketches,* p. 182.

7 DeLancey Ferguson emphasizes Mark Twain's heritage: "They clung to the graces of life. Lavish hospitality, and therefore sufficient means to indulge in it without worry, was part of their dream, and Mark Twain, keeping open house in Hartford in the 1880's, was expressing an essential part of his ancestral tradition." *Mark Twain: Man and Legend,* p. 15.

8 Dixon Wecter, *Sam Clemens of Hannibal* (Boston: Houghton Mifflin Co., 1952), pp. 20–21.

9 Wecter has made the fullest study of John Marshall Clemens. *Supra.*

he continued the search, and he worked hard. By temperamental endowment Sam possessed his father's desire for success, his participation in civic affairs,[10] a natural pessimistic strain, joined by "free-thinking," and most fortunately of all, that fine sense of justice, an abiding interest in right and wrong, which placed all of Mark Twain's thought and action upon a high plane of integrity and honor. The influence of John Marshall Clemens upon his son has only recently been fully appreciated, largely because Mark seldom spoke of him. When he did refer to his father, Mark called him "austere," and though incorporated in a jest, such a passage as "My father and I were always on the most distant terms when I was a boy—a sort of armed neutrality so to speak," seems to reveal the true relationship.[11] The influence of Jane Clemens, however, has been fully recognized, though at times not wisely.

Van Wyck Brooks may be dismissed in the light of testimony from more reliable witnesses. As Annie Webster put it, "I can't imagine where they got the idea that Grandma was so pious and strait-laced."[12] Frustration theories aside, Jane Clemens, Kentucky belle, loved to dance, dress stylishly in bright colors, and she enjoyed a joke; to her we may attribute Sam's similar traits. Of course, she attended church and believed in God; and she tried to rear her son religiously, as do most mothers.[13] Our most recent investigators dismiss the idea of Jane Clemens as a pernicious influence. She was an attractive woman, energetic, fond of life, and at times eccentric—nothing more. We may agree with the critics who derive Mark Twain's humor from his

[10] For instance Mark's attacks on "Boss" Croker, Paine, III, 1145–7.

[11] "A Memory," *Curious Republic of Gondour* (New York: Boni and Liveright, 1919), p. 12.

[12] Webster, p. 226.

[13] The best treatment of Jane Clemens is to be found in Samuel C. Webster, *Mark Twain, Business Man.* A more specific defense appears by Doris and Samuel Webster, "Whitewashing Jane Clemens," *Bookman,* lxi (1925), 531–5.

mother, and we may add his love for colorful clothes, but we should not forget to place full emphasis upon the qualities inherited from his father.[14]

The marriage of John Clemens and Jane Lampton was not loveless, as sometimes misrepresented.[15] Samuel C. Webster has destroyed the basis for such charges by revealing Jane Clemens' senility at the the time she suggested it in old age, telling a story her granddaughter suspected appropriated from another person's experience.[16] The home life appears to have been happy and normal. Unlike the families of Poe and Whitman there is no indication of anything even bordering on the embarrassing. The family, we must admit, was hard up; and it was because of necessity that Orion at the age of fourteen became apprenticed to a printer—a step down for the son of a lawyer.[17] But aside from a natural desire to get on in the world—shared by every healthy person not congenitally lazy—the family seemed unscarred by its financial difficulties. Orion, Pamela, Sam, and Henry were normal children, enjoying a mutual affection, possessing the usual small jealousies, but growing-up sane, healthy, and with no more inhibitions than those of any law-abiding citizen.[18] Through his father and mother Sam fortunately received the inheritance of their English ancestry, transformed through pioneer environment—Anglo-Saxon customs adapted to the Mississippi Valley, where the violence of the frontier contrasted with the culture transported from Virginia.

14 For further information on Mark's ancestry and inheritance see in addition to Paine and Wecter, A V. Goodpasture, "Mark Twain, Southerner," *Tennessee Historical Magazine,* I, 253–260 (July, 1931) and C. O. Paullin, "Mark Twain's Virginia Kin," *William and Mary Quarterly,* XV, 294–8 (July, 1935).

15 Van Wyck Brooks, *The Ordeal of Mark Twain,* p. 47.

16 Webster, p. 224. See also, Wecter, pp. 18–19.

17 Ferguson, pp. 21–22.

18 Paine's narrative of the Clemens' home and Sam's early youth remains a true picture, despite factual corrections added by Brashear, Webster, and Wecter.

Hannibal was a slave-holding community; more than half of its citizens were Southerners. But actually slaves in Hannibal were few, as there were no plantations on the delta scale, only small farms on which the hands worked directly under their owners. In the village itself the Negroes were mostly household servants, happily regarded as such, and consequently treated better than the gangs of slaves impersonally supervised by overseers. Yet Negroes were not recognized as individuals; they were property, regarded as Huck looked upon Jim, despite his personal affection. For Huck's conscience, which plagued him about his duty to Jim's owner, rather than the slave and his family, was actually the conscience of a region. Yet Hannibal was not geographically of the Old South; it differed, despite its customs and its stock.[19]

Across the Alleghenies the stream of Southern culture from the tidewater of the early republic adapted itself to the Mississippi Valley. Amid other soil and climate, confronted by new conditions, it effected a changed way of life, retaining parts of the old, but receiving a new identity. Physically this society became essentially frontier, embracing equalitarianism and individualism, yet with social demarcations. As Mark was to remember:

> In the small town of Hannibal, Missouri, when I was a boy, everybody was poor, but didn't know it; and everybody was comfortable, and did know it. And there were grades of society—people of good family, people of unclassified family, people of no family. Everybody knew everybody, and was affable to everybody, and nobody put on any visible airs; yet the class lines were quite clearly drawn and the familiar social life of each class was restricted to that class. It was a little democracy which was full of liberty, equality and Fourth of July, and sincerely so, too; yet you perceived that the arisocratic taint

19 See Chapter XXXI, *Huckleberry Finn;* also Lionel Trilling's introduction to that title in the Rinehart edition; and Edgar M. Branch, "The Two Providences: Thematic Form in Huckleberry Finn," *College English,* XI, 188–95 (January, 1950).

was there. It was there, and nobody found fault with the fact, or ever stopped to reflect that its presence was an inconsistency.

I suppose that this state of things was mainly due to the circumstance that the town's population had come from slave states and still had the institution of slavery with them in their new home.[20]

That slavery was an evil never dawned upon Hannibal consciousness. Young Sam regarded all the Negroes as friends—so did the rest of Tom Sawyer's band—and with slave boys of his own age romped and played. "We were comrades," said Mark, "and yet not comrades; color and condition interposed a subtle line which both parties were conscious of and which rendered complete fusion impossible."[21] Both slave and master regarded the relationship with equanimity. Certain things were frowned upon: it was not often that Negro families were separated, the practice being generally limited to the settlement of estates. Cruelty to a slave, indeed, brought such retributive unpopularity that it remained rare. If little Sam ever saw a slave auction he never remembered it, although, as he later admitted, it may have been because the spectacle was not unusual. The sight of a chained slave, however, was another matter, for the sad faces of some once seen lived too vividly in his memory to have arisen from a common occurrence. Moreover, Mark reminds us, "The 'nigger trader' was loathed by everybody,"[22] for all, white and black, had a horror of the slave's existence on the huge plantations. The mere threat to sell a slave "down the river," as readers of *Pudd'nhead Wilson* will recall, was sufficient to reform all but the most incorrigible.[23]

20 *Autobiography,* I, 119–20.

21 *Ibid.,* I, 100.

22 *Ibid.,* I, 124.

23 It must be kept in mind that in Hannibal, a small town, all relationships were personal and direct. The impersonal fate of the plantation slave, unknown to his owner, a mere instrument of labor, was as appalling as the complete loss of individuality suffered by the human being becomes under any circumstances.

Although orientated toward the river, Hannibal retained a lifeline to the East, for with slavery the settlers brought also certain intellectual pursuits and something of Cavalier manners. There was a town library; four different bookstores advertised in the newspapers. Books and magazines in fact were plentiful, often of the best. Readers procured journals published by Putnam, Harper, Godey, and Graham, while Shakespeare, Milton, and Shelley were for sale on the book shelves, along with volumes in French, Latin, and Greek. The Bible, of course, was known to all, but the classics were read too, and current literature, especially the typical humorous writings of the section, was plentiful.[24] Despite the distances separating Hannibal and London, many citizens of the village like General Choke in *Martin Chuzzlewit* visited the seat of empire in print, or like Tom Sawyer a Hannibal boy might surrender to the distant glamour of Europe and the Orient until imagination brought the Crusades and characters from the *Arabian Nights* into the Missouri countryside.

Then the surrounding woods with its wild flowers, animals, and birds provided education of still another sort. There one could hunt, fish, or just dream away the calm summer days, for most days were calm, despite flares of violence, such as did occur. The eternal cruelties and passions were present there as elsewhere, breaking forth in perennial crimes; yet for the most part existence was happy. During two or three months each year Sam visited the farm of his uncle, John A. Quarles. Situated four miles from Florida, the farm was worked by about twenty Negroes; one of them, old "Aunt" Hannah, the children believed to be a thousand years old, while the slaves insisted she had talked with Moses and credited her thin hair to fright at seeing Pharaoh drown.

[24] See Brashear, Chapters VI and VII. Also Wecter, Chapters VII and XIII.

"It was a heavenly place for a boy, that farm of my uncle John's," Mark recalled.[25] In summer the family dined in a corridor, open at both ends, which connected the two wings of the house. Mark once recited a typical, sumptuous meal:

Fried chicken, roast pig; wild and tame turkeys, ducks and geese; venison just killed; squirrels, rabbits, pheasants, partridges, prairie-chickens; biscuits, hot batter cakes, hot buckwheat cakes, hot 'wheat bread,' hot rolls, hot corn pone; fresh corn boiled on the ear, succotash, butter-beans, string-beans, tomatoes, peas, Irish potatoes, sweet potatoes; buttermilk, sweet milk, 'clabber'; watermelons, muskmelons, cantaloupes—all fresh from the garden; apple pie, peach pie, pumpkin pie, apple dumplings, peach cobbler—I can't remember the rest. The way that the things were cooked was perhaps the main splendor—particularly a certain few of the dishes. For instance, the corn bread, the hot biscuits and wheat bread, and the fried chicken. These things have never been properly cooked in the North—in fact, no one there is able to learn the art, so far as my experience goes. The North thinks it knows how to make corn bread, but this is mere superstition. Perhaps no bread in the world is quite so good as Southern corn bread, and perhaps no bread in the world is quite so bad as the Northern imitation of it. The North seldom tries to fry chicken, and this is well; the art cannot be learned north of the line of Mason and Dixon, nor anywhere in Europe. This is not hearsay; it is experience that is speaking.[26]

The experience, he might have added, was gained from eating in the finest restaurants of the world. Yet no food ever appealed to him as did those meals at Uncle John's.

There was an orchard, tobacco fields, and a limpid brook, deeply shaded among the trees for wading. Here, also, were swimming pools, more desirable because forbidden. And little Sam played to his heart's delight, climbing the hickory and walnut trees to gather nuts in season, swinging on strands of bark stripped from hickory saplings, or if straw-

25 *Autobiography*, I, 96.
26 *Ibid.*, I, 97.

berries were ripe picking them "in the crisp freshness of the early morning, while the dew beads still sparkled upon the grass and the woods were ringing with the first songs of the birds."[27] All entered into his consciousness as the natural delight of the English countryside impressed itself upon Wordsworth during rapturous boyhood. With night, entertainment shifted to the slave quarters, or the house servants gathered about the open fireplace to tell old tales of African fantasy. While a little boy quivered with mingled fright and delight, Uncle Ned spun a blood-curdling tale to reach the climactic moment of the "Golden Arm."[28]

These old Southern customs of plantation and slave, it must be remembered, existed in a frontier environment. Dixon Wecter reminds us of the element of terror present in both *Tom Sawyer* and *Huckleberry Finn,* not just a boyish fear of ghosts and darkness, but the adult fear in a world prevalent with murder, robbery, assault, lynchings, and feuds.[29] However peaceful Hannibal might be, situated as it was, there was no isolation from intruding violence and crime. Mark remembered the man Fairfax, magnanimously sparing a creature who had just tried to murder him with a pistol that missed fire; the Corsican chasing his daughter with a flogging-rope; poor old Smarr, shot down in the main street at mid-day and dying beneath the oppressive weight of a huge family Bible open on his breast; the slave killed by a lump of slag for a slight offense; the stabbing of the "young Californian emigrant" with a bowie knife; the helpless uncle whose nephews held him and repeatedly tried to kill him with a revolver which missed fire; and the

27 *Ibid.,* I, 106. Wagenknecht compares these passages with Keats: "Not even 'The Eve of St. Agnes' is richer in sense-impressions than those descriptions." p. 7.

28 Mark used this story and Uncle Ned's method as an example in "How To Tell a Story," *The $30,000 Bequest,* p. 263.

29 "Mark Twain" in *A Literary History of the United States* (New York: Macmillan, 1948), II, 933.

drunken ruffian shot down by a widow defending her home.[30] The sight of a pistol blazing or knife flashing, followed by the red blood gushing from a death wound, was actuality to Sam Clemens. But violence though prevalent was not prevailing, and as in the realism of Howells, happiness, not sorrow, was the general rule.

Mark Twain's unpublished papers contain a lengthy list of Hannibal residents, notations about them, and comments on what became of them.[31] If sentimentality must be ascribed to those people generally, they were also endowed with idealism, for Mark remembered their being more interested in deeds of honor than in making money. In the cynicism of old age he charged the new desire for wealth above honor to changes wrought by the forty-nine gold rush. Yet the Hannibal of earlier days as recorded in unpublished manuscripts contained its unpleasant side. Commenting on Zola's *La Terre* Mark declared the vicious and abnormal minority in any American village to be our American equivalent of its naturalistic passages, for insanity, murder, rape, and fanaticism were present in his own Hannibal. A manuscript titled "Villagers of 1840–43" outlines several characters who anticipate the villagers of Sherwood Anderson; one such, a bridegroom, fails to appear for his wedding, and after prolonged search is discovered fully dressed like a bride, locked dead in the family vault.[32] Thus Sam Clemens was aware of the abnormal fringe of humanity, even as Sherwood Anderson, William Faulkner, and Eugene O'Neill. But in the world of Mark Twain as in that of Shakespeare and Chaucer the fringe never be-

30 *Autobiography,* I, 82, 118, 131–132.

31 Mark Twain Manuscripts at the University of California.

32 Dixon Wecter could find no trace of such a person in Hannibal, but many other characters mentioned are traceable. It is of vital interest to the student of realism that Mark saw and recorded the introversion and decay along with the vigor and health of Tom and Huck.

comes the whole cloth; minorities are seen perspectively, not magnified. These manuscripts, for our purpose, are important as proof, nevertheless, that the abnormal was seen and recognized.

In brief, the boy Sam Clemens observed with alert eyes, and from an orchestra seat, as it were, viewed the drama in his town and on the Mississippi. Indigent raftsmen, fast packets of commerce, luxurious side-wheelers, gay show-boats floated past in a fleeting world, romantic to the imagination, yet real and endless. They brought glimpses of a cosmopolitanism which though not of Hannibal was at least seen by the residents, and seeing was believing. The little town, meanwhile, continued to be stirred by the Westward movement without being swept into its rush. St. Louis was only eighty miles away, and all within its orbit felt tremors from the expansion, which brought the customs and manners of other places. Whether from the river traffic or West-bound emigrants, extremes of wealth and poverty and diversity of race were evident. In a way, then, Sam Clemens from early youth was a citizen of the world, not just of Hannibal, and though remaining truly regional he was saved from ignorant provincialism. Viewing society vertically through many stratas, knowing whites, both high and low, Negroes, Indians, and half-breeds, the boy was schooled during his most impressionable years through a broad view of humanity, which helped to produce the world author.

Such education naturally continued through a lifetime as Mark became a part of all he met, encountering probably a greater diversity of experience than any other American author; yet Sam's formal schooling ended when he was about twelve—not at all, it should be mentioned, to his regret. After John Marshall Clemens' death the boy became an apprentice in a printer's shop. Until the winter of 1850–51, when he went to work for his brother Orion on the Hannibal *Journal,* first called *Western Union,*[33] Sam learned the newspaper trade from Joseph P. Ament, owner of the *Missouri Courier.* Under his brother's tutelage Sam rose to sub-editor, but first he served as printer, then learned how to write.[34] The newspapers and periodical exchanges received at the office were filled with humorous anecdotes, burlesque characterizations, and hilarious satires—all brimming with exaggerations and understatements. Such writing flourished in American journalism for three decades before the Civil War: tales of bear-hunters, rivermen, country parsons, gamblers, and trappers told with vigorous, sometimes clamorous, fun. Still in his teens Sam became a part of this tradition, in fact, even contributed to it.[35] Franklin J. Meine says that the young printer became "saturated with this frontier humor."[36] Actually Sam needed no books to acquaint him with jokes and pranks, for he and his associates were constantly indulging in them.[37] Frontier humor was a part of life; the authors simply touched it up for literary consumption. Of course,

[33] Brashear states that Sam went to work for Orion in 1850 (p. 97). However, she also says that it may have been as late as 1851 (p. 101). Pattee says that Mark began work with Ament on the *Courier* in 1848 and transferred to Orion's paper in 1850. Bernard DeVoto states: "The known length of Samuel Clemens' apprenticeship is two years. It was unquestionably served under Ament and ended with the establishment of Orion's Hannibal *Western Union,* whose first number was printed on October 10, 1850" (p. 85). As Ament came to Hannibal in May, 1848, the apprenticeship began about fifteen months after the death of John Clemens. The facts are that nobody really knows exactly when the apprenticeship began and ended, but all agree approximately. Wecter believes Sam joined Orion in 1851 (p. 235).

[34] C. J. Armstrong, "Mark Twain's Earliest Writings Discovered," *Missouri Historical Review,* XXIV, 485–501 (July, 1930). This article furnished material for the discussions in DeVoto and Brashear, the latter having the fuller account, based also on her own research.

[35] See Edgar M. Branch, "A Chronological Bibliography of the Writings of Samuel Clemens to June 8, 1867," *American Literature,* XVIII, 109–159 (May, 1946). The Hannibal writings are listed on pp. 113–17.

[36] *Tall Tales of the Southwest* (New York: Knopf, 1930), p. xv.

[37] Witness the devilish printer who inserted "Jesus H. Christ" in Alexander Campbell's sermon, and Sam's dropping the watermelon on Henry's head, *Autobiography,* II, 279–85.

for the tall tales, the legendary exploits of a mythical Mike Fink or a fictionized version of Davy Crockett they drew the long bow as far as it would go. The bigger the "whopper" the better. But most of the stories of Simon Suggs, Sut Lovingood, and Major Jones have authenticity as social history, and their narrative method furnished Sam Clemens his model.[38]

When Orion from financial necessity journeyed to Tennessee in an effort to sell the Clemens' land there, Sam took charge of the paper, thus starting his literary career.[39] But Orion returned unsuccessful, and the sub-editor decided to look about for pastures greener with currency. His writings in Hannibal, though generally funny, are of interest only because Sam Clemens wrote them; there is nothing to suggest the artist of the future. Brashear groups under four headings all the discovered writings which may be assigned to Clemens with any degree of certainty.

First came a volley of exchanges with the rival Whig newspaper, starting July, 1852, when Higgins, new city editor of the *Tri-Weekly Messenger,* published a warning against mad dogs; Sam promptly retorted in the role of a "Dog-be-deviled Citizen" who mock-seriously advocated canine extermination. The sharp exchanges grew personal, and later when Higgins, disappointed in love, sought to drown himself but lacked the courage, Sam delivered a knockout. The *Journal* carried a woodcut of Higgins, with

38 Walter Blair says that the narrative method of such writers was the "greatest gift of Southwestern humor to Mark," *Native American Humor* (New York: American Book Co., 1937), p. 156. Edgar Branch comments on the potential value of this frontier humor and comedy: "It placed Sam Clemens squarely in the stream of American realism. It led him to make use of the vernacular and ultimately to develop popular speech, as an instrument for character portrayal and effective narrative, to near perfection," *Mark Twain's Literary Apprenticeship* (Urbana: University of Illinois Press, 1950), p. 21.

39 Mark exaggerated his experiences in "My First Literary Venture," *Sketches New and Old,* p. 95, and these experiences also suggested "Journalism in Tennessee," *Ibid.,* p. 35.

head like a dog, wading into the stream, lantern in one hand and cane in the other.[40] The second group of writings probably by Clemens consists of four "feature stories"; one, an account of a drunken brawl, is signed W. Epaminondas Adrastus Perkins, and another "Blabbing Government Secrets," aptly substitutes Blab for Perkins. A third group centers around the poem "To Miss Katie of H——l," Sam cleverly building up a fictitious correspondence over misinterpretations of the last word—an attempt probably to revive flagging interest in the paper. These editorial comments and planted replies did help the subscription list, and May, 1853, Orion introduced Sam in a new feature, "Our Assistant's Column," giving the seventeen-year-old editor a free hand to pun, satirize, or rap at will; for example:

> Miss Lucy Stone is lecturing on Woman's Rights in Philadelphia. Wonder if she wouldn't like to cut wood; bring water; shoe horses; be a deck hand, or something of that sort? She has a right to do it; and if she wants to carry a hod, we say, let her alone.[41]

Mark Twain, when applying his theories to himself, liked to trace developments from a sudden twist of events; one such was the bleak, windy afternoon on the Hannibal streets when a scattering wind swept into his hands the fragment from some story of Joan of Arc. So stirred was the young printer's imagination by this glimpse at history that from a broken bit of dialogue he suddenly began to try his hand at sketching characters and plots.[42] Among the exchanges coming into Orion's office was the *Carpet-Bag,* published in Boston by Benjamin P. Shillaber, creator of the Widow Partington, whose humorous comments reached an amused audience throughout the nation. On May 1, 1852, the *Carpet-Bag* carried a slight, humorous sketch called "The Dandy Frightening the Squatter," signed S.L.C.,

40 Brashear, p. 113. 41 *Ibid.,* p. 131.
42 Paine, I, 81–2.

Sam's earliest known appearance in print[43] (if we except the squibs attributed to him in the Hannibal papers) and therefore Mark Twain's first story.

The next year Sam left Hannibal, lured partly, no doubt, by news of the Crystal Palace Fair in New York, which had aroused Hannibal interest. If Sam had desired the river or Western migration there was little to hinder, but thinking of himself as a newspaperman he turned his eyes toward the Atlantic. Since conditions in the *Journal* office admitted no chance of any personal success, in June, 1853, after solemnly promising his mother not to "throw a card or drink a drop of liquor,"[44] young Clemens set out for New York, allaying fears by announcing his destination as nearby St. Louis. But on August 24, 1853, he wrote home from New York, his first travel letter, to be followed by another within a week, both published by Orion in the *Journal*.[45]

Wanderings

Although Sam Clemens soon found work in New York as a printer and continued to report back home on his progress, within less than two months he went to Philadelphia.[46] October 26, 1853, found him writing to Orion in Hannibal, unaware that his brother had moved to Iowa and bought an interest in the Muscatine *Journal*. There the first forwarded letter was published promptly as "Philadelphia Correspondence," to be followed with others requested by Orion. More vivid in detail than previous efforts, these

43 Franklin J. Meine, who discovered the story, assigns it to Mark on the basis of the initials, the Hannibal setting, manner of telling, and the fact that Mark then working in a printing office would have been familiar with the popular *Carpet-Bag*. *Tall Tales of the Southwest*, p. 445.

44 Paine, I, 93.

45 Brashear, pp. 153–7.

46 Sam's Southern background is evident in his reference to "infernal abolitionists," and in his comment, "I reckon I had better black my face, for in these Eastern States niggers are considerably better than white people." Brashear, p. 154.

letters show progress through accurate descriptions of many features of Philadelphia: Fairmount Park, the Water Works, historic buildings, splendid private residences, and Franklin's grave in Christ Church yard. He was enthusiastic, ". . . I like this Philadelphia amazingly, and the people in it."[47] Though these letters gave Sam a chance to practice descriptive writing, they contain little humor, and read like a travel report. They are, however, clear, straightforward, and free of verbosity. February 18, 1854, Sam was in Washington, where he found expression for his humor in a few sly digs at Congress.[48] Then he decided to head homeward, joining his mother and Orion in Muscatine during the late summer.

Nobody knows how long he remained there before going to St. Louis; later he was to remember Muscatine for beautiful summer sunsets: "I have never seen any, on either side of the ocean, that equalled them."[49] We may assume that Sam worked for Orion on the *Journal,* finding the earnings scarce and life rather dull by contrast with the cities. Soon he was off again to St. Louis, spending the winter and spring of 1855 there, before returning home, this time to Keokuk, where Orion had moved with his brother Henry.[50]

Now Sam seemed completely happy. With Orion married and their mother located in St. Louis, he lived as he pleased in his own quarters at Orion's job office. Popularity was instantaneous, and with congenial companions of his own age Sam was content there about a year and a half.[51] But there was too much of John Marshall Clemens in his

[47] *Letters,* I, 27.

[48] Edgar M. Branch, *Mark Twain's Letters in the Muscatine Journal* (Chicago: Mark Twain Association of America, 1942), pp. 18–22.

[49] *Life on the Mississippi,* pp. 467–8.

[50] Fred W Lorch, "Mark Twain in Iowa," *Iowa Journal of History and Politics,* XXVII, 418 (July, 1929).

[51] Orion's Keokuk Directory was on sale July 12, 1856. Priced at one dollar it sold well enough for a second edition in 1857. The 1856 Directory lists: Samuel L. Clemens, Antiquarian. Lorch, *ibid.,* p. 432.

son to allow pleasure to dominate his actions indefinitely. Working hard and receiving little for it, Sam despite his irresponsible state of happiness thought about advancement. Wanderlust seized him as he began to imagine fortune awaiting him in South America. But how to get there?

Then fate again entered the scene. A wind favorable to Sam blew a piece of paper down Main Street; when he stooped to pick it up, there was a fifty dollar bill. Whether he waited four days for the owner to claim it or left that same day we may never know,[52] but with cash in hand he quickly made plans. Success with the Muscatine *Journal* letters naturally suggested newspaper correspondence as a means of securing money for his projected trip to Brazil, and Sam arranged for a series of travel letters for which George Rees, editor of the Keokuk *Post,* agreed to pay five dollars each. The first letter was written from St. Louis, October 18, 1856;[53] then two more followed from Cincinnati during the winter. Sam adopted the customary pseudonym and illiterate spelling; as Thomas Jefferson Snodgrass he recounted the misadventures of a bumpkin who is ejected from a theatre because he thinks the play is real, makes a spectacle of himself on his first train ride, and trying to do a young woman a favor is left holding a basket containing a baby. When Sam upped his rates on the editor, however, the arrangement was terminated,[54] and Thomas Jefferson Snodgrass' "Dierrea" was never added to the shelf of world travel books.

But the winter in Cincinnati was to prove important for

[52] Mark said that he advertised and waited four days, *Autobiography,* II, 288, also that he advertised and left the same day. *Letters,* I, 35. Fred W. Lorch could not find the advertisements mentioned. *Op. cit.,* p. 436.

[53] Lorch, *ibid.,* p. 438. These letters were collected in a limited edition *The Adventures of Thomas Jefferson Snodgrass,* ed. by Charles Honce (Chicago: Pascal Covici, 1928).

[54] Lorch says that Sam was paid five dollars for the first letter; asked seven-fifty for the second and got it, but was refused when he tried for ten. *Ibid.,* p. 439.

notable association. Although his given name has escaped Twain scholars, all attest the influence of a "Scotchman named Macfarlane."[55] At the cheap boarding-house where Sam lodged, this humorless man, twice his age, exerted an irresistible intellectual appeal. His trade Sam never learned, but Macfarlane's hands were hardened by toil; his mind, however, was a storehouse of knowledge gleaned from serious reading in philosophy, history, and science. And Macfarlane like O. Henry knew the dictionary by heart; not once was Sam able to discover a word unfamiliar to Macfarlane. Prior to Darwin's publication of *The Origin of Species* this independent thinker advanced a similar theory, except that he went further: although life had developed on an ascending scale from a primal seed to man, there the development had stopped and retrogression set in. In lengthy discussions lasting through the evening the Scotchman expounded his philosophy: man he contended had the only bad heart in the animal kingdom; his alone contained malice, envy, and vice; man's intellect was depraved; and consequently man was the moral inferior of the animals. Readers of *What Is Man?* will recognize Macfarlane's lasting influence on the ultimate philosophy evolved by Mark Twain.[56]

For that influence alone the winter in Cincinnati remains memorable, but there is aught else. With cessation of the Snodgrass letters Sam temporarily abandoned literature to revive his dream of cocoa-hunter on the Amazon, a dream growing brighter with the returning spring. April, 1857, found him boarding the *Paul Jones,* bound for New Orleans, and then to South America, where air castles would receive a foundation under them. But presence on

[55] Paine, I, 112–15. Also *Autobiography,* I, 143–7.

[56] DeLancey Ferguson points out that Macfarlane's philosophy about the wickedness of man was not radically different from that of the Presbyterian Sunday School, but Sam was impressed by "Macfarlane's version of Calvinism with God left out." *Mark Twain: Man and Legend,* p. 48.

the boat revived an older dream from boyhood, the ambition of every Hannibal youth to be a pilot. The result was swift; Horace Bixby, one of the pilots, knew the Bowen boys, Will, Sam, and Bart, all of whom had become pilots in realization of the dream Sam Clemens once shared with them as pranking youngsters. By the time the boat reached its destination Bixby had agreed to take Sam Clemens on as a pilot, "learn" him the river, and on credit at that.[57]

The Pilot

It was a deal, and Sam turned to his task innocent of the multitudes of minute detail waiting to confound him. Along with the river's changing shape, assuming shadows by starlight, straightening its banks in pitch-dark, and fading away with the gray mist, the pilot had to know the *real* shape so accurately that he could steer ahead, certain of his course regardless of weather or time of day. In Mark's own words: "It was plain that I had got to learn the shape of the river in all the different ways that could be thought of,—upside down, wrong end first, inside out, fore-and-aft, and 'thort-ships,'—and then know what to do on gray nights when it hadn't any shape at all."[58] No sooner did the cub master this problem than he was staggered by the discovery that he must remember shoal soundings and water marks, exactly as to spot and trip. It was inhuman; Sam despaired, "When I get so that I can do that, I'll be able to raise the dead, and then I won't have to pilot a steamboat to make a living. I want to retire from this business." But Bixby was adamant, "I'll learn him or kill him."[59]

And his pupil finally succeeded in committing to memory

57 Paine, I, 117–120. Sam borrowed a hundred dollars from his brother-in-law, W. A. Moffett, to make a down payment. Four hundred dollars more would be paid when he earned it. Room and board was furnished on the boat free, but Bixby made no provision for expenses on shore.

58 *Life on the Mississippi,* p. 70.

59 *Ibid.,* p. 71.

the minute variations and kaleidoscopic shapes of banks and bed. Notebooks kept at Bixby's advice bristle with entries:

> Had 1/4 less 3 in foot of Cat I, tow-head. . . .
> Hove lead at head of 55—no bottom—ran no channel in it. 8 ft. bank on point opp. Densford's—or rather up shore at head of timber. . . .[60]

No wonder Sam felt that piloting strained the memory as nothing else on earth. But the reward was worth it; a pilot earned from a hundred and fifty to two hundred and fifty dollars per month, he was highly respected, and he ruled the boat. As to what kind of pilot Sam became, conjecture has been raised. Although he had only praise for his former pupil when interviewed by Albert Bigelow Paine, Horace Bixby later disparaged him, "He knew the Mississippi River like a book, but he lacked confidence. . . . No sir, Sam Clemens knew the river, but being a coward, he was a failure as a pilot."[61] What Bixby meant Mark himself has admitted, "The growth of courage in the pilot-house is steady all the time, but it does not reach a high and satisfactory condition until some time after the young pilot has been 'standing his own watch' alone and under the staggering weight of all the responsibilities connected with the position."[62] By this time Mark had left Bixby and was on his own boat. The incident recounted in *Life on the Mississippi* of how Bixby destroyed his cub's confidence, causing him to stop the boat in a clear channel through fear of wrecking her, occurred while Sam was learning, but that seems to be how Bixby remembered him.[63] Sam's record,

60 *Notebook,* pp. 4–5.

61 Quoted by Dudley R. Hutcherson, "Mark Twain as a Pilot," *American Literature,* XII, 354 (November, 1940). Another charge that Mark was an inferior pilot was made in a flippant, gossipy manner by Marquis W. Childs, "The Home of Mark Twain," *American Mercury,* IX, 104 (September, 1926).

62 *Life on the Mississippi,* p. 113.

63 *Ibid.,* pp. 115–18. There is also the possibility that Bixby's memory of Clemens may have been darkened because of a sum of money borrowed from his former pupil. Webster, p. 81.

however, proclaims success rather than failure; for he wrote Orion from St. Louis in 1859, when many young pilots were unemployed, that he was on the *City of Memphis,* a large and difficult boat to handle. And the Tom Sawyer in his nature delighted to allow a glimpse of a hundred-dollar bill in his wallet, while noting the chagrin of those who had predicted his failure at the wheel.[64] As for the charge of cowardice, DeLancey Ferguson points out that Sam Clemens, unlike the assured Bixby, possessed too much imagination—and we might add intelligent concern—to achieve perfect confidence. Where Bixby would shove ahead, never doubting his knowledge or ability, Clemens could foresee the consequences of failure.[65] Dixon Wecter reminds us, also, that Clemens was a "born worrier," to whom responsibility for life and property in his care weighed heavily, perhaps producing over-caution.[66] Whatever pilots delighting in daredevil exploits may have thought of his abilities, Sam continued in his profession, turning his wheel until traffic was ended by the war, drawing good wages, and never having any serious mishaps.

Until his license was granted April 9, 1859, he must have continued as a cub, although it appears that he also piloted a freight boat without a license, such practice being lawful.[67] A picture of the *John J. Roe,* once piloted by Twain shows it to have been a freighter.[68] It was the passenger steamer, however, that appealed to Sam, who enjoyed the "glass temple" pilot house with its "red and gold window-cur-

64 *Letters,* I, 43–4.

65 Ferguson explains: "His courage and self-control were the nervously expensive sort which comes from thrusting back the over-vivid pictures furnished by the imagination. It is not without interest to speculate how long he would have lasted on the river without a nervous breakdown had he continued to be a pilot." *Mark Twain: Man and Legend,* p. 55.

66 "Mark Twain," *A Literary History of the United States,* II, 919.

67 George H. Brownell, "Mark Twain's Pilot License," *Twainian,* I, 1–3 (November, 1939).

68 *Waterways Journal,* LX, 15 (February 5, 1949).

tains," furniture with leather cushions, servants to supply "tarts and ices and coffee," and the glittering, gilded accommodations of the staterooms and saloon. "This was unutterable pomp" to delight the heart of Tom Sawyer; moreover, "a pilot, in those days, was the only unfettered and entirely independent human being that lived in the earth."[69] With boyhood ambition realized, Sam now had plenty of money, and the family looked to him for aid and advice. But the river, a source of danger, even as it was a purveyor of wealth, held terrors as well as pomp and glory. Occasional steamboat explosions, horrible with scaldings, burned flesh, and mangled bodies, inflicted injury and death upon helpless passengers and crew. While still a cub, Sam Clemens himself came close to such catastrophe; an explosion on the steamer *Pennsylvania* killed his brother Henry. Because of a quarrel with a tyrannical pilot named Brown, Sam was put ashore from the *Pennsylvania* to follow on another boat. Henry, blown clear of the wreck by the explosion, although injured internally, bravely swam back to rescue others until his own lungs collapsed from the scalding steam. In his grief Sam reproached himself for the disaster, for he had previously urged his brother to help save the passengers in case of accident. It was he, not Henry, who had been put ashore to safety after the fight in the pilot house, though both were involved. Finally in the hospital at Memphis he accidentally gave Henry an overdose of morphine. Sam blamed himself, but he also questioned the fates. Suppose he had not had the quarrel with its resulting events, or another pilot had been found to replace Brown, as the captain of the *Pennsylvania* had wished. The tragedy preyed on his mind, until unable to sleep at night, he confided to Orion his self-condemnations.[70] For the first time he felt the mood of Melville, for chance and fate had brought

[69] *Life on the Mississippi,* p. 118.
[70] *Paine,* I, 144.

tragedy to which he had unintentionally contributed. Samuel Charles Webster tells us that Clemens was so grief stricken his sanity was feared for; indeed he was not able to travel alone from Memphis to St. Louis but was accompanied by a young man.[71] There vanished now something of his youth; to his sister he wrote, "Mollie, there are gray hairs in my head tonight."[72] However youthful he may have been in temperament in later years, from the time of Henry's death, Clemens began to age in appearance. But he continued on the river, returning as steersman for kindly George Ealer, the idolator of Shakespeare.[73] Securing his license, Sam finally became partner to his old mentor, Horace Bixby. On the *City of Memphis,* "the largest boat in the trade and the hardest to pilot," he must have performed satisfactorily, for we find him happy in his berth and hoping to save about $100 per month from his salary.[74]

Gradually Sam returned to his accustomed gaiety, "dissipating on a ten dollar dinner at a French restauarant—breathe it not unto Ma!"[75] And on a trip which he gave his mother he outraged her Victorian sensibilities by hugging and kissing the girls and dancing the schottische.[76] Visiting in St. Louis, he teased his little niece until she complained to her parents that although everybody else understood about Moses and the bullrushes, she could never make Uncle Sam understand that Moses was not the keeper of the secondhand store on Market Street.[77] And how he enjoyed playing the piano while he sang over and over:

71 *Mark Twain, Business Man,* p. 36.

72 *Letters,* I, 40.

73 *Is Shakespeare Dead?* tells of Ealer's quoting the bard while issuing orders

74 *Letters,* I, 43.

75 This letter to Orion contained a twenty-dollar bill. Sam's sense of obligation is expressed here as elsewhere, for he was always helping his relations. *Ibid.,* I, 48.

76 *Ibid.,* I, 46–7.

77 *Mark Twain, Business Man,* p. 39.

There was an old horse
And his name was Jerusalem.

As a pilot Sam Clemens tasted the sweets of success. It was his first triumph, financially and individually. Naturally while learning the river he had been forced by necessity to give up all thoughts of writing.[78] Now that he had mastered his lessons and achieved boyhood's great ambition, Clemens found himself with leisure time. In 1859 the eternal humorist in Mark Twain found opportunity for expression. Captain Isaiah Sellers, a retired pilot with an inexhaustible memory, who contributed bits of river information to the New Orleans *Picayune,* wrote with an oracular assurance and egotistical manner, irritating to the younger pilots. Sam Clemens, annoyed by having present experiences continually depreciated by comparison with the past, even by one holding the longest service record on the river, seized a chance to retaliate. When Captain Sellers with an air of infallibility estimated the rise of a flood, basing his prediction on memory of experiences since 1815, Sam replied with a satire in the *Daily Crescent* (May 17, 1859). Changing Captain Sellers to "Sergeant Fathom" the oldest "cub" on the river, he attributed Fathom's reputation for safety to "the fact that he seldom runs his boat after early candle-light."[79] Then predicting water on the "roof of the St. Charles Hotel" before the "middle of January," he calmed the inhabitants' fears with an absurd account of a voyage down the river in 1763 by a Chinese captain with a Choctaw crew, concluding with a reference to "When me and DeSoto discovered the Mississippi."[80]

78 On March 9, 1858, Sam had written to Orion, "I cannot correspond with a paper, because when one is learning the river, he is not allowed to do or think about anything else." *Letters,* I, 38.

79 Ernest E. Leisy, "Mark Twain and Isaiah Sellers," *American Literature,* XIII, 403 (January, 1942). Here Twain's burlesque of the old pilot is reprinted. See also Paine, IV, Appendix B.

80 *Ibid.,* p. 404.

Although Sam later thought that Sellers' articles were signed "Mark Twain" and that his own burlesque broke the old Captain's heart, there is no such evidence.[81] As Leisy suggests, the probable explanation is that the use of the name "Fathom" by Clemens caused him to confuse it in memory with the similar river term for the same sounding, "Mark Twain." Paine, who thought Sellers had used the name, believed Sam took it to make amends for a thoughtless injury.[82] But a careful investigation has destroyed this myth, and if there is any connection between Sellers and "Mark Twain" it is an indirect one confused in memory. As Sellers never used the name, Clemens could not have borrowed it from him.[83] The old captain served a more immediate purpose, however, in bringing Sam Clemens momentarily again to newspaper writing.[84]

But apparently he wrote nothing else, although the satire was generally appreciated by his cronies. Clemens' good salary enabled him to assist his relatives, and he continued to have fun, while improving himself with such cultural offerings as Church's painting, "Heart of the Andes," which he took his sister Pamela to see in St. Louis.[85] Sam's letters reveal that he had been reading Hood, Goldsmith, and Cervantes.[86] Although the country was on its tragic way to the War Between the States, there is nothing in Clemens' letters or diary to indicate it.

81 George H. Brownell has revealed that Mark Twain could not possibly have borrowed his name from Captain Sellers as he claimed, for Mark first used the pseudonym in the *Territorial Enterprise,* February 2, 1863, and Sellers did not die until March 6, 1864. Thus the whole story of how Mark adopted the name on his death becomes another bit of fiction. See "A Question as to the Origin of the Name 'Mark Twain,'" *Twainian,* I, 5 (February, 1942).

82 *Mark Twain: A Biography,* I, 150.

83 Leisy, *op. cit.,* p. 399. Ivan Benson, *Mark Twain's Western Years,* p. 155.

84 Actually the river term "Mark Twain" meant two fathoms or twelve feet, safe depth for any boat on the Mississippi.

85 *Letters,* I, 46.

86 *Ibid.,* I, 45.

During the election of 1860 Clemens supported Bell and Everett, his niece remembering that the members of her family were split politically, and that Uncle Sam settled her allegiance with the gift of a Bell-Everett button.[87] John Bell of Tennessee and Edward Everett of Massachusetts were nominated for the presidency and vice presidency, respectively, in Baltimore by the Constitutional Union Party, composed of remnants of the Whigs, Native American Party, and other conservatives who wished to save the Union and halt slavery agitation. Its platform advocated "the constitution of the country, the union of the States, and the enforcement of the laws."[88] Adherents to Bell's candidacy opposed war, not wishing to fight for either side, believing rather in some form of compromise under the Constitution to preserve union and enforce the laws. There were no belligerents among them; thus before civil war began, Sam Clemens had already aligned himself with the pacifists and moderates.

When the war started, Horace Bixby, who declared for the Union, remembered that Sam had gone in the opposite direction. Though little is known, it appears Sam accompanied another pilot, named Montgomery, in supporting the Southern cause. Dixon Wecter suggests that Clemens may have joined the Louisiana Guards in the winter of 1860–61[89] The conjecture arises from the contents of a series of ten letters written for the New Orleans *Daily Crescent* from January 21 through March 30 of 1861.[90] In the first letter, Sam, again using the name "Snodgrass"—now changed from "Thomas Jefferson" to "Quintus Cur-

87 *Mark Twain, Business Man,* p. 47.

88 Oliver P. Chitwood, Frank L. Owsley, and H. C. Nixon, *The United States from Colony to World Power* (New York: D. Van Nostrand Co., 1949), p. 406.

89 *New England Quarterly,* XX, 270 (June, 1947).

90 Ernest E. Leisy, ed., *The Letters of Quintus Curtius Snodgrass* (Dallas: Southern Methodist University Press, 1946).

tius"—narrates in mock-heroic style the discomforts of a bloodless expedition to capture Baton Rouge, in ignorance that the Federal garrison had already capitulated. Throughout the letters Sam satirized regimentation, parodied army discipline, and burlesqued the awkward efforts of the recruits. The first five letters are devoted entirely to humorous comments on getting used to military life, but the sixth takes Snodgrass to see the sights, recounting to his friend Brown a series of adventures in restaurant and theatre, similar to those of his predecessor, Thomas Jefferson Snodgrass. The seventh letter, "Snodgrass Dines with Old Abe," displays the derisive attitude of the Confederates toward the Yankee President. The last three letters return to the difficulties of the civilian to adjust himself to his newly acquired military existence. If Sam Clemens was not actually a member of this military aggregation, at least he was familiar enough with its problems to write accurate burlesque and satire.[91] Yet his interest in the war appears slight, for four days after Lincoln issued his call for troops on April 15, 1861, Sam arrived in St. Louis from New Orleans, where he left the volunteers he had so humorously depicted.[92] On the next day Orion received official notification of his appointment as Territorial Secretary of Nevada.[93] If there had been conflicting opinions of loyalty among the pilots, even as among most citizens of the border states, the same was true in the Clemens family, for while Orion was an out-and-out abolitionist, his mother had a horror of "Black Republicans."[94] Amid the excitement of impending hostility Sam found time, however, to embark

[91] Miss Brashear first discovered four of these letters in the files of the New Orleans *Daily Crescent,* reprinting one and describing the others in *Mark Twain, Son of Missouri,* pp. 181–92. The remaining six letters were found by Professor Leisy and Mr. Thomas Ewing Dabney.

[92] Fred W. Lorch, "Mark Twain and the 'Campaign That Failed,'" *American Literature,* XII, 461 (January, 1941).

[93] Fred W. Lorch, "Orion Clemens," *Palimpsest,* X, 359 (October, 1929).

[94] Webster, p. 64.

upon Masonry, passing to a Fellowcraft degree on the same day, June 12, 1861, that Governor Jackson called the Missouri state militia into active service.[95] At this time Sam returned to Hannibal, formerly pro-Southern, but now controlled by Union Home Guards. With several graduates of "Tom Sawyer's band," among them Sam Bowen and Ed Stevens, he helped to organize a Confederate battalion, a movement carried out secretly to prevent arrest by the Federals.[96] Already apprehensive lest he be forced into Union service and made to pilot Federal steamboats at the point of a pistol,[97] Sam entered enthusiastically upon this new venture. There was no formal enlistment, no oath of allegiance, and no discipline, the men electing their officers subject to dismissal. As DeLancey Ferguson has indicated, Missouri was filled with such groups, many disintegrating like this one, some even becoming outlaw gangs, such as Quantrill's, to rob and murder.[98] Mark Twain told his own story later in "The Private History of a Campaign That Failed," adding his usual fictional embroidery to the facts.[99] Whether disillusioned by mud, briars, and encounters with bull dogs, or weary from saddle-boils and sprained ankle, Sam Clemens was out of the army and back in St. Louis taking a Master Mason's degree on July 10, 1861.[100] The charge has been leveled that Clemens was a deserter from

95 Lorch, "Mark Twain and the 'Campaign That Failed,' " *op. cit.*, p. 461.

96 Paine, I, 164.

97 Webster, p. 60.

98 *Mark Twain: Man and Legend,* p. 62.

99 It was Ab Grimes, who served either with Sam or in a similar organization nearby, that contributed the story of the fall from a hayloft window and the sprained ankle. M. M. Quaife, editor of Grimes' old-age recital, *Absalom Grimes: Confederate Mail Runner* (New Haven: Yale University Press, 1926), doubts the authenticity of a narrative prepared half a century after the events took place. Quaife has stated, "And so we leave it to the reader to determine, if he can, whether the narrative of Captain Grimes or Mark—or neither of them—tells the truth about Mark's sole first-hand contact with life in the tented field." "Mark Twain's Military Career," *Twainian,* III, 7 (June, 1944).

100 Lorch, *op. cit.*, 462.

the colors,[101] that he went West to avoid the draft.[102] But Professor Lorch seems to have stated the problem sensibly and fairly:

> Orion had received what appeared to be, and was, a promising political appointment. With his friend Edward Bates in the Cabinet, and with reasonably good fortune in Nevada, he might well expect higher political offices. Orion's star, so long obscure, appeared now to be clearly rising, while Sam's was declining. The river was closed and the war was definitely on. If Sam now took a job piloting out of St. Louis, it would have to be on a Union boat, but Union or Rebel, salaries had dropped considerably. . . . Troublesome days were ahead with little prospect for employment. To join effective Rebel forces again would have necessitated his going far to the South, for by mid-July St. Louis and northern Missouri were definitely in Union hands. But while Orion had a good office he lacked the money to go to it, except such as he may have arranged to borrow. Sam still had money, saved from his earnings on the river. With the probable aid of his mother and sister, Orion urged Sam to go with him, partly for company, partly for financial aid, and partly to wean Sam from his Rebel sympathies.[103]

When the Union forces occupied the surrounding countryside after routing a Rebel army under General Sterling Price, many hastily organized Confederates, such as Home Guards, became demoralized and filtered home, there being no power to hold them. Sam Clemens' decision to retire from a group which was never a part of the Confederate Army was not desertion. Neither does it appear that he hoped to secure sudden wealth by joining Orion, for employment and a chance to see the country were more probably the magnets.

Agreeing to be the Secretary's secretary, Sam, without assignment of duties or salary, paid both fares ($150 apiece),

101 Fred Lewis Pattee, *Mark Twain: Representative Selections* (New York: American Book Co., 1935), p. xlv.

102 Edgar Lee Masters, *Mark Twain: A Portrait* (New York: Charles Scribners, 1938), p. 34.

103 Lorch, *op. cit.*, p. 464.

and they were off in late July, 1861, on the twenty-day journey immortalized in *Roughing It*.[104] DeLancey Ferguson, however, believes that the secretaryship was a bit of Mark's customary embroidery, that the real reasons for the trip were a desire for adventure and Orion's determination to stop Sam's Confederate activities, something an ardent Unionist and abolitionist could regard only with horror.[105]

The West

On July 18, the brothers traveled by steamboat from St. Louis to St. Joseph, where cowhide boots and flannel shirts replaced their former attire. Leaving by Overland stage, July 26, they reached Carson City, Nevada, on August 14.[106] So completely had they affected the slouchy appearance of frontier dress that the reception committee for the new Secretary was dismayed. Brooks seized upon this change of costume to indicate loss of artistic integrity,[107] but Ferguson seems closer to Mark Twain when observing, "Tom Sawyer could always be counted on to play a role to the limit."[108] Now Sam Clemens was in the West, a frontier unique in time and place, where just twelve years after the gold rush fortunes were still being made, suddenly and when least expected. Sam like everyone else caught the fever, but like the majority he got nothing but excitement. Though the theme of rich prospects runs through all of Clemens' letters from Nevada—prospects which had captured Orion's imagination too—the later dedication of *Roughing It* to Calvin H. Higbie "in memory of the curious time when we two were millionaires for ten days" is nostalgic inaccuracy. The story told in *Roughing It* is,

104 Dixon Wecter, "Mark Twain and the West," *Huntington Library Quarterly*, VIII, 361 (August, 1945).

105 *Mark Twain: Man and Legend*, p. 65.

106 Paine, I, 174.

107 *The Ordeal of Mark Twain*, p. 99.

108 *Op. cit.*, p. 66.

moreover, a composite account put together for fiction.[109] But it was, no doubt, the disappointment suffered through the failure of the Monitor and Wide West claims which extinguished Clemens' hopes of a fortune from the mines.[110] In partnership with Orion, Sam staked out a claim at Esmeralda, going to work upon it, while Orion furnished funds. By now, as his own resources were nearly exhausted, he depended upon his brother until his prospecting and mining efforts should pay off. Meanwhile, in his spare time Sam again took up his pen, for a sore back and blistered hands were all the mine yielded. On May 11, 1862, he mentions to Orion some letters, written for the *Enterprise*—burlesque sketches, says Paine, which were signed "Josh."[111] Soon thereafter all hopes for wealth at Esmeralda dwindled into unpaid debts, with Sam propounding, "But how in the h——l I am going to live on something over $100 until October or November, is singular."[112] Clemens was often Colonel Sellers, but never Mr. Micawber; at once he sought a newspaper connection. Until a file of the *Territorial Enterprise* is discovered, we must rest content with descriptions of the "Josh" letters, one being a burlesque of an egotistical lecturer, "Professor Personal Pronoun," whose speech could not be fully printed, because the "type-cases had run out of capital I's"; another was a burlesque report of a Fourth-of-July oration, beginning, "I was sired by the Great American Eagle and foaled by a continental dam."[113] But the editor of the *Enterprise,* Joe Goodman—urged by Barstow, a business manager with a weather eye for what readers wanted—liked Sam's contributions enough to offer him a job at twenty-five dollars a week.[114] Though badly in need of money, Clemens did not jump at the offer; instead he went away for a week or so, leaving at midnight. Why or

109 *Roughing It,* I, 271–87

110 Ivan Benson, *Mark Twain's Western Years,* p. 47.

111 *Letters,* I, 81.

112 *Ibid.,* I, 82.

113 Paine, I, 203.

114 *Letters,* I, 83.

what for, nobody knows. Speculations run from Paine's statement that he went into the wilderness for a communion with his soul[115] to DeLancey Ferguson's pragmatic guess that he may have heard of a new bonanza and was investigating secretly to avoid a stampede.[116] Whatever the reason, he decided to give up mining, and he had no desire for his old profession, for in a letter to Pamela he declared, "I never expect to do any more piloting at any price."[117] Destiny was in the West, leading him at last to the one occupation he should nevermore forsake.

Arriving one hot, dusty August afternoon, after a hundred-and-thirty-mile walk to Virginia City, Sam entered the *Enterprise* office, where he dropped his pack, sank into a chair, and absently declared: "My starboard leg seems to be unshipped. I'd like about one hundred yards of line; I think I am falling to pieces." Then he added: "I want to see Mr. Barstow, or Mr. Goodman. My name is Clemens, and I've come to write for the paper."[118] It was typical of his humor: the irrelevant beginning, the pause for suspense, and then the dramatic line.

Now Samuel Clemens, ex-printer, ex-pilot, ex-Confederate irregular, ex-miner and prospector, was come into his own. Shortly to emerge as "Mark Twain," he was never again to be other than a professional man of letters, earning his livelihood by his pen, from this climactic moment until the end of his triumphant career.

Although the Comstock Lode derived its name from Henry T. P. Comstock, the real discoverers were two miners, Peter O'Riley and Patrick McLaughlin, who struck the ore at the top of what became the famous Ophir Mine. Whether Comstock had secured previous knowledge of the deposit or not has never been settled—circumstances indi-

115 Paine, I, 204.
116 *Mark Twain: Man and Legend,* p. 76.
117 *Letters,* I, 85.
118 Paine, I, 205.

cate that he did. At any rate, O'Riley and McLaughlin unhappily found their strike to be on land owned by Comstock, who promptly declared himself in for a share. From then on, it was Comstock who was conspicuously present around the Ophir, electing himself superintendent, ostentatiously greeting all visitors, and doing so much talking that people came to regard the lode as his, while the real discoverers were quickly forgotten.[119] Soon a village began to form on the site of Comstock's land, first called Ophir, then changing names several times, to be finally christened by James Fennimore, better known as "Old Virginia," who enjoying a customary spree, lurched to the ground with broken whisky bottle and the cry, "I baptize this ground Virginia." The name stuck, although it came to be called Virginia City.[120]

For the leading characters in the first act of Comstock drama fate quickly dealt unhappy cards. McLaughlin, soon exhausting his share of the claim, drifted to a job as cook in San Bernardino, California, later dying a pauper. Although O'Riley built a hotel in Virginia City, he gambled his money away and ended his days insane in a sanitarium. Comstock, after suffering a series of changes in fortune, finally shot himself in the head near Bozeman, Montana. "Old Virginia" was killed by a fall from a horse, a death more natural than the others since he was, as usual, intoxicated.[121] Thus for all, fame vanished through dissipation and ended in violence.

When Sam Clemens arrived, Virginia City was a rough, masculine community, loud and strong, fond of coarse humor and straight whisky. Next to mining, in fact, its most lucrative enterprise was saloon-keeping. Colorful, fascinating, boisterous, Virginia City had its sordid side also in the

119 Dan DeQuille, *The Big Bonanza,* p. 30.
120 *Ibid.,* p. 32.
121 Ivan Benson, *Mark Twain's Western Years,* pp. 60–1.

gambling halls and numerous houses of prostitution, ranging from "ladies of the evening" in abodes of tapestried walls down to the cheapest harlots in the cribs—practically the only women, by the way, to be found in this masculine territory. True there was a theatre, but its influence was more diverting than cultural, for although it did offer Jenny Lind with her Swedish nightingale songs and Artemus Ward with humorous lectures, the big hit at Piper's Opera House was Adah Isaacs Menken in *Mazeppa,* combining Byron, melodrama, and nudity to produce one of the most effective presentations of sex appeal ever displayed on the American stage.

Mark Twain had seen the less human side of man's nature on the Mississippi; here again, man in his more animal aspects paraded for his education. There were toughs and criminals who killed, sometimes in anger or for pleasure, sometimes to acquire a reputation, for "bad men" were respected and the timid soul was lost.

Amid these conditions during his two-year connection with the *Territorial Enterprise,* Sam played an active rôle in the community. Later he recalled this side of Virginia City:

> Vice flourished luxuriantly during the heyday of our "flush times." The saloons were overburdened with custom; so were the police courts, the gambling dens, the brothels, and the jails —unfailing signs of high prosperity in a mining region—in any region, for that matter. Is it not so? A crowded police-court docket is the surest of all signs that trade is brisk and money plenty.[122]

On its better side Virginia City was lively, fresh, healthy, and fearless, a place where rugged, vigorous men lived according to a code, akin in its cardinal insistence upon loyalty, honesty, and fairness to the chivalry of the Old South, freshly acclimatized into Western setting and garb. No col-

[122] *Roughing It,* II, 76.

lege could have offered the curriculum of human nature furnished by Sam's job with the *Enterprise,* for no faculty could have educated him as did the men in that office. All were exceptional, and what is more important in the career of Sam Clemens, they helped him to develop those inherent qualities, which through his associations on the newspaper naturally grew into those of Mark Twain. From Joe Goodman, his discoverer, Sam not only got his chance to live by his pen, but he learned the force of informed, fearless writing. Dan DeQuille, the best humorous writer on the coast, was his constant companion, a model to follow, and a friendly guide. It was in the manner of Dan that Mark began to achieve his first success beyond the local boundary.[123] Rollin M. Daggett, founder of the *Golden Era,* later U.S. Minister to Hawaii, then writing courageous satires for the *Enterprise,* taught Sam something about fighting corruption. Little Steve Gillis, one of the printers, weighing only ninety-five pounds, but brave as a gamecock, who acted later as second in the Comstock duel and accompanied him to San Francisco, was responsible for the memorable visit to Jackass Hill. Denis McCarthy, part-owner of the paper, became Mark's business manager when the lecture tour of 1866 was inaugurated.[124]

The *Territorial Enterprise,* started by Joseph Goodman and Denis McCarthy, had progressed in two years from shoestring beginnings to its own building with the latest in presses and compositors hired from San Francisco. William Wright (celebrated on the coast under the name of "Dan DeQuille"), chief reporter and feature writer, took Sam home with him, starting an enduring friendship. If Goodman can be called the discoverer of Mark Twain through

[123] Dan DeQuille's "Housekeeping with Mark Twain," reprinted by Franklin Walker in *The Washoe Giant in San Francisco* is so similar in style to the Twain pieces in this volume that it is almost impossible to detect the difference.

[124] Benson, pp. 69–71.

his appreciation of the "Josh letters," to DeQuille goes the credit of breaking him in. In fact, it was due to the need of a substitute for Dan, who was soon to take a vacation, that Clemens was hired. Actually the new writer had plenty of leeway, Goodman's policy being simply a matter of getting facts and printing them in full—then letting the devil take the hindmost. Feuds thus arising were more interesting than the news reports starting them. As DeLancey Ferguson has emphasized, readers of the *Enterprise* were acquainted with the news before the paper came from the press; therefore aside from tips on business deals, what appealed most was the lampoon or the hoax, or lacking that, then a good feud in print.[125]

Sam, the once "Dog-be-deviled Citizen" of Hannibal journalism, needed no instruction in starting a feud or creating a lampoon.[126] Now he was to learn the hoax, a favorite of Western humor, at which DeQuille was past master. But his first hoax about a "Petrified Man" appearing in the *Territorial Enterprise,* October 5, 1862, is indebted to "John Phoenix," the nom de plume of George Horatio Derby, who had died the previous year.[127] Phoenix had written a hoax about finding living specimens of highly unusual animals in Washington territory. Although no evidence exists that it was anywhere taken seriously, the mere fact that the New York *Spirit of the Times* reprinted it without calling it humorous was seized upon in California to indicate a serious reception. From this incident the belief on the coast persisted that Western humorists could fool Eastern and European readers with outlandish tales presented as facts. There is no evidence that Clemens' "A Washoe Joke" about a petrified man was ever taken seriously anywhere, al-

125 *Mark Twain: Man and Legend,* pp. 79–80.

126 Brashear, pp. 112–13.

127 Reprinted by the San Francisco *Daily Evening Bulletin,* October 15, 1862, Vol 15. Most easily secured in Benson, *Mark Twain's Western Years,* p. 175.

though Mark Twain ten years later improved the story and claimed it a successful hoax.[128] But it was popular with Western readers, just as it is amusing today, and Mark probably recalled the legend about how John Phoenix "gulled" the East.[129]

During the last two months of 1862 Clemens convinced Goodman that he possessed the ability to report on the Second Territorial Legislature of Nevada, which met at Carson City. As the *Enterprise* correspondent had just resigned to become legislative clerk, Goodman, despite Sam's ignorance of such matters, decided to give him a chance. The first letters sent back to the paper anonymously contained a number of blunders, arising from a lack of parliamentary knowledge, which Clement T. Rice, a skilful reporter for the rival Virginia City *Union,* quickly made the object of jest. Immediately Sam rejoined that Rice's articles might be parliamentarily correct, but in all other respects were a mass of misstatement, so far from the facts that he dubbed their author "The Unreliable."[130] From then on, Sam never referred to Rice by any other term, a practice which delighted the newspaper fraternity of the coast, to whom Rice became "The Unreliable" for life. Sensing the value of journalistic warfare to keep them before the public, Rice and Clemens, although good friends socially, assumed the feud for their papers.

With his letters being copied up and down the coast, Sam began to wish for more than anonymity, realizing that if he wished to develop his stature as a personality his letters should be associated with a name. Goodman agreed, and on February 2, 1863, Samuel Clemens first signed the name of

128 See "The Petrified Man," *Sketches New and Old,* p. 288.

129 Gladys C. Bellamy, "Mark Twain's Indebtedness to John Phoenix," *American Literature,* XIII, 29–43 (March, 1941).

130 Paine, I, 219–20.

Mark Twain to one of his Carson City letters to the *Enterprise.*[131]

Upon arrival at Carson Sam had again "become the glass of fashion that he had been on the river."[132] He made his home with Orion, whose wife and little daughter had arrived from the States, and who as acting governor of the Territory was a person of importance. And Mark himself, now popular in his profession, was never again to leave the limelight. While depending upon his pen, he continued to dabble in mining stock, successfully augmenting his income. He could renew the old habit of sending money home,[133] several letters revealing an enclosure of twenty dollars, for no matter how much his enjoyment in Carson or Virginia, he did not forget his Missouri relatives.

In May, 1863, Mark and the "Unreliable" Rice visited San Francisco, where a hearty welcome from its citizens and many visitors from Washoe began a round of high, wide, and handsome entertainment—trips across the bay, yachting excursions, champagne suppers—days of eating, drinking, and merry making, until Rice declared: "Oh, no—*we* are not having any fun, Mark—Oh, no, I reckon not—it's somebody else—it's probably the 'gentleman in the wagon'! (popular slang phrase)."[134] Mark continued to enjoy high flying, visiting Steamboat Springs in August, where he shared the fun with the "wealth and fashion" of Virginia City, known to everyone and so widely popular that he wrote his mother, "And I am proud to say I am the most conceited ass in the territory."[135]

Mark was having the time of his life, and on October 28,

131 Paine, I, 222. The letter itself does not exist, and we are forced to accept the testimony of Albert Bigelow Paine. However, an extant piece, written during the early months of 1863 makes use of "Mark Twain," which appears in the text. Kate M. Rabb (ed.) *Wit and Humor of America* (Indianapolis: Bobbs-Merrill Co., 1907), V, 1805–1808.

132 Paine, I, 221.

133 *Letters,* I, 90–1.

134 *Loc. cit.*

135 *Ibid.,* I, 92.

1863, he wrote another hoax for the *Enterprise,* traditionally known as "The Empire City Massacre" or "The Dutch Nick Massacre." Like the story of the petrified man thumbing his nose, the account of its general acceptance as fact was later vivified and enlarged upon by Mark.[136] But it delighted Western readers, who reveled in the gory details that blinded them to the hints that a hoax was being perpetrated. The story created a sensation having nothing to do with Mark's real purpose of condemning the San Francisco waterworks for "cooking" a dividend. When the truth was discovered, the papers which had printed it rebuked Mark to such an extent that he was disturbed by the unexpected reaction, for it appears that he had overstepped the line even for Washoe.[137]

In December, 1863, Clemens met Artemus Ward, master platform performer, who exerted a double influence on his future career: first, by demonstrating how a first rate humorist successfully delivered a lecture, and secondly, by offering encouraging advice which Mark had the good sense to follow. For three weeks Artemus remained in Virginia City, enjoying the companionship of Mark and the others with whom he wined and dined until the early mornings. It was an association of mutual fellowship and esteem, and following Ward's departure Mark heeded his advice by preparing a bit of Comstock humor for Eastern consumption. Probably written in San Francisco during the summer of 1863, "Those Blasted Children" was published in the New York *Sunday Mercury,* February 21, 1864,[138] the first product of Twain's pen to appear in an Eastern journal. It was soon reprinted by the *Golden Era*—proof that Mark's satire was funny on either coast.

Prior to the appearance of this sketch Clemens had been

136 "My Bloody Massacre," *Sketches New and Old,* p. 293.

137 Richard G. Lillard, "Contemporary Reactions to "The Empire City Massacre," *American Literature,* XVI, 198–203 (November, 1944).

138 Franklin Walker, ed., *The Washoe Giant in San Francisco,* p. 17.

honored by his fellow newsmen, who were staging a burlesque of the legislature to raise funds for a church benefit. They elected him "Governor" of this burlesque "Third House," and Mark delivered such a successful speech that his associates presented him with a suitably inscribed gold watch. Indeed he was riding high. Returning to Virginia City, where Adah Menken and her troupe opened at the opera house in March, Mark enjoyed the society of the notorious beauty, wrote some eulogistic reviews of her performance, and gallantly accepted her imitative poetry as the work of a fellow "literary cuss."[139]

When Joe Goodman, during a temporary absence, intrusted Mark with editorship of the *Enterprise,* an unfortunate verbal warfare ensued, reminiscent of the cub days on Orion's Hannibal paper, but this time, unfortunately, not so easily settled. As Mark narrates in *Roughing It,* a sack of flour was auctioned to raise money for the Sanitary Fund, the Civil War equivalent of the Red Cross, sponsored by the ladies of Carson City.[140] Still Southern enough to indulge in anti-Union humor, Mark warned that the contributions would probably be diverted to a "Miscegenation Society somewhere in the East."[141] The storm against Mark immediately broke, and the outraged ladies even ostracized Orion and Mollie, who had recently suffered the loss of an only child. Although Mark sent an apology which modified their wrath, the affair had become so involved through exchanges in print between the *Enterprise* and the *Union* that it could not be terminated gently.[142] Personal insult and charges of cowardice led to preparations for a duel with James L. Laird, the *Union* editor, but the duel

139 Paine, I, 248.

140 Vol. II, 24–31.

141 Ivan Benson, *Mark Twain's Western Years,* p. 111. As DeLancey Ferguson observes: "It was the jest of a Missouri Copperhead; it could not have been worse timed or in worse taste." *Mark Twain: Man and Legend,* p. 93.

142 *Letters,* I, 97–8.

actually never took place.[143] It is too bad that the versions later told by Mark and his second, Steve Gillis, have been rejected by scholarship, for if too good to be true, they are, nevertheless, a contribution to Western mythology.[144] The facts seem to be that Mark by issuing a challenge in print openly violated a newly passed law which made it a felony to send or accept a challenge. The authorities could not ignore a printed challenge, one in fact presenting a test case for their legal innovation. Mark fled, then, to escape arrest; he ended his career at the Comstock in May, 1864, when accompanied by faithful Steve Gillis, Clemens went to San Francisco.[145]

Thus far Mark Twain had been the writer of burlesque and extravaganza, the creator of humor for miners on the Comstock, who reveled in the bloody details of his massacre hoax, or the fantastic idea of a petrified man, thumb to his nose, whose burial could be accomplished only after blasting. But he was a professional writer, and even if a journalist, at least one whose writings had been reprinted in the East and who enjoyed popularity the length and breadth of the coast. Moreover, he had previously written Washoe correspondence for the *Golden Era* and the San Francisco *Morning Call*.[146] Now a resident of San Francisco, Mark went to work writing dramatic reviews, court reports, and local news for the *Morning Call*, a job that probably lasted from early June until about October 15. Mark and Steve Gillis, who roomed together, moved a number of times,

[143] Benson, *op. cit.*, p. 112. See also DeLancey Ferguson, "Mark Twain's Comstock Duel: The Birth of a Legend," *American Literature*, XIV, 66–70 (March, 1942).

[144] Mark first told his version in "How I Escaped Being Killed in a Duel," *Tom Hood's Comic Annual* (London, 1873), pp. 90–91. This seems to be the picturesque source for the account by Steve Gillis as given in Paine, I, 250–52. Mark retold the story himself in the *Autobiography*, I, 354–9.

[145] Benson, *op. cit.*, p. 112.

[146] Franklin Walker, ed., *The Washoe Giant in San Francisco*, p. 13.

living for a while on a bluff in California Street, from which point of vantage they enjoyed hurling an occasional beer bottle on the tin-can roofs below, a sport that became their favorite Sunday amusement.[147] San Francisco appealed to Clemens, who found its climate "mild and singularly equable." Indeed he said, "It is as pleasant a climate as could well be contrived, take it all around, and is doubtless the most unvarying in the whole world."[148] Soon Mark was enjoying life at the Occidental Hotel, calling it "Heaven on the half shell," and savoring the delights of the city with such luminaries of Western literature as Bret Harte, Prentice Mulford, Charles Warren Stoddard, and Orpheus C. Kerr.[149] Fulfilling duties for the *Call,* however, grew irksome, loss of his by-line was not pleasant, and after the freedom of expression on the *Enterprise* Clemens objected to being edited. When articles of indignant protest against the municipal government and the police department went unpublished, Mark, finding a policeman asleep on his beat, gently fanned him with a cabbage-leaf until a large crowd gathered.[150] It was a good joke, known over town by next morning, but it was slight recompense for a printed burlesque with by-line.

Since several of his Washoe writings had appeared in the *Golden Era,* Clemens had no trouble selling that journal two sketches shortly after his arrival.[151] Indeed, a close affinity existed between the *Territorial Enterprise* and the *Golden Era.* Goodman, McCarthy, and Daggett had once been connected with the latter before going to Virginia

147 Paine, I, 255–56.

148 *Roughing It,* II, 127.

149 Dixon Wecter, "Mark Twain and the West," *Huntington Library Quarterly,* VIII, 369 (August, 1945).

150 Paine, I, 258.

151 "The Evidence in the Case of Smith vs Jones" appeared in the *Golden Era,* June 26, 1864, and "Early Rising as Regards Excursions to the Cliff House" July 3, 1864. Both are reprinted by Walker, *The Washoe Giant in San Francisco,* pp. 77–88.

City, and Dan DeQuille still served the *Era* as Virginia City correspondent, in which capacity Mark may even have substituted. But another publication soon caught his fancy, the *Californian,* generally considered superior to the *Golden Era,* which though a magazine in content was still a newspaper in format. An offer of fifty dollars a month for one article a week brought Mark to the *Californian,* although it was the same sum paid him by the *Golden Era.* As he wrote to his mother, the *Era* "wasn't high-toned enough."[152] His first sketch for the *Californian,* "A Notable Conundrum," appeared October 1, 1864, and his contributions continued regularly until he left San Francisco.[153] Simultaneously he continued to report for the *Morning Call* for a few more weeks.[154]

While not allowed by the *Call* to express himself freely on corruption and vice in San Francisco, Clemens, through his connections in Virginia City, furnished the *Enterprise* with blistering attacks, which Joe Goodman printed. Until a file of the *Enterprise* is located, we can only guess at the nature of these philippics, but they were strong enough to cause the San Francisco chief of police to enter libel suit against the paper.[155] Mark then repeated the charges in terms so strong that he doubted Goodman would print them, and the *Enterprise* promptly carried the letter, word for word. At this crucial point, when Mark's unpopularity with the San Francisco police was at its peak, Steve Gillis decided to enjoy a fight, which ended delightfully for Steve, but left his opponent, a big bruising bartender, ready for the hospital. The police now took their revenge for Mark's scathing articles; Steve was promptly indicted on charges

152 *Letters,* I, 100.

153 John Howell, ed., *Sketches of the Sixties* (San Francisco: John Howell, 1927), p. 121. A complete list of Twain's contributions to the *Californian* is given at the end of this volume.

154 The account of his leaving the *Call* in *Roughing It,* II, 143–4, is pure fiction.

155 Paine, I, 264.

of assault with intention to kill, and Mark stood his bond. When it became apparent that the retaliative police intended full criminal prosecution, Steve skipped out, followed shortly by Mark, whose personal property was about to be attached.[156] Steve went to Virginia City, and Mark accepted an invitation from Jim Gillis to take refuge at his cabin on Jackass Hill in the Mother Lode country of California, arriving there December 4, 1864.[157]

Here on Jackass Hill near Tuttletown, California, Mark found a restful haven with congenial companions. Many days (for the rainy season was on) he sat around the fire with Jim, Bill Gillis, and Dick Stoker—Stoker and his remarkable cat to be immortalized in *Roughing It* as Dick Baker and Tom Quartz.[158] Jim Gillis owned many of the standard classics, and in the pleasant solitude of the Tuolumne hills Sam Clemens read before the fire or listened to Jim invent wonderful yarns about Dick Stoker, extravagant adventures told with humor and fancy, also with insistence upon their veracity. And it was Jim, standing back to the fire, who narrated "The Burning Shame" later to enrich our literature as "The Royal Nonesuch" in *Huckleberry Finn*.[159] Some of these yarns were masterpieces to commit to memory, which Sam stored away, remarking later that he never could get them to sound so well as when Jim told them.[160]

156 *Ibid.*, I, 265.

157 Franklin Walker discounts the trouble with the police, believing that Mark's *Enterprise* letters were written later than the incident, and that Jim, a good talker, intrigued Mark with his yarns, an offer of Western hospitality, and the chance for a strike in pocket mining. *San Francisco's Literary Frontier*, p. 192. However, the validity of Paine's account is accepted by Ivan Benson, *Mark Twain's Western Years*, p. 122, DeLancey Ferguson, *Mark Twain: Man and Legend*, p. 101, and Dixon Wecter, "Mark Twain and the West," *Huntington Library Quarterly*, VIII, 370–71 (August, 1945).

158 Chapter XX, vol, II, 158–63.

159 Chapter XXIII.

160 Paine, I, 267. Another of Jim's tales was "Jim Baker's Bluejay Yarn," *A Tramp Abroad*. The peaceful paradise of the surroundings have been pictured by Mark in "The Californian's Tale," *$30,000 Bequest*, p. 184. Also in *Roughing It*, II, 153.

If Artemus Ward had provided instruction in platform technique, here was the art of narration taught by a past master.

When the weather permitted, Jim initiated Mark in the art of pocket mining, a trade providing Gillis all he needed for his simple life; for, like Thoreau, Jim in his Tuolumne Walden required only books, food, and shelter. Always ready to offer hospitality or lend whatever money he possessed, Gillis found no necessity for worldly luxuries. The story of how he and Mark almost made a fortune through a lucky strike, only to lose it because Mark was too cold and tired to wash one more pan of dirt bears the touch of artistic decoration, but both Steve Gillis and Joe Goodman vouched for it, and perhaps they did turn their backs on a gold mine.[161]

The cabin on Jackass Hill was not without neighbors, among them the pretty Carrington girls, whom Bill Gillis and Mark nicknamed the "Chaparral Quails." When not reading, listening to Jim spin yarns, or prospecting, Mark, generally accompanied by Bill, turned his footsteps toward the Carrington cabin, where the two attractive daughters lived with their parents.[162] At other times pocket mining led them farther from camp, and on New Year's night, 1865, Mark then in Calaveras saw a "magnificent lunar rainbow," shortly to prove a good omen.[163] Going on to Angel's Camp, where he was saved from a diet of "dish water and beans" by the timely opening of a new hotel with "good fare and coffee that a Christian may drink without jeopardizing his eternal soul,"[164] Clemens struck literary gold in the person of old Ben Coon, an endless talker loaded with a fund of pointless stories, who was looking for an audience. Mark listened, and was rewarded by a literary nugget he jotted down:

161 Paine, I, 273.
162 *Ibid.*, I, 268.
163 *Notebook*, pp. 5–6.
164 *Ibid.*, p. 7.

Coleman with his jumping frog—bet a stranger $50.—Stranger had no frog and C. got him one:—In the meantime stranger filled C's frog full of shot and he couldn't jump. The stranger's frog won.[165]

This old tale, one Mark probably would not have bothered to record if he had heard of it before, was not utilized for several more weeks. Dick Stoker having joined him at Angel's Camp, Mark initiated him to the four kinds of soup served at the Frenchman's on important occasions: "Hellfire," "General Debility," "Insanity," and "Sudden Death."[166] Then on February 25, 1865, Clemens departed from Angel's for Jackass Hill in company with Jim and Dick, the three of them walking across the mountain tops in a snowstorm, the first Mark had seen in California, impressive indeed in its beauty.[167]

Upon arrival back in San Francisco, Clemens found a three-month's accumulation of letters, among them an invitation from Artemus Ward to contribute to a book he was bringing out. Believing that he still had time, Mark wrote the frog story told by Ben Coon and sent it on, only to have it arrive too late for Ward's publisher, G. W. Carleton, to include in the book. The pages had gone to press, and Carleton gave Mark's contribution to Henry Clapp, who printed it in the New York *Saturday Press*, November 18, 1865.[168] With this story Mark Twain may be said to have entered upon his career in American fiction, for in Jim Smiley and Simon Wheeler he first successfully created characters with colorful and distinct personalities. More than an anecdote, "Jim Smiley and His Jumping Frog"

165 *Loc. cit.* Across this penciled note he later added in ink: "Wrote this story for Artemus—his idiot publisher Carleton, gave it to Clapp's Saturday Press." *Idem.*

166 *Ibid.*, pp. 7–8.

167 *Ibid.*, p. 8.

168 Oscar Lewis, *The Origin of the Celebrated Jumping Frog of Calaveras County* (San Francisco: Book Club of California, 1931), p. 17. Paine, I, 278.

(the original title) immediately received popular acceptance as fictional literature. Now Mark was known in the East as well as on the Pacific coast; the New York correspondent of the San Francisco *Alta* wrote that papers were copying the story far and near,[169] and on December 16, 1865, the *Californian* entitled its reprint "The Celebrated Jumping Frog of Calaveras County."[170] But Mark wrote to his mother and sister that he did not relish a compliment for this "villainous backwoods sketch,"[171] an attitude possibly occasioned by one of his "black moods,"[172] perhaps by chagrin at having been left out of Ward's book,[173] but more probably by the fact that his associates on the *Californian* held the polite Victorian concept of literature, almost ignoring local color, while devoting their efforts chiefly to bringing "culture" to California rather than establishing an authentic California culture.[174] In fact, this idea that literature should conform in subject and style to the accepted tradition of New England and Europe Twain held all his life, causing him to overvalue *Joan of Arc* and *The Prince and the Pauper* to the discredit of his masterpieces created out of native material and American idiom. Thus Mark in conforming to the literary definitions of the *Californian* writers, momentarily undervalued his effort. But it brought him fame, and Clemens had the good sense to capitalize on it.[175] Now that the name of Mark Twain had leaped across the nation on the Calaveras frog he received an invitation to visit the Sandwich Islands (as Hawaii was then called) on the new steamer *Ajax* carrying a select party

169 Paine, I, 279.

170 John Howell, ed., *Sketches of the Sixties,* p. 194.

171 *Letters,* I, 101.

172 Ferguson, p. 105.

173 Benson, p. 131.

174 Franklin Walker, *San Francisco's Literary Frontier,* p. 178.

175 Benson reminds us that if Mark had been ashamed of the "Jumping Frog" he would hardly have used it as the title of his first book and placed it first in that volume. *Mark Twain's Western Years,* p. 131.

for its maiden voyage. At first he refused, but immediately regretted his choice and hastily persuaded the publishers of the Sacramento *Union* to commission him special correspondent reporting on trade, agriculture, and general topics of interest.[176] In "My Debut as a Literary Person" (1899) Mark records his gratitude to the "lovable and well-beloved men" who generously gave him an opportunity which meant so much to him and so little materially to them.[177] Writing home of his good fortune on March 5, 1866, he exclaimed happily over leaving on the morrow with "letters of introduction to everybody down there worth knowing.[178] The regular correspondence for the *Territorial Enterprise* had begun to pall—as all routine tasks did for Clemens. Writing pieces for the *Golden Era* and the more "high toned" *Californian* held no excitements compared with those he anticipated upon viewing the great cataracts and volcanoes of the islands.

Sailing on the *Ajax,* Mark arrived at Honolulu on March 18, saw its beauty, and was conquered. In his letters home *beautiful* became a theme word. "It has been a perfect jubilee to me in the way of pleasure,"[179] he wrote Mollie. And his enjoyment in the islands was enhanced by finding himself a celebrity, sought by the United States Minister to China and the Minister to Japan.[180] From the Sandwich Islands Mark again wrote travel letters, something in which he was to excel; and here he began to reach a more sophisticated audience, embarking upon a course which led to *Innocents Abroad.* During the voyage out he had begun to make humorous maxims:

Rise early. It is the early bird that catches the worm. Don't

176 Paine, I, 282.

177 *The Man That Corrupted Hadleyburg and Other Stories and Essays,* p. 71. The proprietors of the *Union* were James Anthony, Paul Morrill, and Henry W. Larkin.

178 *Letters,* I, 103.

179 *Ibid.,* I, 106.

180 *Ibid,* I, 107.

be fooled by this absurd saw; I once knew a man who tried it. He got up at sunrise and a horse bit him.[181]

Immediately upon arrival he sent his first letter to the *Union,* following it with twenty-four others, twenty-one being travel descriptions and anecdotes of human interest, three being serious statistical reports on trade, and one a sensational scoop of the *Hornet* disaster, not actually a part of the *Union* correspondence.[182] During the four months and a day of his sojourn in Hawaii Mark was captivated; years later, August 31, 1895, found him gazing longingly at Oahu and noting, "If I might I would go ashore and never leave."[183] Although he was to visit the islands just this once, they seem to have remained, as Frear states, an "oasis of golden memory to the end of his life."[184] Clemens was also fortunate in his connection with the most popular paper on the coast, one that like the Virginia City *Territorial Enterprise* held the genuine affection of its readers, who valued its honesty and courage above those of all rivals.[185] When papers were delivered, the *Union* was most often purchased, and Mark's contributions, sometimes given front-page space, reached a wide audience. From Honolulu, June 25, 1866, he scored one of the biggest scoops in newspaper history, assisted by the United States Minister to China, Anson Burlingame. The clipper ship *Hornet* had burned at sea, the survivors had suffered terribly for forty-three days in an open boat, and only the third mate and ten of the seamen arrived at Honolulu. Mark had just returned from a horseback trip and was in bed with saddle boils, but Burlingame had the cot carried

181 *Notebook,* p. 12.

182 G. Ezra Dane, ed., *Mark Twain's Letters from the Sandwich Islands* (Stanford University Press, Stanford University, California, 1938), pp. xi–xii.

183 *Notebook,* p. 249.

184 Walter F. Frear, *Mark Twain and Hawaii,* p. 92.

185 Ella Sterling Cummins, *The Story of the Files* (San Francisco, Columbian Exposition Commission, 1893), p. 102.

to the hospital, where he helpfully questioned survivors while Mark took notes. Then Twain, without stopping for food or sleep, wrote all night to complete a story which was thrown at nine the next morning onto the deck of the *Milton Badger* as she pulled away for California. It was a scoop, given front page prominence by the *Union* in a spread of three and a half columns.[186] Recovering shortly from his illness, Mark continued to enjoy pleasant association with Burlingame's party until they departed; then he himself left July 19, 1866, for San Francisco on a slow-going vessel requiring twenty-five days for the voyage.[187]

Back in San Francisco, however, he felt himself "in prison," surrounded once again with toil and care.[188] Actually Clemens had increased his fame with the letters for the *Union,* whose publishers had paid him $300 extra for the *Hornet* scoop, but the daily task of returning to a newspaper did not appeal.[189] Rather he sought some means of earning a living that would leave him footloose, a desire that led just seven weeks after his return to his lecture on the Sandwich Islands from the stage of Maguire's Academy of Music.[190] The advertisement announcing the lecture on October 2, concluded:

A SPLENDID ORCHESTRA
is in town but *has not* been engaged
ALSO
A DEN OF FEROCIOUS WILD BEASTS
will be on exhibition in the next block
MAGNIFICENT FIREWORKS
were in contemplation for this occasion,
but the idea has been abandoned

186 Frear, *op. cit.,* p. 110. 187 Paine, I, 288.
188 *Notebook,* p. 29.
189 "My Debut as a Literary Person," *The Man That Corrupted Hadleyburg,* p. 73.
190 Paine, I, 293.

A GRAND TORCHLIGHT PROCESSION

may be expected; in fact, the public are privileged to expect whatever they please.

Dress Circle, $1.00 Family Circle, 50c

Doors open at 7 o'clock The Trouble to begin at 8 o'clock

The story of this first lecture seems to have been faithfully recorded in *Roughing It.*[191] Now he was a personality on the platform; "Mark Twain" had come alive from a newspaper by-line as the trade-mark of Samuel Clemens, and he was to proceed on his career as writer and lecturer, the immediate result of his visit to the islands. But one disappointment was to mar his pleasure; a full account of the *Hornet* catastrophe which he had sent to *Harper's,* seeking recognition in an Eastern magazine, appeared unsigned in the December, 1866, number and was credited to Mark Swain in the annual magazine index.[192] One can hear Mark's profanity!

But his lecture led to a successful tour, Denis McCarthy, old friend on the *Enterprise,* serving as manager. Traveling through Nevada, Mark was greeted by enthusiastic audiences, who packed the houses at Virginia and Carson.[193] Here no introductions were needed; when the curtain rose at Virginia City and revealed Twain at the piano, singing "I Had an Old Horse Whose Name Was Methusalem," the applause was spontaneous. At Red Dog on the Stanislaus the audience gave him a shouting reception from the start. Legend tells of one introduction: "Ladies and gentlemen, I know only two things about this man: the first is that he's never been in jail, and the second is I don't know why."[194] After a successful lecture at Gold Hill, Steve Gillis and

191 Vol. II, 291–6.

192 Merle Johnson, *A Bibliography of Mark Twain,* p. 215.

193 Paine, I, 297.

194 *Ibid.,* I, 295.

others of the *Enterprise* staff staged a fake robbery on the return to Virginia City, a joke Mark failed to relish at the time, though he finally forgave his friends.[195] Everywhere during his swing through California and Nevada, old friends greeted him joyfully while receptive houses vocally acclaimed his humor. Returning to San Francisco, he lectured to the enthusiastic delight of the audiences and reviewers.

Only too happy at following Anson Burlingame's advice on travel, Mark next proposed a trip around the world to be financed by a series of travel letters. And the *Alta California* was so enthusiastic over Clemens' success that he secured a commission from that paper. But first he would go home, then around the world, leaving San Francisco December 15, 1866.[196]

When Mark Twain left California he was well known as a journalist, lecturer, and personality, in contrast to the inconspicuous young secretary who had journeyed west with Orion. At Virginia City and in San Francisco he had developed gifts of caricature, humorous exaggeration, and satire which would appear more artistically in his later work; in the Sandwich Islands he successfully wrote travel letters; the *Jumping Frog* was the harbinger of a multitude of portraitures to come; and Mark Twain the personality stood complete upon the lecture platform.

Newspaper apprenticeship had been his secondary schooling, the Mississippi River with its expansive curriculum of human nature had been his college, but it was in the Western school of journalism and humor that his graduate course was taken. In the West and through Western humor Samuel Langhorne Clemens became Mark Twain, professional author, public lecturer, and personality. Back in

195 Recounted in *Roughing It,* II, 297–303.
196 Paine, I, 304.

Hannibal Sam Clemens at seventeen had contributed his bit to the native literature that filled the journals on the Southwestern frontier, such as the characteristic humorous yarn and the tall tale, which derived their form and style from the oral anecdote.[197] Many tendencies of his Washoe period were prevalent during his cub apprenticeship, notably a predilection for humor and satire, the preference for travel letters, and the seeming aptitude for controversy.[198] But in the masculine world of the big bonanza the humorous tradition of the old Southwest grew into literary productions carrying their author onward to the Eastern seaboard.

This anecdotal literature of the South from which Western humor grew was the product of men engaged in their professions who wrote only to amuse. The rough life around them afforded colorful characters to catch the eye of a conscientious observer; there were extremes of emotion and vivid action—excellent material for humor. This frontier was uniquely American, an important phase in our history which, as Franklin J. Meine explains, has no authentic expression in our literature save through the pens of its humorists.[199] In the year of Mark Twain's birth (1835) Augustus Baldwin Longstreet published *Georgia Scenes,* sketches of native characters and racy incidents, told realistically and with rollicking humor. Longstreet's coeditor on *The States Rights Sentinel,* William T. Thompson, published a series of amusing amatory letters as *Major Jones' Courtship* (1844), so popularly received that the Major's adventures were expanded into a book of travel letters called *Major Jones' Chronicles of Pineville* (1845). Then the scene changed from rural life in the Southern plantation country to the disorganized social order of the

197 Franklin J. Meine, *Tall Tales of the Southwest,* p. xv.
198 Ivan Benson, *Mark Twain's Western Years,* p. 153.
199 *Op. cit.,* xvi.

frontier in the *Adventures of Simon Suggs* (1845) by Johnson J. Hooper, a successful, though unattractive, character study of a shifty swindler, set against a provincial background furnishing opportunities for his dishonest, yet amusing practices. In the *Flush Times of Alabama and Mississippi* (1853) Joseph G. Baldwin, having emigrated from the Old Dominion to North Alabama, depicted the exciting and amusing phases of a youthful section then uninhibited by tradition. But more important was *Sut Lovingood's Yarns* told by George W. Harris, which circulated through the newspapers from 1845, finally to appear in book form in 1867. Sut, the mountaineer from the Great Smokies, whisky flask by his side, reveals the frontiersman's natural dislike of "passuns" and everything in general that might be considered either highbrow or moralizing. Sut, perennial prankster, enjoys nothing like good, hell-raising fun, sometimes retaliatory, but seldom mean in nature; and Sut is funny, contriving comic situations, at times with Rabelaisian humor, hearty, gusty, and vigorous. Besides the works of Longstreet, Thompson, Hooper, Baldwin, and Harris there were three collections of tall tales from the pens of various writers, popular stories circulating among the frontier newspapers over a period of years: *The Big Bear of Arkansas* (1845) edited by William T. Porter, who also collected *The Quarter Race in Kentucky* (1846), and *Polly Peablossom's Wedding* (c. 1851) edited by T. A. Burke. The writings of all these frontier humorists appeared first in periodicals, often in newspapers, a daily expression of an era and a social commentary. When Mark Twain went West he carried this tradition along, as did the other humorists of the Pacific slope, and he was not "opening up a new vein of American humor with his first famous story, *Jim Smiley and His Jumping Frog*" as Professor Meine demonstrates, but rather continuing a "kind of story-telling that had its home and earlier vogue in the genial South before the War."[200]

In Nevada, however, Mark succeeding as reporter for the *Territorial Enterprise* eventually discarded all previous pseudonyms to associate his personality with his trade name. The carefree, vigorous, and entirely masculine school of journalism left its imprint on his style. No more did he indulge in the forced misspellings of Snodgrass;[201] under the easy guidance of Joe Goodman Mark turned to getting the facts for informed, interesting writing. From Dan De-Quille, then showing more promise of success than Mark, he learned how to convey serious information while perpetrating hoaxes and filling ironical sketches with droll humor. From the other members of the *Enterprise* staff, Rollin M. Daggett, and Steve Gillis the printer, Mark absorbed the fighting courage that animated both. Freedom, facts, courage, principle, justice, and humor, the latter boisterous with exaggeration and keen with satire—they were the ingredients of Joe Goodman's journalistic wares, as they were those of all his staff; and Mark Twain, these qualities inherent in him, naturally developed.

Ivan Benson says of Mark's associates on the *Enterprise,* "They could jest on occasion, but when principles were at stake their satire and irony invariably worked in the cause of justice, tolerance, loyalty to ideals."[202] In the same way Mark Twain used his pen throughout the remainder of his life. The humor of the Comstock was that of working men intent upon digging their fortunes out of the ground. Their labor was manual, their taste was strong; for in a world lacking refinement, humor was naturally vigorous, robust, and coarse. The miners liked exaggeration, and were not

200 *Ibid.,* p. xv.

201 "Artemus Ward," from the *Golden Era,* November 29, 1863, however exhibits Mark returning momentarily to the use of humorous misspellings. Ivan Benson, *Mark Twain's Western Years,* p. 177.

202 *Ibid.,* p. 71.

without imagination; the petrified man thumbing his nose across the centuries delighted Washoe.[203] Miners roared approval when "Mark Twain, the wild humorist of the Sage Brush Hills," reported from Carson City that in addition to "seventeen hundred and forty-two applications for notaryships already on file in the Governor's office"[204] there are "eleven cords of petitions stacked up in his back yard." On a dismal day when news items were down to nothing save hay wagons in from the Truckee, "a desperado killed a man in a saloon and joy returned once more." Mark reports his gratitude to the stranger for his kindness: "I was in trouble and you have relieved me nobly and at a time when all seemed dark and drear." Then expressing his friendship and turning to writing of the murder with "hungry attention to details," Mark had just one regret—"namely, that they had not hanged my benefactor on the spot, so that I could work him up too."[205] All Washoe understood.

On the *Enterprise* Mark felt no inhibitions; he said what he had to say, enjoying it enthusiastically as his popularity increased. With the transition to the *Golden Era*, the robust, often coarse burlesques, and extravaganzas old as frontier journalism, accompanied him. Social occasions, so minutely depicted by the fashion editors, became fair game for his broad satire, which described a *coiffure* seen at the Lick House Ball as "a simple wreath of sardines on a string,"[206] While a lady of the Pioneer's Ball was pictured attired in "an elegant *paté de foi gras*," and another wearing "her new and beautiful false teeth" could be followed by "the scent of her sozodont-sweetened sighs."[207] Still the masculine reporter from the Comstock, Mark confided how standing on the corner of Montgomery and looking up a steep street, Clay or Washington, one enjoyed a charming

203 *Ibid.*, p. 175.
204 *Ibid.*, p. 179.
205 *Roughing It*, II, 6–7.
206 *The Washoe Giant in San Francisco*, p. 40.
207 *Ibid.*, p. 42.

view of ladies' legs under the bell-shaped, hoop-skirts: "And what handsome vari-colored, gold-clasped garters they wear now-a-days!"[208] An early morning visit to the Cliff House, recounted with emphasis upon a horse-blanket wrapped closely against the cold, produced no ecstasy, only the numbing of all sense, save smell, to which even the flowers had the odor of horse blankets.[209]

Mark gradually introduced more thought into his Carson City reporting, leaning less heavily upon the elemental humor of the Comstock, though never indeed substantially forsaking it. From San Francisco as his *Enterprise* correspondence assumed more and more the form of serious satire, "The Wild Humorist of the Pacific Slope" annexed another title through his campaign against municipal corruption, notably among the police—"The Moralist of the Main."[210]

When Mark turned from the *Golden Era* to the *Californian* and association with Bret Harte, who understood the value of form, his sketches were still breezy and strong. Although years later he credited Harte's refining influence, actually Mark learned little except something of form and aptness of phrasing. He still wrote in Washoe fashion: "The Whale was not a long one, physically speaking—say thirty-five feet—but he smelt much longer."[211] And on the Sandwich Island visit, Mark pretended to treat seasickness by reading emetic poetry: " 'It is enough. God bless you!' said Brown, and threw up everything he had eaten for three days."[212] Old habits of frontier humor were not brushed away so easily as the dust of Washoe. Probably beginning to feel coarseness unbecoming in San Francisco, Mark still enjoyed an occasional outburst, and he seems to have in-

208 *Ibid.*, p. 44. 209 *Ibid.*, p. 85.
210 *Ibid.*, p. 14.
211 *Sketches of the Sixties*, p. 128.
212 *Letters from the Sandwich Islands*, p. 200.

vented Mr. Brown, through whom all vulgarities could be uttered with impunity.[213] Going East from Washoe, this character who had appeared as alter ego in the Sandwich Islands letters continued his irreverent, coarse, down-to-earth comments, while his creator, gradually adapting to another audience, prepared his demise.

Breaking with the West

In a series of twenty-six letters for the San Francisco *Alta California* Mark described his sailing from the Golden Gate to Nicaragua, the crossing of the isthmus, and subsequent grim voyage to New York, the ship invaded by cholera, and nobody knowing who would be stricken next. Skipper of the *America* was Captain Ned Wakeman, "portly, hearty, jolly, boisterous, good-natured," who never drank or played cards, and swore only in privacy with friends, when his flights of profanity created "awe and admiration."[214] And the Captain could spin yarns, wonderful inventions of sea-lore, such as that of the leaky, old tub, loose as a basket, but assured of safety because it had rats aboard—"big as greyhounds and as lean."[215] Ned Wakeman, it appears, was in every way a remarkable character; when a runaway couple pleaded loss of their marriage license, the Captain promptly remedied matters by giving them a wedding with witnesses, and when rumors started that the groom had used an assumed name, the old man hauled them in immediately to repeat the ceremony.[216] To Mark he was a delight, a source of inspiration never to be forgotten.

213 See DeLancey Ferguson, pp. 106–7.

214 *Notebook,* p. 35. Mark used the Captain several times as a character: Captain Ned Blakely in *Roughing It,* Captain Stormfield in *Captain Stormfield's Visit to Heaven,* Captain Hurricane Jones in "Some Rambling Notes of an Idle Excursion," *Tom Sawyer Abroad.*

215 *Ibid.*, p. 37.

216 *Travels with Mr. Brown,* pp. 18–19.

On this journey, lapsing into Esmeralda habits, Mark was twice challenged as a steerage passenger.[217] The choir especially incurred his disapproval for its repertory, "the damnedest, oldest, vilest songs"—"and besides they never invited me to sing, anyhow."[218] While in this mood of everlasting curses he uttered honest imprecations against the inventor of the villainous stateroom lamp. Then suddenly came real disaster for the entire ship to suffer, making such annoyances sink properly to trifles. Several sick cases aboard, previously suspected as nothing more than victims of eating tropical fruit, turned out to be cholera of a malignant type. Though he might have gone ashore at Key West, Mark stuck to the ship, continuing on to New York, while the melancholy vessel became a floating hospital, from which its dead were buried at sea.

After his arrival in New York, and a brief visit to his boyhood home in the Middle West, Mark settled down to report on the metropolis for his California readers, while also making plans for the trip abroad.[219] At first he is full of criticism; he doesn't like the crowds, he is annoyed by omnibuses, prices are too high, but gradually as he becomes accustomed to New York City the complaints become fewer, finally to be replaced by praise.

He liked the chic, New York-look of the women, whom he found, "Charming, fascinating, seductive, bewitching!" He visited clubs like the Century, where one met distinguished authors and artists, and was delighted to find an

217 *Notebook*, p. 39.

218 *Ibid.*, pp. 40–1. When the choir sang "What Is Home Without a Mother" Mark commented: "Home without a mother may not amount to much, but there is no use in aggravating the thing with such a tune as that." *Travels with Mr. Brown*, p. 28.

219 The first account of Twain's letters from New York was written by Professor Blair. See Walter Blair, "Mark Twain, New York Correspondent," *American Literature*, XI, 247–59 (November, 1939). Blair summarizes and quotes from the New York letters. The entire correspondence is given in *Mark Twain's Travels with Mr. Brown*, edited by Franklin Walker and G. Ezra Dane (New York: Alfred A. Knopf, 1940).

exclusiveness that insisted upon brains as well as bank accounts and pedigrees.[220] Always interested in the clergy, Mark arose one freezing day, "earlier than any Christian ought to be out of his bed on such a morning," to crowd into the church of Henry Ward Beecher, whom he confessed he was in a "pious frenzy" to hear.[221] Listening to the "poetry, pathos, humor, satire" blended into an "earnest exposition of the great truths," Mark felt like applauding.[222] He was so pleased that he then went to hear Bishop Southgate, whose sermon he liked, finding it enhanced by the beautiful music of the choir.[223]

Mark was attracted by the theatre, one of his perpetual delights, although he was shocked, or pretended to be, by displays of feminine nudity. Ever in the role of moralist, Twain warned against exposing on the stage "beautiful clipper-built girls," who wore barely enough clothes "to be tantalizing." It was the *Black Crook* specifically, so he said, that touched his "missionary sensibilities," for its scenic effects, ballets, and tableaux rivaled the *Arabian Nights,* while "seventy beauties . . . bare-legged girls . . . a wilderness of girls . . . change their clothes every fifteen minutes for four hours, and their dresses become more beautiful and more rascally all the time." Indeed, the "Moralist of the Main" declared, "the scenery and the legs are everything," and nobody noticed the absence of an adequate plot.[224] The way things were going, he told his California readers, the popular taste demanded feminine beauty and nudity, and although Edwin Booth and the legitimate drama still played to full houses, Mark prophesied that "he will have to make a little change by-and-by and peel some women."[225]

220 *Travels with Mr. Brown,* pp. 88–9.
221 *Ibid.,* p. 92.
222 *Ibid.,* p. 94.
223 *Ibid.,* p. 97.
224 *Ibid.,* pp. 85–6.
225 *Ibid.,* p. 87.

These letters, written over a period of six months after leaving San Francisco, are the prologue to *Innocents Abroad.* They ended on the eve of the *Quaker City's* sailing from New York and link the *Letters from the Sandwich Islands* with the *Alta California* correspondence, which was to be rearranged into Clemens' first travel book. As biography they record Twain's perceptions of beauty in the Nicaraguan jungle, his initial depression in the great Eastern metropolis, followed by visits to St. Louis, where Civil War animosity blurred memories of pilot-days on the river, and to Hannibal, now enduring hard times, almost finished by competition and war. Yet he enjoyed it all, for old friends recalled the past, and he lectured twice in St. Louis in the Mercantile Library Hall before large and appreciative audiences.[226]

However "ups and downs" may have affected Hannibal and Keokuk, Quincy still impressed him as a "wonderful place," and indeed his entire journey back to New York left him with an impression of progress and prosperity. Civil strife and its aftermath, together with the decline of steamboating, may have left the Mississippi Valley in depression, but "Such wonderful cities as we saw, all the way through Ohio, New York and New Jersey."[227] Back in our greatest city once more, Mark, now free of prejudice, turned his pen to praise.

"Make your mark in New York," he advised, "and you are a made man."[228] At the same time he mentions his Cooper Institute speech on the Sandwich Islands, saved from fiasco by free tickets given to the school teachers, who packed the house and received him with delight. The papers were kind, and enough seats were actually sold to yield about $300 and save the sponsor, Frank Fuller, an old friend from Utah, who had hired the largest hall in

226 *Ibid.,* p. 136. 227 *Ibid.,* p. 155.
228 *Ibid.,* p. 176.

town in a burst of enthusiasm. Established with the public, Mark then lectured in Brooklyn and again in New York, coming off handsomely.[229] Scant time remained before his boat sailed, but he was asked to lecture in other nearby towns. This was in May, the month his first book was published, *The Celebrated Jumping Frog of Calaveras County and Other Sketches*.[230] May also marked the date of his arrest and overnight confinement in jail.[231] Yet even this could not turn him against New York now; later on he praised the weather for its variety and contrast of four distinct seasons, each one a delight. And the best New York hotels received his acclaim, especially for their dining rooms: no "army of hyenas camped around you, grinding bones and clattering spoons and forks;" instead he found "tables clad in snowy cloths and garnished like a jeweler's window, and everything quiet, and genteel and orderly."[232] Twain, as here, frequently exhibited the best of taste, long before meeting Mrs. Fairbanks or Livy, something often forgotten by critics who remember only his lapses, as in art or music. These he never hid: "I am glad the old masters are all dead, and I only wish they had died sooner," he exclaimed frankly after seeing a picture of a "naked infant that was not built like any infant that ever I saw, nor colored like it, either."[233] Soon he was to face the old masters in Europe with equal candor, which if brash or ignorant, was at least honest.

229 Paine, I, 317. See also Ferguson, p. 119.

230 The Frog again brought Mark's name before the public, but he made nothing financially. It was published by Charles Henry Webb, former editor of the *Californian,* who backed it and offered to pay the author a royalty of ten cents a copy, but Mark later had to pay Webb $800 to regain copyright to the material. Ferguson, p. 117.

231 Mark's story goes thus: "I was on my way home with a friend a week ago—it was about midnight—when we came upon two men who were fighting. We interfered like a couple of idiots, and tried to separate them, and a brace of policemen came up and took us all off to the Station House." *Travels with Mr. Brown,* p. 187.

232 *Ibid.,* p. 201.

233 *Ibid.,* p. 239.

The proprietors of the *Alta California,* having paid $1250 for his passage, Mark Twain sailed June 8, 1867, on the *Quaker City,* a pleasant, satisfactory vessel capable of making ten knots an hour under steam with the help of her auxiliary sails.[234] Although most of the excursionists were ministers or middle-aged people—the Holy Land visit had been extensively advertised and the expenses were high—Mark found a number of congenial associates, among them Dan Slote, his "splendid, immoral, tobacco-smoking, wine-drinking, godless room-mate";[235] Dr. A. Reeves Jackson, nemesis of guides in *Innocents Abroad;* Jack Van Nostrand (Jack); and Julius Moulton (Moult). It was sinful Jack credited by Twain with the remark to the deacons on the exorbitant boat fares at the Sea of Galilee: "Well, Denny, do you wonder now that Christ walked?"[236] And there was Emeline Beach, destined to remain a friend for more than forty years,[237] and especially "Mother" Fairbanks, herself an able correspondent for her husband's Cleveland *Herald,* who understood and encouraged him. While exercising critical judgment over his correspondence, Mrs. Fairbanks exerted a refining influence Mark had the good sense to accept.[238] Another was Bloodgood H. Cutter ("Poet Lariat" of the *Innocents*), an old-fashioned farmer with an obsession for rhymes, who generally found Mark writing, partly, no doubt, to escape hearing Cutter's jingles. But then, it was not all play for the *Alta* correspondent, who had plenty of work ahead: fifty-three letters to the *Alta* within five months and six to the *Tribune.*[239]

The more pious travelers were often shocked by Mark's irreverence, for he doubted the authenticity of relics, joked

234 Paine, I, 326. 235 *Ibid.,* I, 322.

236 *Ibid.,* I, 337.

237 Bradford A. Booth, "Mark Twain's Friendship with Emeline Beach," *American Literature,* XIX, 219–30 (November, 1947).

238 Paine, I, 327. 239 *Ibid.,* I, 331.

about Biblical characters, and made notations like this: "Where Baalam's ass lived, holy ground."[240] Yet others saw, too, the strength of character that loyally stuck to a friend; when Dan Slote, sick with cholera, was about to be abandoned by the other tourists, Mark declared: "Gentlemen, I understand that you are going to leave Dan Slote here alone. I'll be d——d if I do."[241] And there he remained until his friend recovered. It was Mark, chosen in spite of his irreverence, who drafted the address to the Emperor of Russia on that auspicious occasion when a *Quaker City* "pilgrim" inquired of the Grand Duke in a resonant stage whisper: "Say, Dook, where's the water-closet?"[242] The voyage was a great experience; from Gibraltar to Athens, from Egypt to Rome, Spain, France, the Holy Land—Mark poured it all into his *Alta* letters while experience was vivid.[243]

Yet the most important incident of the journey occurred quietly one day in the stateroom of a young man, Charles Langdon, Mark's junior and admirer, who exhibited an ivory miniature of his sister. There in the Bay of Smyrna Samuel Clemens fell in love with the likeness of Olivia Langdon; each time he visited her brother afterward, he asked to see it, even begged for it. And there he resolved to meet the girl whose face was so delicately tinted on the dainty ivory, who so evoked his admiration and reverence.[244]

When the *Quaker City* docked in New York, November 19, 1867, Clemens found himself a celebrity. His final letter, written for the New York *Herald,* was uproariously

240 *Notebook,* p. 88. 241 Paine, I, 337.

242 *Notebook,* p. 80.

243 See the notes to *Mark Twain to Mrs. Fairbanks,* edited by Dixon Wecter, for additional information on the *Quaker City* voyagers.

244 Paine, I, 339. Dixon Wecter describes the miniature, *Love Letters of Mark Twain,* p. 2.

funny but personally satirical, causing offense to the stodgy ones who had almost turned the pleasure excursion into a funeral procession.[245] But Mark did not wait for retributive wrath; the next day found him in Washington, secretary to a senator, an arrangement concluded from Naples, unhappily not destined to last. Senator Stewart refers unpleasantly to Mark, in his memoirs, uttering charges that do not square with the facts. The job was soon terminated; for covering sessions of Congress, answering letters from constituents, and interviewing job seekers proved too irksome. One reason Twain had accepted the position was to secure a place for Orion, and the resulting failure was a keen disappointment. Yet it really seems that the senator and his secretary were born incompatibles; soon Mark was publishing "My Late Senatorial Secretaryship" and "Facts Concerning the Recent Resignation," good-humored fun which reflected on nobody, as he changed his employer's name to Jim Nye in these sketches.[246]

Clemens was already established as a Washington correspondent, receiving contracts from the New York *Tribune* and the *Herald,* while numerous others sought his services. Then came a letter from Elisha Bliss, Jr., inquiring if he would be interested in writing a book for the American Publishing Company; Mark replied that he would like to rewrite his *Alta* correspondence into a travel volume. Since the *Alta* had few exchanges in the East, Clemens doubted if many readers there had seen the originals. As Paine observed, then began "one of the most notable publishing connections in American literary history."[247] But the book was not immediately forthcoming; Bliss became

245 Paine, I, 345.

246 See *Sketches New and Old.* Ferguson says the secretaryship lasted about a week. *Mark Twain: Man and Legend,* p. 128. Effie Mona Mack, however, thinks two and a half months. *Mark Twain in Nevada,* p. 345.

247 Paine, I, 351.

ill and there was further delay in discussion over the percentage of royalty.

Meanwhile, Dan Slote invited his *Quaker City* friend to spend Christmas in New York, an invitation which led to a meeting with the lovely girl of the ivory miniature. The Langdons, it so happened, were visiting in New York, where Mark was introduced to them two days after Christmas at their hotel, the St. Nicholas.[248] Years later Mark said of this meeting with Olivia: "It is forty years ago. From that day to this she has never been out of my mind."[249] On January 2 or 3, Charles Dickens, wearing a black velvet coat decorated with a red flower in his buttonhole, read the death scene of Steerforth from *David Copperfield* in Steinway Hall, but impressive as he was, Mark remembered better the twenty-two-year-old Olivia, with whose family he had attended the lecture.[250] On New Year's Day he had seen her also, paying a call as was the fashion, where Olivia was receiving with a niece of Henry Ward Beecher. Soon he was to dine with Beecher himself at a dinner party including Harriet Beecher Stowe and his steamship friends, Moses S. Beach and his daughter Emeline. It was a gay evening, and Mark remaining overnight at Beecher's invitation exclaimed in a letter to his mother and sister, "Henry Ward is a brick."[251]

Returning to Washington, where a lecture was arranged by a friend—one "not entirely sober at the time"—Mark confronted with all details, hardly knowing what he was going to talk about, managed to improvise something called "The Frozen Truth." He trusted to luck to carry him through and it did; the lecture was subsequently given in several other places. At the same time correspondence with Bliss brought him to Hartford for an interview, which left

248 *Love Letters,* p. 5. 249 Paine, I, 353.
250 *Idem.* Dixon Wecter established the correct date, *Love Letters,* p. 6.
251 *Letters,* I, 143.

the publisher dissatisfied with Mark's traveling suit and fragrant pipe, but highly impressed with his personality. Turning down an outright offer of ten thousand dollars cash for his copyright, Twain accepted a proposition paying instead five per cent royalty.[252] Now he turned to the job of preparing the *Alta* correspondence, revising, editing, and supplementing, a task which engaged his attention for six months.[253] In the meantime, he returned to Washington, where he produced newspaper correspondence and sketches, intent upon earning something while finishing the book. With that inexhaustible energy Clemens could at times exhibit he also agreed to a syndicate arrangement with John Swinton to furnish several other newspapers with letters.[254]

Suddenly came bad news from Joe Goodman; the *Alta* publishers, holding copyright to the letters, were thinking of bringing them out as a book. It was a bombshell, and Mark poured out his wrath to Orion upon the thieves who sought to swindle him! Immediately he telegraphed, then wrote, and receiving no satisfactory answer he left for San Francisco in March to meet "those Alta thieves face to face."[255] Financed with an advance royalty from Bliss, Mark again crossed the isthmus and arrived by steamer in San Francisco, where all problems about the letters were quickly settled to everyone's satisfaction. But before returning, Twain decided to increase his funds with a lecture tour around the old circuit of two years ago, where he was received in triumph by old friends of Virginia, Carson, and elsewhere. Again in San Francisco for his last California lecture, he advertised it in the form of a purported protest

252 Paine, I, 356–7.

253 Leon T. Dickinson, "Mark Twain's Revisions in Writing *The Innocents Abroad*," *American Literature*, XIX, 139 (May, 1947).

254 Paine, I, 359. Mark Twain's newspaper correspondence from Washington lies buried in undiscovered files, awaiting excavation.

255 *Ibid.*, I, 361.

from leading citizens against further infliction, ending with fictitious signatures of business firms, newspapers, and the clergy, with the final word:

You had *better* go. Yours, Chief of Police[256]

It was a great success, and Mark sailed July 6, his financial status considerably improved and the manuscript of his book ready for delivery to the publishers at Hartford. Yet the last hurdle was still to come; the directors of the American Publishing Company, suddenly discovering the nature of the venture, decided against publication. As Mark later remembered it, the contract date for the issue of the book arrived with no book or any explanation. Going to Hartford, he had talked with the "staid old fogies" who feared the taint of humor, and we might add the wrath of stodgy piety. After talking with the "remains" of one of the "old relics" on the board of directors, Mark warned Bliss to go ahead or expect trouble. This warning produced page proof, followed by yet another delay without explanation. A threat of suit for damages if the book were not on sale within twenty-four hours, broke the log-jam, with the resulting popular reception by the public.[257] That was how Mark recalled it, but Paine adds that Bliss, who believed in the book, forced the directors to publish it by a threat of resignation.[258]

While awaiting publication of *The Innocents Abroad,* Mark visited the Langdons in Elmira—of course, to pay court to Olivia. It was a gay and happy week. The home of Jervis Langdon, a prosperous business man whose mines produced the coal sold by his firm, was handsome and hospitable. When Samuel Clemens discovered how deeply he was in love with Olivia, he confided his feelings to her

256 Paine, I, 365.

257 *Mark Twain in Eruption,* p. 146–8.

258 Paine, I, 365. Paine declares that Mark did not threaten suit, as he remembered it. *Ibid.,* I, 381.

brother, at the same time declaring that he *ought* to leave. The alarmed Charley Langdon, who thought nobody good enough for Livy, hastened the departure, but as the light two-seated carriage started quickly from the gate, the rear seat, left unbolted, fell backward carrying Mark with it. Unhurt, he did not recover too quickly, but allowed himself to be carried into the house, where his presence was now enforced for a day or two.[259]

After a Cleveland trip to confide his courtship to "Mother" Fairbanks, Clemens returned to Hartford for conference with his publishers. Now he met the Rev. Joseph H. Twichell, pastor of a wealthy and fashionable Congregational church, who became his fast friend. Twichell was a man—physically, mentally, and spiritually; he had been chaplain for General Sickles during the Civil War, and he was so generous that his charitable nature proved his financial undoing. Strong and athletic, he loved life with an understanding of human nature and a keen sense of humor.[260] One of many ministers who admired Mark Twain, Twichell met him on the common grounds of humanity and manhood.[261] Twichell's house became his home whenever he was in Hartford.

But once again Mark was away on a lecture tour, this time directed by James Redpath of the Boston Lyceum Bureau, with a new and immensely popular lecture on "The Vandal Abroad." The newspapers, and his audiences, were enthusiastic over the subject and manner of delivery.[262] Popular and successful, earning more than a hundred

[259] Paine, I, 369. See also *Mark Twain to Mrs. Fairbanks,* pp. 39–40. Dated letters to Mrs. Fairbanks and Olivia Langdon reveal that he did not remain longer.

[260] Paine, I, 371.

[261] Paine reminds us that the Rev. Mr. Rising of the Comstock was Mark's friend, as was Henry Ward Beecher before Twichell. While they might not approve of his irreverence, they valued his creed of "liberty and justice"—in short, "humanity." *Idem.*

[262] *Ibid.,* I, 374.

dollars an evening on many a successive night, Mark returned to Elmira whenever possible to persist in his suit, until finally he broke down all resistance and the engagement was announced February 4, 1869. Closing his lecture tour in March with a profit of around $8,000 Clemens returned to Elmira, where his fiancée assisted him with proof reading. The book finally appeared July 20, 1869, in an edition of 20,000 copies.[263]

Now author of a best seller, Mark began to prospect for a lucrative newspaper connection; a third interest in the Buffalo *Express* could be purchased for $25,000. To secure the money, he launched plans for an extensive tour of the Pacific coast, when Mr. Langdon, having completely accepted his future son-in-law, insisted upon advancing the needed funds. All inquiries about repayment of the loan remained unanswered by Jervis Langdon, but Clemens determined to give a note to the firm's business agent, and paid the interest as it fell due.[264] Mark's assumption of editorial duties did not prevent his leaving in October on a lecture tour through New England, where the reception was quite as enthusiastic as in the West. Clemens made his tour-headquarters in Boston; there he met William Dean Howells, assistant editor of the *Atlantic Monthly,* and James T. Fields, its editor.[265] So anxious was he to earn all he might to pay off his debts that the wedding was postponed from Christmas; and Mark continued on the lecture platform until February, recalling jokes about stewed plums and that night at Angel's Camp with the story of the frog. A few days before the wedding he wrote his old friend Jim Gillis how he wished that Jim and Dick Stoker could be there to see his bride—"lovelier than the peerless 'Chapparal [sic] Quails.' "[266]

On February 2, 1870, Joe Twichell arrived in Elmira to

263 *Ibid.,* I, 380–1.
264 *Ibid.,* I, 386.
265 *Ibid.,* I, 390.
266 *Letters,* I, 171.

help the Rev. Thomas K. Beecher perform the ceremony. Pamela with her daughter Annie came from St. Louis, and Mrs. Fairbanks from Cleveland. The wedding took place in the Langdon home before a few guests, followed by a wedding-supper and dancing during which the bride's father danced with her. On the next afternoon the gay party set out for Buffalo, where Mark expected to carry his bride to a boarding-house, unaware that his father-in-law had bought and furnished a fine place on Delaware Avenue as a gift. Arriving to be met by servants who ushered them into the newly decorated rooms, Clemens recovered from his amazement to say to his benefactor, "Mr. Langdon, whenever you are in Buffalo, if it's twice a year, come right here. Bring your bag and stay overnight if you want to. It sha'n't cost you a cent."[267]

SELECTED BIBLIOGRAPHY

HANNIBAL

Bidewell, George Ivan. "Mark Twain's Florida Years," *Missouri Historical Review,* XL, 159–73 (January, 1946).

[Formative influences from Florida, Missouri, on Clemens.]

Brashear, Minnie M. "Mark Twain Juvenilia," *American Literature*, II, 25–53 (March, 1930).

[Describes earliest journalism of Clemens and shows the cultural importance of Hannibal as a town.]

——. *Mark Twain, Son of Missouri.* Chapel Hill: University of North Carolina Press, 1934.

[Invaluable for formative influences.]

Clemens, Cyril. *Young Sam Clemens.* Portland, Maine: Leon Tebbetts Editions, 1942.

[Adds nothing to our knowledge of Clemens.]

Dugas, Gaile. "Mark Twain's Hannibal," *Holiday,* II, 102–7 (April, 1947).

[Hannibal is now a shrine of American boyhood.]

Ferguson, DeLancey. *Mark Twain: Man and Legend.* Indianapolis: Bobbs-Merrill Company, 1943.

[Good account of the formative influences.]

267 Paine, I, 396.

Lorch, Fred W. "Mark Twain and the 'Campaign That Failed,'" *American Literature,* XII, 454–70 (January, 1941).

[A comprehensive examination of the facts and a sound evaluation.]

——. "Orion Clemens," *The Palimpsest,* X, 353–386 (October, 1929).

[A brief account of Twain's brother.]

Mark Twain's Autobiography, with an Introduction by Albert Bigelow Paine. 2 vols. New York: Harper & Brothers, 1924.

[Indispensable.]

Paine, Albert Bigelow. *Mark Twain: A Biography.* 3 vols. New York: Harper & Brothers, 1912. Revised in 2 vols., 1935.

[Still a useful source.]

Paullin, Charles O. "Mark Twain's Virginia Kin," *William and Mary College Quarterly,* XV, 294–8 (July, 1935).

[Traces Clemens' genealogy.]

Quaife, M. M. "Mark Twain's Military Career," *Twainian,* III, 4–7 (June, 1944). Discovery of James Bradley's *The Confederate Mail Carrier* (1894) indicates that *Absalom Grimes, Confederate Mail Runner* (1926) is no more reliable than Mark's own version of his military episode.

Roberts, Harold. "Sam Clemens: Florida Days," *Twainian,* I, 4–6 (March, 1942).

Twainian, published by the Mark Twain Society, formerly at Elkhorn, Wisconsin, now Perry, Missouri.

[This journal is invaluable for facts about Twain's boyhood.]

Wecter, Dixon. *Sam Clemens of Hannibal.* Boston: Houghton Mifflin Co., 1952.

[The definitive study.]

WANDERINGS

Branch, Edgar M., editor, *Mark Twain's Letters in the Muscatine Journal.* Chicago: Mark Twain Association of America, 1942.

[Shows development in style.]

Brashear, Minnie M. *Mark Twain, Son of Missouri.* Chapel Hill: University of North Carolina Press, 1934.

[Chapter V is helpful for this period.]

Ferguson, DeLancey. *Mark Twain: Man and Legend.* Indianapolis: Bobbs-Merrill, 1943.
[Sound and interesting for these years.]

Flanagan, John T. "Mark Twain on the Upper Mississippi," *Minnesota History,* XVII, 369–84 (December, 1936).

Paine, Albert Bigelow. *Mark Twain: A Biography.* 3 vols. New York: Harper & Brothers, 1912. Revised in 2 vols., 1935.
[Still a good source.]

THE PILOT

DeVoto, Bernard. *Mark Twain's America.* Boston: Little, Brown, and Company, 1935.
[Discusses Twain on the river.]

Eskew, Garnett L. "Mark Twain, Steamboat Pilot," *Coronet,* VIII, 100–106 (May, 1940).
[Suggests jealousy in antagonisms to Twain's reputation as a pilot.]

Ferguson, DeLancey. *Mark Twain: Man and Legend.* Indianapolis: Bobbs-Merrill Co., 1943.
[Chapter III contains all the known facts on Twain as a pilot.]

Hutcherson, Dudley R. "Mark Twain as a Pilot," *American Literature,* XII, 353–5 (November, 1940).
[Cites opinion that Twain was unsuccessful as a pilot.]

Leisy, Ernest E. "Mark Twain and Isaiah Sellers," *American Literature,* XIII, 398–405 (January, 1942).
[The Clemens burlesque of Sellers, the facts of the case.]

Mark Twain's *Life on the Mississippi* (printed in numerous editions).
[Mark's own account of his cub days on the Mississippi remains our fullest source.]

Twainian, published by the Mark Twain Society, now in Perry, Missouri.
[Important for facts of this period.]

Wecter, Dixon. "Mark Twain's River," *Atlantic Monthly,* CLXXXII, 45–7 (October, 1948).
[A trip down the Mississippi by towboat in August, 1947, by the literary editor of the Mark Twain Estate.]

THE WEST

Altrocchi, Julia C. "Along the Mother Lode," *Yale Review* XXIV, 131–145 (September, 1934).
[Follows the trail of Clemens and Bret Harte in California.]

Benson, Ivan. *Mark Twain's Western Years.* Stanford University, California: Stanford University Press, 1938.

[The standard work on this period.]

Branch, Edgar Marquess. *The Literary Apprenticeship of Mark Twain.* Urbana: University of Illinois Press, 1950.

[Definitive study of Mark's apprenticeship development.]

Brooks, Van Wyck. *The Times of Melville and Whitman.* New York: E. P. Dutton & Company, 1947.

[Treats Twain in the West.]

DeQuille, Dan (William Wright). *The Big Bonanza.* New York: Alfred A. Knopf, 1947.

[An important book on Virginia City and the Comstock Lode, written by Mark's old friend on the *Territorial Enterprise.* Splendid for the Western background.]

DeVoto, Bernard. *Mark Twain's America.* Boston: Little, Brown and Co., 1932, revised 1935.

[Traces the Western influence, important.]

Ferguson, DeLancey. *Mark Twain: Man and Legend.* Indianapolis: Bobbs-Merrill Company, 1943.

[Important; corrects Paine and the *Autobiography.*]

——. "Mark Twain's Comstock Duel: the Birth of a Legend," *American Literature,* XIV, 66–70 (March, 1942).

[Facts contradict the *Autobiography* version.]

——. "The Petrified Truth," *Colophon,* II, 189–196, (Winter, 1937).

[Uses stories by Twain and Dan DeQuille to show fiction of Mark's Comstock tales.]

Frear, Walter Francis. *Mark Twain and Hawaii.* Chicago: The Lakeside Press, 1947.

[Definitive for the visit to Hawaii.]

Gillis, William R. *Goldrush Days with Mark Twain.* New York: Albert and Charles Boni, 1930.

[Inaccurate, of no biographical value.]

Goodwin, C. C. *As I Remember Them.* Salt Lake City: Salt Lake Commercial Club, 1913.

[Accurate.]

Loomis, C. G. "Dan de Quille's Mark Twain," *Pacific Historical Review,* XV, 336–47 (September, 1946).

[The association of William Wright and Clemens.]

Lorch, Fred W. "Mark Twain's Early Nevada Letters," *American Literature,* X, 486–8 (January, 1939).

[Corrects sequence of letters as given by Paine. Shows Clemens' interest in mining earlier than Paine supposed.]

Lyman, George D. *The Saga of the Comstock Lode.* New York: Charles Scribners' Sons, 1934.

[Interesting contribution.]

Mabbott, Thomas O. "Mark Twain's Artillery: A Mark Twain Legend," *Missouri Historical Review,* XXV, 23–29 (October, 1930).

[Amusing article on Twain from Carson City *Appeal* of 1880.]

Mack, Effie Mona. *Mark Twain in Nevada.* New York: Charles Scribner's Sons, 1947.

[Full account of the Washoe environment.]

Mark Twain's Letters, arranged with comment by Albert Bigelow Paine. 2 vols. New York: Harper & Brothers, 1917.

[Helpful for these years.]

Paine, Albert Bigelow. *Mark Twain: A Biography.* 3 vols. New York: Harper & Brothers, 1912. Revised in 2 vols., 1935.

[Interesting, but often inaccurate.]

Twainian, first published at Elkhorn, Wisconsin, now at Perry, Missouri.

[Important source for facts and uncollected items by Twain while in the West.]

Walker, Franklin. *San Francisco's Literary Frontier.* New York: Alfred Knopf, 1939.

[Twain in San Francisco.]

Wecter, Dixon. "Mark Twain and the West," *Huntington Library Quarterly,* VIII, 359–77 (August, 1945).

[The best single article on Clemens in Nevada and California.]

BREAKING WITH THE WEST

Blair, Walter. "Mark Twain, New York Correspondent," *American Literature,* XI, 247–59 (November, 1939).

[The travel letters written for the San Francisco *Alta California* in 1867, just before the *Innocents Abroad* voyage.]

Brownell, George H. "The First of Series II, American Travel Letters, in *Alta California,*" *Twainian,* VI, 1–3 (May–June, 1947).

[Uncollected Twain letters of 1867.]

——. "The Home of the Prodigal Son," *Twainian,* II, 1–3 (April, 1943).

[Reprints sketch in *Alta California,* February 9, 1868, omitted from the *Innocents.*]

——. "More Twain Found in New York Weekly," *Twainian,* III, 1–4 (March, 1944).

[Five letters on Sandwich Islands printed in New York *Weekly* in 1867 described.]

——. "Seven New Twain Tales Discovered by Chance," *Twainian,* III, 3–6 (November, 1943).

[Describes two tales in the Washington *Weekly Chronicle* and five in the New York *Sunday Mercury.*]

——. "Two Hitherto Unknown Twain Tales Found in New York Tribune," *Twainian,* V, 1–2 (November, December, 1946).

[Two tales, published December 12, 1868, and December 18, 1867.]

Clemens, Cyril. "Mark Twain's Washington in 1868," *Mark Twain Quarterly,* V, 1–16 (Summer, 1942).

[Newspaper correspondence, unfortunately not arranged in order.]

Dickinson, Leon T. "Mark Twain's Revisions in Writing *The Innocents Abroad,*" *American Literature,* XIX, 139–157 (May, 1947).

[Reveals Twain's revisions as he made the *Alta* letters into a book for Eastern readers.]

Ferguson, DeLancey. *Mark Twain: Man and Legend.* Indianapolis: Bobbs-Merrill, 1943.

[As elsewhere, valuable.]

——. "Mark Twain and the Cleveland Herald," *American Literature,* VIII, 304–5 (November, 1936).

[Brief note on Mark's interest in joining the *Herald.*]

Lorch, Fred W. " 'Doesticks' and *Innocents Abroad,*" *American Literature,* XX, 446–9 (January, 1949).

[Letters to a minor humorist show that Mark thought of making travel letters into a book prior to *Quaker City* departure.]

——. "Mark Twain's Orphanage Lecture," *American Literature,* VII, 453–5 (January, 1936).

[Material from Cleveland *Daily Leader* concerning Twain's lecture there on January 22, 1869.]

——. "Mark Twain's Sandwich Islands Lecture in St. Louis," *American Literature,* XVIII, 299–307 (January, 1947).

[Reprints a lecture given in March, 1867.]

Mark Twain's Travels with Mr. Brown, edited by Franklin

Walker and G. Ezra Dane. New York: Alfred A. Knopf, 1940.

[Very important link in Twain's development.]

Paine, Albert Bigelow. *Mark Twain: A Biography*. 3 vols. New York: Harper and Brothers, 1912. Revised in 2 vols., 1935.

[Still valuable, though sometimes inaccurate.]

Vogelback, Arthur L. "Mark Twain: Newspaper Contributor," *American Literature,* XX, 111–28 (May, 1948).

[Discusses Twain's press writings in the decade following the *Innocents.*]

CHAPTER III

THE MAN OF LETTERS

THE EAST: BUFFALO

ONCE MARRIED and settled in his home, Mark turned diligently to his newspaper work; somehow despite the success of *The Innocents* he did not yet regard himself as an author. Meantime he would advance in his journalistic profession, not only writing editorials and satires for the Buffalo *Express,* but accepting an offer from a magazine, the *Galaxy,* to supply monthly contributions called "Memoranda" at a stipend of $2400 per annum. His working hours, though irregular, were long and hard (often from eight in the morning until eleven at night) while he sat at his desk, gradually removing coat, vest, collar, and finally shoes—anything to insure comfort.[1] Editorials from his pen—he always defended the oppressed—were scathing, fearless, and sincere in his attacks upon injustice and violations of liberty. And he also produced humorous sketches, among them "Journalism in Tennessee" and "A Curious Dream," the latter a satire directed at cities allowing graveyards to fall into decay and ruin.[2] Yet the *Galaxy* contributions appealed to him more; soon he was sending it his better sketches, many of them courageous attacks upon prominent persons, selected as targets because of their injustices. Two of these were the renowned minister DeWitt Talmage, then at the peak of popularity, and another fashionable churchman named Sabine, but Twain was not concerned over

1 Paine, II, 398.

2 See *Sketches New and Old,* p. 227.

alienating readers or making enemies—not with a principle involved.[3] But some of his efforts were just pure fun, devoid of seriousness, such as "How I Edited an Agricultural Paper,"[4] or the plain fooling of a "Burlesque Map of Paris" reprinted from the *Express*.

And his home life was happy; from the beginning Mark adored Olivia, so much so that he accepted for a time, at least, such customs as family worship, grace before meals, and Bible readings. Joe Goodman visited Buffalo shortly after the wedding and was astounded to hear Mark ask the blessing and read from the Bible.[5] But Livy's Victorian crusade in favor of piety and against tobacco soon came to naught; the Bible readings went first, to be followed by a resumption of smoking and eventually swearing. Indeed, as DeLancey Ferguson invites our attention, the household was run to suit Mark's desires rather than Livy's; he smoked in the presence of ladies, lounged before the fire in slippers, and did and said whatever he pleased.[6] At first, however, he strove his best to conform with Victorian standards of propriety, and even after this conformity ceased, he allowed his wife to lecture him and admitted his short comings, only to continue the practices. Again Ferguson wisely reminds us: "It relieved Livy's mind and it didn't bother him."[7]

The auspicious beginnings of life in Buffalo unfortunately were short: first came the serious illness of Mr. Langdon, who was so stricken with cancer early in the spring that in June Clemens and his wife went to Elmira to aid in the task of day and night nursing demanded by the patient's critical condition. On August 6, Jervis Langdon died. To Olivia, physically exhausted, it was a crushing blow emotionally.[8] Plans for a summer in England or joining the

[3] Paine, II, 406.
[4] *Sketches New and Old*, p. 280.
[5] Paine, II, 411.
[6] *Mark Twain: Man and Legend*, p. 152.
[7] *Ibid.*, p. 153.
[8] Paine, II, 416.

Twichells in the Adirondacks were forgotten, as it seemed best to remain quietly at home. Actually, it was the worst thing they could have done, for fate, as if ironically stacking the cards, ordained that an old school chum of Livy's, Emma Nye, should become dangerously ill with typhoid fever while visiting them. Another long siege of nursing ensued, ending tragically September 29 with the death of Miss Nye.[9] Olivia was now ill herself from anxiety and nursing; the death of her friend in the new home, following so closely upon that of her father, had been too much. Yet fate still had more ironic trumps concealed: when another friend, invited to cheer her, departed hurriedly to catch a train, Olivia, accompanying her guest to the station, was so prostrated by the jolting of the cab that her first child, Langdon, was prematurely born, November 7, 1870. Both mother and child passed through a crisis of five days before Mark felt they were safe enough for him to write friends of his son's arrival. With so much disaster Mark and Livy naturally found Buffalo uncongenial and gloomy; somehow they had never really managed to feel themselves a part of the community, Mark's venture with the *Express* had not worked out as anticipated, and they were both ready to move elsewhere.

Meanwhile, however, his career had brought fortunate changes in the lives of his relatives; not far from Buffalo was a little city, Fredonia, where Jane Clemens and Pamela moved at Mark's request. Now that they were settled, all that remained was to take care of Orion, which was done in time by securing him a position originally offered to Sam himself, the editorship of a new paper *The Publisher,* just established by Bliss, who was prevailed upon to give Orion the job.[10]

His relations provided for, and anxious to follow up the success of *The Innocents* with another book, Mark logi-

9 *Ibid.,* II, 417.

10 *Ibid.,* II, 425.

cally caught upon the idea of writing up his Western journey to Nevada and California, places about as strange to Eastern readers as Constantinople—if not more so. To facilitate sales of *The Innocents,* which within a year passed the 67,000 mark and continued at a rate of several thousand copies each month, he reverted to his sage-brush days with a hoax. Mark "reproduced" in the *Galaxy* a purported article on the *Innocents* from the English *Saturday Review,* which was actually a delightful burlesque pretending to treat the humorous situations with deadly seriousness. But the hoax backfired, readers accepting it as a genuine English criticism, but regarding it as humor which Mark had failed to perceive. This was too much; and he rushed into print with an explanation, one many failed to accept, the Cincinnati *Enquirer* being particularly objectionable about it.[11]

April, 1871, found Clemens giving up his work for the *Galaxy* entirely and with no regrets, the same month in which he disposed of his interest in the *Express* at a loss of $10,000 under the purchase price. As soon as Livy and little Langdon were able to travel they moved to Elmira, going at once to Quarry Farm, the home of Mrs. Clemens' sister, where they remained through the summer.[12] With the health of his wife and baby improving Clemens found that his work on the book was going well. At first it had progressed slowly, but a visit from Joe Goodman provided the needed enthusiasm, Joe carefully reading the manuscript and declaring that it was a great book.[13] In February, 1871, while still in Buffalo, Mark had his third book published, but it was an unpretentious little volume, which he later regretted and tried to suppress by buying up the plates.[14]

[11] *Ibid.,* II, 430.

[12] *Ibid.,* II, 434.

[13] *Ibid.,* II, 436.

[14] This volume: *Mark Twain's Burlesque Autobiography and First Romance* is described by Merle Johnson, *A Bibliography of the Works of Mark Twain,* pp. 12–13; and by Paine, II, 433.

Working steadily on what he hoped would be a fitting companion to *The Innocents,* Twain's spirits rose as manuscript accumulated and family health improved; he would produce a readable, "starchy" book, with the following dedication, alone considered worth the price of the volume:

TO THE LATE CAIN

THIS BOOK IS DEDICATED

not on account of respect for his memory, for it merits little respect; not on account of sympathy with him, for his bloody deed placed him without the pale of sympathy, strictly speaking, but out of a mere humane commiseration for him, in that it was his misfortune to live in a dark age that knew not the beneficent insanity plea.[15]

Truly his stock was looking up; with the book proceeding well, offers were flooding in for articles, almanacs, other books, and lecture tours. Twain did find time from his major project to write several sketches, sending three to Bliss during June, while he also contrived an automatically adjusting vest-strap, one of the many inventions he was always perfecting.[16] Reconsidering the decision to forsake the platform, Mark agreed finally with James Redpath for another season. Then he went to Hartford, where he and Livy had both decided they wished to live, largely because of the Twichells, although his publishers were also located there. Arrangements were completed for a house on Forest Street on the first of October, where his neighbors would be Charles Dudley Warner and Harriet Beecher Stowe. After the disposal of his Buffalo property, Clemens shipped the furnishings away from the bridal home that had seen so much sorrow.[17]

The question has been raised concerning the effect of Mark Twain's residence in the East upon his art. Stephen

[15] *Letters,* I, 188. [16] Paine, II, 440.
[17] *Ibid.,* II, 442.

Leacock, for instance, believed that Howells, Twichell, and Mrs. Clemens imposed a censorship that was damaging.[18] "What would please his Hartford neighbors, who had taken him into *their* hearts and homes?" deprecates Van Wyck Brooks, "—that was the point now."[19] Brooks indeed became convinced that Clemens actually failed as a satirist because "he accepted the code of his wife and his friends."[20]

According to Van Wyck Brooks Olivia Langdon killed whatever artistry in Mark Twain the frontier had not obliterated. "There is something for the gods to bewail," he charged, "in the sight of that shorn Samson led about by a little child who, in the profound somnolence of her spirit, was merely going through the motions of an inherited domestic piety."[21] Actually, however, the record proves the opposite; Mark's influence on Livy far outweighed hers upon him. As Dixon Wecter emphasizes, Mark's apparent submission during his courtship and early marriage soon evaporated, with the old habits of smoking, drinking, and excursions into profanity returning, never more to depart. In fact, the whole Clemens household was adapted to suit the husband, for Livy "surrounded him with a gracious social life in which he was always cast as the prima donna."[22] So far as Mark was concerned Livy was perfection, nothing about her needed change; and as for Livy's desires to "reform" him, the result was that she gradually ended by making concessions until Mark had his way. He dressed as he pleased, smoked when he wished, lounged with his leg over the chair arm, and comported himself generally after his own fashion. To all of which Livy quietly assented. Samuel C. Webster tells us that Twain liked to complain about Livy's tyranny "but only in

18 *Mark Twain* (New York: Appleton, 1933), p. 69.
19 *The Ordeal of Mark Twain,* p. 285.
20 *Ibid.,* p. 288.
21 *Ibid.,* p. 147.
22 *The Love Letters of Mark Twain,* p. 11.

Livy's presence"—a joke some theory-ridden biographers have failed to perceive.[23]

Mark simply adored her. "My own dear little darling," he wrote her from London, telling how he had returned to the parlor at 2 a.m. to look once more at her picture; and there is no sentimentality but the truth of spiritual affinity in his declaration, "I simply worship you, Livy dear. You are all in all to me."[24] Once when Clemens was joked about sending a Merry Christmas telegram to her—a remark being made that it was more the sort of thing for a sweetheart than wife—Mark promptly demanded an apology. Indeed, they were sweethearts from first to last.[25]

Of course, the major charge against Livy—with Brooks the chief prosecutor—is that of emasculating Mark's style, an indictment no longer taken very seriously by Twain scholars. Wagenknecht observes that Mrs. Clemens used her influence "against burlesque, against extravagance, against blasphemy and irreverence of all kinds."[26] Yet he adds, "After all, he did attack the missionaries, he did write *Huckleberry Finn,* he did formulate his philosophy of determinism."[27] It is Wagenknecht's conviction that Mark had too much virility to be "pushed very far from his native bent;" moreover, his obvious faults do arise from too much burlesque and extravagance—exactly the major targets of Mrs. Clemens' criticism. DeLancey Ferguson goes even further in rebuttal: "Detailed study of the manuscript of his greatest books, in short, reveals no evidence of blighting censorship."[28] And Ferguson credits Livy with saving Mark's readers from "boresome minutiae" in many of his books, at the same time averring that the few "strong" words she deleted have been magnified in the minds of her

23 *Mark Twain, Business Man,* p. 113. 24 *Love Letters,* p. 186.
25 *Ibid.,* p. 189.
26 *Mark Twain: The Man and His Work,* p. 174.
27 *Ibid.,* p. 185.
28 *Mark Twain: Man and Legend,* p. 227.

critics.[29] Bernard DeVoto, who finds "considerably less bowdlerization" in Twain's writings than frequently inferred, believes "the greater part of it was Mark's voluntary act, in obedience to his own judgment and his own conception of propriety and public taste."[30] Professor Pattee's blunt answer to the charge that Livy, abetted by neighbors, kept Mark from writing as he wished, is simply, "Nonsense! Twaddle!"[31] Dixon Wecter, while freely admitting the censorship of Livy and Howells over "certain vivid words and phrases," believes that Mark proved to be "his own most attentive censor," because he realized the curtailed expression of Victorian print, a curb to which "in the main he gave unstinting consent."[32] In a word, those who have studied the Twain papers and manuscripts find that Livy did change words or phrases, but that in the main her alterations oftener saved Mark from bad judgment rather than weakened his style; there is no evidence of anything more.

Hartford

After the new home had been opened in Hartford during the fall of 1871, Clemens left almost immediately upon an extended lecture tour to finish paying his debts incurred through the family illnesses and the unfortunate sacrifice sale of his Buffalo interests. Nothing was more to his distaste than the inconvenience of a tour, but he could not afford to overlook a means of quick and ready income, even though he was hustled about, here and there, from Boston to Chicago. Yet there were some compensations not monetary, for Mark did enjoy the triumph of an enthusiastic reception, and congenial company awaited him at the Ly-

29 *Ibid.*, p. 273.

30 *Mark Twain at Work,* p. 85.

31 *Mark Twain: Representative Selections,* ed. by Fred Lewis Pattee (New York: American Book Company, 1935), p. xxvii.

32 "Mark Twain," *Literary History of the United States,* II, 925.

ceum headquarters in Boston, where Petroleum V. Nasby and Josh Billings, fellow humorists and good friends, met to exchange pleasantries.[33] They along with Mark were pioneers in reverse, bringing the humor of the Old Southwest and the frontier into the Atlantic States.

And Boston offered other pleasant associations, for there was William Dean Howells, and Thomas Bailey Aldrich, and Mark's old associate on the *Californian,* Bret Harte, who had won his literary way across a continent to become a contributing editor of the *Atlantic* at a salary of $10,000 a year for whatever he might choose to write.[34] There were pleasant, informal occasions when Clemens met with Aldrich, Fields, Harte, and Howells, dinners made enjoyable by good stories, wit, and aimless fun.

Yet Mark was never quite accepted in Boston as Bret Harte was, the reason being, as explained by Albert Bigelow Paine, that Harte was understood, a part of the convention, while Twain was not. The creator of "The Outcasts of Poker Flat," despite his Western humor, spoke their language through his pathos and his Victorian sentimentality, his art being essentially close to that of Charles Dickens, while the "Wild Humorist of the Pacific Slope," on the other hand, was something yet to be classified.[35] Among the traditionalists of the Brahmin caste only Charles Eliot Norton and Francis J. Child welcomed Mark Twain with unqualified approval.[36]

By the end of February Clemens was completing the lecture tour, made more difficult by the task of reading proof for the new book as he jumped from place to place. The Cain dedication was discarded in favor of one with no humor but genuine sentiment:

33 Paine, II, 446.

34 Fred Lewis Pattee, *The Development of the American Short Story* (New York: Harpers, 1923), p. 220. 35 Paine, II, 451.

36 *Idem.* See also Howells, *My Mark Twain,* p. 46.

To Calvin H. Higbie of California, an Honest Man, a Genial Comrade, and a Steadfast Friend, this Book Is Inscribed by the Author in Memory of the Curious Time When We Two Were Millionaires for Ten Days.

But now he was out of debt, the advanced sales of *Roughing It* (1872) were large enough to rival his earnings from *The Innocents,* and Twain's mind was made up to follow authorship alone as his profession. Yet the new book, despite the fact that it dealt with one of the most picturesque phases of American history, failed to attain the popularity of *The Innocents,* its sale gradually diminishing after the first three months until ten years were required to reach the mark of one hundred thousand copies attained by the former book in three.[37] This disappointment was not great, but again as in Buffalo, fate prepared to deal another blow.

With the birth of their first daughter, Susan Olivia, at Elmira, March 19, 1872, the Clemens family appeared to be happily progressing, but on June 2, in the new home at Hartford occurred the death of little Langdon, for which Mark Twain reproached himself as the sole cause. Actually the child was so delicate that his life had often been uncertain, but because he was intrusted to his father at a time when the carriage-robes slipped, exposing him to the chilling air and causing a cold which developed into diphtheria, Mark felt the blame, a remorse that dwelt with him to the end. This second loss coming so soon after the death of her father made Mrs. Clemens feel as if death were pursuing them. Thinking that the air of the seashore would be good for the baby, they spent the summer at Saybrook, Connecticut, while Orion, to whom Mark had generously sent $1,000 for aiding him with *Roughing It,* took charge of the house at Hartford.[38] Naturally Clemens did very

[37] *Ibid.,* II, 455.

[38] *Ibid.,* II, 457. Orion had assisted his brother in recalling incidents and places of their Western journey.

little writing that summer, yet possibly to forget his grief he turned to the invention of the "Mark Twain Scrapbook." Its pages were covered with strips of dry glue to be moistened when used, a device which was successfully marketed by Dan Slote of the *Quaker City* party, whose stationery firm paid royalties on it of around $2000 a year.[39] Although this profit continued through 1881, Mark felt that it should have been three times as much, and as the returns grew smaller after that, his friendship with Dan was eventually disrupted.[40]

As creative energy returned Mark decided to write another travel book, this time about England, and he began to make plans. Ostensibly, however, the reason for his trip would be to protect his copyright against English book pirates. No international copyright law then existed, and the legal vacuum encouraged publishers to have more respect for profits than morality, but British law did grant copyright to any book first published there. Consequently *Roughing It* had been brought out by Routledge in London prior to the American publication, and although Twain had not been a British resident at the time, nobody challenged the legality by pirating an edition.[41]

Having sailed alone on the *Scotia,* August 21, 1872, Mark Twain arrived in Liverpool and took the train to London; his first glimpse of the English countryside filled him with "rapture and ecstasy," words he admitted too poor to convey his actual delight, but the best he could find at the moment.[42] The first meeting with his publishers, occurring just as they were about to sit down to lunch, lasted until after dinner that evening as Mark talked on and on to their cordial enjoyment. Finally leaving the establishment, all went to the Savage Club, where Stanley the explorer, Sir

39 Samuel C. Webster, *Mark Twain, Business Man,* p. 160.

40 *Ibid.,* pp. 201–3.

41 Merle Johnson, *Bibliography,* p. 16.

42 Paine, II, 458–9.

Henry Irving, Harry Lee, and the younger Tom Hood, joined enthusiastically in the welcome. Indeed literary London subsequently followed suit, with the White Friars' Club and others honoring Clemens with banquets, while his jokes circulated everywhere.[43] London had not forgotten Artemus Ward, nor Bret Harte, while Joaquin Miller had put on an act in professional Western garb that was as dramatic in its way as Buffalo Bill's Wild West Show. Yet here was something entirely different; most of our American writers had their English counterparts, but Twain was completely and distinctly American. When he returned to his own country in November, loaded with Christmas presents for friends and relations, Clemens realized for the first time that he was a literary figure. Boston might not accept him as the equal of Holmes and Lowell, but London acclaimed him their superior, whom he transcended as Lincoln did an academic Seward.

The book about England, however, never was written; perhaps, as Paine says, because he enjoyed England too much to write humorously about a "country so beautiful that you will be obliged to believe in fairy-land," where he had "a jolly good time," and where he declared, "I would a good deal rather live here if I could get the rest of you over."[44] Ferguson, however, seems more penetrating with the explanation that since his focus was London there was no framework of narrative, no pattern of movement upon which to construct a narrative as in the *Innocents* or *Roughing It*.[45] Whatever the reason, the book was never written, though it was not long before Mark found himself involved in another task arising from a boast similar to James Fenimore Cooper's that he could write a better novel than the one he and his wife were reading. During the winter of 1873 when the Clemens' household seemed settled happily into

[43] *Ibid.*, II, 461. [44] *Ibid.*, II, 470.
[45] *Mark Twain: Man and Legend,* p. 165.

its first real home life since their early months in Buffalo, they enjoyed a particularly intimate friendship with the Warners. One evening at the dinner table, Clemens and Warner's light treatment of certain novels read by their wives provoked the retort to furnish the public with better ones, a challenge mutually accepted on the moment to do a novel in partnership.

For some time Mark had hesitated to undertake an extended work of fiction, although he had in mind a tale about James Lampton, his mother's visionary cousin. Now when Warner approved the idea and agreed to help, he immediately set to work. The first eleven chapters of the book, written by Mark in a burst of enthusiasm, were then read to Warner, who continued the story through the next twelve chapters.[46] The book was to be evenly divided; however, the work was not entirely separated into sections, for a number of passages written by one were rewritten by the other, portions were alternately added, and as the manuscript accumulated the separate contributions became more intimately interwoven. As Mark Twain's own annotated copy of *The Gilded Age* reveals, the task was evenly but not clearly divided: a chapter mapped out by him was actually written by Warner, each made paragraph interpolations throughout, and although labors of both are evident, they also become inextricable.[47] The separate division of chapters recorded by Paine, while originally intended, did not work out in practice.[48] Whenever Mark saw a chance to enliven the dialogue or expose abuse he did so, while Warner, on occasion, modified some of Twain's wrath, or even set down an incident told him by his collaborator.

The Gilded Age, begun in February, was rapidly completed during April;[49] and though only partly by Clemens,

46 Paine, II, 477.

47 Ernest E. Leisy, "Mark Twain's Part in *The Gilded Age,*" *American Literature,* VIII, 445–7 (January, 1937).

48 Paine, II, 477.

49 *Ibid.,* II, 478.

stood as a *fait accompli* of fiction writing; he was now a novelist, a creator of characters and deviser of plot. If today its melodrama seems to damn it, yet it has successfully characterized and accurately named an era of graft, greed, and corruption, a period of exploitation in our national life when a policy of "anything goes" was producing personal fortunes on the one hand at the expense of public welfare and natural resources on the other. Moreover, there is delightful humor in many passages, such as that of the Negroes and the steamboat, while the character of Laura Hawkins—though like her descendants Scarlett and Amber reminiscent of Becky Sharp—stands out vividly; and of course, there is Colonel Sellers, immortal visionary. But it is the Tennessee land, that will-o-the-wisp of his father's futile dreams, that furnished the theme for the book, finally paying off in fiction what it had never yielded in reality. There was another co-worker on *The Gilded Age,* J. Hammond Trumbull, who prepared the chapter headings in many and diverse languages, a humorous contrivance that missed fire. Trumbull was a learned linguist, who "according to Clemens could swear in twenty-seven languages."[50]

That same winter Mark and Livy purchased a lot on Farmington Avenue, preparatory to building a new home, but in May while it was still under construction, Mark and his family, accompanied by Livy's girlhood chum, Clara Spaulding, went to England. This second visit, like the first, turned into a round of enthusiastic receptions, entertainments so numerous that Livy begged Mark to cancel further engagements and slip away quietly to Scotland. Unfortunately they did not go before the effects of social stress left her ill in Edinburgh; there they formed a warm friendship with the well-known author and physician, Dr. John Brown, who became a devoted playmate for Susy.[51] The

[50] *Ibid.,* II, 477–8. [51] *Ibid.,* II, 488.

entire family, as a result, remembered Edinburgh with pleasure. They left for a brief stop in Glasgow and a short trip to Ireland, then returned to England, where they visited the beautiful Cholmondeley estate, Condover Hall, near Shrewsbury. Before the end of the six-month vacation in England, a trip to Paris with sight-seeing and shopping added zest, but even so, Livy was becoming homesick.[52]

Not wishing to endanger copyrights by returning to the States before his next book appeared, Mark on October 13 lectured on "Our Fellow Savages of the Sandwich Islands" to a large audience in Queen's Concert Rooms, Hanover Square. He was greeted on five successive nights and a matinee with delighted roars of laughter.[53] Yet lingering only long enough to repeat the lecture once in Liverpool, Clemens sailed home with his family on October 21 to be met by Orion, November 2. The older brother was just then characteristically engaged inventing a flying machine, writing a Jules Verne-type novel, reading newspaper proof, and contemplating a lecture tour.[54] Mark was received with acclaim, so surrounded by admirers that the president of the Mercantile Library Association tried vainly four times to reach him with offers of a lecture tour. Going to see Booth in *Hamlet* that evening, Mark was invited behind the scenes; when he proposed to add a new character to the play, a bystander who makes humorous comments, Booth was not shocked but "laughed immoderately."[55]

Within a month, Mark was once more in England, lecturing again, this time with "Roughing It on the Silver Frontier." Again he rode the crest of popularity: the Athenaeum Club made him a visiting member, he was feted everywhere, callers besieged him, and—the humorist's ac-

52 *Ibid.*, II, 489.

53 *Ibid.*, II, 492.

54 *Ibid.*, II, 495.

55 *Idem.* Mark did write such a play, adding the character of a book salesman. The Ms. is in the papers of the Mark Twain Estate.

colade—he was quoted by *Punch.*[56] The poet Charles Warren Stoddard then in London acted as Clemens' secretary, even patiently collecting the daily news reports of a now forgotten legal farce, the Tichborne trial. To Mark, however, this case recalled the claimant in the Lampton family, who continued to supplicate for aid in a futile effort to establish himself as Earl of Durham, a character later utilized in *The American Claimant.*

When *The Gilded Age* appeared a few days before Christmas, Clemens sailed home on the *Parthia,* January 13, 1874. By the end of January, 26,000 copies of the new book were sold, sales later increasing to 40,000 a month; with the new home nearing completion and the family in good health, prospects for the coming year seemed bright.[57] Though at first refusing, Mark later agreed to lecture for Redpath—"a persistent devil"—who arranged dates here and there during February and March.[58] Then in April the family moved to Quarry Farm, where Mark worked in a separate study, a small room filled with windows like a pilot house. Here he began another autobiographical book, but not of travel this time; he would convert actual experiences into fiction. More than four years ago Clemens had written an old friend about their boyhood pranks, schoolday episodes, and childhood games in the woods on Holliday's Hill; now old days and old faces began once more forming in his memory.[59] And as happy recollections bodied forth into the idyll of youth in pre-industrial America, Twain turned to the writing of *Tom Sawyer.* Immersed in the subject, oblivious to everything else, Mark accumulated manuscript at the rate of fifty pages a day.[60]

That June Clara was born, and the family enjoyed occa-

56 *Ibid.,* II, 496. 57 *Ibid.,* II, 500.
58 *Ibid.,* II, 502.
59 *Mark Twain's Letters to Will Bowen,* pp. 18–20.
60 *Letters,* I, 224.

sional holidays, mostly Sundays, when Clemens ceased work for relaxation with the children or reading with Livy. Yet with prodigious creative power, in addition to *Tom Sawyer,* he also produced a play based on *The Gilded Age,* written for the actor, John T. Raymond, who performed the part of Colonel Sellers, though not to Mark's satisfaction.[61]

Despite Mark's disapproval of Raymond, who debased Colonel Sellers into low-comedy, it appears to have been his acting and knowledge of theatre audiences which turned a rather poor play into a profitable venture. The play was founded upon a plot constructed by Gilbert Densmore, a script Mark not only frankly admitted using, but paid for accordingly, causing Densmore himself to refer to the "very handsome manner in which you have acted in this matter."[62] Meanwhile Clemens achieved the distinction of joining the contributors to the *Atlantic Monthly,* which accepted for publication in November, 1874, "A True Story, Repeated Word for Word as I Heard It." As Mark stated when submitting the manuscript to Howells, the story was written just as he heard an old Negro servant, "Auntie Cord," tell it, only starting with the beginning rather than the middle as she did.[63]

Upon Twain's return to Hartford, the new home though pronounced "ready" was still filled with workmen, causing Charles Dudley Warner, then visiting in Egypt, to send humorous condolences on Mark's discomfort. Finally the place was finished, everything in order, and a charming, happy homelife began. The house was spacious, including a large hall, parlor, billiard room, library, conservatory, numerous bedrooms and baths, the whole as individual and original as Mark Twain's home should be. Once asked why the kitchen was built toward the street he replied: "So the servants can see the circus go by without running out into

61 *Autobiography,* I, 89–90. 62 Paine, II, 518.
63 *Ibid.,* II, 514.

the front yard."[64] In the library a mantel brought from Scotland presented the appropriate motto: "The ornament of a house is the friends that frequent it."[65] Filled with Oriental rugs, handsome draperies, fine paintings and statuary, the home was worthy of its frequent visitors, among them Twichell, Howells, and Aldrich, who took their ease before the English fireplace beneath a window, where they could watch at once the cheerful fire and falling snow. Or if it were autumn, guests visited the upper balconies to enjoy the hazy tints so beautiful in that section.

With Joe Twichell Mark delighted to walk—the only exercise he ever cared for—a pleasure, however, which led them to an ambitious trip from Hartford to Boston. At an inn they encountered a profane hostler whose blasphemy delighted Mark proportionally as it gave Twichell discomfort; there, too, a solicitous drunk recommended kerosene for stiffness, claiming it had cured him after lying out all night in the cold.[66] It was a memorable journey, and upon reaching Boston, they found Howells waiting with good food and company. Next day Mark anticipated Edward Bellamy's *Looking Backward* with a letter to Livy—purportedly written from Boston in 1935—describing the country as an absolute monarchy.[67] Already his anxiety over dictatorship had awakened.

Shortly, when Howells requested something for the January number of the *Atlantic Monthly,* Mark at first declined. Then during a walk with Twichell, conversing about old days on the Mississippi as seen from the pilot house, Mark received an enthusiastic response, "What a virgin subject to hurl into a magazine!"[68] So it was—its very newness pleased Mark. Immediately he wrote Howells, "I am the

64 *Ibid.,* II, 521.

65 *Ibid.,* II, 522. The motto is from R. W. Emerson's "Domestic Life" in *Society and Solitude.*

66 *Ibid.,* II, 528.

67 *Letters,* I, 231.

68 Paine, II, 531.

only man alive that can scribble about the piloting of that day—and no man ever has tried to scribble about it yet."[69] Then Clemens at once produced seven installments, the first appearing in January and the last in August under the heading "Old Times on the Mississippi."[70] Mark grew so enthusiastic that he proposed taking Howells on a trip to refresh his memory and add to his material. But Howells, unable to leave his desk at the *Atlantic,* declined; Osgood was invited, then John Hay. When none could go, it finally proved seven years before the trip materialized.[71] Now, however, the piloting chapters surging forth from memory appeared in the *Atlantic Monthly,* the best writing he had achieved up to that time, destined to take their place among the classic pages of American letters. Successful at once, they were reprinted everywhere by the newspapers, even pirated into book form in Canada.[72] Here was the raw material from which *Huckleberry Finn* later grew, and with it Mark began for the first time to work that source of inspiration for his greatest books—Sam Clemens' boyhood in the great Mississippi Valley during pre-industrial days. Indeed, the first half of *Life on the Mississippi* is devoted to the boy serving an apprenticeship, for it is the cub rather than the pilot there pictured.[73] The contributions to the *Atlantic* from which the book grew were retained as Chapters IV–XVII.[74] They are not a factual history of the times, rather the pure gold of actual experience lifted into the realm of art by the creative force of gifted imagination. If crime is ignored and sex unmentioned, it is done with deliberation; Mark was uninterested in the sordid side of river traffic. What absorbed him were his boyhood ambitions arising from environment, his efforts as a cub to master a difficult

69 *Letters,* I, 236.

70 Edward Wagenknecht, Introduction, *Life on the Mississippi* (New York: Heritage Press, 1944), p. vii.

71 Paine, II, 533.

72 *Ibid.,* II, 534.

73 Ferguson, *op. cit.,* p. 212.

74 Wagenknecht, *op. cit.,* p. viii.

profession, the customs of piloting, and varied aspects of human nature ranging from the kindly George Ealer to the venomous, inverse class-hatred of the tyrant Brown. Mark was just as aware of vice and crime as a Caldwell or a Steinbeck, but like Henry James he preferred to select his materials. And if his book paints only part of the picture, it is a glorious depiction of those aspects to which his memory was so magnetically drawn. Perhaps the criminals and prostitutes did not overshadow the beauty, grandeur, and romance of the mighty Mississippi for Mark Twain in retrospect, because they had held little interest for Sam Clemens at the actual time. In fact as Wagenknecht states, ". . . he had from the beginning, this boy of the frontier, a certain fastidiousness of character that made many of the grosser temptations no temptations for him."[75] Nevertheless, he saw and understood the wide gamut of humanity passing in review, until he could later say of any character encountered in fiction or biography: "I have known him before—met him on the river."[76] Yet dregs played no part in the glorious river days of Mark's memory, though realism of fact furnished stage props for the setting of imagination. Who, for instance, can forget taunting, class-conscious Brown venting hatred born of mediocrity upon one whom he felt to be his social superior; surely, this is no Eden happily free of serpents.[77] Yet through the glow of imagination, aided by sense perceptions as rich as those of Keats and a feeling for beauty akin to Spenser, the final boyhood days of Sam Clemens merging into manhood as cub pilot on the Mississippi reveal an epic quality arising from the sweeping scene against which they are placed by fine narrative art.

In January, 1875, the Sellers play was performed in the Hartford Opera House with every seat sold. Raymond by

[75] *Ibid.*, p. ix. [76] *Life on the Mississippi*, p. 163.
[77] *Ibid.*, pp. 164–8.

now acted his role to perfection, Kate Field played Laura Hawkins, while a young man from Hartford, William Gillette, was also in the cast.[78] The play was successful wherever it went; all in all a hundred thousand dollars was divided between actor and author.[79]

Accepted now by Hartford socially and intellectually, Mark was received into the Monday Evening Club, composed of the best minds of the community; among them were Warner, Twichell, Professor Calvin E. Stowe, Dr. Horace Bushnell, and J. Hammond Trumbull. Elected just after his first trip to England, Mark made his debut with a paper on the "License of the Press."[80] Another paper prepared for club reading was "The Facts Concerning the Recent Carnival of Crime in Connecticut," one of Mark's delvings into the problem of man versus conscience, something of a self-chiding allegory.[81] Later he talked on "What Is Happiness?," which presented the theory he was to develop into his "gospel," the basic idea of "What Is Man?" Yet the Club came eventually to bore him, for saving his own contributions there appears to have been little life or exhilaration.[82] And Mark finally suggested that "these tiresome damned prayer-meetings might better be adjourned to the garret of some church, where they belonged."[83]

Psychic theories and mental telegraphy (his own phrase) fascinated Twain. One morning while lying in bed, as he recalled, "suddenly a red-hot new idea came whistling down into my camp."[84] It was to get his old friend Dan DeQuille

78 Gillette was a Clemens protege. He later vindicated Mark's faith in his ability by succeeding with distinction as actor and playwright.

79 Paine, II, 540. Arthur Hobson Quinn writes of "the tradition of the remarkable performance of John T. Raymond as Colonel Mulberry Sellers." *A History of the American Drama from the Civil War to the Present Day* (New York: F. S. Crofts and Company, 1937), p. 114. Montrose J. Moses adds, "Raymond, in the public eye, was *Mulberry Sellers.*" *The American Dramatist* (Boston: Little Brown and Company, 1925), p. 185.

80 Paine, II, 542.

81 *Tom Sawyer Abroad,* p. 302.

82 Paine, II, 542.

83 *Autobiography,* I, 305.

84 Paine, II, 543.

to write a book about the Comstock lode; the time was ripe and Dan was the man. Promptly Mark prepared a detailed plan, holding it only until he could talk with his publishers, but within a week a letter arrived addressed by Dan's hand, bearing a Nevada postmark. Mark turned to a visitor saying he would perform the miracle of revealing the date, contents, and signature of the letter without opening it, which he did. The incident, along with others, is recorded in "Mental Telegraphy."[85] Of more interest to posterity, however, is that Dan accepted Mark's invitation to be his guest and write the book. *The Big Bonanza,* though not the best-seller Mark or Dan expected, was successfully published by Bliss and remains a valuable and entertaining book on the shelf of Americana.

Meanwhile the "inspiration tank," as Mark liked to call it, having filled up again, the story of Tom and Huck progressed steadily. The family did not visit Elmira that summer, going instead to Bateman's Point, Rhode Island.[86] Then during the fall (1875) appeared the book contracted for five years before, *Sketches New and Old.*[87] Mostly made up of sketches originally published with the *Jumping Frog,* selections of "Memoranda," and contributions to the Buffalo *Express,* it contained a few new items, one being "Some Fables for Good Old Boys and Girls," a satiric account of a scientific investigation into the ways of men conducted by wood creatures. Although given a laudatory review by Howells, *Sketches,* after an initial sale of twenty thousand copies, made a rather poor showing. The public seemed to sense that it was not in the same class with the *Innocents* or *Roughing It,* for the original sales presumably were based more on the author's reputation than the contents. And

85 *In Defense of Harriet Shelley,* p. 111. See also "Mental Telegraphy Again," *Ibid.,* p. 138, and in *Following the Equator* Mark records other such happenings.

86 Paine, II, 549.

87 Johnson, *Bibliography,* p. 24.

the public was right; indeed Mark himself declared most of it should never have been collected.[88]

In the above mentioned review Howells had commented on the more serious side of Twain exhibited in "A True Story," and in the October (1875) *Atlantic* Mark contributed "The Curious Republic of Gondour," his own version of a Utopia secured through intellectual qualifications for voting. It was unsigned—Clemens sometimes felt that his *nom de plume* might suggest a hoax—but it delighted Howells, who wished continued reports from the model republic. By now, however, Mark's fancy had been caught with a jingle composed by Noah Brooks and Isaac Bromley, who had seen a placard posted in the street cars for the information of passengers and conductor. The chorus, so Mark pretended, kept running through his brain to the exclusion of everything else; all he could think of was:

> Punch, brothers! Punch with care!
> Punch in the presence of the passenjare!

The result, "A Literary Nightmare," published in the February (1876) *Atlantic,* started an epidemic of horse-car poetry. Howells' children recited it in chorus, and going out to dinner, he found the Longfellow ladies knew it by heart. From Boston it swept across the nation, even carrying its nonsense jingles into Europe.[89]

Yet *Tom Sawyer* remained unpublished, despite Howells' admonition to hurry—"That boy is going to make a prodigious hit,"[90] he wrote Mark. But Tom's creator was first anxious to find a means of outwitting the book pirates, especially in Canada, who grabbed everything in the *Atlantic* or elsewhere. He therefore gave the manuscript to Moncure D. Conway, who carried it to London, where arrangements were made for publication with Chatto & Windus. Thus

88 Paine, II, 551.
89 *Ibid.*, II, 557.
90 *Ibid.*, II, 570.

began a friendly business relation between Twain and his English publishers, which lasted throughout his life.[91] Although *Tom Sawyer* was not to appear on the American market until the end of the year, it came out in England on June 9, 1876.[92]

During that centennial summer the Clemens family sought refuge at Elmira, where the children could romp on the shady lawn of Quarry Farm, while Mark returned to his study. Susy, his favorite, was growing up, a thoughtful, remarkable child. Once when a grand display of fireworks was seen from the town, Susy objected to being put to bed, saying, "I wish I could sit up all night, as God does."[93] Mark took the children for extended walks, actually completing little that summer save a burlesque "The Canvasser's Tale."[94] But far more important, he had begun work on a manuscript destined to become an American classic and one of the great volumes in world literature—*The Adventures of Huckleberry Finn*. For a time he was enthusiastic over this sequel to *Tom Sawyer*, especially about narrating the story in the first person, but gradually his interest flagged. Declaring that he liked it "only tolerably well," he pigeonholed the half-completed manuscript and let it lie unfinished for years.[95] Now his imagination, stimulated by reading Pepys' *Diary*, turned to the court manners and conversations of olden times. He would try his hand at the days of Queen Elizabeth, recording conversation with outspoken frankness and coarseness.[96] Written in a letter to good old Joe Twichell, whose reverend

[91] Idem. [92] Johnson, *Bibliography*, p. 29.

[93] Paine, II, 577.

[94] Published in the *Atlantic*, December, 1876. Now in *Tom Sawyer Abroad*, p. 369.

[95] Paine, II, 578.

[96] Mark later made a good yarn, saying: "I sent it anonymously to a magazine—and how the editor abused it and the sender. But that man was a praiser of Rabelais, and had been saying 'Oh, that we had a Rabelais.' I judged I could furnish him one." *Notebook*, p. 151.

profession had not weakened his robust sense of humor, this sketch of manners and talk among a group of courtiers and ladies in the presence of Queen Elizabeth was called at first *Fireside Conversation in the Time of Queen Elizabeth,* later *1601*. Before mailing, it was shown to David Gray, who urged Mark to sign it and print it, declaring, "You have never done a greater piece of work than that."[97] In due time *1601* reached John Hay, who hailed it as a classic. Four years later Hay, also, allowed proofs to be made of it, from which a very private circulation followed.[98] Eventually it escaped into the public domain, and a number of editions have since been printed.[99] Too much has been made of this bit of ribaldry, both by enthusiasts who claim literary qualities it does not possess and the Freudians who see it as the way Mark would have always written if unhampered. Neither is correct, yet it remains an amusing story for the smoking room. Moreover, it is funny and illustrates the coarse strain of Mark's nature, but its literary importance is minor.

Eighteen seventy-six, besides being the centennial of American Independence, marked the presidential campaign between Hayes and Tilden. Clemens, like his friends Twichell and Howells, voted for the Republicans. Howells wrote a campaign biography for Hayes, and Mark spoke at a rally over which he also presided.[100] Yet later in life Clem-

97 Paine, II, 580.

98 "The copies were distributed as follows: one to Hay, two to the author and one kept by the publisher, Gunn," Johnson, *Bibliography,* p. 35. About 1882 when Mark visited the Military Academy at West Point he requested the Adjutant, Charles Erskine Scott Wood, to print a few copies of it for him. This was done with special type and some editing to make it "antiqued," from fifty to a hundred copies being struck off on varying sizes of paper. *Ibid.,* p. 37.

99 By all odds the best of these is by Franklin J. Meine, *1601; or, Conversation as It Was by the Social Fireside in the Time of the Tudors* (Chicago, 1939).

100 Paine, II, 582.

ens declared this election "one of the Republican party's most cold-blooded swindles of the American people."[101]

Following his election activities, Twain appeared on the lecture platform in Boston and Philadelphia, but refused to go farther from home because he was having a portrait painted. The artist, Frank Millet, young, handsome, and vivacious, had become so popular with the entire family that Mark hated to part from his company, while the children included his name in the blessings of their nightly prayers. When the first sketch was finished, Livy was so delighted that she would not allow Millet to touch it again for fear of some possible alteration. A second portrait, however, turned out to be another excellent likeness, although the young artist was disappointed with it because Mark had his hair cut in the interval between sittings.[102] Meanwhile literary activities continued.

The Adventures of Tom Sawyer appeared on the market probably about the second week in December (1876) in an edition of about five thousand copies.[103] With it Twain added his first volume to the classic shelf of American fiction, as well as contributing in Tom and Huck two immortals to the portrait gallery of permanent literature. Though destined to be overshadowed by its sequel, *Tom Sawyer* is a masterpiece; here is the idyll of boyhood, the charm of a past era—all portrayed through vivid, lifelike characterization and a plot at times reaching dramatic intensity. There are few more dramatic incidents in American literature than the graveyard scene in which Injun Joe murdered Dr. Robinson,[104] or Tom and Becky trapped in the cave with Tom's one mortal enemy.[105] And Mark's imagination, so often fantastic, is here restrained by a purpose as serious as its expression is humorous: it truthfully

[101] *Mark Twain in Eruption,* p. 287.
[102] Paine, II, 583.
[103] Johnson, *Bibliography,* p. 29.
[104] *Tom Sawyer,* Chapter IX.
[105] *Ibid.,* Chapter XXXI.

recalls the memory of his own boyhood in Hannibal. From that solid base of actuality his imaginative faculty created the wonderful episodes of whitewashing the fence, Huck and the wart-cure, Aunt Polly and the pain-killer, Tom's schoolboy love-affair, and all those glorious happenings among the pirate band. There is magic, too, in the descriptions, often verging on poetry; the delightful humor of the whitewashing episode is thus delicately prefaced:

> The locust-trees were in bloom, and the fragrance of the blossoms filled the air. Cardiff Hill, beyond the village and above it, was green with vegetation, and it lay just far enough away to seem a Delectable Land, dreamy, reposeful, and inviting.[106]

Destined to reach the highest sales to date of all Twain's books, *Tom Sawyer* was issued by subscription, the same form of door-to-door sale, which had so successfully launched the *Innocents*. When this method was finally abandoned in 1904, its grand total, including many moderate-priced editions, rose to more than two million.[107] The book retains to this moment its wide appeal for all ages; popular as a "children's classic," its magnetism is equally great to those adults who still remember childhood.[108] In fact, when Mark finished the manuscript he wrote to Howells: "It is *not* a boy's book, at all. It will only be read by adults. It is only written for adults."[109] And Howells, while designating it a boy's story, declared adults would enjoy it no less, admitting he had sat up fascinated until one a.m. to

106 *Ibid.*, p. 12.

107 Frank Luther Mott, *Golden Multitudes* (New York: Macmillan, 1947), p. 157. Since 1932 *Tom Sawyer* has been free of copyright, although it cannot be issued with the trade mark, Mark Twain, except by arrangement with the Mark Twain Company.

108 A prominent Philadelphia physician told me that the first book he read upon discharge from the army in 1945 was *Tom Sawyer*. And the success of two motion picture versions, one in technicolor, depended upon an adult as well as juvenile audience.

109 *Letters,* I, 258.

finish it.[110] Indeed the author's purpose expressed in the preface seems successfully achieved, "to pleasantly remind adults of what they once were themselves, and of how they felt and thought and talked, and what queer enterprises they sometimes engaged in."[111] Or as industrialization circumscribes us, the reminder is perhaps of days desired but unrealized in a never-to-be-again land, a past projected by great art into our living present.

While waiting for *Tom Sawyer* to make its debut, Mark confided to Howells: "Bret Harte came up here the other day and asked me to help him write a play and divide the swag, and I agreed."[112] Mark was to put in Scotty Briggs (of the Buck Fanshaw funeral episode in *Roughing It*), and Bret was to develop a wonderfully funny Chinaman. The two authors wrote separate plots, so they could "gouge from both and build a third." Wishing to keep the whole transaction secret Mark requested Howells to get the title "Ah Sin, a Drama" printed on a page for him, the rest of the application for copyright being allowable in longhand.[113] Both Mark and Bret worked hard on the play until it was finished. Yet when *Ah Sin* opened at the National Theatre in Washington, May 7, 1877, Twain was unable to attend because of bronchitis, and Charles T. Parsloe, who played the Chinese laundryman, found Harte unbearably annoying.[114]

Mark prepared two curtain speeches, one in case of failure, one for success. When the audience kindly decided in favor of the latter Parsloe read a witty address explaining how the manager had aided the authors:

> So he cut out, and cut out, and the more he cut the better the play got. I never saw a play that was so improved by being cut down; and I believe it would have been one of the very best

110 *Ibid.*, I, 266.
111 Preface to *Adventures of Tom Sawyer.*
112 *Letters,* I, 287.
113 *Ibid.*, I, 288.
114 Paine, II, 588.

plays in the world if his strength had held out so that he could cut out the whole of it.[115]

Ah Sin was not a success; when produced in New York by Augustin Daly at the Fifth Avenue Theatre, July 31, 1877, it enjoyed only a short run, followed by a career equally brief on the road. Indeed the curtain speech was the best thing connected with the whole performance.[116] Perhaps this tended to increase the friction, arising between the authors during its composition, a mutual antagonism destroying their former friendship and making future association impossible. While writing the play Harte made sarcastic remarks about the Clemens home, finally uttering a disparagement which Mark thought aimed at Livy. This was too much; Harte was ordered from the house, never to return. Mark henceforth had nothing but contempt for the man,[117] a hearty dislike he did not fail to express publicly and in strong language.[118]

Soon, however, Mark was off on a delightful holiday to Bermuda, accompanied by Joe Twichell, a real pleasure trip marred only because Howells could not be with them. The *Notebook* records the sensitivity with which Twain reacted to the beauty of the spot with its houses like marble, only "whiter, daintier, richer—white sugar is the nearest to it."[119] On returning to Hartford, undaunted by *Ah Sin,* he finished another play *Simon Wheeler, the Amateur Detective,* which he submitted to Dion Boucicault. Others read the play, too, and while all agreed that the dialogue was entertaining and the situations well constructed, somehow or other it just would not act. Like many another novelist, Twain was unable to transfer the dramatic inci-

115 Johnson, *Bibliography,* p. 140.

116 Johnson declares that *Ah Sin* was neither printed nor published. A manuscript copy, perhaps a prompt book, was sold at the American Art Association Galleries and is now in private hands. *Ibid.,* p. 141.

117 *Mark Twain in Eruption,* p. 278. 118 See Ferguson, pp. 187–88.

119 *Notebook,* p. 124.

dent from the printed page to actual sound and motion before the footlights. Fortunately he did not pursue theatrical activities further at this point, but probably realizing that playwriting was not his forte turned to a more profitable venture in fiction. While reading Charlotte M. Yonge's *The Prince and the Page,* Clemens suddenly received a parallel idea from her plot of a prince who disguised himself as a blind beggar.[120] Why not add also a beggar disguised as a prince, giving a double plot and a new twist to the situation? Thus began the composition of *The Prince and the Pauper,* about four hundred pages of manuscript being finished that summer, before faltering inspiration caused him to lay aside the task, not to be touched again for more than three years.

During that winter occurred perhaps the greatest *faux pas* in Mark Twain's entire life. The *Atlantic Monthly* staff proposed to honor John Greenleaf Whittier on his seventieth birthday with a banquet; it was to be a great occasion, the literary elite would be there, and Clemens, among others, was invited to speak. With the distinguished guest list headed by Emerson, Longfellow, and Holmes, Mark, happy to be included, determined to give them one of the funniest speeches of his career. Anywhere else it would have been funny, but the unfortunate subject matter was as out of place as making fun of Robert E. Lee at a Confederate reunion. Boston and Cambridge had gathered to honor not only Whittier but New England literature. It was a tribute to their cultural heritage, embodied in the venerable figures of the poets who graced the banquet on this auspicious evening. Each speaker in turn paid his respects to the poets present and the environment that had nurtured them; then to quote Howells: "the amazing mistake, the bewildering blunder, the cruel catastrophe was upon us."[121] Mark began a story about a miner whose lonely

120 Paine, II, 597.

121 *My Mark Twain,* p. 60.

cabin had been invaded by three literary men, "Mr. Longfellow, Mr. Emerson, and Mr. Oliver Wendell Holmes—consound the lot." At those words the audience froze, and as the story proceeded with a description of the supposed Emerson as "a seedy little bit of a chap, red-headed," the pretended Holmes as "fat as a balloon; he weighed as much as three hundred, and had double chins all the way down to his stomach," and the bogus Longfellow "built like a prize-fighter" the atmosphere grew colder with every word. The speaker sensed the trouble at once, but there was nothing to do but spin the yarn about their drinking, gambling, and quarreling.[122] Emerson was described "a-whetting his bowie on his boot" and Longfellow was depicted stealing the miner's boots to leave footprints on the sands of time. All present were silent, shocked—all, that is, save one guest who laughed and shrieked throughout! We shall never know this person, hysterical from laughter, whose name, said Howells, "shall not be handed down to infamy."[123] The next day, abject with apology, the unhappy speaker sent letters to Emerson, Longfellow, and Holmes, beseeching pardon, which the three, being gracious gentlemen, quickly granted. This did not ease his mind, however, for Clemens, still mortified, feared lest Howells exclude his future writings from the pages of the *Atlantic.* Though he finally got over feeling disgraced, in later years even declaring it a funny speech, at the time he was overcome by chagrin and shame.[124]

Perhaps this unhappy occurrence had something to do with Twain's decision to revisit Europe, where he resolved to spend a year or two, but there were other reasons, one being the demand for another travel book. About this time, also, Clemens had given way to a tendency to invest money

122 This speech is available in Paine, IV, 1643–7.

123 *My Mark Twain,* p. 60.

124 The best account of this incident is given by Bernard De Voto, *Mark Twain's America,* pp. 196–204.

in numerous enterprises, most of which involved him in vexatious patent rights, but yielded no profits. All this consumed time and prevented completion of a half dozen manuscripts already started.[125] Social events were frequent, and now since he had determined to live awhile in Germany, he began to study the language. Though he had no chance to write, he characteristically found time to read a manuscript for Orion and offer suggestions about its publication. Their correspondence reveals that Mark had probably already written part of *Captain Stormfield's Visit to Heaven,*[126] which he had been revising from time to time for about five years.

The Clemens family accompanied by Miss Clara Spaulding sailed for Hamburg on the *Holsatia,* April 11, 1878, a miserable voyage with screaming children, crashing crockery, lurching ship, and a "special hell" added—a piano![127] But however rough and noisy, the ship's company, at least that provided by Bayard Taylor, recently appointed Minister to Germany, and Murat Halstead, was pleasant. Taylor, quite a linguist as well as popular poet, entertained by reciting German folk-songs and singing the "Lorelei."[128] From Hamburg, where they rested a few days, the party proceeded through Hanover and Frankfort to Heidelberg; there Clemens took accommodations at the Schloss Hotel, which afforded the visitor one of the most beautiful views to be found in Germany. Twain wrote enthusiastically to Howells how the view by day changed from "one enchanting aspect to another" and how Heidelberg by night became "a cobweb, beaded thick with lights."[129] Selecting a house across the river, Mark rented a room in which to write: all seemed perfect. Yet the beauty of the landscape did not ease the struggles with the awful German language, though one

125 *Letters,* I, 320.
126 *Ibid.,* I, 323.
127 *Notebook,* p. 133.
128 Paine, II, 618.
129 *Letters,* I, 330.

suspects an exaggeration of the difficulties. There are many amusing incidents and comments, enough to indicate that Mark was having a battle with cases and genders.

Twichell joined Clemens for a walking tour through the Black Forest into Switzerland, where they escaped from public attention. On this journey Mark experienced several startling instances of what he called "mental telegraphy," the most striking being their meeting a man at the turn of a path just a few seconds after talking about him.[130] It was a gay holiday, and Mark abandoned himself with delight. Twichell records how he excitedly ran after some driftwood in a stream, laughing, shouting, and jumping as the wood went over a fall. Also, his friend remembered Clemens' sensitive nature, courtesy to people, and consideration of animals.[131] As ever, Twain was absorbed by the natural beauty, its vistas, trees, and especially flowers. Twichell found him an ideal companion, for Mark reacted with such sensitivity and expressed himself so picturesquely that he "nearly did justice to the things we saw."[132] As the holiday ended they joined Mrs. Clemens at Lausanne, Twichell set out for home by way of England, and the Clemens party wandered down into Italy. At Rome and Florence they visited art galleries, and occasionally made purchases for their home. In Venice they bought a massive carved bed with serpentine columns surmounted with rosewood cupids, a bed perhaps three hundred years old, abandoned from a Venetian palace. It became a custom in their family, for the children when ill to enjoy the privilege of occupying this bed and having one of the cupids removed to play with.[133]

Although Mark did not dislike the old masters so intensely as when he viewed them as an Innocent, he still could not approach them with the same reverence as Livy

130 Paine, II, 628.
131 *Ibid.*, II, 629.
132 *Ibid.*, II, 630.
133 *Ibid.*, II, 633.

and Miss Spaulding. Once accompanied by Sarah Orne Jewett, Mark declared that if the old masters had labeled their fruit, one "wouldn't be so likely to mistake pears for turnips," a witticism quickly reproved by Livy, to which Miss Jewett added, "Now, you've been spoken to."[134] Leaving Italy and the old masters, Clemens, acting as his own courier, finally arrived at Munich after suffering bad connections and weary delay.

That winter in Munich work progressed well, while the children enjoyed the German Christmas with its decorations, trees, and toys. The language, too, seemed to hold no troubles for the youngsters, although their father, finding that he could not possibly write and study German at the same time, finally gave up the latter. The family decided to spend the spring in Paris and unhappily encountered the longest spell of winter ever to curse a visitor there. Sitting before a roaring fire on June first, while "this vindictive winter continues," no doubt influenced Mark's comment, "France has neither winter nor summer nor morals—apart from these drawbacks it is a fine country."[135] When they could stand the cold and rain no longer, Clemens moved to Brussels, then to Antwerp, followed by rapid visits to Rotterdam, Dresden, and Amsterdam. They arrived in London on July 29 (1879) amid more rain and cold, which seemed to characterize the weather of all Europe that summer.

To Twain London always meant a series of brilliant functions with notable associates. Now he met Whistler and Henry James, and before leaving took a trip up to Windermere Lake to see the "great Darwin."[136] Sailing from Liverpool August 23, homeward bound, Clemens again saw a lunar rainbow, a brilliant, complete arch. Back in New York, September 3, 1879, they went directly to Quarry Farm, ever a delight, now after long absence a "fore-

[134] *Ibid.*, II, 634.
[135] *Notebook*, p. 153.
[136] Paine, II, 647.

taste of Heaven."[137] But by November Mark was in Chicago, delivering a speech at the reception for General Grant by the Army of the Tennessee, an occasion memorable with historic names, and one at which Clemens delivered an address that shook the crowd, brought praise from Sherman, and acknowledgment from Grant himself.[138] Never had the boy from Hannibal dreamed of greater success, and soon thereafter came an opportunity to redeem his one public humiliation, the fiasco of the Whittier birthday speech. The *Atlantic Monthly* honored Dr. Holmes with a breakfast, another notable gathering at which Emerson, Longfellow, Whittier, and Parkman were present; Clemens, who accepted at the insistence of Warner and Howells, this time made a very careful tribute, gracious with praise and salted with just the proper touch of humor. And so the year closed happily for him.

Once again at home a chief pleasure became the acting of charades invented by Clemens, who also costumed the performers, and frequently participated with enthusiasm. Other times Mark played and sang spiritual and jubilee songs loved from boyhood, while the children joined in the melody. And, of course, he liked nothing better than to read aloud; it appears that this first winter back in the States began the custom of reading his manuscripts to Mrs. Clemens and the children.[139] Twain was just then resuming work on *The Prince and the Pauper,* which he read with pleasure as each chapter was completed. But his other project, *A Tramp Abroad,* had become a nightmare; when it was finally finished Mark expressed to Howells "the unutterable joy of getting that Old Man of the Sea off my back, where he has been roosting for more than a year and a half."[140] Delight with *The Prince and the Pauper,* however, was as great as his boredom with *A Tramp Abroad;*

137 *Ibid.,* II, 650.
138 *Letters,* I, 371–2.
139 Paine, II, 662.
140 *Letters,* I, 376.

whereas the travel book had taxed him to fill out the necessary pages, the novel gave him so much pleasure that he worked enthusiastically.

When *A Tramp Abroad* appeared, March 13, 1880, there was an advance sale of 25,000 copies.[141] An added satisfaction was a proposal by Tauchnitz to issue an illustrated edition in Germany, in addition to the regular printing. Though Howells reviewed it favorably and Brander Matthews gave it critical acclaim, yet it remains today one of Twain's books less likely to live. It lacks the gusto, the joy, the sheer genius of the important books. Entertaining in spots, humorous at times, on the whole it is a manufactured piece of work, turned out for the trade, uninspired, and holding no more interest for the reader than it held for its reluctant author. The wonderful "Jim Baker's Bluejay Yarn," the search for the lost sock in the dark, and some fine word-pictures continue to gleam, but the three to one sales preference expressed by the public for the *Innocents* seems sound criticism.[142]

At Elmira, July, 1880, Jean, a third daughter, was born. Clemens alternated work that summer, turning first to *The Prince and the Pauper,* then to the story begun four years earlier, the saga of Huck Finn, suddenly now of new interest for him. Yet he did not read the Huck manuscript aloud to his family, rather it was the lesser novel that he considered his major task and read for approval as the manuscript accumulated at the end of each day. It was a pleasant summer. The cats at the farm were a delight with outlandish names, such as Sour Mash, Sin, and Satan. Susy once remarked: "The difference between papa and mama is, that mama loves morals and papa loves cats."[143]

Later that year Mark was agitating for international copyright, making at least one trip to Washington to see

141 Paine, II, 665. 142 *Ibid.,* II, 671.
143 *Ibid.,* II, 684.

his old friend, Rollin M. Daggett, now a congressman, who offered to introduce any bill that the authors agreed upon. But Mark could scarcely agree even with himself for long on the copyright question, and soon he was turning his interests to the presidential election in support of Garfield. Clemens made a campaign speech to a packed house in Hartford on October 26, one long remembered there and showing how seriously Twain took politics at this stage.[144] During the year he decided to change publishers; feeling that the American Publishing Company had not earned all the profits he was entitled to, Mark gave *The Prince and the Pauper* to James R. Osgood, thereby starting an association which inspired Mark to devise new publishing methods and ventures. In fact, Clemens had actually, without realizing it, become his own publisher; for he advanced the money to meet publication costs and paid Osgood a royalty for selling the book, a reversal of the usual procedure.[145] When he decided to go further with the publishing business by having Osgood bring out a *Library of Humor,* to be edited by Howells and Charles Hopkins Clark, Clemens actually became a business man.

Next summer, June 8, 1881, Twain emerged more prominently into public life by speaking at a dinner in Hartford for General Sherman and Secretary of War, Robert Lincoln, travelling in their private car to address the military students at West Point.[146] That summer President Garfield was assassinated (July 2, 1881) and was succeeded in office by Chester A. Arthur, a change which caused Howells to worry over his father's being continued as consul at Toronto. An appeal to Mark, who took the matter to Grant had the desired results; not only was Mark active in public affairs—he also had influence.[147]

Meanwhile *The Prince and the Pauper* was published in

144 *Ibid.,* II, 694.
145 *Ibid.,* II, 707.
146 *Ibid.,* II, 710.
147 *My Mark Twain,* p. 71.

England, December 1, 1881, and to insure Canadian copyright Clemens resided in Montreal for two weeks, only to find that he still must rely upon the previous publication in England to secure his rights.[148] Paine states that the book also appeared in Germany early in December, 1881.[149] Perhaps Mark Twain's best constructed plot, *The Prince and the Pauper,* remains as its subtitle explained, "A Tale for Young People of All Ages." It is a charming romance and historical novel, both dramatic and humorous, having as its deeper current the underlying theme of democracy.

About this time Mark became involved in a multiplicity of interests other than literature. A patent steam generator absorbed part of his bank account, to be followed by a steam pulley which cost him $32,000, and a watch company which did not exist long enough to pay dividends. Ironically, when a young inventor, Alexander Graham Bell, tried to interest him in a telephone, Mark, momentarily fed up with wildcat speculation, declined.[150] He continued to write, giving Osgood a collection of sketches called *The Stolen White Elephant,* but a far more important project was in mind—the completion of a book on the Mississippi River. Osgood agreed to a trip to renew inspiration and get the river atmosphere once more; starting down stream on the steamer *Gold Dust* they concealed their identity, but Mark was quickly recognized both on boat and ashore. At New Orleans Clemens met Bixby, now captain of the *City of Baton Rouge,* one of the last imposing steamboats on the river, and he arranged to make the up-river trip on Bixby's boat. In New Orleans Clemens delighted in exploring the old French Quarter with George W. Cable and Joel Chandler Harris.[151]

148 Johnson, *Bibliography,* p. 41.

149 Paine, II, 716. Although the title page of the first edition in the United States carries the date, 1882, Johnson says it was published actually about the middle of December, 1881. *Bibliography,* pp. 40–41.

150 Paine, II, 726.

151 *Ibid.,* II, 739.

After a trip of copious note-taking back up the river to St. Paul, during which he enjoyed three days in Hannibal, Mark started to write, a task made difficult by a time limit, something which always seemed to shackle his creative force. Finally the book was completed and handed to Osgood, although the real work of publishing descended upon the shoulders of Charles L. Webster, newly added to the firm; Webster was also the husband of Twain's niece. Osgood spent most of his time with Clemens playing billiards, a business method much to Mark's taste, while Webster put the book through the press, and it appeared about the middle of May (1883).[152] Although *Life on the Mississippi* had a good sale at first, it has been the steady sale throughout the years, including numerous recent editions, which has put it in the best-seller category.[153] And as time goes on, its importance increases; though a collection of facts, regional sketches, and humorous anecdotes, it preserves the story of an era and the flavor of a profession. Here is the epic of the Mississippi pilot, as he was then, a figure against the sky. While the book was going through the press it seemed advisable to omit one chapter (48) because of hostile feelings it might cause in the South.[154] Yet the wild attack on Sir Walter Scott was retained, one of the most far-fetched theories Mark ever propounded, for he forgot that an author may feed an appetite already existing rather than be the creator of a new one. Scott was popular in the Old South because chivalry was a part of the code most ladies and gentlemen lived by and for, not because he had presented

152 *Ibid.*, II, 745.

153 Frank Luther Mott, *Golden Multitudes* (New York: Macmillan, 1947), p. 157.

154 Caroline Ticknor, "Mark Twain's Missing Chapter," *The Bookman*, XXXIX (1914), 298. See also Edward Wagenknecht's introduction, *Life on the Mississippi* (New York: Heritage Press, 1944), pp. xii–xiv. This edition which contains the deleted chapter is the only "complete" one.

an innovation.[155] With the incorporation into the new book of "Old Times on the Mississippi" all the charm, poetic values, and social history of the *Atlantic* contribution is permanently preserved. This is the chief value of the work, written when Mark was enthusiastic over a virgin subject with the glow of imagination which transmutes facts into higher truths and clothes memory at times with glorious unreality; the factual section of the volume, written under pressure, cannot compare with the earlier idyll of youthful ambition and success on the mighty river.

To insure copyright Clemens made another trip to Canada, where he was entertained by the Marquis of Lorne, the son-in-law of Queen Victoria, then Governor-General. That summer, back on Quarry Farm, Mark toyed with a number of ideas for books, among them "Captain Stormfield's Visit to Heaven," but the only immediate result was a play with Howells as collaborator.[156] The plot concerned Colonel Sellers in his comic aspect with all of his marvelous schemes and his impractical inventions. Howells says that he and Twain wrote scenes in turn until the final play emerged.[157] No producer would take it, however, and no actor would play it; yet Clemens, and Howells too, for that matter, refused to give up, finally resorting to having an elocutionist put it on as a burlesque of Raymond in the role of Sellers. Although they talked Daniel Frohman into promoting this double burlesque, when Howells saw the actuality his enthusiasm turned to suffering, and Mark, summoned from Hartford, readily agreed to pay for the theatre, release the actors, and call it quits.[158]

Yet the footlights continued to fascinate him, for Twain sought next to dramatize both *The Prince and the Pauper*

[155] One must not forget Twain's pre-war politics. He belonged to the Southern party opposed to war and for preservation of the Union, hence his dislike of what he blamed for the conflict, a seemingly outmoded code.

[156] Paine, II, 755.

[157] *My Mark Twain,* p. 24.

[158] Paine, II, 762.

and *Tom Sawyer.* He even made extensive plans for writing about the Sandwich Islands, another project to be turned into a play, this last again with the help of Howells.[159] Though his dramatic efforts failed because Clemens possessed no practical knowledge of stagecraft, this particular winter of 1883–4 proved, nevertheless, one of entertainment and gaiety.

By spring, 1884, Mark had his publishing business definitely under way with Charles L. Webster and Company located at 658 Broadway. But he was suffering trouble with the proof sheets of *Huckleberry Finn,* from which Howells offered to help extricate him.[160] *Huckleberry Finn* received ample notice from time to time in the press; selections appeared in the *Century,* and in January and February, 1885, Twain read passages during his lecture trip with George W. Cable in Iowa.[161] The book was illustrated by E. W. Kemble, later a foremost cartoonist, whose successful drawings for the portions appearing in the *Century* promised well for the book.[162]

The Adventures of Huckleberry Finn, though officially published in England and America, December, 1884, was not in the hands of the salesmen until February, 1885.[163] Delays arose from a last minute decision of Mark's to use as frontispiece a picture of his bust executed by Gerhardt, and from an unfortunate incident of a damaged plate which gave one illustration such an off-color meaning that it had to be withdrawn for correction.[164] Despite the advance build-up, at the time of *Huck Finn's* appearance only one

159 *Ibid.,* II, 764.

160 *Letters,* II, 442.

161 Fred W. Lorch, "Mark Twain in Iowa," *Iowa Journal of History and Politics,* XXVII, 533 (October, 1929).

162 Selections from *Huckleberry Finn* appeared in the *Century* during December, 1884, January and February, 1885. Arthur L. Vogelback, "The Publication and Reception of *Huckleberry Finn* in America," *American Literature,* XI, 261 (November, 1939).

163 Paine, II, 793.

164 Johnson, *Bibliography,* pp. 46–50.

reviewer noticed it, T. S. Perry writing a favorable review in the *Century*.[165] More helpful, however, was the banning of the book by the Concord, Massachusetts, Public Library, which led the New York *Tribune* to predict an immediate rise in sales.[166] With an advance order for 40,000 copies, and interest stimulated by the Concord ban, *Huckleberry Finn* was off to a good start; yet in total sales it did not surpass *Tom Sawyer,* still the best seller of all Mark Twain's books.[167] Indeed, critical as well as general readers, with slight exception, seemed unaware that a masterpiece had appeared. The epic picture of the life of an entire region, the preservation of the customs of a vanished day, the realistic depicting of both people and places, were perhaps not sufficiently removed in time to impress Twain's contemporaries as they do us. Moreover, *Huckleberry Finn* was not in the genteel tradition, something which still causes a juvenile approach to the book on the part of people who prize formality above vitality in language, who do not see that Huck's sense perceptions are those of a poet, while his loyalty is that of a hero. For the adolescent the book abounds in good fun and adventure, and as such it may be read and enjoyed; but for the adult there is the vast panorama of humanity in all its virtues and vices, its ideals and shams, its nobility and stupidity. Here Mark Twain approaches the art of Shakespeare and Chaucer, that catholicity of mind which takes in not just a part of the scene but the entirety. In breadth and inclusion there are few books its equal, and in depth there are few more penetrating studies than that of Huck's moral struggle with his conscience and his decision to remain loyal to Jim and go to hell for it.[168] With irony Twain shows how the morality of

165 Vogelback, *op. cit.,* p. 266. 166 *Ibid.,* p. 265.

167 Frank L. Mott, *Golden Multitudes,* p. 157.

168 See Edgar M. Branch, *The Literary Apprenticeship of Mark Twain,* pp. 206–16.

a slave community had made Huck inhuman in his attitude toward Jim, although his natural self remained uncorrupted, finally winning over prejudice.

And here are Twain's greatest character creations: Huck, of course, and Tom, while Jim rises to heights of natural dignity, just as "Pap" Finn sinks to the lowest state of degraded humanity. Indeed, the real hero of the book is Jim, who excels even Huck in faithfulness and kindness. When Tom, suffering from fever, needs a nurse, it is Jim who braves capture to succor him. Jim is generous, sincere, courageous, ever showing fidelity and gratitude—all tempered by the quality of endurance. Moreover, those rascals, the King and the Duke, take their rightful places in the portrait gallery of unforgettable creations; their like we probably shall not see again. Colonel Grangerford remains a fine portrayal of the Southern gentry, even as the village loungers depict the worst of a region, *Huckleberry Finn* in its sweeping compass vindicating the validity of the polar extreme scopes of both Thomas Nelson Page and Erskine Caldwell.

A masterpiece of great character painting, filled with sensitive passages of rare poetic quality, *Huckleberry Finn* recounts in vigorous style the social history of an era and the atmosphere of a region. However much the reading public at large failed to see this at the time, the humor and the adventure appealed enough to insure financial success. Then came another publishing venture, this time the memoirs of General Grant, for which the contract was closed, February 27, 1885.[169] Clemens inadvertently learned from Richard Watson Gilder, editor of the *Century*, that Grant, who had written three war articles for that magazine, was preparing a fourth. When Gilder, innocent of true value, mentioned that he paid five hundred dollars for each article, Mark was amazed; but when he stated further that

169 Paine, II, 807.

the General was in need and happy to make some "trifle of bread and butter money," Mark sought to rectify a grave mistake.[170] Since neither Grant nor Gilder sensed the immediate sales value of the articles, Mark offered the amazed General $25,000 in advance on the manuscript of each volume of his personal memoirs.[171] Realizing that he had a best-seller, Mark through the Webster Company employed sixteen general agents and ten thousand canvassers on the advance sales; by May sixty thousand sets were sold.[172] Twain himself records the subscription to 320,000 sets by October 26, 1885.[173] The venture was a great success: the time was ripe for such a book, Grant's courageous fight against illness and poverty created a sympathetic reception, and the business details were handled admirably by the Webster Company. On February 27, 1886, General Grant having died, his widow received a check for $200,000, the largest single royalty ever paid in America up to that time.[174] The publishing of the Grant *Memoirs,* the making of a bust of the General by Clemens' young friend Gerhardt, and the long illness of a man whom he greatly admired combined to prevent Mark from doing any writing of his own. Other than dictating a few chapters of his *Autobiography*—a method suggested to him by Grant's dying difficulties—and writing the "Private History of a Campaign That Failed,"[176] he was too occupied with furthering the sale of the *Memoirs* to think of much else.

PUBLISHING VENTURES: THE TYPESETTER

Now at the age of fifty, Twain was not only a popular writer; he appeared also to be a successful business man. His birthday, one of the happiest, brought a number of

170 *Autobiography,* I, 32.
171 *Ibid.,* I, 39.
172 Webster, p. 312.
173 *Notebook,* 189.
174 Webster, p. 352.
175 Published in the *Century,* December, 1885. Now in *The American Claimant and Other Stories and Sketches,* p. 255.

greetings and poems from such notables as Oliver Wendell Holmes, Frank R. Stockton, Charles Dudley Warner, Joel Chandler Harris, and Andrew Lang. Though his hair was now iron-gray, Mark still looked young, for he was youthful in both spirit and vigor. Susy tells how that summer he blew soap-bubbles for the children, filling the airy fancies with tobacco smoke, and how he frolicked with the kittens and even attempted to ride Jean's donkey.[176] No wonder his favorite child recorded, "We are a very happy family!" And her description of his "beautiful curly grey hair . . . kind blue eyes . . . wonderfully shaped head and profile" leaves us with the impression of a fine looking person, just as her adoration of his character is an even greater compliment.[177] Loved by his family, liked by the public, Mark Twain at fifty stood upon a pinnacle of success with the vista of boundless others ahead.

Yet the turning point to a down grade was close at hand. It started with an unfortunate publishing venture, one that Mark with Sellers-like optimism thought would be a greater success than the Grant *Memoirs*—a life of the Pope, to be written with the blessings of his Holiness himself.[178] The contract was made in Rome, April, 1886, Webster being granted the special honor of a private audience; plans were made to launch the book simultaneously in six languages, each purchaser to receive a volume blessed by the sovereign pontiff.[179] Mark was having as much excitement in the game of business as ever Tom Sawyer had enjoyed with his escapades. But going into business multiplied responsibilities; Mark found it necessary to employ an agent, F. G. Whitmore, to handle the inquiries from ambitious authors, supplications from charities, and general correspondence from cranks of all sorts. About this time, also, the villain in Mark Twain's life appeared, the destroyer of

176 Paine, II, 821–2.
177 *Idem.*
178 *Ibid.*, III, 832.
179 *Ibid.*, III, 855.

his happiness, and the drainer of his resources—the Paige typesetting machine. On December 1, 1885, Clemens enthusiastically listed in the Notebook an account of this machine's assets.[180] From then on his belief in its potentialities caused him to sink a fortune into what might well have proved a profitable venture, but which unfortunately led to disaster. Actually the idea of a typesetter was good, and at the time Mark became interested it could have been marketed, but Paige, the inventor, insisted upon improvements. While these were made from time to time over a period of four years (and always at great expense), Twain finally found that he had spent $190,000 with nothing to show for it.[181] Yet in 1885 Mark thought he had a gold mine through mechanical invention, one such as prospecting in Nevada had failed to bring. And his home life was never happier. Katy Leary tells of quiet evenings when Mark read to the children until bedtime, afterwards reading Browning to Mrs. Clemens. Or sometimes delightful private theatricals took place on Saturdays, with a stage erected in the schoolroom, scenery painted by Gerhardt, and the children performing their own compositions. If it was a special occasion, the library and dining room were utilized for *The Prince and the Pauper,* in which Mark acted, and there were parts, too, for Katy and for George, the colored butler. "Oh, those was [sic] happy, happy times," affirmed Katy, "it was a wonderful life they led, Mr. and Mrs. Clemens."[182]

In his enthusiasm over the Grant book, Clemens seems to have forgotten his own; the only writing project which appeared to attract him was *Captain Stormfield,* the manuscript of it remaining locked away in a safe. But there was another book he expected to write, one that he may have begun as early as November, 1884, and upon which he

180 *Notebook,* p. 181. 181 *Autobiography,* I, 76–8.
182 Mary Lawton, *A Lifetime with Mark Twain,* p. 41.

worked now and then for about five years—*A Connecticut Yankee.*[183] About this time the Browning readings began, lasting through the winter of 1886–7, during which Mark conducted a sort of class, among which were members from the Saturday Morning Club as well as the family. Finally the Browning readings tapered off into a German class; out of this grew Clemens' three-act play *Meisterschaft,* a humorous and picturesque mixture of German and English. The class twice performed it successfully; it appeared in the *Century* (January, 1888),[184] and subsequently found its way into the collected works.[185]

Other interests, though far from literary, lodged successively in his head: there was the "mind cure" which had the whole family running around without glasses, and which healed everything from stomach aches to common colds. Not just the family, but everybody, including Howells and Twichell were invited to try the "mind cure."[186] Then there was Professor Loisette's school of memory, where one learned the art of never forgetting.[187] It is amazing that a person with Twain's penetrating insight into the human mind and his profound understanding of human beings could at times follow such inane fads—another proof of the complexity of the man.

The publishing business still continued a major interest. The *Library of Humor,* edited by Howells and Clark, with which Mark had little to do save write a "Compiler's Apology," sold fairly well—not so well as hoped—but well enough to insure a profit and a subsequent printing by Harper in 1906.[188] And a book by General Sheridan sold profitably, as did the ten-volume *Library of American Lit-*

183 John B. Hoben, "Mark Twain's *A Connecticut Yankee:* A Genetic Study," *American Literature,* XVIII, 198–9 (November, 1946).

184 Paine, III, 849.

185 *The American Claimant,* p. 341.

186 Paine, III, 842–3.

187 *Ibid.,* III, 850.

188 Harold Blodgett, "A Note on Mark Twain's *Library of Humor,*" *American Literature,* X, 78–80 (March, 1938).

erature; but unfortunately *The Life of Pope Leo XIII* was not a best-seller, not even popular, though it did earn something. Not so fortunate, however, were the books by Rollin M. Daggett and General Hancock, neither of which managed to get out of the red.[189] What the publishing house really needed was another book by Twain himself.

Such a work, however, was long appearing; by November, 1886, Mark had managed to write only two or three chapters of the new story, not intended as a satire at this stage, but only as a contrast between life in Arthur's day and now.[190] Then, it would appear, the caustic criticisms upon America uttered by Matthew Arnold gradually kindled Twain's wrath until he decided to strike back with satire upon certain British institutions.[191] But there was a purpose other than mere antagonism to Arnold, for as the book progressed it turned into an attack upon all special privileges, and through his hero, the Yankee mechanic, Mark poured forth his indignation upon universal evils.

While the *Yankee* was in progress Twain met Robert Louis Stevenson, with whom he shared a bench in Washington Square, exchanging ideas about people and books.[192] Mark was made a charter member of the Players, that delightful club founded by Edwin Booth in the old brownstone building at Gramercy Park; and in June, 1888, Yale honored him with a Master of Arts degree.[193] The following summer, 1889, Clemens first met Rudyard Kipling, then a young man fresh from newspaper work, to whom Mark talked freely for two hours explaining his philosophy, to which the visitor from India applied the word "Kismet."[194]

189 Paine, III, 856.

190 *Mark Twain to Mrs. Fairbanks,* p. 258.

191 Hoben, *op. cit.,* p. 211.

192 Paine, III, 859.

193 *Ibid.,* III, 867.

194 Rudyard Kipling, *From Sea to Sea* (New York: Doubleday and McClure, 1899), II, 175.

For several reasons Mark wished *A Connecticut Yankee* to appear in the best possible format: the publishing house needed a book badly—it was Mark's first in five years—and finally here were his mature opinions upon democracy and humanity at large. Dan Beard was selected as illustrator, a most happy choice, for the pictures in the *Yankee* not only catch the eye but illuminate the text. As Paine said, "Beard realized the last shade of the author's allegorical intent and portrayed it with a hundred accents which the average reader would otherwise be likely to miss."[195] When the *Yankee* appeared at the end of 1889[196] not enough readers perceived its universal plea for human rights over property, or social progress over special privileges; what was seen was the broad burlesque with its attack upon heredity and monarchy. Especially was this true in England, where Twain's publishers suggested revising so as not to offend a monarch-minded reading public. Mark, however, flatly refused, insisting that the *Yankee* appear as he wrote it. When it did, there was a protest generally denouncing the book as vulgar, and Twain finally wrote to Andrew Lang for assistance. Declaring that he had "never cared what became of the cultured classes," Clemens avowed that never once had he tried to cultivate them further, but had written for the general public.[197] Lang responded with an article in the *Illustrated London News* praising Twain as a writer and declaring *Huckleberry Finn* the "great American novel," but even he could not bring himself to speak for the *Yankee;* indeed he confessed not having read it.[198]

In a land where one never jokes about the king, the irreverent aspects of Twain's satire upon monarchy seemed vulgar, just as his bitter attacks upon an established church were likely to give offense to a devout Catholic. It is unfortunate, for Mark told a delightful fantasy of a Connecticut

195 Paine, III, 889.

196 Johnson, *Bibliography,* p. 50.

197 *Letters,* II, 528.

198 XCVIII, 222 (February 14, 1891).

Yankee suddenly swept back into the days of chivalry, a fine comic situation that has proved popular on both stage and screen.[199] Moreover, it is a great declaration of democratic principles, and in the final analysis it is not just the court of King Arthur that is exposed to the light of the truth, but the "damned human race."

Following publication of the *Yankee* Clemens suffered an attack of rheumatism in his arm, making writing difficult. For relief he wished for some German baths, especially as Livy also suffered occasionally with the same trouble. Yet business affairs would not permit; instead the family went up to the Onteora Club at Tannersville in the Catskills, where they took a cottage for the season. With Brander Matthews, who occupied a place nearby, there were frequent visits, generally at the Bear and Fox Inn, their favorite spot. Susy, now eighteen, was brilliant and charming, Clara entertained with amusing impersonations of Modjeska or Ada Rehan, while Jean, only ten, amused herself going barefoot and riding her pony. At evening often before the fire, Mark told wonderful stories, once favoring them with the thrilling climax of the Golden Arm. Each day pantomimes and charades, and burlesque races with Twain as starter[200] added light-hearted amusement.

Yet the gay season ended sadly; Mark was summoned to his mother's bedside in Keokuk, and on October 27 Jane Clemens died. Then shortly afterward Livy's own mother died in Elmira, and at the same time Jean became suddenly ill. The typesetter continued to cost money, while the publishing company made little or none. No wonder that Mark, exasperated by the end of the year, (1890) wrote to Hall, his publishing manager, "Merry Christmas to you, and I wish to God I could have one myself before I die."[201] With Susy

199 There have been three motion picture versions and a musical comedy, which enjoyed a long run and a successful revival.

200 Paine, III, 900.

201 *Ibid.*, III, 901.

away at Bryn Mawr the house seemed lonesome, and Twain found it difficult to work. As a diversion he engaged Charles Noel Flagg to paint his portrait, something he always enjoyed, for he could talk and smoke while acquiring information about the artist's profession.[202]

The typesetter continued to drain Mark's resources and fray his nerves; each time completion seemed near its inventor sought another improvement. Once it was working fine, and the New York *Herald* in the market for its purchase, when Paige suddenly decided to add an air-blast attachment, something quite unnecessary and requiring months to perfect. With delay the customers lost interest.[203]

Financial strain and worry were aggravated by recurrent attacks of rheumatism; then came news from the publishing company that the *Library of American Literature,* sold on the installment plan, required cash to meet costs of production until the monthly driblets should accrue.[204] But one dependable source for revenue was left, and Mark seized his pen, turning the old play about Colonel Sellers and the claimant to a dukedom into a novel. He even ransacked his desk for anything that might sell immediately; the old article, "Mental Telegraphy," was expanded and sent to *Harper's,* as was another old sketch entitled "Luck." To counteract the impediment of rheumatism Twain tried dictating into a phonograph, finally compromising on writing by hand until forced from pain to turn to dictation. Yet the claimant story went on, with the McClure syndicate eventually paying twelve thousand dollars for the serial rights.[205] McClure also agreed to join W. M. Laffan of the *Sun* in paying a thousand dollars each for six travel letters to be written on a trip which Clemens was then planning.[206]

Since both Mark and Livy continued to suffer from rheumatism, Livy also being bothered by a heart disturbance,

202 *Ibid.,* III, 902.
203 *Ibid.,* III, 911.
204 *Ibid.,* III, 914.
205 *Ibid.,* III, 919.
206 *Loc. cit.*

the European baths seemed necessary. The cost, too, of maintaining the Hartford house was exceeding the income derived alone from writing. Thus a period of happy associations and prosperity ended; among the servants Katy Leary alone was personally retained—for the rest, the gardener and his wife were left in charge of the house, while other places were found for George and Patrick. When Patrick McAleer drove them from the door for what proved to be the last time, they embarked upon a far longer journey than any of them realized. On June 6, 1891, the *Gascogne* bore them toward Le Havre, whence they proceeded immediately to Paris.[207] Soon in Geneva, then quietly resting awhile at Aix, afterwards visiting Bayreuth with its Wagner festival, they finally came to Marienbad in Bohemia.[208] At Aix, Clemens recovered the use of his arm and at once began his first travel letter. From Bayreuth he wrote "At the Shrine of St. Wagner."[209] But believing it easier to write a book than independent and complete articles he determined to write no more for serial publication than the six promised letters.

Leaving the family behind, Clemens engaged Joseph Very, courier of earlier travels recorded in *A Tramp Abroad,* and embarked upon a journey during which they spent the night in the old castle of Chatillon before reaching the Rhone, where Twain indeed found it "too delicious, floating with the swift current under the awning these superb, sunshiny days in deep peace and quietness."[210] After his return from Switzerland and France, the family spent the winter in Berlin, enjoying an eventful social season, the high point being a dinner with Emperor William II, at which Mark was the guest of honor—pomp and circumstance enough to delight even Tom Sawyer. Yet Twain was just as pleased with a compliment on *Old Times*

[207] *Ibid.,* III, 921.
[208] *Loc. cit.*
[209] *What Is Man? Etc.,* p. 209.
[210] Paine, III, 924.

on the Mississippi from the *portier* at his hotel[211] as he had been with praise for the same volume from the Emperor. As a Christmas gift for the children Mark Twain translated *Der Struwwelpeter,* reading aloud to his daughters the rhymes of Slovenly Peter, from a manuscript he had placed under the tree, wrapped in a huge red ribbon.[212]

When Twain's health (one reason for the trip to Europe) failed to improve satisfactorily, he set out for Mentone in the south of France accompanied only by Livy. After a month of second honeymoon there, as it were, they went to Pisa, then to Rome to join the rest of the family. Sightseeing in Venice for a fortnight, they traveled by way of Lake Como to Lucerne, finally through Berlin to Bad Nauheim, where the family spent the summer. But Twain now felt business affairs demanded his presence in America; though the publishing company remained in straits, at long last it seemed the typesetter was about to reach the stage of manufacture.[213] Hurrying to Chicago, where a factory really did exist capable of manufacturing fifty machines, Mark then returned to Nauheim for a summer of rather steady writing. As his arm improved he completed several short articles while beginning work on *Tom Sawyer Abroad,* and upon what finally became *Those Extraordinary Twins,* then a part of *Pudd'nhead Wilson.* And there he met the Prince of Wales, later Edward VII, who enjoyed Mark so much that he invited him to supper, followed by a pleasant evening of conversation.[214]

The American Claimant was published in May (1892), following a little volume called *Merry Tales,* issued shortly before; yet neither was up to standard.[215] Naturally the returns on both were slight, and Mark still losing money on

211 *Ibid.,* III, 944.
212 Published later as *Slovenly Peter* (New York: Harper & Brothers, 1935).
213 Paine, III, 947.
214 *Ibid.,* III, 952.
215 Johnson, *Bibliography,* p. 52.

the typesetter and making no progress in the publishing business, had to work even harder at his writing. That winter spent at the Villa Viviani in Florence, Twain largely completed the *Personal Recollections of Joan of Arc.* There also, he finished *Tom Sawyer Abroad, The £1,000,000 Bank-Note,* and—more important—went back to the original story of *Pudd'nhead Wilson.*[216]

Though living abroad, Clemens retained his keen interest in American politics, as indicated by the following entry in his *Notebook:*

> Settignano, March 4, 1893: 9:30 P.M. Mr. Cleveland has been President now two or three hours, no doubt.[217]

Soon Mark ferried back across the Atlantic, for the country descended into one of its worst depressions, further deteriorating the publishing business. To the typesetter he looked for financial help; once again fifty machines were about to be manufactured, and Mark's spirits rose. In May, however, at the Villa Viviani Mark found that he could do little save figure up his indebtedness. Again the family moved, settling in Munich for awhile, until Twain, finding he could stand it no longer, once more sailed for New York (August 29, 1893).

Then one night at the Murray Hill Hotel, one of the most fortunate incidents in Clemens' whole life occurred: Dr. Clarence C. Rice introduced him to Henry H. Rogers, long an admiring reader, who had heard Mark lecture on the Sandwich Islands. As the conversation progressed with Twain telling a number of amusing stories and with Rogers thoroughly enjoying them, it was as if the two had known each other for years.[218]

Rice later suggested to Rogers that Mark's finances needed looking into; actually from that moment financial

216 Paine, III, 957.
217 *Notebook,* p. 228.
218 Paine, III, 970.

reverses were halted. For although Clemens was to lose practically everything temporarily, his future affairs through Rogers' capable handling led to sound prosperity. But the present found Mark fighting to save the publishing house and salvage something from the typesetter, tasks, no doubt, impossible without the fortuitous assistance of Rogers. However, even financial worry by day could not stop the social activities by evening—so numerous, gay, and important that Mark was dubbed "The Belle of New York."[219] In Boston, where he lectured for charity, a dinner was given him at the Fields home, at which Dr. Oliver Wendell Holmes, now eighty-four, was such a delighted guest that he overstayed his time, twice refusing his coachman's solicitous suggestions of lateness. Traveling to Chicago, Twain and Rogers enjoyed the private car of the president of the Pennsylvania Railroad, whose orders were to stop the train for anything Mark might wish that was not aboard.[220]

The first of March Clemens hurried across the ocean for a three-weeks' visit with his family in France, then arrived back in New York the middle of April, only to find the publishing business backed against the wall. On April 18, 1894, the firm of Charles L. Webster & Company closed its doors, and a meeting of creditors was called with Rogers serving as Twain's representative.[221] And wisely so, for Mark would have been picked clean but for Rogers' acumen in pointing out that Livy, who had lent the firm sixty thousand dollars, was now preferred creditor and thereby entitled to the assignment of copyrights until her claim should be paid in full. Other claims amounted to a hundred thousand dollars to be settled at the rate of fifty cents on the dollar; Mark declared that he would work until he had fully paid his entire debt, but this only he and Livy believed possible. The creditors, according to Rogers, were "bent on devour-

219 *Ibid.*, III, 972.
220 *Ibid.*, III, 982.
221 *Ibid.*, III, 984.

ing every pound of flesh in sight and picking the bones afterward," but by saving the copyrights (which then did not appear so valuable) as well as the Hartford home, Twain was not left penniless.[222]

On the very day of the failure *Tom Sawyer Abroad,* the last book issued by Webster, was filed for copyright in Washington.[223] Now seeking a publisher for *Pudd'nhead Wilson,* Clemens, fortunately through the offices of Frank Bliss, again secured the American Publishing Company to bring forth his books after a lapse of twelve years. The failure of Webster and Company demonstrated to Twain how many sincere friends he possessed, for several immediately offered financial aid, Poultney Bigelow and Douglas Taylor each sending him a check for one thousand dollars, while a number of creditors urged him to forget their claims until such time as he might be able to take them up unburdened. Although Livy wrote her husband encouraging letters, actually she was horrified at the "hideous news," for she said to her sister, "business failure means disgrace."[224] Mark hastened back to Paris, soon taking the family to a quiet watering-place in the south of France, finally settling down in Étretat. In July (1894) "In Defense of Harriet Shelley" appeared in the *North American Review,*[225] one of the finest pieces of critical analysis Mark ever wrote, delightful with wit, and illuminating with penetrating insight. For Mark understood Shelley—perhaps Brooks' comparison is valid in their basic similarity—and he revealed the poet's great qualities of generosity and magnanimity, as well as those adverse traits arising from a negated childhood. And the characterizations are apt—of Godwin, from whose "point of view the last syllable of his name was surplusage,"[226] or Mary, his daughter, with her

[222] *Idem.* See also Clemens' own statement, *Love Letters,* pp. 306–7.

[223] *Ibid.,* III, 985.

[224] *Ibid.,* III, 987.

[225] Johnson, *Bibliography,* p. 246.

[226] *In Defense of Harriet Shelley,* p. 47.

masculine will, "a child in years only."[227] Here in this essay Twain demolished the "literary cake-walk" of Dowden's stilted prose, along with the specious defense of Shelley at the expense of Harriet's reputation. Although some critics have dismissed this essay as an example of Victorian chivalry on Mark's part, the fact remains that he reached the same conclusions arrived at by later efforts in scholarship.[228]

At Étretat in Normandy work progressed on *Joan of Arc,* interrupted momentarily by news of the failure of the typesetting machine, a disaster Mark could scarcely believe; yet he soon recovered to commence writing again. Not only *Joan,* but *Tom Sawyer, Detective* poured forth from the inspiration tank, now rapidly filling since entirely released as a literary reservoir. Settled down in Paris for the winter, Twain finished *Joan of Arc* there and sent it to *Harper's.* Accepted promptly for serialization, *Joan,* however, was published anonymously; Mark feared if it appeared over his name that people would expect a humorous story. Disappointed readers he wished to avoid, but as he avowed to Rogers sales did not interest him—"it was written for love."[229]

Yet, just then he needed a best seller, or something more, for debts continued heavy. Neither conscience nor sense of honor could rest until the slate was clean, a condition only to come, it seemed, if Twain resorted to the lecture platform. Although an abhorred thought, it had proved salvation in the past, and Clemens now arranged with J. B. Pond for a tour. Then suddenly a better idea evolved: Why not lecture his way around the world, at the same time acquiring material for a new book? Back in the States at Quarry Farm Mark planned the trip around the world; Susy was to remain at home with her aunt and Jean, while Clara was

227 *Ibid.*, p. 45.

228 Professor Newman Ivey White told me during August, 1948, that he considered Twain's conclusions valid.

229 *Letters,* II, 624.

to go with her parents. When they left Elmira on July 14, (1895) they did not dream that the sight of Susy waving good-bye would be the last they should ever have of her.[230]

Lecturing Around the World

Faced with either touring India during the hot season or beginning his lectures in America during July, Mark chose the latter as the lesser evil. For thirty-three days they travelled through blistering heat from Elmira to Vancouver, with readings in Cleveland, Duluth, Minneapolis, St. Paul, Winnipeg, and Butte. Before sailing, August 23, Twain announced to the press that the profits of his tour should go to his creditors, for honor demanded one hundred per cent settlement of all debts.[231] Then began the long tour to Australia, New Zealand, India, and South Africa.

Though the first month of lecturing returned a net profit of five thousand dollars, which was applied to the indebtedness, this was partially offset for Mark by keen disappointment at not being able again to visit the Sandwich Islands, where his scheduled lecture at Honolulu was prevented by an outbreak of cholera. Yet they could gaze at the shoreline, which seemed to him "just as I had seen it long before, with nothing of its beauty lost, nothing of its charm wanting."[232] Indeed Clemens declared that he would like to "go ashore and never leave." But it was not to be; soon they sailed away crossing the equator on September 5. "Clara kodaked it,"[233] said her father.

In Australia, they were royally received with crowded houses, ovations, and lavish entertainment, which delighted Twain and served the more practical purpose of clearing another two thousand dollars to apply on his debts.[234] At

[230] Paine, III, 1002.
[231] *Ibid.*, III, 1007.
[232] *Ibid.*, III, 1008.
[233] *Notebook*, 251.
[234] Paine, III, 1010.

Melbourne even lancing a carbuncle could not dampen Clemens' enthusiasm, which continued as he lectured his way across Australia and New Zealand. With the New Year they were off to Ceylon, thence across India from Bombay to Calcutta, with Mark delighting in all the old romantic atmosphere of Lahore, Delhi, and Lucknow. Nor could the discomforts of travel change his happy mood; of a thirty-five-mile descent in a hand-car down the Himalayas he acclaimed, "the most enjoyable time I have spent in the earth."[235] All of India he saw from the vantage point of a tour for which government officials and native potentates outdid themselves to make it worth remembering for a lifetime. The Clemens family were entertained in Arabian Nights fashion by Prince Kumar, whose servants piled bales of rich goods before them for the selection of whatever presents they desired.[236] They lunched at the Governor's House, and Mark delivered a lecture in the great hall of the palace where the Durbars were held.[237] Yet this did not shut his eyes to the abject position of the Indian subjects, for Twain commented upon the Hindu servant squatting barefooted on the cold tiles outside his master's door, and the parched earth with mud villages crumbling into decay impressed him as "a sorrowful land—a land of unimaginable poverty and hardship."[238]

Twain next visited South Africa, just after the Transvaal invasion had been repulsed and the Jameson raid had ended disastrously with fifty or more prisoners in jail at Pretoria. Clemens gave a number of readings, paid a visit to the Kimberley diamond mines, and had an audience with President Kruger.[239] Here as elsewhere Twain's poetic perception of natural beauty is revealed: "I think the Veldt in its sober winter garb is as beautiful as paradise."[240] Fi-

235 *Ibid.*, III, 1012.
236 *Ibid.*, III, 1014.
237 *Notebook*, p. 273.
238 *Ibid.*, 276.
239 Paine, III, 1019.
240 *Notebook*, 296.

nally just one year exactly after leaving home (July 14, 1896) Clemens sailed with his family for England, where they arrived at Southampton, having actually circumnavigated the globe.[241]

It had been arranged for Katy Leary to bring Jean and Susy to England; instead a letter came announcing Susy's illness. Mrs. Clemens and Clara immediately decided to return home, leaving Mark alone to write the book based on his recent travels. Just three days after they sailed on August 15, the solitary father received the saddest message that could have reached him: "Susy was peacefully released today."[242] She was his favorite, the one most nearly like himself; with her he had so much in common, and now she was gone. Other hard blows Twain had taken in stride, but this shattered his defenses. Susy's final illness had been one of raging fever, turning into delirium, until blind from brain infection, she had groped for Katy Leary's face and said, "Mamma."[243] The death of Susy brought to the surface all the latent pessimism in his nature; whereas before it had been confined chiefly to private utterance, henceforth it was to appear more openly, though the most bitter expressions were not to be published until after his death.

Seeking seclusion, the Clemens family hid away that winter at 23 Tedworth Square in London. Mark tried to escape his sorrow in work; it was the best way out, and besides debts still remained to be liquidated. Yet his own troubles did not prevent his helping Helen Keller, the little girl who though stone deaf and blind managed partially to overcome her muteness. Through Mrs. H. H. Rogers, Twain managed to secure funds to enable this "marvelous child" to continue her studies for a college degree.[244] The death of

[241] Paine, III, 1019. It was from Southampton that Twain had sailed from England to start his tour in America.

[242] *Ibid.*, III, 1021.

[243] *Love Letters*, p. 319.

[244] *Letters*, II, 638.

Susy, however, continued to weigh so heavily that he wrote to Joe Twichell, "I did not know that she could go away, and take our lives with her, yet leave our dull bodies behind"; then finally he despairingly asked, "Why am I robbed, and who is benefited?"[245] Slightly over a month later he wrote Howells that he was indifferent to everything but work, which he did "without purpose and without ambition; merely for the love of it."[246] He knew this mood of sadness would pass eventually, but Livy must recover first. For the present they were "dead people who go through the motions of life," but with Clara and Jean it was different—"They have youth—the only thing that was worth giving to the race."[247]

About this time a rumor that Twain and his family were living in poverty became so persistent that the New York *Herald* launched a public benefit fund with a subscription of one thousand dollars, to which Andrew Carnegie promptly added another thousand. When Mark learned of it he was privately enraged, yet he publicly thanked his would-be benefactors, telling them he was able to care for his family by his own efforts.[248] During this time occurred, also, the incident of the young reporter instructed by his paper to cable five hundred words if Twain were actually dying in poverty and one thousand if already dead. When the green youth unthinkingly showed Mark the message, the humorist composed the famous reply to the effect that "the report of my death was an exaggeration."[249]

With passage of time Clemens once more appeared socially; the Savage Club elected him to honorary life-membership, and by summer he was in the mood to write for the Americans papers about the Queen's Jubilee, June 22, 1897, being the day the sixty-year reign was celebrated.[250]

245 *Ibid.*, II, 641. 246 *Ibid.*, II, 643.
247 *Idem.* 248 Paine, III, 1026. See also *Notebook,* p. 327.
249 *Notebook,* p. 328. See also *Twainian, VI,* 2 (Nov.–Dec., 1948).
250 Paine, III, 1043.

Finally after careful manuscript reading by Livy, with more profit from deletion of boring details than suffering from prudery, *Following the Equator* was finished. There is neither the freshness of the *Innocents* nor the gay burlesque of *A Tramp Abroad,* for Mark put more padding into this book than he had ever used before, no doubt because of his weary desire to bring the task to a close. The chapter mottoes from Pudd'nhead Wilson's calendar, however, are both amusing and bitter, for he had looked upon much exploitation during his course around the earth, seeing social and political injustices to make a Christian blush. *Following the Equator* is of more interest as a storehouse of Mark's mature judgments than anything else, but when it appeared, November, 1897,[251] it enjoyed an early sale comparable with *Roughing It.* People were anxious to aid a man who had the honor to pay his debts, especially when that author was Mark Twain, a name synonymous with good reading.

All royalties went to Rogers for liquidating debts, which were cleared by the end of January, 1898.[252] Clemens was a free man again, and he now took his family to Vienna, where they enjoyed, as usual, a series of brilliant social gatherings. More than once, however, politics intruded, for it was the eve of the Spanish-American war and most Austrians were in sympathy with their fellow Europeans. Though he would change his mind later, at the outset Mark thought the American cause righteous.[253]

Mark never worked harder than he did during this period following his freedom from debt. There were many false starts, but not all, for two of his finest pieces were produced that winter: *The Man That Corrupted Hadleyburg* and *The Mysterious Stranger.* The former represents Twain's pessimistic attitude toward the human race, an

251 Johnson, *Bibliography,* p. 66. 252 Paine, III, 1056.
253 *Letters,* II, 663.

attitude which included himself, and which if the reader is honest and objective is seen to embrace him, too; for it is the corruption and the downfall of an entire town that is depicted, the yielding to temptation of once honest people who succumb through weakness to the lure of wealth. It is a bitter denunciation of self-righteousness, rationalization, and the failure of people to resist temptation when the price is high enough. Yet it was in the latter story that Mark embodied his philosophy of man, displaying that miserable creature in his pygmy form as he appeared in his impersonal state before the eyes of Satan. Here in these two tales the bitter, penetrating, and unadorned truth about human kind was set forth as it appeared to one who had looked at life for many years.

Yet as pessimism increased in Twain's mind, material prosperity returned. Now the family actually had $107,000 on deposit in the bank, the house in Hartford with all its furnishings was clear of debt, while income from English and American copyrights was equal to the returns upon a $200,000 capital investment.[254] But mental repose did not accompany material wealth. For some time all had been distressed over a marked change in Jean's nature, her naturally friendly and kindly disposition suffering spells of arrogance, turning her from a lovable to an unfriendly person. During the spring or summer of 1896 she had experienced convulsions, and an actual epileptic fit had occurred while she was at school.[255] Now Jean's epilepsy took a turn for the worse, forcing Clemens to take her to Sweden for treatment at Dr. Kellgren's sanitarium at Sanna, where she remained from July until October (1899). Hoping that osteopathy might succeed where medical science had failed Mark even tried the treatment himself. In order to allow his afflicted daughter to continue the cure Clemens settled

[254] Paine, III, 1073.

[255] Mss. of the Twain Estate.

his family in London, where Kellgren maintained another institution; and there they spent the winter of 1899–1900, seeing the new century appear as hope for Jean's recovery vanished.

Mark finished an essay "St. Joan of Arc," which Douglas Hyde took the liberty of editing, thereby drawing upon his head the full wrath of a temper risen to "104 in the shade." At this "long-eared animal—this literary kangaroo—this illiterate hostler with his skull full of axle-grease" Mark stormed as he withdrew the piece, which several years later appeared in *Harper's*.[256] A few unimportant articles constituted the rest of his output that winter. Twain had other reasons than the ill health of his daughter to make him unhappy, for the two wars then in progress were disheartening.[257] Although he had at first regarded the Spanish-American war as a noble crusade for the freedom of Cuba, the subsequent military operations in the Philippines had embittered him, while the only comfort the Boer war with England could bring was that at least England herself must be upheld as a nation with free institutions. And as usual the social life of London, unabated by the war, was not conducive to hard work; the final result was very little accomplished.

At this time S. S. McClure tried to interest Mark in the editorship of a magazine and was almost successful, but when he realized that he would be harnessed with all managerial details, and that it was not a matter of having a magazine to write for as the spirit moved him, Mark lost interest.[258] Still clinging to any faint hope that Jean's condition might be improved by Kellgren, Twain remained in England during the summer, taking a beautiful residence surrounded by trees just outside of London, Dollis Hill

256 Paine, III, 1090–1.

257 William M. Gibson, "Mark Twain and Howells: Anti-Imperialists," *New England Quarterly*, XX, 435–70 (December, 1947).

258 Paine, III, 1101.

House,[259] which had once been a vacation spot for Gladstone. The entire family found it a paradise, but toward the end of summer their anticipation of returning home became more compelling than their attachment to the old English manor.

Home Once More

And America received Mark Twain like a returning conqueror. If there were any doubts about his permanent hold upon the public they were now dispelled. But though again home, the family was still homeless, for they could not bear to look upon the house at Hartford; it held memories too sad, suddenly made more so by the death of an old neighbor, Charles Dudley Warner, only five days after their landing. On his way to serve as pall-bearer, Twain looked into the old home, coming away with the feeling that "if we ever enter the house again to live our hearts will break."[260] Through Frank N. Doubleday a house was secured at 14 West Tenth Street in New York, where Mark immediately moved without the formality of signing a lease. Once Doubleday had straightened this out, his troubles had only begun, for Mark found fault with everything from the windows to the furnace and sent the unhappy Doubleday a daily postal card of complaint as though he were responsible.[261] Clara Clemens has recorded how this place soon became the most popular house in the city with guests calling at all hours, reporters seeking interviews, and the telephone ringing until the butler hardly had time to do anything but answer it.[262]

Mark thought his reasons for not returning to Hartford were only the ghosts haunting him with memories of happy associations, yet it is doubtful if he could have remained long from a metropolis; he had become so accustomed to

259 *Ibid.*, III, 1108.
260 *Ibid.*, III, 1112.
261 *Ibid.*, III, 1113.
262 *My Father, Mark Twain*, p. 217.

being in the centers of world activity that he would probably have gravitated to New York anyway. Here the many dinners and speech-makings forced Mark to adopt a habit of arriving too late for food but in time to talk. One club after another plied Twain with honors, one of the most lavish being a dinner at the Lotos Club, where Mark with characteristic generosity told his audience how considerately he had been treated by his creditors.[263]

And the American people acclaimed him in the role of common sense philosopher, just as a quarter of a century later, Will Rogers would fill a similar position via newspapers, stage, and radio, but without Clemens' literary art. Mark, now old enough to be accepted as a sage, fitted into the part naturally, for the "moralist of the main," as San Francisco's literary pioneers had dubbed him, needed only the passing of time to become the counselor to his countrymen on everything from the weather to foreign affairs. He became a sort of general spokesman, and the average man applauded when Twain defined a classic as "something everybody wants to have read and nobody wants to read."[264] And Mark in the tradition of rail-fence philosopher reminded the Public Education Association of the old farmer's remark that nothing was to be gained financially from closing schools because "every time a school was closed a jail had to be built."[265] American imperialism in the Philippines, the English brand of the same offense in South Africa, and the wholesale application of it by the European powers in China, all drew from him characteristic and apt criticism. When the City Club held a municipal reform meeting, January 4, 1901, Mark's statement that forty-nine men out of fifty were honest, with dishonest government arising because the forty-nine were disorganized, became a slogan.[266]

263 Paine, III, 1116.

264 *Speeches,* p. 210.

265 *Ibid.,* 213.

266 Paine, III, 1122.

One of the most interesting speeches Mark ever made was an introduction for Colonel Henry Watterson at a Lincoln birthday celebration in Carnegie Hall, during which Twain referred openly to his own service for the Confederacy and spoke of "you of the North and we of the South," as he paid his respects to Lincoln and expressed his faith in the future of a united country.[267] He continued to call public attention to evils and abuses. "To the Person Sitting in Darkness," which appeared in the *North American Review,* February, 1901, was a scorching indictment of injustice and hypocrisy, cleverly achieved by placing against the complacent Christmas Eve editorial of the New York *Tribune* several clippings from the *Sun* which juxtaposed the "contentment and happiness" of the former with the human degradation appearing in the latter.

At Saranac Lake in June the Clemens family lived in a log cabin, which Mark called "The Lair," swimming, boating, and taking long walks through the woods. It was a happy summer free from visitors and newspapers, during which Mark did no writing except *A Double-Barrelled Detective Story,* written in six days and dispatched immediately to *Harper's.* For this burlesque of Sherlock Holmes Jean acted as her father's secretary;[268] it contained one of Twain's most fortunate parodies, a take-off on the fine writing so popular with the Victorians, in which a "solitary esophagus" was introduced into a paragraph of lilacs and laburnums.[269]

When summer ended, the family, after a week in Elmira, settled at Riverdale-on-the-Hudson, within easy access to New York. Fall and winter were filled with activities leaving scant time for writing. In October Yale conferred upon Clemens the degree of Doctor of Letters, an honor

267 *Ibid.,* III, 1124. 268 *Ibid.,* III, 1135.

269 *The Man That Corrupted Hadleyburg and Other Essays and Stories,* p. 304.

also shared by his old friend Howells. Then with characteristic desire to help the human race—however much he might protest that it was irrevocably damned—Mark threw himself into a fight for municipal reform. Anxious to defeat Tammany Hall and "Boss" Croker, Twain delivered a serious, denunciatory speech at the old Waldorf-Astoria, in which he impeached Croker after the fashion of Burke's attack upon Warren Hastings.[270] Hundreds of thousands of copies of this speech were printed and distributed, and Mark put his heart and soul into the campaign. Marching in a procession up Broadway, making a speech for which he arose from a sick bed, Twain did his full part for the reform ticket, which carried the field on election day.

Meanwhile, the American adventure in the Philippines produced an action which many praised but which Mark denounced with furious invective—the betrayal and capture of Aguinaldo by General Frederick Funston.[271] Mark's anger, filled with cold scorn and fury, poured forth in a bitter castigation of the treachery. Funston was not to blame for his act, because he was born as he was and his disposition lacked moral perception. Such irony was scathing, and Mark had the courage to challenge public opinion by denouncing a popular triumph as treachery.

Twain then turned from serious matters to seek recreation with Henry Rogers on the latter's yacht, sailing to Nova Scotia, August, 1901. Joe Twichell, who was invited but unable to go, received a joking note from Mark, "We had a noble good time in the yacht, and caught a Chinese missionary and drowned him."[272] Another voyage to the West Indies followed in April, a delightful trip for Mark, devoted mostly to draw poker, at which Tom Reed, Speaker

270 Paine, III, 1145.

271 "A Defense of General Funston," *North American Review*, CLXXIV, 613–24 (May, 1902).

272 *Letters*, II, 712.

of the House of Representatives, succeeded in winning twenty-three pots in a row.[273]

Finally, at long last, the University of Missouri, following in the wake of Yale, honored Clemens with an LL.D. Arriving in St. Louis at the end of May, Mark met his old pilot-friend, Horace Bixby, who escorted him to the Pilots Association rooms, where several old companions were still on hand to greet him. Then came five days in Hannibal, a triumphant return to meet the survivors of his youth, during which he visited the old home on Hill Street, met Buck Brown, his rival in spelling bees, walked over Holliday's Hill with John Briggs from Tom Sawyer's band, shook hands with Jimmy McDaniel, to whom he had first told the story of Jim Wolfe and the cats, talked with Laura Hawkins, and was escorted to the churches and Sunday schools by John RoBards. Just before Mark left, Tom Nash, long stone deaf from a skating escapade when he and Sam crashed through the ice, pushed forward and unknowingly shouted as he indicated the crowd, "Same damned fools, Sam."[274]

At every station along the line from Hannibal to Columbus crowds acclaimed him, a dramatic recognition climaxed on June 4, 1902, with the bestowal of the honorary degree by the University of Missouri.[275] When Clemens returned home, the family moved for the summer to York Harbor, Maine, with Howells nearby at Kittery Point. But the season was blighted by Livy's becoming seriously ill, an illness so alarmingly persisting that it was not until December 30 that Mark was allowed to see her, and then only for five minutes.

Shortly before Christmas Jean developed pneumonia, sinking so dangerously as to require constant attendance. It was imperative to keep her condition secret from Livy, a circumstance which eventually developed its amusing

273 Paine, III, 1163.
274 *Autobiography,* II, 99.
275 Paine, III, 1172.

side. Clara, the only member of the family permitted to see Mrs. Clemens daily, had to prevaricate—something she enjoyed a reputation for never doing. Amused by his veracious daughter's predicament, Mark questioned Clara after each visit so that he might corroborate her deceptions in the little notes he sent his wife. As spring approached, Livy gradually improved until the physicians held out hopes for recovery in a milder climate. Memories of Villa Viviani turned their thoughts toward Florence, where Mark was willing to spend the rest of his days if it would only prolong Livy's life. After selling the house purchased the previous summer at Tarrytown, they reached Quarry Farm by the first of June; here Livy spent three peaceful months recuperating, and Mark again occupied the old octagonal study, the birthplace of Tom and Huck.[276] But little writing came forth, only "A Dog's Tale" being completed, and that written to please Jean, who abhorred vivisection of animals.

It was October 22, 1903, however, that Henry Rogers completed negotiations with Harpers to publish all of Twain's books and guarantee the author at least $25,000 each year.[277] Actually the books sometimes earned twice that much, freeing Mark of financial worry and leaving him more time to devote to Livy, with whom he promptly sailed for Genoa on the *Princess Irene*.

Abroad Again

Taking residence in the Villa Quarto, located in a picturesque garden of ancient trees and crumbling walls, looking towards Florence and the Chianti Hills, they immediately suffered disappointment from the weather which brought more fog than sunlight. And there were other dissatisfactions over the barnlike aspect, and general dearth

[276] *Ibid.*, III, 1206. [277] *Ibid.*, III, 1207.

of modern improvements.[278] Yet the place gradually won them. By January, 1904, Livy's health grew better as the weather improved, and Mark completed some magazine articles for *Harpers,* one of them "The $30,000 Bequest." Now he could turn to the autobiographical writing in which he was more interested, but which should not see print until after his death. For this he tried dictation at first, which proved unsuccessful, because the amanuensis could not write shorthand.

But Livy's seeming improvement revealed itself a false hope; as she alternately appeared better one day and retrogressed the next, the spirits of the family rose and fell. On June 5, 1904, Mark found her looking "bright and young and pretty,"[279] so much so that on that very day he and Jean enthusiastically selected a new villa for their home and found her animated over the prospects. That evening, because she seemed improved, Mark remained with her longer than usual, talking over old times; then blowing a kiss until his return to say goodnight, he went to the piano and softly sang the spirituals Susy had so loved. Hearing the distant music Livy said, "He is singing a good-night carol to me."[280] A moment after the music ceased she died, though Mark did not discover it until he came to say goodnight and found Clara and Jean standing dazed by the bed. In his *Notebook* he wrote: "At a quarter past 9 this evening she that was the life of my life passed to the relief and the peace of death after 22 months of unjust and unearned suffering." Then to his old friend Joe Twichell, he said, "How sweet she was in death, how young, how beautiful, how like her dear girlish self of thirty years ago, not a gray hair showing." To Howells he confided, "I am tired and old; I wish I were with Livy."[281]

278 Clara Clemens, *My Father, Mark Twain,* pp. 241–3.
279 Paine, III, 1216. 280 *Ibid.,* III, 1218.
281 *Ibid.,* III, 1219.

Indeed Livy's illness had been pitiful, for she feared death from strangulation, having suffered five spells of "choking horror" each lasting an hour or more.[282] Clemens and the children sailed for home to bury her beside Susy and Langdon, taking passage on the *Prince Oscar,* June 29, for although the *Princess Irene* sailed earlier they could not bear to return on the boat that brought them over. The funeral was held on July 14 at the old home in Elmira, where Joe Twichell, who had performed the marriage ceremony thirty-four years ago, now rendered the last service. At the grave Clemens placed a simple marker which gave only her name and the dates of birth and death, followed by this expressive line in German: *Gott sei dir gnadig, O meine Wonne.*[283]

As if the loss of Livy were not enough to bear, fate promptly dealt a series of disasters. Clara, who had borne the brunt of her mother's long illness, now that the strain was past, suffered a nervous collapse, which necessitated her being taken to a sanitarium, where she remained for a year of rest. Jean, out for a moonlight ride with a group of friends, suffered bruises and a broken tendon in her ankle when her horse collided with a trolley car, an accident which killed the animal and knocked Jean unconscious. She was taken to a hospital, and when the news reached Twain he was completely prostrated. Only a short time before he had put out a fire because he remembered the birds had built a nest in the chimney, but now he rushed to Clara with news of the accident when his actual intentions were to hide it from her.[284] Then on September 1, Pamela, his sister, died at age 73. It was a disastrous year through personal losses and illness.

282 *Love Letters,* pp. 348–9.
283 "God be merciful to thee, Oh, my Rapture," Paine, III, 1223.
284 Clara Clemens, *My Father, Mark Twain,* p. 256.

New York

But Clemens managed to move to New York in the fall, where he took a house at 21 Fifth Avenue on the corner of 9th Street, and there the furniture, stored at Hartford for thirteen years, was placed in its new surroundings by faithful Katy Leary, who with Jean constituted the household. For once Mark wished seclusion. Restless and disturbed he wrote but little, though he did furnish the *North American Review* one of his best papers on the copyright problem.[285] And Paine believed that he now began, or at least contemplated, *Eve's Diary*, which closes with Adam speaking the sentiments of Sam Clemens for Livy: "Wheresoever she was, *there* was Eden."[286]

Feeling the need for solace, Twain purchased an Aeolian Orchestrelle, for however much he derided his own taste in music, the stately and harmonious did appeal to him.[287] To Mrs. Crane Mark confided his feelings that "Tannhaüser" was "solemn and impressive and so divinely beautiful," while to Jean he said that his favorite piece of music was Beethoven's Fifth Symphony.[288] Consolation came through these majestic melodies, and though he went out but little that winter, Clemens gradually assumed something of his former habits, attending an intimate dinner of friends at the Metropolitan Club, and turning his attention once more to world affairs. A massacre of Jews in Moscow brought forth "The Tsar's Soliloquy," a withering satire on Russian despotism, and the atrocities perpetrated by

285 "Concerning Copyrights," published January, 1905, Johnson, *Bibliography*, p. 246.

286 *The $30,000 Bequest*, p. 381.

287 Frank M. Flack says that Mark, unlike most of his countrymen, who had no liking for operatic or symphonic music, "gradually obtained a more intimate knowledge of higher musical art." "Mark Twain and Music," *Twainian*, II, 3 (October, 1942). During his last years Twain found pleasure in the works of Beethoven, Brahms, Chopin, and Schubert. *Ibid.*, p. 4.

288 Paine, III, 1227.

King Leopold in the Belgian Congo produced "King Leopold's Soliloquy," so blistering that it was not thought suitable for magazine publication but was issued as a pamphlet by the Congo Reform Association.[289] The policies of our own government aroused Mark's anger to the point of his denouncing President Roosevelt in a letter to Twichell, in which he expressed admiration for Theodore Roosevelt the man but stated his intense dislike of him as the politician.[290] Most scathing of all, however, was the "War Prayer," which he read to Dan Beard and to Jean, but which he felt too contradictory of the illusions and traditions of mankind to be published.[291]

With the coming of summer Twain took a house at Dublin, New Hampshire, where he turned his attention to a lengthy satire "3,000 Years Among the Microbes," the fantastic autobiography of a microbe living on the person of a tramp, Blitzowski, upon which human continent all the seething problems of life occur in a Lilliputian satire upon social and political problems.[292] Although he tired of it before completion, it served the purpose of diverting his mind from personal sorrows. To oblige Mrs. Minnie Maddern Fiske, who was crusading against bull-fighting in Spain, Mark wrote "A Horse's Tale," which pleased Mrs. Fiske but added no more to his reputation than it hindered bull-fighting.[293]

Returning to New York in the fall, Mark entered naturally again into public life. When his seventieth birthday arrived, Colonel Harvey arranged a celebration at Delmonico's to be held December 5, 1905, so as not to conflict with the Thanksgiving holidays. Most of the leading authors of the day gathered to honor Clemens; to him Howells said, "I will not say, 'O King, live forever,' but 'O King,

[289] Johnson, *Bibliography,* p. 81. [290] Paine, III, 1232.
[291] Published in *Europe and Elsewhere* (1923), p. 394.
[292] Paine, IV, Appendix V, 1663–70. [293] *Ibid.,* III, 1246.

live as long as you like!' " and when Twain arose before that audience including such old friends as Joe Twichell, Brander Matthews, and Henry Rogers, he made his greatest speech, closing unforgettably:

"Threescore years and ten! It is the scriptural statute of limitations. After that you owe no active duties; for you the strenuous life is over." Then he thanked them for still keeping him in remembrance, but reminded, "I am seventy; seventy, and would nestle in the chimney-corner, and smoke my pipe, and read my book, and take my rest, wishing you well in all affection, and that when you in your turn shall arrive at Pier 70 you may step aboard your waiting ship with a reconciled spirit, and lay your course toward the sinking sun with a contented heart."[294]

Letters from all over the world arrived at 21 Fifth Avenue; a group of English authors cabled their congratulations; and the Society of Illustrators honored him with a banquet, at which a pretty girl costumed as Joan of Arc stepped forward to a trumpet flourish and crowned him with a laurel wreath. Yet amid all this fanfare of popular acclaim and the sincere expressions of love from intimate friends and admiration from a multitude of readers, Twain probably wrote the closing chapter of *The Mysterious Stranger,* in which his despair was embodied in narrative:

"It is all a dream—a grotesque and foolish dream. Nothing exists but you. And you are but a *thought*— a vagrant thought, a useless thought, a homeless thought, wandering forlorn among the empty eternities!"[295]

It was January 3, 1906, at a Players Club dinner with Brander Matthews presiding, that Albert Bigelow Paine, then unknown to Clemens, gathered courage to ask permission to call upon him. A friend suggested that Paine approach Clemens about a biography, and the interview at

294 *Ibid.*, III, 1252.
295 *The Mysterious Stranger*, p. 140.

Twain's home ended with Mark saying, "When would you like to begin?"[296] Thus the authorized biography started; soon Paine engaged a stenographer to take dictation, and Mark plunged into his autobiography, though actually he revealed little of his inner thought while unhappily dwelling on much of only transitory interest. Paine soon discovered, also, that many of Mark's self-dramatizations "were not safe to include in a record that must bear a certain semblance to history,"[297] for Mark adorned and improved with magical imagination and the great gift for the dramatic which he had exercised too long to cast aside in the interest of mere facts.

This same winter Clemens placed flowers upon the grave of an old and valued servant, his coachman Patrick McAleer. Shortly thereafter he concluded a speech delivered to the Young Men's Christian Association in New York with this encomium: "He was all honor, honesty, and affection. . . . I have been asked for my idea of an ideal gentleman, and I give it to you—Patrick McAleer."[298]

Mark was a democrat in the best sense of the word, which led him to value each individual on his merits, and to advocate equality of opportunity everywhere. This sympathetic attitude made him espouse the efforts of Maxim Gorky, recently arrived in America to secure funds for the cause of Russian emancipation. With Howells Mark lent his support until he was suddenly embarrassed by news that Gorky had been put out of his hotel for having with him a woman not his wife, a Russian actress who was also a leader in the cause of freedom. Soon an army of reporters besieged Clemens and Howells, who however much they sympathized with the Russian serfs, could not condone the flouting of custom.

It was April 19, 1906, that Twain gave his farewell lec-

296 Paine, IV, 1264.

297 *Ibid.*, IV,1269.

298 *Ibid.*, IV, 1278.

ture at Carnegie Hall for the benefit of the Robert Fulton Memorial Association. As Mark entered, the band played "America," while the audience, including General Grant and his uniformed staff, rose to greet him. Thus Samuel Clemens, relating the old tales that had proved so popular in his long trip around the world, closed a chapter in his career, first opened in San Francisco forty years before.[299]

Those in his immediate household who saw Mark in his rich dressing-robe, propped against the pillows of his massive bed, started calling him "the King," a habit soon taken up by most of his admirers. And like a king he received the devotions of his followers. Once when a woman who had requested the privilege of just seeing him face to face, murmured, "How God must love you!" Mark said after her departure, "I guess she hasn't heard of our strained relations."[300]

Twain liked dictating to his biographer while striding up and down, smoking as he talked. Sometimes he would pause in the midst of a narrative to expound upon the failings of the human race, though most of his dictations at this time were about Susy, filled with self-reproaches for denying her encouragement and attention. More than once he exclaimed that all the misfortunes his family had suffered were solely his own fault.[301]

This same year Clemens determined upon a private printing of his "Gospel" for distribution among a few intimate friends. Frank Doubleday, who took charge of the matter, arranged with the De Vinne Press for two hundred and fifty numbered copies printed on hand-made paper and published anonymously under the title *What Is Man?* In this form it appeared August 20, 1906.[302] That same summer Twain yielded to Colonel Harvey's persuasions to publish some selections from the *Autobiography* in the *North*

299 *Ibid.*, IV, 1290.
300 *Ibid.*, IV, 1292.
301 *Ibid.*, IV, 1299.
302 Johnson, *Bibliography*, p. 83.

American Review, in return for which Mark was paid thirty thousand dollars. Promptly thereafter he began plans to build a house at Redding, located on a beautiful hilltop, affording so delightful a view that Twain wrote Howells begging him to build nearby and make the situation perfect.[303]

But until the house should be completed, Mark returned to New York. Now learning that Mrs. Rogers intended giving him a billiard table for Christmas, he could not restrain himself, quickly hinting that he would like to have it right away. Soon it was installed, and all else became of secondary interest, as Paine let biography wait while he and Mark played billiards, sometimes until three or four o'clock in the morning. Even then Twain would beg for one more game. Sometimes when things went awry Mark would fly into a rage from which he always recovered a bit ashamed of himself, realizing that he had made an amusing spectacle.[304]

After his seventy-first birthday he made up his mind to wear nothing but white clothes in the future, save for evening dress and a gray suit or two for travel.[305] Like Tom Sawyer he loved spectacular costume, and when he later visited Oxford he was fascinated by a party of Indian princes in gorgeous court dress, which he admiringly declared he would like to wear himself.[306] This decision to dress in white came upon the eve of a journey to the nation's capital to lobby in behalf of copyright.

Mere convention never fazed Mark, as it never daunted Tom Sawyer, and he appeared everywhere thus conspicuously dressed. Paine tells how Clemens went into the Plaza Hotel one Sunday, postponing a stroll down Fifth Avenue until the crowds should come out of church.[307] And again

303 Paine, IV, 1323.
304 *Ibid.,* IV, 1329.
305 *Ibid.,* IV, 1342.
306 *Ibid.,* IV, 1386–7.
307 *Ibid.,* IV, 1416.

how he insisted upon walking down the long "Peacock Alley" of the Willard Hotel in Washington, when he might have entered the dining room by a more direct but less public approach.[308] On this same expedition to the capital Twain engaged in one of his most impressive outbursts of profanity. Turning on the faucet to shave, he met a flow of boiling water. Hardly recovered from this mishap, Mark encountered a slopping milk pitcher which caused further exasperation. "I get so damned short of profanity at a time like this," he concluded.[309] Mark occupied the private room of Speaker "Uncle Joe" Cannon, while a procession of congressmen filed through to meet him and listen to his proposals. He left the Capitol highly elated to dine that evening at the home of Thomas Nelson Page. The following morning, with Paine he hired a carriage and drove out to Rock Creek Cemetery to see the Saint-Gaudens "Adams's Memorial," before which Clemens removed his hat in silent tribute.[310]

Though at the peak of a long life's achievement, Mark at this time confided to intimates that not a month passed without his having a recurring dream of being in reduced circumstances and forced again into piloting to earn a living. Usually in this unpleasant dream he was just about to go into a black shadow without being able to distinguish between a solid bluff and the darkness of night. But another persistent dream, even more nightmarish, was that he had been compelled to return to the lecture platform, where he tried to say funny things without success until the audience walked out leaving him alone in semi-darkness. And a third dream equally persistent carried Mark to a brilliant gathering in his night-clothes, where people looking suspiciously in his direction refuse to believe he is Twain, finally leaving him standing alone ashamed.[311]

308 *Ibid.*, IV, 1347–8.
309 *Notebook*, p. 397.
310 Paine, IV, 1351.
311 *Ibid.*, IV, 1368–9.

Yet fortune and acclaim continued for Clemens despite the nightmares; he lived extravagantly, his household expenses now amounting to more than fifty dollars a day.[312] But though he lived on a lavish scale, enjoying the best and giving his money away liberally, Mark was never wasteful, for his Boswell records that he was careful to turn down the gas-jets, objected violently to any over-charge, and abhorred any visible waste.[313] For an old friend, however, generosity was never lacking, as shown by his sending an expensive set of his books, each volume autographed, to Steve Gillis in California when Steve wrote that he was now an invalid with plenty of time to read Sam's books if he only had them.[314]

Christian Science appeared February 7, 1907.[315] Parts of the book were originally published in *Cosmopolitan* and the *North American Review,* but everything following the first hundred pages was entirely new.[316] In fact, there is evidence that Twain changed his mind during its course of preparation, for though the earlier portions are in a comic vein, the later portions are a serious estimate of Mrs. Eddy and her influence. The healing principle of Christian Science, or the importance of mind over matter, Mark never undervalued, but for the "ignorant village-born peasant woman" whose shrewdness had enabled her to capitalize on its principle by making it into a religion and a well-paying source of income he had only contempt; she was "a tramp stealing a ride on the lightning express."[317]

During the winter of 1907 Clemens went with Joe

312 *Ibid.,* IV, 1371.

313 *Idem.*

314 *Ibid.,* IV, 1373.

315 Johnson, *Bibliography, p.* 87.

316 The articles appeared in *Cosmopolitan,* October, 1899, and in the *North American Review* for December, 1902, and January, February, and April, 1903.

317 "Letters," *Portable Mark Twain,* p. 786. Here in a letter first published, Mark made a final reaffirmation of his opinion on the subject, August 7, 1909.

Twichell on a brief trip to Bermuda, their first since thirty years ago when they had been so charmed by the fresh greenness and full bloom of the island. Now they walked and drove about, happy as before. In March of the same year Albert Bigelow Paine made a journey to Hannibal which took him along the Mississippi to the cave and Holliday's hill, and then following the trail of Twain lore to the far West, he went in company with Joe Goodman to Jackass Hill for an unforgettable visit with Steve and Jim Gillis. Steve, now a hopeless invalid, sent Clemens this message: "Tell Sam I'm going to die pretty soon, but that I love him; that I've loved him all my life, and I'll love him till I die. This is the last word I'll ever send to him."[318] On his return from this trip, while coming up the river on one of the old steamers, Paine read in the paper that Mark Twain was to receive an Oxford degree. "I never expected to cross the water again, but I would be willing to journey to Mars for that Oxford degree," said Mark on Paine's arrival, then immediately fell to talking of Steve and Jim Gillis, recalling the days when Jim had stood back to the fire, improvising endless flights of grotesque fancy.[319]

On arrival in England Mark was again acclaimed everywhere, the climax being reached on June 26, 1907, when at the Sheldonian Theatre, to the strains of "God Save the King" he marched in the procession headed by Lord Curzon to "receive the highest academic honors which the world has to give."[320] Amid a cyclone of cheers from an enthusiastic audience came the shouts of the undergraduates: "Have you brought the Jumping Frog with you?" "Where is the Ascot Cup?"[321] During this visit Mark was honored by the Athenaeum and Garrick clubs in London, and elabo-

318 Paine, IV, 1377.

319 *Ibid.*, IV, 1379.

320 *Ibid.*, IV, 1393.

321 A newspaper placard had juxtaposed the headlines: "Mark Twain Arrives. Ascot Cup Stolen." *Ibid.*, IV, 1384.

rately entertained at the Dorchester House by the American ambassador. Clemens attended the King's garden party at Windsor Castle; he was also honored guest at a luncheon given by the Pilgrims at the Savoy. After reviewing the Oxford pageant from a box with Rudyard Kipling and Lord Curzon, Mark went to a dinner given by the Lord Mayor of London at the Mansion House. So many social functions were held in his honor that it was not until July 13 that he finally sailed for home.[322]

The following winter *Captain Stormfield's Visit to Heaven* appeared in *Harper's Magazine* for December, 1907, and January, 1908, without causing any furor. Originally intended as a burlesque of Elizabeth Stuart Phelps' *The Gates Ajar,* this extravaganza built upon Captain Ned Wakeman's dream was no longer blasphemous or irreverent to readers whose ideas about Christian orthodoxy had modified greatly since Clemens' youth.

With the death of Edmund Clarence Stedman on January 18, Mark was again reminded that he and Howells were the last lingering leaves from the literary tree of the past century. And as a bronchial cough threatened, Twain sailed that same month for Bermuda, where his cold disappeared the first day, leaving him free to enjoy the sunlight in the company of a delightful child, Margaret Blackmer, whom he adopted as a granddaughter after meeting her in the hotel dining-room.[323] Entertaining this youngster no doubt carried his memory back to days in Elmira when he had devised similar games for his own little girls. Twain enjoyed his stay in Bermuda so much that upon returning to New York and finding Mr. Rogers also suffering from poor health he persuaded his friend to return to Bermuda for another holiday. There they both enjoyed one of the happiest of vacations; referred to as "the King" and "the

[322] *Ibid.,* IV, 1403.

[323] *Ibid.,* IV, 1435.

Rajah" the two were the center of an admiring audience wherever they went, with Mark creating his following of young girls into an "Angel Fish Club."[324]

Though retired from the lecture platform, Twain continued to make a number of public addresses during the spring of 1908, his most impressive appearance being at the dedication of the City College of New York on May 14, during which the students gathered around shouting "Twain, Twain, Twain" followed by cheers for Tom Sawyer, Huck Finn, and Pudd'nhead Wilson. That night during a banquet at the Waldorf Mark spoke to them and advocated that the college found a chair of citizenship.[325]

Shortly thereafter the new house at Redding was completed and ready to receive him on June 18. Actually Mark had taken small part in planning the establishment beyond stipulating a large living room for the orchestrelle, a large billiard room which must be in red, and ample accommodations for guests. Otherwise he declared he did not even wish to see the place until the cat was purring on the hearth. When he did arrive Clemens declared, "It is a perfect house—perfect, so far as I can see, in every detail. It might have been here always."[326] There on that first evening Dan Beard, founder of the American Boy Scouts, led the other neighbors in a celebration of fireworks as Twain was welcomed to his new home.

The end of June saw the dedication of the Aldrich Memorial Museum. Mark has recorded his distaste for the vanity that inspired Mrs. Aldrich to dedicate such a memorial in the first place, and the shabby treatment accorded the guests, who were left to pay for what they had supposed to be a special train provided by the poet's wealthy widow.[327]

324 Elizabeth Wallace, *Mark Twain and the Happy Island* (Chicago: A. C. McClurg and Company, 1913), pp. 76–8.

325 Paine, IV, 1444.

326 *Ibid.*, IV, 1450.

327 *Mark Twain in Eruption*, pp. 298–9.

In August Clemens was shocked to receive news of Samuel E. Moffett's death by drowning, for this was his nearest male relative, Pamela's son, and a favorite nephew. Twain returned from the funeral greatly depressed; a day or so later he suffered an attack of illness which he thought biliousness, but which was perhaps the heart ailment that eventually caused his death. By now Clemens had determined to live the year round at "Stormfield"—the name given to the house because a wing was constructed with money received from the Captain's adventure—, and the house on Fifth Avenue was vacated. Now he spent most of his time playing billiards, reading, and entertaining guests, living a tranquil existence, bothered little by interest in public affairs or politics. Life at "Stormfield" was one of individual convenience, with guests eating when or where they pleased, while the afternoons were devoted to games—hearts or billiards.[328] And Mark usually spent the forenoon in bed, reading or looking over his mail. As summer turned to autumn he delighted in the changing colors of the Connecticut landscape; the red tones in the foliage pleased him so that he referred to the windows in his room as the picture gallery.

A procession of visitors called, and Mark delighted in the guest book, often making entries himself if somebody failed to supply all the information desired. When Billie Burke, the actress, signed the guestbook, December 27, 1908, Mark added: "Billie Burke, the young, the gifted, the beautiful, the charming, was the last guest to cross this threshold in 1908, thus she has a page to herself. . . . Her name is a pleasant one to close a pleasant year with."[329] Yet the social activities of Stormfield did not prevent his interesting himself in local community affairs. One of his first neighborly acts was to throw the new house open for inspection, and

[328] Paine, IV, 1461.
[329] Guest Book in Twain Collection at Berkeley, California.

not long afterward a gay party was held for everyone who had taken any part whatsoever in the building. Wishing to contribute permanently to the lives of his neighbors, Clemens thought of a public library to which he would give the surplus books flooding him from authors and publishers. An unused chapel was secured, which became the Mark Twain Library of Redding with a duly appointed librarian and elected officers, but Mark, anxious to have a more suitable building, hit upon the plan of asking contributions from his guests, who were admonished to contribute a dollar or go away without their baggage.[330]

When winter arrived with bad weather, Twain amused himself with the Shakespeare-Bacon problem; he had read *The Shakespeare Problem Restated* by George Greenwood, which seemed to him to clinch the argument of authorship in favor of Lord Verulam. Another book then in press, *Some Characteristic Signatures of Francis Bacon* by William Stone Booth, added the final touch of conviction, and Twain eventually published a small volume of his own on the subject, *Is Shakespeare Dead?* Though it contains no new arguments, it gives an amusing presentation of the old ones.[331] Like everyone else swept away by the desire to attribute authorship of the plays to others than the actor, Mark was not a profound student of Elizabethan drama as a whole; Shakespeare he knew, but not Dekker, Middleton, Webster, and the rest.

On a trip to Norfolk, Virginia, to speak at the opening ceremonies of the Virginia Railway, Clemens used the occasion to pay his personal respects to Henry H. Rogers, telling of Rogers' aid to Helen Keller, the deaf and dumb child who had learned to communicate her thoughts. Later in the same month H. H. Rogers died while Twain was on his way to meet his good friend and benefactor in New York,

330 Paine, IV, 1472. 331 *Ibid.*, IV, 1479.

the news reaching him as he alighted from the train. Mark, who served as pall-bearer at the funeral, felt the loss too deeply to talk about it.[332]

On the brighter side that year, a copyright bill was passed for which Twain had been fighting since his visit to the capital in 1906. Largely through the efforts of Champ Clark a bill had been forced through Congress to extend the copyright privileges for an extra fourteen years, and though not the bill Mark wished for, it was such an improvement that he accepted it gladly.[333]

Twain visited Baltimore, June 8, 1909, to address the graduating class of a little girl he had met in London two years earlier. On this trip he suffered the first definite attack of the heart disease which was to cause his death. But he quickly recovered to deliver at St. Timothy's School a delightful address in which he advised the girls not to smoke—to excess; not to drink—to excess; not to marry—to excess.[334]

That summer at Stormfield, to be his last, passed quietly, for Clemens seemed uninterested in company. Clara was preparing a concert tour, and Mark, eager for her success, urged her to spend her time in study. Jean, who now suffered from recurring attacks of epilepsy, spent most of her time collecting poultry and caring for animals. Though enduring attacks of angina which crumpled him with pain, Twain continued to walk about a good deal and to play billiards, never complaining of his ailment. Once he remarked, "I came in with Halley's comet in 1835. It is coming again next year, and I expect to go out with it."[335] Though he actually stated it would be a great disappointment not to depart from the earth with the comet, he discussed with Paine plans for finishing *The Mysterious*

[332] *Ibid.*, IV, 1492.
[333] *Ibid.*, IV, 1495.
[334] *Ibid.*, IV, 1498. See Mark Twain's *Speeches* (1910 edition), p. 107.
[335] *Ibid.*, IV, 1511.

Stranger, which existed in several forms, one of which his biographer advised working to a conclusion. And he continued to devise moral ideas, as he called them, a series of stories about Little Bessie, who plagued her mother with unorthodox questions about the scheme of things.[336]

The marriage of Clara to Ossip Gabrilowitsch, the concert-pianist, took place October 6, 1909, a perfect day of peaceful autumn. Only a few friends and relatives were invited, and Joe Twichell performed the ceremony. By request Mark wore his brilliant Oxford gown over his white clothes, and it was a happy occasion, one he declared Livy would have enjoyed.[337]

Now with Clara away and Jean unable to look after affairs Mark suffered the misfortune of a betrayal of trust from his private secretary. The young woman in question went on a three-day drunk, and it then came to light that she had been robbing him of money all along. Mark, however, refused to prosecute a woman, and simply turned all settlements over to Paine, who took charge as secretary and reduced monthly expenses to less than a third of what they had been.[338] The humiliation of a betrayed trust, another example of human perfidy, influenced Twain no doubt to write for his own satisfaction a book he felt could never stand publication, *Letters from the Earth.* Most of the ideas were ones he had long ago exhausted, but here with no restrictions of print he let his fancy free and exuberantly reveled in irreverence.

In the middle of November, 1909, Twain again visited Bermuda. Just the day before sailing, word came that Rich-

336 Though Paine declares these "Little Bessie" stories "not within the privilege of print," it is hoped that lapse of time has brought them from limbo. Professor Norman H. Pearson may give us an edition of them in the near future.

337 Paine, IV, 1524.

338 Paine said that he could run Stormfield, even with the family there, for $10,000 per year. *Twain Mss.*

ard Watson Gilder was dead, and the next morning brought news of the death of another friend, William M. Laffan. The leaves were now falling fast, but though he experienced an occasional paroxysm, none was severe and Mark enjoyed driving about the island, discussing philosophy or history and talking of a book which fascinated him, *The Pith of Astronomy*. Here he spent his seventy-fourth birthday, playing hearts by the fireside with no visitors save Helen Allen, one of the "Angel-fish" to whom he read several favorite passages from *Tom Sawyer*.[339] Of course, there was a cake, but no celebration, as cigars and fireside conversation quietly closed the evening.

In Bermuda Mark completed his last article for publication, "The Turning-Point of My Life," valuable as a final summation of his general philosophy, though as autobiography it was more entertaining than accurate. Interesting indeed, however, is his statement: "To me, the most important feature of my life is its literary feature. I have been professionally literary something more than forty years."[340] Deciding to return home for the holidays he found that rumors of ill health had preceded him. To these Mark cheerfully replied: "I hear the newspapers say I am dying. The charge is not true. I would not do such a thing at my time of life. I am behaving as good as I can. Merry Christmas to everybody!"[341]

Ironically, the last secretarial act of Jean for her father was telephoning his message to the associated press, for on Christmas Eve she was found dead in her bathtub, a victim of epileptic convulsion. And on Christmas day Jean's body was carried away amid a snowstorm such as had always delighted her, while Twain, too feeble in health himself to attend the funeral, stood sadly at the window of his empty

339 Paine, IV, 1545.

340 "The Turning Point of My Life," *What Is Man? and Other Essays*, p. 130.

341 Paine, IV, 1549.

house.[342] Next day as the snowstorm turned bitterly into a blizzard Mark composed a tribute to Jean, tenderly and sadly. It was, he said, the last of his autobiography.

Twain remained at Stormfield for ten days after Jean's death, the extremely cold weather persisting; then with Claude, his butler, Mark sailed again for Bermuda. There he was contented, and though he suffered occasional spasms of pain, his health seemed to improve in the mild climate. Among those visiting Twain at the Bay House was Woodrow Wilson, with whom pleasant hours were passed at miniature golf. Once when Wilson had beaten him Mark said, "Wilson, you will be the next President of the United States."[343] Clemens refused to allow his physical condition to dampen his enthusiasm or stifle his humor; but though he seemed all right, Paine noticed in March that his letters were dictated. When in April Paine learned that Twain's bronchial trouble had become serious, he proceeded straightway to Bermuda, at the same time advising Clara and her husband to sail at once from Europe.[344] Twain suffered several sinking spells during the journey home, which Paine feared they might not complete. Though Mark himself thought death near, he was calm and undismayed, showing consideration for his companion and regret at being such a care. Finally, the trip over, he was carried back to Stormfield, where upon arrival he insisted upon stepping from the carriage unaided, although he was then carried to his room by Paine and his man-servant.[345]

Halley's comet appeared in the sky, April 20, and next morning though clear in mind Twain had trouble speaking. He tried to write requests for his spectacles and a glass

342 Mark wrote in the Guest Book: "Night—at 6 p.m. the hearse and carriages moved toward the station. Jervis and Katy will take Jean to Elmira, where her mother, Susy and Langdon lie buried. A snow storm was raging. Clara is in Germany."

343 Paine, IV, 1560. 344 *Ibid.*, IV, 1563.

345 *Ibid.*, IV, 1574.

pitcher. Just after midday he reached to take Clara's hand, "Goodbye dear, if we meet," he said, and then passed into a doze lasting until about sunset, and at that time on April 21, 1910, Mark Twain peacefully died.[346]

From every corner of the earth condolences reached his daughter; newspapers round the world paid him tributes. Dressed in the white he had enjoyed, Twain was carried to the Brick Church in New York, where Dr. Henry van Dyke spoke briefly and Joseph Twichell delivered a prayer, broken with grief. As he lay in state thousands filed by the flower-covered bier, people from all walks of life, wishing to pay their devotion to a great author, a lovable personality, and a noble gentleman. Sunday afternoon, April 24, Clemens was quietly buried at Elmira, New York, by the side of his loved ones, while a slow, steady rain fell.[347]

Paradox: Romanticist and Realist

Mark Twain, in more ways than most authors, presents a paradox, for he appeared upon the world's stage in different rôles. In Hannibal he was Tom Sawyer gathering his band to adventure on Holliday's Hill; in Philadelphia, Keokuk, and Muscatine he was the journeyman printer observing while earning his way; on the mighty Mississippi he was the pilot, solvent and imposing, as the world passed in review; Nevada saw him in the rôles of miner and frontier journalist; California received him as a lecturer and author; and finally to the East came the pilgrim from his Innocent voyage to become the professional man of letters, the popular personality, and the genial ambassador at large to creation.

Indeed Mark Twain contained multitudes, and like the Whitman of "Song of Myself" was full of contradictions. The diversity of the human race he felt within, for there

346 Clara Clemens, *My Father, Mark Twain,* p. 291.
347 Paine, IV, 1580.

were no traits that he did not feel at times to be his own. Did he not say, "If the desire to kill and the opportunity to kill came always together, who would escape hanging?"[348] No doubt, much of the paradox arises from the very breadth of Twain's humanity; his stature does not admit the neat classification of a lesser figure; and because he observed from so many coigns of vantage, experience broadened his vision, intensified his feelings, deepened his sympathies. Sensitive by nature, aware by intellect, Clemens saw life more fully than the mere naturalist, more circumspectly than the unworldly idealist, for Mark Twain was both romanticist and realist, both idealist and satirist. And he was pessimist and optimist.

It was the romantic in him, the idealist, the optimist that produced *Tom Sawyer, Life on the Mississippi,* and *Joan of Arc.* It was the realist, satirist, and pessimist who wrote *The Mysterious Stranger, The Man That Corrupted Hadleyburg,* and *What Is Man?* But it was the combination of all that went into his masterpiece *The Adventures of Huckleberry Finn.* Through eyes of idealism boyhood Hannibal glowed until imagination bodied forth Tom Sawyer's band in those halcyon days of youth, preserved neverfading in the pages of that idyll. Yet it was the penetrating eye of the realist that pierced through the placid surface to picture the ugly and frightening violence present in certain episodes, and especially in the sequel.

Perhaps nowhere do the realist and idealist meet more abruptly in Clemens' writing than in *Those Extraordinary Twins,* a farce of little value except that it exemplifies Twain's methods and attitudes. One twin is an idealist, the other immersed in the material, both unfortunately inhabiting the same body and exemplifying concretely the duality of human nature. In the same manner the realist in Clemens caused him to see the evils, oppressions and

348 *Following the Equator,* II, 98.

corruptions, the faults, foibles, and vices of those about him; the idealist in his nature enabled him to perceive the qualities of truth, courage, and endurance by which the great souls advance the rest of humanity.

For all his pessimism about the human race at large Twain never lost his faith in the individual. His books are filled with nobility of character: Jim, Huck's companion on the raft, gentle, kind, and true; the Yankee, who went "grailing" at Arthur's court in devotion to democratic ideals; Miles Hendon, steadfast and loyal to the little pauper-prince; and Joan of Arc, culmination of all faith in the ultimate good of the human race.

Mark liked to disparage romance, even going so far as to accuse the romanticism of Sir Walter Scott of causing the Civil War. Romanticism in this sense dwelt in a world of shadows weaving its magic but futile web, totally apart from any realization of actuality. Such was Sally Sellers, kept from being a useful woman by dreams as unreal as any fabricated by the Lady of Shalott.[349] Mark disliked this romanticism because it did not front facts; it pretended things were not what they seemed. When it began to upset judgment, especially moral attitudes, Twain turned stoutly against it. In "A Curious Experience" he pictured a boy so completely confused by the cheap romance of dime novels that the world of imagination blinded him to the real. In the same vein, the hero and heroine of *The $30,000 Bequest* are utterly ruined by daydreaming. When romance began to envelop life with a deceptive haze, when it began to distort moral values, then Mark turned to tilt against it.

Mark Twain knew that the past should not be venerated simply because it was forever gone, but because it had possessed truth and beauty. The old orders change, and as

349 Sally appeared in *The American Claimant.* More recently Tennessee Williams has treated this theme in *The Glass Menagerie* and *A Streetcar Named Desire.*

Twain looked in retrospect he could not descry any one custom good enough to be held incorruptible. History was filled with crime, murder, robbery, and vice—all ages and all stratas. Yet amid this muck there arose from time to time a noble figure; such was the hope for humanity, not the mass but the individual who would hold to his ideals through fire and famine. For what the past had to offer that was inspirational Twain held high regard; he simply insisted upon examining antiques to determine if they were beautiful before he wasted his sentiments on old junk. Thus there appears what on the surface might be paradox, but which actually is not. Twain detested shams, he abhorred crimes, and along with them the false "romanticising" which turned black into white. But he did venerate the good, true, and beautiful, and he knew that genuine romance can ennoble. What he asked was that we look upon the past as it was, not as we would like to believe it to have been.

The realist in Twain made him a satirist, but his temper frequently diverted him to fulmination. As he confided to Howells, "a man can't write successful satire except he be in a calm, judicial good-humor."[350] And generally when Mark turned to satire he ended either with the uproarious burlesque so frequent in the *Yankee* or the bitter invective of *The Mysterious Stranger*. Yet there is satire directed against the cowardice, injustice, and stupidity of the human race, even though it generally takes the form of exuberant extravaganza or ironic denunciation. Such is the satire of *The Gilded Age* with its shots directed at politicians, speculators, and lobbyists, while the American juryman's tendency to yield to insanity pleas came in for a final blast. And the *Yankee,* burlesque extravaganza that it is, contains moral indignation dramatically presented; for it was the romanticist and idealist in Twain which made him yearn

350 *Letters,* I, 339.

for perfection and scorn ignobility, but it was the realist in his nature which perceived sham, pretense, and humbug. The aspirations of the romantic Mark knew from his own heart, but the counterbalance of realism prevented his sinking into sentimentality. The true realist in Clemens saw that this world is made of many shades and moods, verging close upon each other, until the wide gamut from the ideal height to the sorry dregs of animal naturalism are encompassed. This is the world of Shakespeare and Chaucer, alike the most romantic and real because of its sweeping inclusiveness, and it is also the world of Twain and Whitman. Perhaps the paradox in Samuel Clemens is explained by the paradox in nature, which old Walt so fully understood.

Sources of Pessimism

Mark Twain's pessimism, nevertheless, has been variously explained. The disasters of his later years alone seem sufficient to account for these dark moods; yet the prescience of world disaster is an equally valid explanation. Moreover, black moods alternating with lightheartedness appear a part of Mark's nature, and later in life as personal sorrow and world catastrophe weighed upon him they became more frequent. Back in 1876 he had written Mrs. Fairbanks a gloomy letter almost prophetic of his own personal disasters, one in which he expressed despondency over life and declared death a bringer of contentment.[351] Talking with Paine he declared that "the man who *isn't* a pessimist is a d——d fool,"[352] an expression of sentiment directly occasioned by reading about the murder of a woman engaged in settlement work among the Chinese. Though such pessimism was often the immediate result of some such personal reaction, there is also behind this tragic concept a broader view governing his general idea of life.

351 *Mark Twain to Mrs. Fairbanks,* pp. 199–200.
352 Paine, IV, 1508.

When Mark said that life would be infinitely happier if we could only begin at the age of eighty and approach eighteen,[353] he was not thinking of a loss of experience or the exchange of animal spirits for wisdom. Though fully aware of the growth of the individual mentally and spiritually, Twain was sensitive to the physical decay which must lead finally to mental impairment if the subject only lives long enough. Indeed, is not man eventually "the animal of the wig, the ear-trumpet, the glass eye, the porcelain teeth, the wooden leg, the trepanned skull, the silver windpipe—a creature that is mended and patched all over from top to bottom."[354] And nature, be it said, seems to delight in his discomfort:

> What is his beard for? It is just a nuisance. All nations persecute it with the razor. Nature, however, always keeps him supplied with it, instead of putting it on his head, where it ought to be. You seldom see a man bald-headed on his chin, but on his head. A man wants to keep his hair. It is a graceful ornament, a comfort, the best of all protections against weather, and he prizes it above emeralds and rubies, and Nature half the time puts it on so it won't stay.[355]

Of those compensatory attributes accruing with age, wisdom, experience, and the happiness growing therefrom, Mark was fully aware, for he himself possessed them. Yet he could not avoid feeling sorrowful that a man once strong, handsome, and virile should become a dotard, dependent upon those about him. At the same time he realized that youth may remain in spirit: "The heart is the real Fountain of Youth. While that remains young the Waterbury of Time must stand still."[356] Nobody better exemplified this than Clemens himself, or was likely to value it higher. Indeed, Livy always called him "Youth." Yet he

[353] This remark was quoted by William Lyon Phelps, *Autobiography With Letters* (New York: Oxford Press, 1939), p. 965.

[354] Paine, IV, 1363.

[355] *Ibid.*, IV, 1362.

[356] *Notebook*, p. 346.

could not escape the fact that the spirit, howsoever young, must remain with the body, which grows older with each passing day.

The origin of Mark's pessimism, however, was more than ontogenetic. Had not the course of human history been one of strife and bloodshed?—all ages had been filled with crime, ignorance, cowardice, and violence. His Yankee at the Court of Arthur encountered superstition, oppression, and injustice on every hand, while Joan of Arc, personification of idealism, suffered death at the stake. Reading history, Clemens found the human race selfish, stupid, bungling in the main, rescued from its bondage at times through the efforts of a few noble souls who offered their lives in atonement. But the race itself never improved; individual crime and mass murder through war persisted in spite of science and enlightenment. Intellectual progress was only perverted to wicked use for material gain and selfish power through exploitation. Every age had its prejudices, its own particular brand of witch-hunting: "The very ink with which all history is written is merely fluid prejudice."[357]

If the human race ought to be damned, then the blame must rest on the individual: "Every man is in his own person the whole human race, with not a detail lacking. I am the whole human race without a detail lacking; I have studied the human race with diligence and strong interest all these years in my own person; in myself I find in big or little proportion every quality and every defect that is findable in the mass of the race."[358]

Quick to blame himself, to make self-accusations, holding a rigid standard of high conduct, Mark Twain became convinced that he had failed even as the race itself. He blamed himself for Henry's death, he reproached himself

[357] *Following the Equator,* II, 366.
[358] *Mark Twain in Eruption,* p xxix.

for carelessness he imagined led to the fatal illness of his own son; he was saddened by the business failure which took him away to lecture at the time of Susy's death—always it had been his own shortcomings. In his moods of despair his faults, real or imagined, glared at him.

Closely intwined with feelings of self-reproach was the sense of personal misfortune. Here was a success story of monetary achievement, literary fame, individual popularity, world acclaim, and a beautiful, happy marriage,—success apparently in all respects; yet actually Twain felt himself cursed by the fates.[359] The deaths in his own family—Langdon, Susy, Livy, and Jean—left him with a sense of irretrievable loss; the financial disaster sending him back to the wearisome toil of the lecture platform, together with his failing health in old age, contributed to a general feeling of misfortune. Like Captain Ahab he cursed the fates.

Yet still another factor must be considered: perhaps the same which later caused T. S. Eliot to see a sterile wasteland from which mankind could be saved only by courageous efforts devoted to spiritual ideals; perhaps the same which led Robinson Jeffers to deplore the perishing republic, filled with violence and introversion. No doubt the pessimism of Twain bore kinship with the later ironies found in Robinson, Frost, and F. Scott Fitzgerald. Even Walt Whitman in his old age had lost some of his optimism over the future of the great democratic experiment. Mark deplored the plutocracy—so contrary and inferior to an aristocracy—which had replaced the ruling class of the early republic and the democracy of Jackson and Lincoln with the selfish and stupid money grabbers of the Gilded Age.[360] It was not the idea of capitalism, but the misuse of power that caused Twain to believe, as Jeffers was to assert

[359] See Bernard De Voto, "The Symbols of Despair," *Mark Twain at Work,* pp. 105–30.

[360] "The Plutocracy," *Mark Twain in Eruption,* pp. 61–70.

later, that our country was moving away from the democratic principles of the republic toward the evils of dictatorship. And it was not America alone that had deteriorated. Though he did not say it in so many words, Mark must have felt with Eliot that through Christianity lies the salvation of the race, for it was with the nations holding in belief—if not always in practice—to those principles that he placed his hopes for the future. "England must not fall," he declared; "it would mean an inundation of Russian and German political degradations which would envelop the globe and steep it in a sort of Middle-Age night and slavery which would last till Christ comes again."[361] Just four years after Clemens' death the German government, in defiance of its pledged treaty, hurled its armies against those who believed in a civilized world of law and order. Twenty-five years later occurred the second act in this savage drama of conquest.[362] One cannot ignore the element of prescience in Mark's despair for the human race.

SELECTED BIBLIOGRAPHY

THE MAIN EDITIONS OF TWAIN'S WRITINGS
(Listed Chronologically)

The Celebrated Jumping Frog of Calaveras County, and Other Sketches. New York: C. H. Webb, 1867.

The Innocents Abroad, or *The New Pilgrims' Progress.* Hartford: American Publishing Co., 1869.

Mark Twain's (Burlesque) Autobiography and First Romance. New York: Sheldon and Co., 1871.

Roughing It. Hartford: American Publishing Company, 1872.

The Gilded Age, in collaboration with Charles Dudley Warner. Hartford: American Publishing Company, 1874.

361 *Letters,* II, 693.

362 Winston Churchill in a speech at Massachusetts Institute of Technology March 31, 1949, deplored that this age of the common man had seen more mass-murder through scienific warfare than any other age in history.

Sketches, New and Old. Hartford: American Publishing Company, 1875.

The Adventures of Tom Sawyer. Hartford: American Publishing Company, 1876.

A True Story and the Recent Carnival of Crime. Boston: James R. Osgood and Co., 1877.

Punch, Brothers, Punch! and Other Sketches. New York: Slote, Woodman and Company, 1878.

1601, or *Conversation as It Was by the Fireside in the Time of the Tudors.* Cleveland edition of 1880, no publisher, n.p., n.d.

A Tramp Abroad. Hartford: American Publishing Company, 1880.

The Prince and the Pauper. Boston: James R. Osgood and Company, 1882.

The Stolen White Elephant. Boston: James R. Osgood and Company, 1882.

Life on the Mississippi. Boston: James R. Osgood and Company, 1883.

Adventures of Huckleberry Finn. New York: Charles L. Webster and Company, 1885.

A Connecticut Yankee in King Arthur's Court. New York: Charles L. Webster and Company, 1889.

Merry Tales. New York: Charles L. Webster and Company, 1892.

The American Claimant. New York: Charles L. Webster and Company, 1892.

The £1,000,000 Bank-Note and Other New Stories. New York: Charles L. Webster and Company, 1893.

Tom Sawyer Abroad. New York: Charles L. Webster and Company, 1894.

The Tragedy of Pudd'nhead Wilson and the Comedy Those Extraordinary Twins. Hartford: American Publishing Company, 1894.

Personal Recollections of Joan of Arc. New York: Harper and Brothers, 1896.

Tom Sawyer Abroad, Tom Sawyer, Detective, and Other Stories. New York: Harper and Brothers, 1896.

How to Tell a Story and Other Essays. New York: Harper and Brothers, 1897.

Following the Equator. Hartford: American Publishing Company, 1897.

The Man That Corrupted Hadleyburg and Other Stories and Essays. New York: Harper and Brothers, 1900.

How to Tell a Story and Other Essays. Hartford: American Publishing Company, 1900.

English as She Is Taught. Boston: Mutual Book Company, 1900.

Edmund Burke on Croker and Tammany. New York: Economist Press, 1901.

A Double Barrelled Detective Story. New York: Harper and Brothers, 1902.

My Debut as a Literary Person with Other Essays and Stories. Hartford: American Publishing Company, 1903.

A Dog's Tale. New York: Harper and Brothers, 1904.

Extracts from Adam's Diary. New York: Harper and Brothers, 1904.

King Leopold's Soliloquy: a Defense of His Congo Rule. Boston: P. R. Warner Company, 1905.

Eve's Diary. New York: Harper and Brothers, 1906.

The $30,000 Bequest and Other Stories. New York: Harper and Brothers, 1906.

Christian Science. New York: Harper and Brothers, 1907.

A Horse's Tale. New York: Harper and Brothers, 1907.

Is Shakespeare Dead? New York: Harper and Brothers, 1909.

Extract from Captain Stormfield's Visit to Heaven. New York: Harper and Brothers, 1909.

Mark Twain's Speeches. New York: Harper and Brothers, 1910.

The Mysterious Stranger. New York: Harper and Brothers, 1916.

Mark Twain's Letters. New York: Harper and Brothers, 1917.

What Is Man? and Other Essays. New York: Harper and Brothers, 1917.

The Curious Republic of Gondour and Other Whimsical Sketches. New York: Boni and Liveright, 1919.

The Mysterious Stranger and Other Stories. New York: Harper and Brothers, 1922.

Europe and Elsewhere. New York: Harper and Brothers, 1923.

Mark Twain's Speeches, revised edition. New York: Harper and Brothers, 1923.

Mark Twain's Autobiography. New York: Harper and Brothers, 1924.

Sketches of the Sixties by Bret Harte and Mark Twain. San Francisco: John Howell, 1926. Revised, enlarged edition, 1927.

The Adventures of Thomas Jefferson Snodgrass. Chicago: Pascal Covici, 1928.

Mark Twain's Notebook. New York: Harper and Brothers, 1935.

Slovenly Peter (Der Struwwelpeter) translated by Mark Twain. New York: Harper and Brothers, 1935.

The Washoe Giant in San Francisco, Sketches for the *Golden Era.* San Francisco: George Fields, 1938.

Mark Twain's Letters from the Sandwich Islands. Palo Alto: Stanford University Press, 1938.

Letters from Honolulu. Honolulu: Thomas Nickerson, 1939.

Mark Twain's Travels with Mr. Brown. New York: Alfred A. Knopf, 1940.

Mark Twain in Eruption. New York: Harper and Brothers, 1940.

Mark Twain's Letters to Will Bowen. Austin: University of Texas, 1941.

Republican Letters. Webster Groves, Missouri: International Mark Twain Society, 1941.

Mark Twain's Letters in the Muscatine Journal. Chicago: The Mark Twain Association of America, 1942.

Washington in 1868. Webster Groves, Missouri: International Mark Twain Society, 1943.

The Letters of Quintus Curtius Snodgrass. Dallas: Southern Methodist University Press, 1946.

Mark Twain in Three Moods. San Marino: Huntington Library, 1948.

Mark Twain to Mrs. Fairbanks. San Marino: Huntington Library, 1949.

The Love Letters of Mark Twain. New York: Harper and Brothers, 1949.

Report from Paradise. New York: Harper and Brothers, 1952.

STANDARD SETS

The Writings of Mark Twain, Uniform Edition, 25 vols. New York: Harper and Brothers, 1899–1910.

The Writings of Mark Twain, Definitive Edition, 37 vols. New York: Gabriel Wells, 1923–1925.

[This edition contains a page bearing the autograph and signed pseudonym of the author; it was limited to 1024 sets. Although it was called "Definitive," actually no such edition of Twain exists.]

Mark Twain's Works, Stormfield Edition, 37 vols. New York: Harper and Brothers, 1929.

Numerous sets of Twain have been issued, such as the Limp Leather Edition and Mississippi Edition, but there is none in print now. For a description of some of the more interesting ones see Merle Johnson's *A Bibliography of the Works of Mark Twain,* pp. 150–3.

IMPORTANT EDITIONS OF SEPARATE VOLUMES

Huckleberry Finn in *Four Great American Novels,* edited by Raymond W. Short. New York: Henry Holt & Co., 1946.

[An illuminating introduction, useful to the student.]

Huckleberry Finn in *The Portable Mark Twain,* edited by Bernard De Voto. New York: Viking Press, 1946.

[Prints the raftsman's passage in Chapter XVI, which is always omitted and placed in *Life on the Mississippi,* where Mark used it, although it was originally written for Huck.]

The Adventures of Huckleberry Finn, with Introductions by Brander Matthews and Dixon Wecter. New York: Harper and Brothers, 1948.

[Two interesting comments by two acute critics of different generations.]

The Adventures of Huckleberry Finn, Introduction by Lionel Trilling. Rinehart & Company, 1948.

[The finest essay yet on the true greatness of Twain's masterpiece.]

The Adventures of Huckleberry Finn, Introduction by T. S. Eliot. New York: Chanticleer Press, 1950.

The Adventures of Tom Sawyer, Introduction by Bernard DeVoto. New York: Limited Editions Club, 1939.

Life on the Mississippi, edited by Willis Wager, with an Introduction by Edward Wagenknecht. New York: Heritage Press, 1944.

[The complete edition, based on the manuscript.]

Life on the Mississippi, Introduction by Dixon Wecter. New York: Harper and Brothers, 1950.

[Important introduction.]

UNCOLLECTED WRITINGS AND MANUSCRIPTS

For the uncollected writings of Mark Twain the student should consult the bibliographies in Albert Bigelow Paine's *Mark Twain: A Biography,* Edward Wagenknecht's *Mark Twain: The Man and His Work,* DeLancey Ferguson's *Mark Twain: Man and Legend,* Kenneth R. Andrews' *Nook Farm: Mark Twain's Hartford Circle,* and the files of *The Twainian.*

The most important manuscript collection is that of the Mark Twain Literary Estate, University of California at Berkeley, which contains vast unpublished materials. Other important collections are at Yale University and in the New York Public Library.

THE MAN OF LETTERS

Andrews, Kenneth R. *Nook Farm: Mark Twain's Hartford Circle.* Cambridge, Massachusetts: Harvard University Press, 1950.

[Detailed study of Twain's Connecticut environment and its influence.]

Anon., "Dan Beard Tells All About Those 'Yankee' Pictures," *Twainian,* III, 4–5 (October, 1943).

[The artist's notes on the Yankee illustrations.]

Bellamy, Gladys Carmen. *Mark Twain as a Literary Artist* Norman: University of Oklahoma Press, 1950.

[Useful and stimulating.]

Blodgett, Harold, "A Note on Mark Twain's Library of Humor," *American Literature,* X, 78–80 (March, 1938).

Brooks, Van Wyck. *The Ordeal of Mark Twain.* New York: E. P. Dutton & Company, revised edition, 1933.
[More perceptive of Twain's feelings than of his thought or action.]

——. *The Times of Melville and Whitman.* New York: E. P. Dutton & Co., 1947.
[Interesting treatment by a severe critic.]

Brownell, George H. "Kipling's Meeting with Mark Twain," *American Book Collector,* IV, 191–2 (September–October, 1933).
[Based on Kipling's account in the New York *Herald,* August 17, 1890.]

——. "Mark Twainiana," *American Book Collector,* V, 124–6 (April, 1934).
[Twain's contacts with some contemporary journalists.]

Burton, Richard. "Mark Twain in the Hartford Days," *Mark Twain Quarterly,* I, 5 (Summer, 1937).
[Personal recollections.]

Clemens, Clara. *My Father, Mark Twain.* New York: Harper & Brothers, 1931.
[A valuable intimate picture by Clemens' daughter.]

Clemens, Cyril. *Mark Twain the Letter Writer.* Boston: Meador Publishing Company, 1932.
[Newspaper stories about Twain and bits of letters, not arranged in order.]

DeVoto, Bernard. *Mark Twain at Work.* Cambridge, Massachusetts: Harvard University Press, 1942.
[Not biography, but an interesting account of how Clemens wrote, and a penetrating analysis of his pessimism.]

Donner, Stanley T. "Mark Twain as a Reader," *Quarterly Journal of Speech,* XXXIII, 308–11 (October, 1947).

Eastman, Max. "Mark Twain's Elmira," *Harper's Magazine,* CLXVI, 620–32 (May, 1938).
[Important article on the social and religious attitudes of the Langdons and their friends.]

Ferguson, DeLancey. "The Case for Mark Twain's Wife," *University of Toronto Quarterly,* IX, 9–21 (October, 1939).
[Further refutation of the Brooks thesis.]

——. "Mark Twain's Lost Curtain Speeches," *South Atlantic Quarterly,* XLII, 262–9 (July, 1943).

[Reprints three speeches at presentations of *The Gilded Age* and *Ah Sin.*]

——. *Mark Twain: Man and Legend.* Indianapolis: Bobbs-Merrill, 1943.

[Good narrative, based on facts.]

Flack, F. M. "About the Play 'Roughing It' as Produced by Augustin Daly," *Twainian,* V, 1–3 (July–August, 1946).

Gates, William B. "Mark Twain to His English Publishers," *American Literature,* XI, 78–81 (March, 1939).

[Four Twain letters showing a cordial relationship with Chatto and Windus.]

Hemminghaus, Edgar H. *Mark Twain in Germany.* New York: Columbia University Press, 1939.

[Discusses Twain's ideas which appealed to the German mind.]

Henderson, Archibald, *Mark Twain.* New York: Frederick A. Stokes Company, 1911.

[Discusses Twain as sociologist and philosopher.]

Howells, Mildred. *Life in Letters of William Dean Howells.* Garden City, N.Y.: Doubleday, Doran & Co., 1928.

[Contains Twain items.]

Howells, William Dean. *My Mark Twain.* New York: Harper & Brothers, 1910.

[Twain's mind as revealed to an intimate friend.]

Lawton, Mary. *A Lifetime With Mark Twain.* New York: Harcourt, Brace & Company, 1925.

[The memories of Katy Leary, for thirty years a servant in the Clemens household, an interesting contribution.]

Leacock, Stephen. *Mark Twain.* New York: D. Appleton & Co., 1933.

Lemonnier, Léon. *Mark Twain: L'Homme et Son Oeuvre.* Paris: Librairie Artheme Fayard, 1946.

[Briefly treats Twain's thought.]

Liljegren, S. B. *The Revolt Against Romanticism in American Literature as Evidenced in the Works of S. L. Clemens.* Upsala: Lundequistska Bokhandeln, 1945.

[Relates Clemens to the stream of European realism.)

Lorch, Fred W. "Lecture Trips and Visits of Mark Twain in Iowa," *The Iowa Journal of History and Politics,* XXVII, 507–547 (October, 1929).

[Details of Twain's Iowa visits from 1867 to 1890.]

——. "Mark Twain in Iowa," *The Iowa Journal of History and Politics,* XXVII, 409–56, 507–47 (July, 1929).

[New facts of biography on Muscatine and Keokuk periods, 1853–55. First printing of two letters to Annie Taylor and three "Snodgrass" letters.]

The Love Letters of Mark Twain, edited by Dixon Wecter. New York: Harper & Brothers, 1949.

[Valuable addition to our knowledge of Twain's ideas, especially religion and politics.]

Mark Twain's Autobiography, edited by A. B. Paine. New York: Harper & Brothers, 1924.

[Must be checked always against other sources.]

Mark Twain in Eruption, edited by Bernard DeVoto. New York: Harper & Brothers, 1940.

[Autobiographical papers from the Clemens Literary Estate, a valuable contribution to our knowledge of Twain's mind and thought.]

Mark Twain's Letters, edited by A. B. Paine. New York; Harper & Brothers, 1917.

[Useful, but not complete.]

Mark Twain's Letters to Will Bowen, edited by Theodore Hornberger. Austin: University of Texas, 1941.

[Sixteen letters from Twain to "My First & Oldest & Dearest Friend," interesting for reminiscences about Hannibal.]

Mark Twain to Mrs. Fairbanks, edited by Dixon Wecter. San Marino, California: Huntington Library, 1949.

[Interesting correspondence adding to our knowledge of Twain's mind.]

Mark Twain's Notebook, prepared for publication by Albert Bigelow Paine. New York: Harper & Brothers, 1935.

[Selections from Twain's journals, brief and sketchy but important.]

Mark Twain's Speeches, with an Introduction by Albert Bigelow Paine, and an Appreciation by William Dean Howells. New York: Harper & Brothers, 1923.

[A selection of Twain's speeches, not complete.]

Matthews, Brander. "Memories of Mark Twain," *The Tocsin of Revolt.* New York: Charles Scribner's Sons, 1922, pp. 253–94.

[Interesting biographical contribution.]

Masters, Edgar Lee. *Mark Twain: A Portrait.* New York: Charles Scribner's Sons, 1938.

[Repeats all the fallacies of the Brooks theory; of no value to the student of Twain.]

Paine, Albert Bigelow. *Mark Twain: A Biography.* New York: Harper & Brothers, 1912. 3 vols., revised in 2 vols., 1935.

[Invaluable; intimate and full account by Clemen's personal secretary.]

Parrington, Vernon L. "The Culture of the Seventies" in *Main Currents in American Thought.* New York: Harcourt, Brace & Co., III, 86–101.

[Still an interesting appraisal of Twain's mind.]

Peabody, E. F. "Mark Twain's Ghost Story," *Minnesota History,* XVIII, 28–35 (March, 1937).

[Comments on the Twain-Cable lecture tour in Minnesota, 1884–5.]

Pellowe, William C. S. *Mark Twain: Pilgrim from Hannibal.* New York: Hobson Book Press, 1945.

[Fullest discussion of Twain's religion.]

Phelps, William L. "Mark Twain," *Yale Review,* XXV, 291–310 (Winter, 1936).

[Presents Twain as a shrewd observer and a great artist.]

Quick, Dorothy. "My Author's League with Mark Twain," *North American Review,* CCXLV, 315–29 (Summer, 1938).

[Twain's friendship for a little girl and letters to her.]

Schönemann, Friedrich. *Mark Twain als literarische Persönlichkeit.* Jena: Verlag der Frommanschen Buchhandlung, Walter Biedermann, 1925.

[The most important German study of Twain's ideas.]

Schultz, John R. "New Letters of Mark Twain," *American Literature,* VIII, 47–51 (March, 1936).

[Letters to Bayard Taylor in 1878 about experiences in Germany and difficulties with the language.]

Taylor, Walter Fuller. *The Economic Novel in America.* Chapel Hill: University of North Carolina Press, 1942.

[Fullest discussion of Twain's economic thought; refutes charge of not expressing his opinions.]

Underhill, Irving S. "The Haunted Book: A Further Exploration Concerning Huckleberry Finn," *Colophon,* I, 281–91 (Autumn, 1935).

[Bibliographical details of the first edition.]

Vogelback, Arthur Lawrence. "The Publication and Reception of *Huckleberry Finn* in America," *American Literature,* XI, 260–272 (November, 1939).
[Indicates failure of the critics to perceive a masterpiece.]

Wagenknecht, Edward. *Mark Twain: The Man and His Work.* New Haven: Yale University Press, 1935.
[Important; examines Twain's mind and work.]

Wallace, Elizabeth. *Mark Twain and the Happy Island.* Chicago: A. C. McClurg & Company, 1913.
[A charming picture of Clemens' visits to Bermuda.]

Webster, Samuel Charles. *Mark Twain, Business Man.* Boston: Little, Brown, and Company, 1946.
[Adds to our knowledge of Mark's environment.]

CHAPTER IV

MIND AND ART

SOURCES

TWAIN, LIKE all writers, drew source material from experience, either through actual contact or vicariously from reading. Perhaps more than any other American author of first rank his work assumes autobiographical characteristics; yet evidences of source materials from books are not infrequent.

More than twelve years prior to Mark's "Jumping Frog" the Sonora *Herald* printed "A Toad Story," probably written by the editor, Walter Murray.[1] Something over five years later Samuel Seabough printed a frog yarn in the San Andreas *Independent* (1858). However, the Sonora *Herald* version is the merest sketch with no characters developed, while Sam Seabough's tale, though more elaborate, remains a brief sketch of similar type. It is evident that the frog story was known in California, but only locally, for it awaited the pen of Mark Twain to give it currency on both coasts.[2] There is no evidence, by the way, that Clemens ever saw either one of these sketches.[3] The source for the story, on the other hand, was really old Ben Coon, garrulous derelict of Jackass Hill, who spun the yarn for

[1] Oscar Lewis, *The Origin of the Celebrated Jumping Frog of Calaveras County* (San Francisco: Book Club of California, 1931), p. 9. "A Toad Story" appeared June 11, 1853.

[2] Twain's story printed in the New York *Saturday Press,* November 18, 1865, was copied in a dozen Pacific coast journals within a few weeks, including the *Californian* and the *Golden Era. Ibid.,* p. 19.

[3] *Ibid.,* p. 8.

Mark's ears as it had been told around the campfires of mining camps for decades.[4]

DeLancey Ferguson points out that the realistic, unpoetic Mr. Brown, pervading Mark's humor throughout the Sandwich Island journey, even continuing into the trip that produced the *Innocents,* obviously derived from Oliver Wendell Holmes' *The Autocrat of the Breakfast Table.*[5] In fact, Mark later unconsciously borrowed his dedication for the *Innocents* from a volume of Dr. Holmes' poems.[6] For like everyone else Twain read the popular New Englander, who in the *Autocrat* created a young character named John to provide humor through a crude and materialistic interpretation of the older man's more ideal philosophizing. And Mark saw how such a creation of his own, Mr. Brown, might serve equally as a projected, though detached, aspect of his nature, through whom bodily vulgarities and mental crudities could be expressed.[7]

Though the *Innocents Abroad* is obviously based upon Clemens' journey to Europe and the Holy Land, even it had forerunners, which may have served as sources, for instance Samuel Fiske's *Mr. Dunne Browne's Experiences in Foreign Parts,* published in Boston, 1857, which presented a traveler who found a great deal of fault with European art, even as he mistook the Thames for a creek.[8] Likewise J. Ross Browne, whose earlier life had been rather similar to Twain's, had written satires of travel literature in *Yusef* (1853).[9] Whether or not Mark read these books we do not

4 Mark's own notation of the plot appears in *Notebook,* p. 7.

5 *Mark Twain: Man and Legend,* p. 106. See also Bradford A. Booth, "Mark Twain's Comments on Holmes's *Autocrat,*" *American Literature,* XXI, 456–463 (January, 1950).

6 *Autobiography,* I, 238–242.

7 See *Mark Twain's Travels with Mr. Brown.* Though Brown disappears from the *Innocents* he may be found in the *Alta California* letters.

8 Walter Blair, *Native American Humor* (New York: American Book Co., 1937), p. 155.

9 *Ibid.,* p. 158.

actually know, for especially in the case of J. Ross Browne, the similarities in outlook could have arisen from their common background of frontier environment. However, one definite source, at least as it furnished inspiration for burlesque, was William C. Prime's *Tent Life in the Holy Land,* of which Mark wrote to the *Alta:*

> I have read all the books on Palestine, nearly, that have been printed, and the authors all wept. When Mr. Prime was here, before he wrote his curious "Tent Life in the Holy Land," he wept, and his party all wept, and the dragoman wept, and so did the muleteers, and even a Latin priest, and a Jew that came straggling along. It would have been just as cheap to believe that the camels and the asses wept also, and fully as likely; and he might as well have added them to the water company likewise. Prime got such a start then that he never could shut himself off; and he went through Palestine and irrigated it from one end to the other.[10]

Even as his *Yusef* had anticipated the *Innocents,* J. Ross Browne was in the field of Western writing ahead of Mark with *Adventures in the Apache Country* (1869), using the same tricks of humor and employing the same journalistic appeal as may be found in *Roughing It.*[11] And there were other sketches by Browne—depictions of his fellow travelers, tales of the great rush to Washoe, incidents found on the Comstock Lode—all in *Crusoe's Island* (1864).[12] Again we do not actually know if Twain was indebted to his forerunner, who won slight recognition and dropped from view, for both covered the same ground under very similar circumstances.

With *The Gilded Age,* however, there is more definite evidence. DeVoto believes that J. M. Field's *The Drama in Pokerville* (1847) furnished most of the details for Chapter IV of that volume, in which Laura is brought into the

10 Leon T. Dickinson, "Mark Twain's Revisions in Writing *The Innocents Abroad,*" *American Literature,* XIX, 155 (May, 1947).

11 Blair, *op. cit.,* p. 158.

12 Effie Mona Mack, *Mark Twain in Nevada,* p. 28.

story.[13] And Franklin Walker reminds us of a notorious trial that took place in San Francisco, certain details of which bear marked similarities to the plot and characterization in *The Gilded Age*.[14] In a general manner, however, the character types and contrasts may have derived from Thackeray's *Vanity Fair*.[15] Wagenknecht, by the way, sees a similarity to Dickens in Sellers' description of the clock in Chapter VII, while he believes that Senator Dilworthy's speech in Chapter XXII, Volume II, might have been directly modeled on that of the Rev. Mr. Chadband in Chapter XIX of *Bleak House*.[16]

Though Mark has told us how he based *The Adventures of Tom Sawyer* upon his own youth, there is here again evidence of other sources.[17] Walter Blair points out the similarity of Aunt Polly to Shillaber's Mrs. Partington.[18] Franklin J. Meine discovered, moreover, that the identical picture of Shillaber's character was used to illustrate Aunt Polly in Tom Sawyer; they even look alike.[19] Will D. Howe noticed several decades ago that Mrs. Partington and Aunt Polly held a similar Calvinistic attitude toward punishing their respective nephews, Ike and Tom, for their acts of mischief.[20] Walter Blair in further substantiation parallels a passage from Chapter III of *Tom Sawyer* with a similar conversation in Shillaber's *Knitting-Work* (1859).[21] Chapter XVIII of Mark's story, on the other hand, suggests the inventive boy of Longstreet's "Georgia Theatrics," who triumphantly defeated an imaginary opponent.[22] Another

13 *Mark Twain's America*, pp. 253–4.

14 Franklin Walker, "An Influence from San Francisco on Mark Twain's *The Gilded Age*," *American Literature*, VIII, 63–66 (March, 1936).

15 DeLancey Ferguson, *Mark Twain: Man and Legend*, p. 170.

16 *Mark Twain: The Man and His Work*, p. 270.

17 *Autobiography*, I, 102–5.

18 *Native American Humor*, p. 151.

19 *Idem.*

20 *The Cambridge History of American Literature* (New York: Macmillan, 1918), II, 155.

21 *Op. cit.*, p. 152.

22 *Ibid.*, p. 153.

Southwestern humorist, George W. Harris, may also have contributed to the plot with a sketch suggesting the boys in the loft who played jokes on the teacher in Chapter XXI.[23] Then Mark's own sketches written for the *Golden Era,* such as "Those Blasted Children," may have been a reminder to him—not alone in themselves—but to recall humor of a kindred pattern. Yet memories were varied, for Mark read Poe during his days in Keokuk and "The Gold Bug" seems to have lent its influence on Tom Sawyer's treasure hunt.[24]

It was a juvenile volume, an English story concerning the thirteenth century by Charlotte M. Yonge, *The Prince and the Page,* which gave Clemens the idea for *The Prince and the Pauper.* Albert Bigelow Paine, however, declared that all Twain received from the earlier volume was mere suggestion.[25] Actually Clemens made greater use of *The English Rogue* by Richard Head and Francis Kirkman, first published in London, 1665–1680, from which he acquired a general knowledge of the lower social orders. Several passages about beggars in *The Prince and the Pauper* closely parallel similar ones in *The English Rogue.*[26] Twain wished this novel to be considered seriously as social history, and since he believed fiction based on fact superior to that based on imagination, he drew upon *The English Rogue* for atmosphere and specific customs which he incorporated into the pauper backgrounds. He probably used a four-volume reprint, published in 1874.

For many devices in *Life on the Mississippi,* DeVoto believes that Twain went directly to the humorists who pre-

[23] "A Razor-Grinder in a Thunder Storm," which has the same tone. *Ibid.,* p. 155.

[24] DeLancey Ferguson, *op. cit.,* p. 26. Van Wyck Brooks finds further influence from Poe in the macabre humor of "Aurelia's Young Man," and the hoaxes, such as "The Petrified Man" and "My Bloody Massacre." *The Times of Melville and Whitman,* p. 286.

[25] Paine, II, 597.

[26] Leon T. Dickinson, "The Sources of *The Prince and the Pauper,*" *Modern Language Notes,* LXIV, 104 (February, 1949).

ceded him, even though the indebtedness shades into generalizations.[27] The misquotations, ramblings, and garrulities may be traced to Longstreet and Hooper. The tall talk, such as in the raftsmen passage, has the ring of authentic reporting, yet numerous examples existed in the Davy Crockett books, in the "Polly Peablossom's Wedding" of T. A. Burke, and in the type-specimen of them all, *The Big Bear of Arkansaw*. For the rest of his narrative Mark drew his material from his own contributions on piloting, published in the *Atlantic* in 1875.

Life on the Mississippi presents the raw material from which Twain's masterpiece *Huckleberry Finn* was made. For instance, the feud between the Darnells and the Watsons in Chapter XXVI of the former improved through artistic transmutation to become the Grangerford-Shepherdson episodes.[28] But there were outside sources. Blair believes that the passage about Huck's trip to the circus may have come from one of the frontier humorists: W. T. Thompson, G. W. Harris, or Richard Malcolm Johnston, though the evidence indicates strongest probability of Johnston, whose "The Expensive Treat of Col. Moses Grice" was well known to Huck's creator.[29] DeVoto, on the other hand, thinks that this same passage "rests solidly" on William Tappan Thompson's "The Great Attraction."[30] And DeVoto believes also that the playbill produced by the Duke of Bilgewater derived from J. M. Field's *The Drama in Pokerville,* while the mutilated Shakespeare speech composed for the King to render as Juliet was perhaps from one

27 *Mark Twain's America,* p. 256.

28 Edward Wagenknecht, Introduction to *Life on the Mississippi* (New York: Heritage Press, 1944), p. vii.

29 *Native American Humor,* p. 154.

30 *Mark Twain's America,* p. 254. D. M. McKeithan sees the influence of Thompson in the first Snodgrass letters. "Mark Twain's Letters of Thomas Jefferson Snodgrass," *Philological Quarterly,* XXXII, 353–65 (October, 1953).

of the books by Sol Smith, *Theatrical Apprenticeship* (1845) or *Theatrical Journey Work* (1854).[31] The King's visit to the camp meeting has marked identity with Chapter X of *The Adventures of Simon Suggs* by Johnson J. Hooper, the only instance, by the way, in which DeVoto thinks Twain failed to surpass his original.[32]

We should not forget Jim Gillis of Jackass Hill, at this point, for Jim's artistic narration of "The Burning Shame" was to assume literary permanence in Chapter XXIII of *Huckleberry Finn*.[33] Then there are the scholarly considerations of Olin H. Moore, who sees the influence of Cervantes and believes that Mark made Huck into "a prosaic Sancho Panza, a foil to the brilliant Tom Sawyer."[34]

A Connecticut Yankee in King Arthur's Court has, as DeVoto suggests, affiliations with the Jack Downing letters.[35] Here is political and economic satire, present in Down East humor before it reached amplification through the authors of the Old Southwest and the literary comedians, but it is now given expression of genius.[36] Miss Constance Rourke perceives even more of the native humor tradition in the sources for this book, believing that Twain wrote the *Yankee* in the same spirit as the *Innocents*, something of a grotesque naturalism, critical of ancient myth. She sees the Boss akin to "such creatures of the American fancy as Sam Slick and Sam Patch."[37] Of course, as both Paine and Clemens have told us, it was the reading of

31 *Idem.*

32 *Ibid.*, p. 255.

33 DeLancey Ferguson, *op. cit.*, p. 102.

34 Professor Moore believes, also, that Cervantes influenced *The Innocents Abroad, Life on the Mississippi, Tom Sawyer,* and *A Connecticut Yankee*. "Mark Twain and Don Quixote," *Publications of the Modern Language Association,* XXXVII, 324–46 (June, 1922).

35 *Mark Twain's America,* p. 272.

36 DeVoto mentions Simon Suggs and Crockett's campaign documents as part of a fecund tradition. *Idem.*

37 *American Humor,* p. 215.

Malory's *Morte d'Arthur* which first stimulated his imagination.[38]

Always interested in inventions, Twain as early as 1868 toyed with the idea of a story about a balloon trip, but it was not completed until *Tom Sawyer Abroad* appeared in 1894. The title page announced that the book was by Huck Finn, edited by Mark Twain, and many of the incidents are from the same sources that furnished the inspiration for Mark's earlier volumes about Tom and Huck; but D. M. McKeithan has demonstrated that there is also an indebtedness to Jules Verne's *Five Weeks in a Balloon.*[39] An English translation of Verne's romance was published in the United States in 1869, and its similarities to some of the balloon adventures of Tom, Huck, and Jim are close enough to indicate that Clemens had read it. But the most valuable parts of *Tom Sawyer Abroad,* the characters and their conversations, are Twain's own creations.

Of *Tom Sawyer, Detective,* Twain himself stated, "It transfers to the banks of the Mississippi the incidents of a strange murder which was committed in Sweden in old times."[40] Actually it was in Denmark in the seventeenth century. In a footnote to this story when published Twain affirmed the incidents to be facts, "even to the public confession of the accused."[41] Taking the strange events recorded in the story of this criminal trial, Mark claimed that he merely changed the characters and scenes to America.[42]

38 Paine, II, 790; *Notebook,* p. 171. See, also, Robert H. Wilson, "Malory in the Connecticut Yankee," *University of Texas Studies in English,* XXVII, 185–205.

39 "Mark Twain's *Tom Sawyer Abroad* and Jules Verne's *Five Weeks in a Balloon,*" *University of Texas Studies in English,* XXVIII, 257–270 (1949).

40 *Letters,* II, 623. 41 Quoted in Johnson, *Bibliography,* p. 63.

42 Steen Steenson Blicher's *The Parson of Vejlby* has the same plot as *Tom Sawyer Detective.* Mark never read it, but heard the story from an acquaintance. See J. Christian Bay, "Tom Sawyer Detective: the Origin of the Plot," *Essays Offered to Herbert Putnam by His Colleagues and Friends on His Thirtieth Anniversary as Librarian of Congress* (New Haven: Yale University Press, 1929), pp. 80–88.

For *Joan of Arc* Clemens did more research than for any other book. Mentor L. Williams summarizes the works used in preparation for the *Personal Recollections:*

In 1850, J. E. J. Quicherat examined and edited the original documents connected with Joan's rehabilitation. Jules Michelet's moving and sympathetic story, *Jeanne d'Arc,* appeared in 1856; H. A. Wallon's unbiased, objective history was published in 1876; and Janet Tuckey's biography in 1880. Joseph Fabre reworked Quicherat's materials into a masterpiece of historical writing in 1883, and Lord Ronald Gower's biography appeared in 1893.[43]

Mark once said that for the first two-thirds of the book he used "only one French history and one English one," but for the last third he resorted to "five French sources and five English ones." Characteristically he adds, "and shoveled in as much fancy work and invention on both sides of the historical road as I pleased."[44] Indeed he did; DeVoto finds examples of the tall tale, as in Chapter VII, where "the Paladin is embroidering the narrative with yarns that are in the strict tradition,"[45] while Sut Lovingood furnished the incident of Uncle Laxart and the bull.[46]

The Gates Ajar by Elizabeth Stuart Phelps, which Twain sought to satirize, suggested the idea of utilizing a dream recounted by Captain Ned Wakeman, the result of these combined sources being *Captain Stormfield's Visit to Heaven.* Here, however, as in all the discovered sources used by Clemens, the material seen or heard outweighed in importance anything derived from reading. Twain's reading often suggested a plot or a germinal idea, but the stuff that went into the flesh of the characters—the things they did, what they thought and said—more frequently came from

43 "Mark Twain's Joan of Arc," *Michigan Alumnus,* LIV, 243 (May 8, 1948).

44 *Letters,* II, 624.

45 DeVoto, *op. cit.,* p. 244.

46 *Joan of Arc,* II, 60–63. See E. Hudson Long, "Sut Lovingood and Mark Twain's *Joan of Arc,*" *Modern Language Notes,* LXIV, 37–9 (January, 1949).

memories stored within, recollections of the great valley or of Washoe.[47]

Folklore

Of more importance is the folklore so often present in Twain's writings, the common beliefs and superstitions of the Mississippi Valley during the nineteenth century. Reminiscences and survivals from other lands mingled there, adapted to local conditions and customs. Similarities in folk beliefs always interested Clemens, who inquired into the customs of foreign lands with the interest of an anthropologist. In India he sought the facts of caste, suttee, thuggee, while admitting that to comprehend such customs truly one must have an understanding of the *how* and *why* lacking to an outside observer.[48] So it is with the folklore of his own region.

With *The Prince and the Pauper,* as with *A Connecticut Yankee,* Mark drew upon the deadening effects of superstition upon intellect. Here many superstitions of early England are dramatically presented; some instances of magic and enchantment are derived from Malory, but Mark himself simply stated: "It is not pretended that these laws and customs existed in England in the sixth century; no, it is only pretended that inasmuch as they existed in the English and other civilizations of far later times, it is safe to consider that it is no libel upon the sixth century to suppose them to have been in practice in that day also."[49] Again it is human nature rather than scholarship furnishing materials, for no one can read *A Connecticut Yankee* without feeling the continuity of human failings reaching into the present.

[47] There may be an interesting point of comparison here between Clemens and Chaucer; Professor Manly with the skill of a detective has theorized that Chaucer based his Canterbury Pilgrims upon actual people. *Some New Light on Chaucer* (New York: Henry Holt and Company, 1926).

[48] *Following the Equator,* II, 130.

[49] *A Connecticut Yankee,* p. ix.

Joan of Arc, however, as Victor R. West reminds us, turns to Continental folklore.[50] Fairies were not common in the folklore of Missouri, either among Negroes or whites, yet Mark makes use of the traditional fairy tree, showing in his opening incident the relationship of Joan and her playmates to the fairies, whose banishment Joan so strongly deplored.[51] In this fictionized biography of the Maid of Orleans channels were already charted by history and tradition, and it is interesting to note that this alone of all Twain's writings shows any interest in fairy lore. For it was the folklore of his youth which he knew at first hand, acquired unconsciously, and therefore embodied throughout his work with natural artistry.

Much of this folklore came to him through childhood association with the Negroes. Long years afterward Mark recalled,

> I know the look of Uncle Dan'l's kitchen as it was on the privileged nights, when I was a child, and I can see the white and black children grouped on the hearth, with the firelight playing on their faces and the shadows flickering upon the walls, clear back toward the cavernous gloom of the rear, and I can hear Uncle Dan'l telling the immortal tales which Uncle Remus Harris was to gather into his book and charm the world with.[52]

Some of these stories which impressed him so deeply—"I can feel again the creepy joy which quivered through me when the time for the ghost story was reached."[53]—he was to tell again to audiences as rapt with interest as that of the children who had squatted before the cabin fireplace of his youth. Such was "The Golden Arm," which Mark told to an audience at Vassar, so effectively his daughter

[50] *Folklore in the Works of Mark Twain* (University of Nebraska Studies in Language and Literature, X, Lincoln, Nebraska, 1930), p 8.
[51] *Joan of Arc,* I, 9–14. [52] *Autobiography,* I, 112.
[53] *Idem.*

Susy said that "he startled the whole roomful of people and they jumped as one man."[54]

In Hannibal belief was common that a departed person's spirit took form as a ghost; the night of John Clemens' funeral when Sam walked in his sleep, both his mother and sister had at first mistaken the white-clad figure for a ghost.[55] Moreover, popular superstition, held by white and black, assumed that the ghost would look just as it did in life. Thus the "awful scream" of Nigger Jim upon beholding Tom Sawyer's white face when he thought the boy had plunged to death from the balloon. And Huck, who holds similar beliefs, understands at once, "He thought it was Tom's ghost, you see."[56] Further along in this narrative Jim is frightened by a mirage, because "hit's a *ghos'*, dat's what it is," he wails with fright; "de lake's dead, en we's seen its ghos."[57] In *Life on the Mississippi* the raftsmen recount the story of a ghost-barrel bringing ill-fortune upon any unlucky vessel it chances to follow.[58] And the pilots added their tales of the supernatural, to those implanted in youthful breasts by the Negroes. One was about a phantom steamer, lost because her swearing pilots uttered a wish that they might never get out of a perplexing cut-off. "More than one grave watchman has sworn to me," says Mark, "that on drizzling, dismal nights, he has glanced fearfully down that forgotten river as he passed the head of the island, and seen the faint glow of the specter steamer's lights drifting through the distant gloom, and heard the muffled cough of her 'scape-pipes and the plaintive cry of her leadsmen."[59]

The *Adventures of Tom Sawyer,* with its sequel *Huckleberry Finn,* presents Twain's three chief purveyors of ghost-

[54] *Ibid.,* II, 170. "The Golden Arm" is preserved in "How To Tell a Story," *The $30,000 Bequest,* p. 263.

[55] Paine, I, 75.

[56] *Tom Sawyer Abroad,* p. 35.

[57] *Ibid.,* p. 68.

[58] Chapter III, *Life on the Mississippi.*

[59] *Ibid.,* p. 158.

lore, Tom, Huck, and Jim. All know the intricate ways of ghosts and how to detect their presence. When Huck suggests leaving the treasure spot because "Injun Joe's ghost is round about there, certain," Tom reminds him, "Looky here, Huck, what fools we're making of ourselves! Injun Joe's ghost ain't a-going to come around where there's a cross."[60] And Huck sees the point immediately. Yet some problems remain unsettled; in the graveyard at night Tom asks, "Say, Hucky, do you reckon Hoss Williams hears us talking?" When Huck replies in the affirmative, Tom says, "I wish I'd said *Mister* Williams."[61]

Haunted houses, also, were believed in and avoided by people. Tom tells us "mostly because they don't like to go where a man's been murdered." But in a particular case blue lights have been seen, which means one thing only to Huck, for "where you see one of them blue lights flickering around, Tom, you can bet there's a ghost mighty close behind it."[62] A haunted house serves as a useful prop in *Pudd'nhead Wilson;* once its reputation was established "Nobody would live in it afterward, or go near it by night, and most people even gave it a wide berth in the daytime."[63] Here Roxy's false son based his thieving operations with impunity.

As would be suspected, dwarfs, giants and a forest denizen appear through dreams and superstitions in *The Prince and the Pauper, A Connecticut Yankee,* and *Joan of Arc.* Even Satan is mentioned in *Tom Sawyer.* When Injun Joe perjures himself with impunity during his murder trial, Tom and Huck "expecting every moment that the clear sky would deliver God's lightnings upon his head" become frightened by his immunity, for "plainly this miscreant had sold himself to Satan and it would be fatal to meddle with

60 *Tom Sawyer,* p. 275.
61 *Ibid.,* p. 82.
62 *Ibid.,* p. 208.
63 *Pudd'nhead Wilson,* pp. 69–70.

the property of such a power as that."[64] In addition to credence in a personal devil, the boys harbor belief in devils in general, some of whom were expected to come after the spirit of Hoss Williams on his burial; however, devils have no power until midnight, and Hoss buried on Saturday was safe until Monday, for Huck reminds Tom, "Devils don't slosh around much of a Sunday, I don't reckon."[65]

Witchcraft also appears in Clemens' writings. When Mark visited the witch's cave at Endor he noted the repellent appearance of the place with "camel dung on the roofs and caked against the houses to dry."[66] Accusation of witchery naturally was included in *A Connecticut Yankee;*[67] of course, *Joan of Arc* employs a similar belief. The English soldiers think of Joan, "surely this *is* a witch, this is a child of Satan!"[68] And at the end of her conviction, the populace hears, "*The witch's time has come!*"[69] But in humorous vein, there is the belief expressed by Nigger Jim when Tom and Huck take his hat off and hang it on a limb: "Afterward Jim said the witches bewitched him and put him in a trance, and rode him all over the state, and then set him under the trees again, and hung his hat on a limb to show who done it."[70] Jim's story was so favorably received by the other Negroes that he enlarged the territory covered until the witches "rode him all over the world, and tired him most to death, and his back was all over saddle boils."[71] Another Negro, Nat, falls easy prey to suggestions about witches, who worry him extremely. "Dey's awluz at it, sah," he laments, "en dey do mos' kill me, dey sk'yers me so."[72] Yet Huck and Tom, for all their fooling, believe exactly as the Negroes under frightening conditions. Huck says, "We

[64] *Tom Sawyer,* p. 100.
[65] *Ibid.,* p. 59.
[66] *Notebook,* p. 94.
[67] P. 357.
[68] *Joan of Arc,* I, 251.
[69] *Ibid.,* II, 258.
[70] *Huckleberry Finn,* p. 8.
[71] *Idem.*
[72] *Ibid.,* p. 329.

can't ever tell the right time, and besides this kind of thing's too awful, here this time of night with witches and ghosts a-fluttering around so."[73] Tom, who agrees with Huck, replies, "Yes, but Huck, ghosts don't travel around only at night. They won't hender us from digging there in the daytime." Sometimes, so superstitions ran, witches intervened in the course of affairs, and something of this nature happened to Tom Sawyer, who employed a charm to be sure. Tom called the doodle-bug out of his sandy hole, only to have the insect dart back in again; whereupon Tom declared, "He dasn't tell! So it *was* a witch that done it."[74] When Huck, on another occasion, meets a bad omen, he hastens to take precautions; "I got up and turned around in my tracks three times and crossed my breast every time; and then I tied up a little lock of my hair with a thread to keep witches away."[75] The Negro Nat also used the latter safeguard: "his wool was all tied up in little bunches with thread. That was to keep witches off."[76] Roxy, however, in *Pudd'nhead Wilson* employs the more familiar device of a horseshoe to guard against dangers of witchcraft through Wilson's hobby of fingerprinting.[77] There was superstition enough in general among all classes through the entire region of Sam Clemens' boyhood, and it was not confined to witches or devils.

Huck Finn, as DeVoto so rightly observes of his first appearance in *Tom Sawyer,* "wanders into immortality swinging a dead cat."[78] Though Tom recommends spunk water used with proper incantations to cure warts, Huck places

[73] *Tom Sawyer,* p. 206.

[74] *Ibid.,* pp. 76–7.

[75] *Huckleberry Finn,* p. 5.

[76] *Ibid.,* p. 327. Mark was drawing on actuality here, for he had known an old slave, Aunt Hannah, who employed the charm: "Whenever witches were around she tied up the remnant of her wool in little tufts, with white thread, and this promptly made the witches impotent." *Autobiography,* I, 99–100.

[77] P. 24.

[78] *Mark Twain's America,* p. 73.

his faith in the cat.[79] Both agree, however, about unlucky days; says Huck, "There's some lucky days, maybe, but Friday ain't."[80] To which Tom retorts, "Any fool knows that." Dreams, moreover, are important omens. Huck tells us: "I had a rotten bad dream last night—dreampt about rats." And Tom comforts him by saying that since the rats did not fight in the dream "it's only a sign that there's trouble around, you know. All we got to do is to look mighty sharp and keep out of it."[81]

Signs, portents, and omens figure prominently in responses by Huck, Tom, and Jim, whose thinking, we may be sure, is representative. Many of these signs portended bad luck, few indicated good; for as Jim proclaims, "What you want to know when good luck's a-comin' for? Want to keep it off?"[82] Yet he does admit some use in the signs of future wealth conveyed by his own "hairy arms en a hairy breas," which he explains: "You see, maybe you's got to be po' a long time fust, en so you might git discourage' en kill yo'sef 'f you didn' know by de sign dat you gwyne to be rich bymeby."[83] Bad luck might be avoided, however, if one were careful not to do certain things: "And Jim said you mustn't count the things you are going to cook for dinner, because that would bring bad luck. The same if you shook the tablecloth after sundown."[84]

But many signs had nothing to do with luck, good or bad. Bees, according to Jim, would not sting idiots, to which Huck confides, "but I didn't believe that, because I had tried them lots of times myself, and they wouldn't sting me."[85] Birds flying a yard or two at a time indicated rain; as did young chickens so behaving; and to catch one of them would surely bring death.[86] From Jim, too, Huck

[79] *Tom Sawyer,* pp. 55–7.
[80] *Ibid.,* p. 209.
[81] *Ibid.,* pp. 209–10.
[82] *Huckleberry Finn,* p. 63.
[83] *Idem.*
[84] *Idem.*
[85] *Idem.*
[86] *Idem.*

learned that it was bad luck to talk about a dead man who might have been murdered.[87] Some taboos carried greater portent than others; Jim bewailed Huck's handling of a snake-skin: "He said he druther see the new moon over his left shoulder as much as a thousand times than take up a snake-skin in his hand."[88] Which shows what "awful bad luck" it proclaimed, for dire were the disasters of so looking upon the moon:

> Old Hank Bunker done it once, and bragged about it; and in less than two years he got drunk and fell off of the shot-tower, and spread himself out so that he was just a kind of a layer, as you may say; and they slid him edgeways between two barn doors for a coffin, and buried him so, so they say, but I didn't see it. Pap told me. But anyway it all come of looking at the moon that way, like a fool.[89]

Yet handling a snake-skin was more disastrous, for Huck says, "Anybody that don't believe yet that it's foolishness to handle a snake-skin, after all that snake-skin done for us, will believe it now if they read on and see what more it done for us."[90]

Victor Royce West in the most comprehensive survey of folklore in Twain's writings tells us that all "crawly things" were supposed to be ill omens, pointing out that Huck upon suffering the misfortune of killing a spider invoked the aid of witchcraft.[91] West further reveals that in the folk beliefs of the Southern Negro it was a sign of death to see a gray mare. Mississippi steamboat captains did not consider the gray mare alone so dire an omen, but if one were combined with a preacher, then calamity was imminent. An old river-man of long standing stated:

> I went down the river in such company. We grounded at Bloody Island; we grounded at Hanging Dog; we grounded just below this same Commerce; we jolted Beaver Dam Rock;

87 *Ibid.*, p. 72.
88 *Ibid.*, p. 74.
89 *Idem.*
90 *Ibid.*, p. 130.
91 *Op. cit.*, p. 59.

we hit one of the worst breaks in the "Graveyard" behind Goose Island; we had a roustabout killed in a fight; we burst a boiler; broke a shaft; collapsed a flue; and went into Cairo with nine feet of water in the hold—may have been more, may have been less. I remember it as if it were yesterday. The men lost their heads with terror. They painted the mare blue, in sight of town, and threw the preacher overboard, or we should not have arrived at all. The preacher was fished out and saved. He acknowledged, himself, that he had been to blame. I remember it all as if it were yesterday.[92]

And Mark recalls:

I myself remember a case where a captain was warned by numerous friends against taking a gray mare and a preacher with him, but persisted in his purpose in spite of all that could be said; and the same day—it may have been the next, and some say it was, though I think it was the same day—he got drunk and fell down the hatchway and was borne to his home a corpse.[93]

Tom and Huck, even as young Sam Clemens, are learned in the lore of animal omen. When a dog "set up a long, lugubrious howl" both realize immediately that death is meant for one of them should the dog prove to be a stray. At first Tom thinks he recognizes the animal, but when he discovers his mistake, the boys believe death is meant for them together. Huck moans, "Oh, Tom, I reckon we're goners. I reckon there ain't no mistake 'bout where *I'll* go to. I been so wicked." And Tom agrees, "Dad fetch it! This comes of playing hookey and doing everything a feller's told *not* to do." To which he hopefully adds, "But if I ever get off this time, I lay I'll just *waller* in Sunday-schools"; then the boys discover that the stray dog has his back to them, which means the death omen is for someone else.[94]

When the boys discover Injun Joe's guilt but decide against telling, they revert to the ancient covenant of blood.

[92] *Life on the Mississippi,* p. 212. [93] *Ibid.,* pp. 212–213.
[94] *Tom Sawyer,* p. 94.

On a shingle Tom scrawls: "Huck Finn and Tom Sawyer swears they will keep mum about this and they wish they may drop down dead in their tracks if they ever tell and Rot."[95] Using the ball of his finger for a pen, each affixes his initials in blood, and belief is firm that if either tells he will actually fall dead on the spot. And another ancient superstition that a corpse will bleed in the presence of its murderer appears when Injun Joe helps to raise the body of his victim; but so firmly is suspicion centered on Muff Potter that the sign is mistaken, people remarking, "It was within three feet of Muff Potter when it done it."[96]

Mark Twain's folklore, like his plots and characterizations, exhibits the first-hand knowledge of intimate association. Through companionship with the Negroes and through saturation of boyish beliefs, founded upon slave-lore and upon common grounds of superstition, Samuel Clemens knew that children and the uneducated believed in ghosts, signs, and portents. These folk elements he introduced into his fiction with the naturalness of art that springs spontaneously from organic truth. Later, as West tells us, there appeared "the second-hand information gained from wide and intelligent inquiry during his later travels, and what might be called the third-hand or literary knowledge gleaned from the many books to which his lively interest in the subject directed him."[97] Interesting they are, but far more important is that lore which permeates the thought of Tom, Huck, and Jim, and which plays so large a part in the minds of many around them, the firm beliefs found in the folk thinking of the old-time Negro in the Mississippi valley.

95 *Ibid.*, p. 92.
96 *Ibid.*, p. 101.
97 *Op. cit.*, p. 77. These traditions and superstitions, which West wisely distinguishes from those of Twain's own early environment, appear largely in *Following the Equator, A Tramp Abroad, A Connecticut Yankee, The Prince and the Pauper,* and *Joan of Arc.*

Literary Sources

The influence of books on Mark Twain began with his youthful reading in Hannibal. There through the promptings of his mother and his sister little Sam began his acquaintance with the Bible.[98] He had read it through, reluctantly no doubt, before he was fifteen years of age, and Wagenknecht agrees with Paine that much of the beauty of Twain's style came from that common inspiration for so much that is great in English literature.[99] Mark simply takes for granted his reader's knowledge of scriptures; Charles W. Stoddard has described how Twain one night in London thrilled his listeners with a beautiful reading from the Book of Ruth.[100] In all, it appears that Clemens made more references to the Bible than to any other work, 124 such allusions appearing in his books.[101]

Along with an early reading of the Bible Sam became conversant with his father's copy of *Don Quixote,* an influence which both Wagenknecht and Moore regard as next in importance.[102] DeLancey Ferguson, also, believes that the boy absorbed Cervantes thoroughly, and he indicates that a pervasive influence of Poe appears in certain parts of *Tom Sawyer.*[103] There is no doubt that Mark Twain read a great deal in his youth, and Miss Brashear has devoted an entire chapter to a description of the material then available in Hannibal—journals as well as books—for a boy so inclined.[104] Even though Mark said that he could never read Dickens, both Ferguson and Wagenknecht feel certain that he did.[105] Writing to Orion in 1860 Sam tells his

98 DeLancey Ferguson points out a number of Biblical allusions in his writing, *Mark Twain: Man and Legend,* p. 26.

99 *Mark Twain: The Man and His Work,* p. 44.

100 *Idem.*

101 Wagenknecht quotes Pochmann, *Ibid.,* p. 43.

102 *Ibid.,* p. 44.

103 Ferguson, p. 26.

104 "Sam Clemens's Reading," *Mark Twain, Son of Missouri,* pp. 196–224.

105 Ferguson, p 45; Wagenknecht, p. 270.

brother of reading Tom Hood's letters, confiding at the same time that his "beau ideals of fine writing" are *Don Quixote* and Goldsmith's "Citizen of the World." While on the river Sam read *Paradise Lost,* remarking upon "the Arch-Fiend's terrible energy";[106] there too he read Shakespeare, who was to furnish him with humor in an early Snodgrass letter, who was to be burlesqued in the *Californian,* and who was finally to become the subject of a volume, *Is Shakespeare Dead?*[107] During cub days on the river Sam read Tom Paine's *Age of Reason;*[108] after moving East he read Carlyle's *French Revolution,* both exerting a permanent influence upon his thinking.[109] The latter was one of the few books Twain reread every year, others being Lecky's *History of European Morals,* Pepys' *Diary,* and Suetonius' *Lives of the Caesars.* Mark's interest in evolution led him to *The Universal Kinship* by J. Howard Moore, to whom he wrote an appreciative note saying the book had stated his own "long-cherished opinions and reflections and resentments."[110] Though he could not bear most of Scott—he found *Rob Roy* and *Guy Mannering* a blight—when he read *Quentin Durward* Mark confessed delight, qualified by the query, however, "I wonder who wrote *Quentin Durward?*"[111] At the same time Twain was charmed—"enchanted" was his word—with Helen Keller's *The Story of My Life,* the wonderful achievements by the blind girl through the help of her teacher, Miss Sullivan; this book appealed to his sense of courage and devotion.[112] The *Literary Essays* of Professor William Lyon Phelps held Clemens'

106 Paine, I, 146.

107 Aside from this monograph Pochmann lists twenty allusions to Shakespeare in Twain's works, twice the number to any other writer. Quoted by Brashear, p. 215.

108 Paine, IV, 1445.

109 *Letters,* II, 490.

110 Paine, IV, 1363.

111 *Ibid.,* III, 1198.

112 *Idem.*

attention until he finished the book without putting it down.[113]

During the winter of 1886–7 Twain earnestly turned to the poetry of Robert Browning, conducting a group who gathered to hear him read the verses he had so carefully studied until obscurity disappeared through the clear insight of the reading. Admitting Browning's many dark intervals Clemens stated that these were broken by great passages like "a splendor of stars and suns."[114] But for Meredith Twain could experience no such enthusiasm; when the family read *Diana of the Crossways,* he said: "The author keeps telling us how smart she is, how brilliant, but I never seem to hear her say anything smart or brilliant. Read me some of Diana's smart utterances."[115]

Mark read Macaulay on English history, rereading him again in old age.[116] Thomas Hardy's *Jude the Obscure* impressed Clemens so favorably that he urged his biographer to read it, the moral problems presented in this, his last continuous reading, being the chief matter of interest.[117] Pepys' *Diary,* always a favorite, Mark read yearly, once determining to write something similar—but the result was *1601,*[118] One summer when Howells' *Foregone Conclusion* was running in the *Atlantic Monthly,* Mark followed the serial; and though he seldom read fiction, on this exception he complimented his friend highly.[119] Similar praise went to Elizabeth Robbins, whose *Open Question* moved Mark to write her, "I have not been so enriched by a book for many years, nor so enchanted by one."[120] When Twichell lent Twain a copy of Jonathan Edwards' *Freedom of the Will,* Clemens was led to set down some theology of his own in dialogue form, a colloquy between the Master of the Uni-

[113] *Ibid.,* IV, 1562.
[114] *Ibid.,* III, 847.
[115] *Idem.*
[116] *Ibid.,* IV, 1565.
[117] *Ibid.,* IV, 1567.
[118] *Ibid.,* II, 580.
[119] *Ibid.,* II, 510.
[120] *Ibid.,* III, 1089.

verse and a Stranger, for although he heartily approved Edwards' contention that mankind never creates an impulse itself, from there on Clemens suffered a "haunting sense of having been on a three days' tear with a drunken lunatic."[121]

But Lowell's *Letters,* read while smoking, were more congenial matter.[122] Mark also once expressed admiration for Coventry Patmore's *The Angel in the House.* At the same time he objected to the obscurity in Elizabeth Barrett Browning's *Aurora Leigh.* While the "Recording Angel" passage in Sterne's *Tristram Shandy* once drew his praise, on the whole he found the book too coarse, at least to be read by Livy.[123]

When Edward Everett Hale died, Clemens expressed privately that he held "the greatest admiration for his work."[124] But for Jane Austen, he exclaimed that when he read one of her books, ". . . such as *Pride and Prejudice,* I feel like a barkeeper entering the kingdom of heaven."[125] *Gulliver's Travels,* read in boyhood, furnished greater pleasure as he grew older, despite his dislike of Swift as a man.[126] And *Don Quixote,* an influence already noted, Twain early praised as "one of the most exquisite books that was ever written, and to lose it from the world's literature would be as the wresting of a constellation from the symmetry and perfection of the firmament."[127] Yet Clemens was alert to the work of new, young writers, discovering a poem by Willa Cather, "The Palatine," in the *Saturday Times Review,* which brought his praise and revealed foresight in discovering one who was to prove an important figure in American letters.[128] Andrew D. White's *Science and Theology,* a his-

121 *Ibid.,* III, 1157.

122 *Ibid.,* IV, 1488.

123 *Love Letters,* p. 34.

124 Paine, IV, 1498.

125 *Ibid.,* IV, 1500.

126 Coley B. Taylor, *Mark Twain's Margins on Thackeray's Swift* (New York: Gotham House, 1935), p. 55.

127 *Love Letters,* p. 76.

128 Paine, IV, 1501.

tory of the warfare between science and unenlightened theological beliefs, Twain read and reread, calling it a "lovely book."[129] Charles Kingsley's *Hypatia* Mark found too tiresome to continue; however, *The Cloister and the Hearth* by Charles Reade he read with all the enchantment that O. Henry found in the same volume.[130]

Interest in contemporary literature led him to Booth Tarkington, whose *Beasley's Christmas Party* actually brought tears from Twain; Tarkington's work in general pleased the older writer. Another book read with great pleasure for its subtle art, *Chivalry,* by James Branch Cabell, also drew expressions of high praise.[131]

On the table by his bed, as on the billiard-room shelves, Twain kept those books he constantly returned to: the three volume *Memoirs of Saint-Simon,* Suetonius, and Carlyle's *French Revolution.*[132] Henry H. Breen's *Modern English Literature—Its Blemishes and Defects* furnished Mark with enough examples of slipshod English for a paper on that subject, read before the Saturday Morning Club. It was Greville's *Journal of the Reigns of George IV and William IV,* much read and annotated, containing an adverse comment on Byron, which drew one of Mark's most characteristic comments in the margin:

> But, dear sir, you are forgetting that what a man sees in the human race is merely himself in the deep and honest privacy of his own heart. Byron despised the race because he despised himself. I feel as Byron did, and for the same reason. Do you admire the race (and consequently yourself)?[133]

Twain's copy of Plutarch revealed frequent usage, and Mark's catholicity of taste appeared in the equally thumbed pages of the *Life of P. T. Barnum, Written by Himself.* The before-mentioned *Letters* of Lowell furnished frequent en-

129 *Ibid.,* IV, 1506.
130 *Love Letters,* p. 126.
131 Paine, IV, 1535.
132 *Ibid.,* 1536–7.
133 *Ibid.,* IV, 1539.

joyment, as did one of the few novels he ever cherished, Richard Henry Dana's *Two Years Before the Mast.* Several books of an introductory nature on astronomy and geology seem to have held his interest, and though he came to peruse it less in old age, a much-read book from earlier days, Darwin's *Descent of Man,* furnished influence through its very presence. Albert Bigelow Paine tells us that during the days of his association with Clemens the latter read steadily not much besides Suetonius, Pepys, and Carlyle, though the *Morte d'Arthur* and Kipling's poems were kept where he might reach them.[134]

It would appear that to the end of his days Mark's taste altered scarcely from the earlier sentiments expressed in an interview with Rudyard Kipling, "Personally I never care for fiction or story-books. What I like to read about are facts and statistics of any kind."[135] Twain once set down a literary declaration: "I like history, biography, travels, curious facts and strange happenings, and science. And I detest novels, poetry, and theology,"[136]

Sources from Life

The most vital sources in Clemens' writings came from personal experiences. For his first novel, the collaboration with Warner, Twain depended upon family reminiscences to write about Jamestown, the unmaterialized boom-town of dashed hopes from the Tennessee land. But the character of Colonel Sellers, that enthusiastic optimist—"There's millions in it!"—was modeled from life upon a favorite cousin of Mark's mother, James Lampton. And this impossible character, this extravagant invention, so Twain insisted, was no creation. "I merely put him on paper as he was," Mark said; "he was not a person who could be exag-

134 See the chapter "Mark Twain's Reading," *Ibid.,* IV, 1536–40.

135 Rudyard Kipling, *From Sea to Sea* (New York: Doubleday and McClure, 1899), II, 180.

136 Paine, II, 512.

gerated."[137] Clemens further claimed that all the impossible, extravagant incidents of *The Gilded Age,* in both novel and play, merely seemed so, for he had actually seen them, or at least believed he had, even to the turnip-eating episode.[138] Years later during a lecture tour with George W. Cable, James Lampton called upon Twain, immediately expounding upon a "small venture" he had begun, elaborating the possibilities until they exceeded imagination, only to close with the comment that it was a mere trifle. After Lampton's departure, Cable, for whose benefit Mark had left the door ajar, remarked through the opening, "That was Colonel Sellers."[139]

The farm of John A. Quarles, where Sam visited for several months each year until he reached his teens, was generously utilized for *Huckleberry Finn* and *Tom Sawyer, Detective;* in these works Mark moved it from Missouri down to Arkansas, saying "It was all of six hundred miles, but it was no trouble; it was not a very large farm—five hundred acres, perhaps—but I could have done it if it had been twice as large. And as for the morality of it, I cared nothing for that; I would move a state if the exigencies of literature required it."[140] And he added in nostalgic mood, "It was a heavenly place for a boy, that farm of my uncle John's."[141] On the farm was an old Negro, regarded affectionately as good friend and adviser to all the children, "Uncle Dan'l," who was an old time Southern darky like Uncle Remus, one Clemens recalled "whose sympathies were wide and warm, and whose heart was honest and simple and knew no guile."[142] Shearing away the years to create physical vigor, Twain turned "Uncle Dan'l" into Jim, and "carted him all around—to Hannibal, down the

137 Autobiography, I, 89.

138 "In fact," Mark stated, "I was myself the guest who ate the turnips." *Idem.*

139 *Ibid.*, I, 93.

140 *Ibid.*, I, 96.

141 *Idem.*

142 *Ibid.*, I, 100.

Mississippi on a raft, and even across the Desert of Sahara in a balloon—and he has endured it all with the patience and friendliness and loyalty which were his birthright."[143]

From his boyhood, also, came the impressions of Sunday School later expressed in *Tom Sawyer* and *Huck Finn,* for as DeLancey Ferguson observes, "Sam heard long expositions of predestination and hell-fire, which began by scaring and ended by boring him."[144] Naturally, in spite of later associations with scholarly ministers, Twain continued to associate theology with the dull long-winded sermons of boyhood.

From youthful memories, too, came the episode of whitewashing the fence in *Tom Sawyer,* Mark recalling that he had once so tried to impose on a little slave named Sandy, upon whom the ruse failed to work.[145] And the villain "Injun Joe" was an actual half-breed, once lost in the cave near Hannibal, where he would have starved if the bats had run short. From him young Sam heard the story, confessing years later. "In the book called *Tom Sawyer* I starved him entirely to death in the cave, but that was in the interest of art; it never happened."[146] Mark suggests, though only by implication, that Pap in *Huck Finn* may have been based upon the town drunkard, Jimmy Finn, whose predecessor, "General" Gaines, may also have figured in the characterization. In fact, the "General" like "Injun Joe" became lost in the cave, where he effected escape by pushing his handkerchief through a hole miles from the entrance, the good fates causing somebody to see it and dig him out. But Mark observed, "There is nothing the matter with his statistics except the handkerchief. I knew him for years and he hadn't any. But it could have been his nose. That would attract attention."[147] As Ferguson notes, all of *Tom Sawyer* may

143 *Idem.*

144 *Mark Twain: Man and Legend,* p. 25.

145 *Autobiography,* I, 102.

146 *Ibid.,* I, 105.

147 *Idem.*

be autobiographic through its characters, altered or colored for dramatic purposes.[148]

Twain once flatly stated that Huck Finn was based on Tom Blankenship, saying "I have drawn Tom Blankenship exactly as he was. He was ignorant, unwashed, insufficiently fed; but he had as good a heart as ever any boy had."[149] Tom's father, moreover, at least in Mark's memory, had been a town drunkard like "General" Gaines and Jimmy Finn, and one gathers that Finn perhaps filled that office with greater competency than the others. As Mark observed "he was not finical; he was not hypercritical; he was largely and handsomely democratic—and slept in the deserted tanyard with the hogs." This together with Mark's passing reference to an unsuccessful attempt on his own father's part to reform Jimmy indicates a bequest of more than surname to the character of Pap. John Clemens, in whom the spirit of reform was only spasmodic, once tried to rehabilitate "Injun Joe," a failure which relieved Sam and his chums from anxiety. "For Injun Joe, drunk, was interesting and a benefaction to us, but Injun Joe, sober, was a dreary spectacle."[150] The half-breed's death, however, occurring at night during a violent thunder storm, impressed Sam forcibly. As lightning flashed and rain lashed against the windows, the boy was sure Satan had come for Injun Joe; indeed, he remembered "I should have thought it strange and unaccountable if Satan had come for him in a less spectacular way." Which led Sam to repent his sins, lest one more chance for salvation be lost, a mood quickly wearing off with sunrise—"But in the morning I saw that it was a false alarm and concluded to resume business at the old stand and wait for another reminder."[151]

148 *Op. cit.*, p. 29. Cf. Dixon Wecter, *Sam Clemens of Hannibal* for a full discussion of Twain's use of real persons.

149 *Autobiograpy,* II, 174.

150 *Ibid.*, II. 175.

151 *Ibid.*, II, 176.

And there were other perfect memories from youth incorporated into the saga of Tom and Huck, when Twain conveyed the actual description of Dawson's schoolhouse to the pages of *Tom Sawyer,* just as he employed "that distant boy-Paradise, Cardiff Hill" from whence the "drowsy and inviting summer sounds" floated through the school windows.[152] Yet more inviting was the countryside near his uncle's farm:

> I can see the woods in their autumn dress, the oaks purple, the hickories washed with gold, the maples and the sumachs luminous with crimson fires, and I can hear the rustle made by the fallen leaves as we plowed through them. I can see the blue clusters of wild grapes hanging among the foliage of the saplings, and I remember the taste of them and the smell.[153]

But comic incidents mingled with happy memories of nature, as the story of Jim Wolfe illustrates; that painfully bashful boy's episode with the cats Mark used several times, in the pages of the *Californian* and the *Golden Era,* and in speeches.[154]

And other real people appear in Twain's literary portrait gallery; the original of Becky Thatcher in *Tom Sawyer* was Laura Hawkins, the little girl with whom Sam Clemens went to school in Hannibal.[155] She bears no resemblance, however, to Laura Hawkins of *The Gilded Age,* beautiful but dangerous adventuress, who committed a murder, for perhaps the original of that icy brunette was Laura Dake, whom Sam once found fascinating and may have been trying to write out of his system.[156]

In some ways, at least, Mark's mother served as the model for his portrait of Tom's Aunt Polly,[157] while Pamela

152 *Ibid.,* II, 179. 153 *Ibid.,* I, 110.

154 Johnson, *Bibliography,* p. 229. The full account appears in *Autobiography,* I, 135–9.

155 Paine, I, 68.

156 Samuel C. Webster, *Mark Twain, Business Man,* p. 58.

157 Paine, I, 35.

Clemens in her gentle fashion became Cousin Mary.[158] Sam's brother, Henry, was utilized for the Sid of *Tom Sawyer,* though Henry was in every way a finer lad than Sid.[159] Moreover, many of the incidents of that book—the shirt sewed with colored thread, the pain-killer administered to the cat—actually happened, or Mark thought they had.[160] To his old friend, Will Bowen, Clemens once wrote of a conscious effort to recall the old days at Dawson's school, now fading from his "treacherous memory," though one incident vividly protruded, Will's buying a louse of "poor Arch Fuqua."[161]

From the verdant solitude of the Tuolumne hills came the stories of Tom Quartz the cat,[162] the Jaybird and Acorns,[163] and the cameleopard skit in *Huckleberry Finn,* bowdlerized from the "Burning Shame" as narrated by Jim Gillis.[164] Angel's Camp, where the weather was bad as the beans and dish-water served three times a day, furnished the story of "Coleman with his jumping frog," while from the same locality came a story which grew many years later into "The Californian's Tale."[165] Though derived at second hand from Joe Twichell the Biblical explanations of Captain Ned Wakeman were incorporated into "Some Rambling Notes of an Idle Excursion."[166] The old seaman, unaware of his passenger's identity, undertook a logical clarification of the miracles, his profanity in full swing.

The incident of the lost sock in *A Tramp Abroad* was another story derived directly from experience, Mark transferring the scene from Munich to Heilbronn and substi-

158 *Ibid.,* I, 36.

159 *Ibid.,* I, 52.

160 *Ibid.,* I, 53.

161 *Mark Twain's Letters to Will Bowen,* p. 17.

162 "The Prejudiced Cat," *Roughing It,* Vol. II, Chapter XX.

163 "Baker's Bluejay Yarn," Chapter III, *A Tramp Abroad,* Vol. I.

164 Paine, I, 267. The skit appears in Chapter XXIII, *Huckleberry Finn.*

165 *Notebook,* p. 7.

166 Letters, II, 708. "Some Rambling Notes" first appeared in *The Stolen White Elephant;* now it is in the volume entitled *Tom Sawyer Abroad.*

tuting Twichell for Livy as his travelling companion. The whole episode was written immediately after it happened, as Mark's subsiding anger gave way to perception of the literary values in the ridiculous situation of a person fully dressed save for one sock crawling about in the darkness of a hotel room in a futile search for the missing article.[167] It is difficult to evaluate Twain's own statements of his sources for the same reasons that his *Autobiography* must be carefully weighed on the scales of established fact. But when all scholarly returns are in and the counts of his literary sources are tallied, the essential truth, if not always the actual fact, of Mark's indebtedness to his own experiences persists. It is in the world of memory recorded in the *Autobiography* that the primary sources of his major contributions may be found, the world of Hannibal, of John Quarles' farm, of old times on the Mississippi, and of tumultuous days in Washoe.

Vocabulary

The accuracy with which Twain recorded the speech of boys reveals patient observation and a keen ear. Like the writers of the frontier tradition preceding him, Mark followed the colloquial idiom and colloquial syntax, and it is not only in the conversation of youngsters, but in that of adults, that the flow of language in his books follows the stream of life. Never addicted to bookish speech, Twain had as early as the Philadelphia travel letters shown a tendency to vigorous writing, for a comparison with their sources reveals that the young printer valued simplicity and directness of style.[168] And Sam Clemens, like Emerson, who listened to the live language of teamsters, and Robert Bur-

[167] Paine, II, 639. See Chapter XIII, *A Tramp Abroad.*

[168] Fred W. Lorch points out ten parallel passages to show how Clemens substituted direct expression for the florid style of R. A. Smith's *Philadelphia As It Is in 1852.* "Mark Twain's Philadelphia Letters in the Muscatine *Journal,*" *American Literature,* XVII, 348–352 (January, 1946).

ton, who listened to the bargemen, perceived the vitality of common speech, transferring it to the printed page.

From his early youth Sam had listened to talk between untutored men, he had heard the dialect of Negro slaves, and he knew how the general person spoke in his everyday conversation. Before him, moreover, was the entire tradition of frontier humor, told in the language of a Sut Lovingood or a Simon Suggs, a tradition devoted to realism, one quick to laugh at any affectation. In maturity Twain criticized Professor Dowden's biography of Shelley as a "literary cake-walk"; Mark's strictures on Dowden's style tell us conversely something of his own: "The ordinary forms of speech are absent from it. All the pages, all the paragraphs, walk by sedately, elegantly, not to say mincingly, in their Sunday-best, shiny and sleek, perfumed, and with *boutonniéres* in their buttonholes; it is rare to find even a chance sentence that has forgotten to dress."[169] Here is insistence on realism of speech, the absence of which aroused Twain's ire toward James Fenimore Cooper, of whose dialogue Mark said: ". . . when the personages of a tale deal in conversation, the talk shall sound like human talk, and be talk such as human beings would be likely to talk in the given circumstances, and have a discoverable meaning, also a discoverable purpose, and a show of relevancy, and remain in the neighborhood of the subject in hand, and be interesting to the reader, and help out the tale, and stop when the people cannot think of anything more to say."[170]

Clemens' precise ear is evident in his comments on the differences between our language as spoken in England and as used in the Southern and Western portions of the United States: "The languages were identical several generations ago, but our changed conditions and the spread of our people far to the south and far to the west have made many

169 *In Defense of Harriet Shelley and Other Essays,* p. 3.
170 "Fenimore Cooper's Literary Offenses," *Ibid.,* p. 61.

alterations in our pronunciation, and have introduced new words among us and changed the meanings of many old ones."[171] And Mark's understanding of the value of the spoken words of the majority is also clear: "It is not simply a manner of speech obtaining among the educated handful; the manner obtaining among the vast uneducated multitude must be considered also."[172] For this latter Twain became the literary spokesman.

If there are less dialect variations in *Huckleberry Finn,* for instance, than Mark imagined, and those rendered into print more haphazardly than painstakingly, the very lack of a studied conformity, as Katherine Buxbaum observes, makes for vigor, vividness, and imagination; for Twain's dialect is natural, real, with a "wealth of clear-cut, pointed phrases."[173] Out West he took the strong, racy slang of the miners, contrasting it with accepted, literary usage when Scotty Briggs in *Roughing It* sought a parson for Buck Fanshaw's funeral:

"Are you the duck that runs the gospel-mill next door?"

"Am I the—pardon me, I believe I do not understand?"

With another sigh and a half-sob, Scotty rejoined: "Why you see we are in a bit of trouble, and the boys thought maybe you would give us a lift, if we'd tackle you—that is, if I've got the rights of it and you are the head clerk of the doxology-works next door."

"I am the shepherd in charge of the flock whose fold is next door."

"The which?"

"The spiritual adviser of the little company of believers whose sanctuary adjoins these premises."

Scotty scratched his head, reflected a moment, and then

[171] "Concerning the American Language," *Tom Sawyer Abroad and Other Stories,* p. 407.

[172] *Ibid.,* p. 409.

[173] Katherine Buxbaum, "Mark Twain and American Dialect," *American Speech,* II, 236 (February, 1927).

said: "You ruther hold over me, pard. I reckon I can't call that hand. Ante and pass the buck."

That was the extreme, yet even the slang employed by Clemens—nothing is more ephemeral than slang—is clearly understood today. It is when Mark turns to the colloquial, however, that we are most indebted to him for broadening the scope of dialogue in American letters. "You don't know about me," says Huckleberry Finn, "without you have read a book by the name of *The Adventures of Tom Sawyer*; but that ain't no matter. That book was made by Mr. Mark Twain, and he told the truth, mainly. There was things which he stretched, but mainly he told the truth." And as Huck continues, "Now the way that book winds up is this: Tom and me found the money that the robbers hid in the cave, and it made us rich,"[174] we have authentic, native American idiom used for the first time in a masterpiece of world literature.

For Mark knew how boys talked, and he could reproduce the speech used by their elders, as in this conversation between "Squire" Hawkins and his wife:

"For goodness sake, Si—"

"Wait, Nancy, wait—let me finish—I've been secretly boiling and fuming with this grand inspiration for weeks, and I *must* talk or I'll burst! I haven't whispered to a soul—not a word—have had my *countenance* under lock and key, for fear it might drop something that would tell even these animals here how to discern the gold-mine that's glaring under their noses."[175]

In his descriptions Clemens was as accurate as in dialogue, making language fit the subject perfectly. Here is Hannibal:

> After all these years I can picture that old time to myself now, just as it was then: the white town drowsing in the sun-

[174] *The Adventures of Huckleberry Finn,* p. 1.
[175] *The Gilded Age,* I, 7.

shine of a summer's morning; the streets empty, or pretty nearly so; one or two clerks sitting in front of the Water Street stores, with their splint-bottomed chairs tilted back against the walls, chins on breasts, hats slouched over their faces, asleep—with shingle-shavings enough around to show what broke them down; a sow and a litter of pigs loafing along the sidewalk, doing a good business in watermelon rinds and seeds; two or three lonely little freight piles scattered about the "levee"; a pile of "skids" on the slope of the stone-paved wharf, and the fragrant town drunkard asleep in the shadow of them; two or three wood flats at the head of the wharf, but nobody to listen to the peaceful lapping of the wavelets against them; the great Mississippi, the majestic, the magnificent Mississippi, rolling its mile-wide tide along, shining in the sun; the dense forest away on the other side; the "point" above the town, and the "point" below, bounding the river-glimpse and turning it into a sort of sea, and withal a very still and brilliant and lonely one.[176]

Such diction is evocative; we see the sights and colors, hear the sounds, and sense movements. It is all told in language that is clear, vivid, lucid; in a style that is realistic and factual, yet at the same time poetic, beautiful, and true.

In picturing his region Twain naturally introduced the language of the Negro, which he depicted with an art, equalled for accurate representation only by that of Joel Chandler Harris and Thomas Nelson Page. In *The Gilded Age* he had presented Uncle Dan'l, who knew how to quote scripture to his purpose:

"Goodness sakes, Mars Clay, don't de Good Book say? 'Sides, don't it call 'em de *he*-brew chil'en? If dey was gals wouldn't dey be de she-brew chil'en? Some people dat kin read don't 'pear to take no notice when dey *do* read."[177]

Of course, it was with Jim, Huck's companion on the raft, that Mark pictured the language of the Negro of that time most fully. Huck with his untutored speech, Jim with his slave dialect, Tom with the natural colloquial talk of a

[176] *Life on the Mississippi,* p. 32–3.
[177] Chapter III, p. 24.

village boy never become confused in their creator's mind, for the artist in Twain rendered dialogue as truthfully as it presented human actions.

Structure

Mark Twain once spoke of Bret Harte "who trimmed and trained and schooled me patiently until he changed me from an awkward utterer of coarse grotesquenesses to a writer of paragraphs and chapters that have found a certain favor in the eyes of even some of the very decentest people in the land."[178] Yet when Clemens came to write the *Innocents Abroad* there was nothing of Harte's method in his architectonics, for as DeLancey Ferguson observes, "The continuity of the *Innocents* is the continuity of the tour it records, nothing more."[179] Here, however, is the method Twain was to follow generally throughout his career, and in this first venture boyhood days obtruded into his narrative with the memory of his rapid departure through the window of his father's office upon discovery of a corpse,[180] with the memory, too, of the boulder bounding to the foot of Holliday's Hill, narrowly missing disaster.[181] Sam Clemens was even then, despite fresh materials of the excursion, finding his deepest reservoir in boyhood memories, the same that were to make *Tom Sawyer, Huck Finn,* and the *Autobiography* great books. Yet as Bernard De Voto says, this is the method of genius, rather than of a conscientious literary craftsman, and Twain often worked on several projects at once, taking up whichever he found stimulating, only to abandon it for another when enthusiasm flagged. Sometimes a project would be laid aside for long intervals; Mark returned to several manuscripts after twenty years had lapsed, even taking up one thirty years

178 *Letters,* I, 182–3.
179 *Mark Twain: Man and Legend,* p. 137.
180 *Innocents Abroad,* I, 173–5.
181 *Ibid.,* II, 381–2. Paine, I, 58–9.

later.[182] And always experience, unconscious absorption, played its rôle. Of the letters of Walpole, read by Clemens as a boy, he said, "I absorbed them, gathered in their grace, wit, and humor, and put them away to be used by-and-by. One does that so unconsciously with the things one really likes."[183] And Mark frequently reworked his own materials; for instance there was the famous storm scene of *Following the Equator,* given first in his speech on New England weather.[184] Then the final development of the "Boy's Manuscript" of 1870 into *Tom Sawyer* shows the full extent to which Twain could elaborate and improve his own suggestion.[185]

Experience was the rough diamond; but the final artistic embodiment came through the glow of imagination, which turned actualities into the glorious world of dreams and fancy. "Get your facts first," Mark told Rudyard Kipling; "then you can distort 'em as much as you please."[186] And this method held even for historical romance, where the tall tale of frontier humor might intrude for no reason of history or form; witness *Joan of Arc,* where, as De Voto says, "Narrative obligations count for little when a chance offers for Papa D'Arc, a relative of Uncle Silas's, to remember the bull that overturned some beehives."[187]

In the preface to *Those Extraordinary Twins* Mark made a frank statement about the troublesome times arising when one tries to build a novel; the writer's problems Mark knew by experience:

> He has no clear idea of his story; in fact he has no story. He merely has some people in his mind, and an incident or two, also

182 *Mark Twain at Work* (Cambridge: Harvard University Press, 1942), p. 3.

183 Mark Twain's *Speeches* (1910 ed.), p. 215.

184 *Speeches* (1923 ed.), pp. 56–7. *Following the Equator,* II, 256–9.

185 Bernard De Voto, *op. cit.,* pp. 3–24.

186 *From Sea to Sea,* II, 180.

187 *Mark Twain's America,* p. 281.

a locality. He knows these people, he knows the selected locality, and he trusts that he can plunge those people into those incidents with interesting results. So he goes to work.[188]

But as the tale progresses and grows in length the original motif often disappears, as happened in *Pudd'nhead Wilson,* which began as a farce but changed to tragedy—all without intent by the author. Twain, as he frankly tells us, found himself with two plots on his hands, hopelessly intermingled and cluttered, with no alternative save to separate them, leaving tragedy dominant in *Pudd'nhead Wilson* and relegating the farce to another story, *Those Extraordinary Twins.* Into the farce about an Italian "freak," begun as extravaganza, other characters began to intrude, Pudd'nhead Wilson, Roxana, Tom Driscoll, who pushed themselves so prominently into the plot the others fell by the wayside; and Mark confesses:

> Before the book was half finished those three were taking things almost entirely into their own hands and working the whole tale as a private venture of their own—a tale which they had nothing at all to do with, by rights.[189]

Clemens also found that he had a defective plot, "two stories in one, a farce and a tragedy." In *Joan of Arc, The Prince and the Pauper,* and *A Connecticut Yankee,* intrusion of farce upon serious plot recurred frequently with Clemens. Here in this admixture, however, Twain managed to effect a neat dichotomy, the result being the serious plot of *Pudd'nhead Wilson* and the utter farce of *Those Extraordinary Twins.*

The mingling of diverse elements arose naturally in this instance, as often in Mark Twain's writings, from the unchartered manner of composition; it was his belief that

> . . . narrative should flow as flows the brook down through the hills and the leafy woodlands, its course changed by every

[188] Preface to *Those Extraordinary Twins,* now printed with *Pudd'nhead Wilson,* p. 207. [189] *Ibid.,* p. 209.

bowlder it comes across and by every grass-clad gravelly spur that projects into its path; its surface broken, but its course not stayed by rocks and gravel on the bottom in the shoal places; a brook that never goes straight for a minute, but *goes,* and goes briskly, sometimes ungrammatically, and sometimes fetching a horseshoe three-quarters of a mile around, and at the end of the circuit flowing within a yard of the path it traversed an hour before; but always *going,* and always following at least one law, always loyal to that law, the law of *narrative,* which *has no law.* Nothing to do but make the trip; the how of it is not important, so that the trip is made.[190]

Here we see Clemens in his insistence upon matter over manner, upon the organic over mechanics, nature over art —the opposite in many respects, of Hawthorne, Poe, and James. Yet in his very insistence upon the importance of making the trip successfully there is a realization of art; indeed what Clemens seems to be saying here is that each narrator must proceed after his fashion, his own being to let the narrative flow like the stream of life, which often diverts, eddies, and swirls before reaching its climax. While dictating his memoirs Twain made a statement equally valid for his fiction: "*The thing uppermost in a person's mind* is the thing to talk about or write about."[191] But it is the notice prefixed to *Huckleberry Finn* which states most forcefully Clemens' thoughts about preconceived plots: "persons attempting to find a plot in it will be shot."[192] In Mark's workshop the author held the pen while the stories told themselves. This he believed the only true art; of a writer who tried to substitute a fabricated narrative for facts transfigured through imagination, Twain said, "The result is a failure. It is a piece of pure literary manufacture and has the shopmarks all over it."[193] Mark seldom knew where his plot was going, if we may accept his own state-

190 *Autobiography,* I, 237.

191 *Ibid.,* I, 327.

192 "Notice," *Huckleberry Finn.*

193 *Mark Twain in Eruption,* p. 244.

ment that the author is unfamiliar with the future of his tale, "and can only find out what it is by listening as it goes along telling itself."[194]

Fortunately for American letters, the boyhood period of Hannibal recollected through a haze of memories and dreams came to appeal more and more to the mature imagination of Samuel Clemens. As Dixon Wecter tells us, the first hint occurs in one of the New York letters to the *Alta California* during the spring of 1867, a reference to the town drunkard, Jimmy Finn, together with an account of the Cadets of Temperance, joined by young Sam in order to wear a red scarf when marching in funeral processions.[195] This was to appear later in *Tom Sawyer*. And several of Tom's adventures were in a letter to Will Bowen, "My First & Oldest & Dearest Friend," when on a February day of 1870 in Buffalo Mark Twain recalled the old days and old faces from childhood.[196]

Just as Chapter XXII of *Tom Sawyer,* telling of Tom and the temperance society, was prefigured in the *Alta California* newsletter of 1867; the tale about the tick and a schoolroom game (Chapter VII) appeared briefly in a Congressional dinner speech delivered in Washington during 1868; the Robin Hood games of Chapter VIII were earlier described, though briefly, in the letter to Will Bowen;[197] the Sunday School scene of Chapter IV was first narrated in a letter to Annie Taylor in 1856, the so-called "bugs letter."[198] Naturally the *Innocents Abroad* drew upon Mark's own travel letters for subject matter, though we have already noted that even here Clemens recurred to memories of Hannibal, and in *Roughing It* he turned to his Califor-

194 Preface to *Those Extraordinary Twins,* p. 207.

195 *A Literary History of the United States,* II, 929.

196 *Mark Twain's Letters to Will Bowen,* pp. 18–21.

197 *Loc. cit.*

198 Printed by Fred W. Lorch, "Mark Twain in Iowa," *Iowa Journal of History and Politics,* XXVII, 422–5 (July, 1929).

nia newspaper work of 1863 for materials which he incorporated into Chapters VIII, XI, and XIII. Other parts of *Roughing It* were revisions of some of the Sandwich Island letters, showing that the young author realized the value of utilizing pertinent material already written. We see, then, that many of Twain's books were rehearsed, as it were. For instance, in *Roughing It,* the young man, Johnny, on the trip to the lake is treated in much the same manner as Brown in the Sandwich Island letters.[199]

Structurally *The Innocents Abroad* is a narrative of stories strung on the autobiographical thread of a journey. The momentum of the narrative is one of travel, while the stories—mostly in the manner of the frontier anecdote—are interspersed with descriptive passages, some indeed of beauty. Bernard De Voto says of the burlesque passage on Heloise and Abelard, which leads to the traditional attempt of a tourist to get an American drink:[200] "The passage is typical and the point need not be labored; . . . It is Mark discoursing in the manner of the pilot house; he has found a technique completely adapted to his qualities."[201] A similar framework encloses the structure of *Roughing It;* yet here, too, it is travel which takes the story forward, brings it to a close, and energizes throughout.[202] When Twain came to write *A Tramp Abroad, Following the Equator,* and the first half of *Life on the Mississippi,* again movement from place to place supplied the framework. Setting his characters on journeys supplies the structure or channel for the narratives of *Huckleberry Finn, A Connecticut Yankee, Joan of Arc,* and *The Prince and the Pauper;* only *Tom*

199 *Roughing It,* I, Chapters XXII and XXIII.

200 *Innocents Abroad, I,* Chapter XV.

201 *Mark Twain's America,* p. 246.

202 DeVoto, who feels that the momentum of the *Innocents* is supplied largely by anecdote, says naturally that in *Roughing It* the same motive power is employed to far greater results. *Idem.*

Sawyer and *Pudd'nhead Wilson* stand outside this device, and even these not entirely.

For the rules of Aristotle Mark had no regard; for rules in general he held no brief: what he did seek consistently was natural organic expression, not rules but natural laws. It was his conviction that execution transcends design, that a tale must tell itself, growing naturally from within until the ideal narrative, informal like actual life or talk, flows along, perhaps digressive yet ever fresh and vigorous. As Feinstein observes, "Literary form is plainly for him a function of personality rather than of genre."[203] Thus it is true that *Life on the Mississippi,* for instance, does not fit completely into any category—history, travel, or novel—being more an expression of Samuel Clemens' personality than anything else. Unity of time, place, or action means no more to Twain than it did to Shakespeare, while the tonal unity of Hawthorne or Poe struck him, it must be admitted, as artificial.

Yet Mark Twain did achieve a structural form, as the research of Trilling, Branch, Bellamy, and Blair reveals. It has been the fashion, because of Mark's insistence upon natural, organic outgrowth in expression, to say that his work is formless, but Walter Blair has demonstrated that *Tom Sawyer* has one narrative, artistically developed: the growth of a boy from adolescence toward maturity. Within this central theme are four "units of narrative, the lines of action": (1) the story of Tom and Becky, (2) the narrative of Tom and Muff Potter, (3) the Jackson Island episode, (4) the series of happenings which may be called the Injun Joe story. Of the 35 chapters comprising the novel only four fail to deal with one of these four plots, while eight chapters contain elements uniting two of the lines of action. The theme of *Tom Sawyer,* the single line of develop-

203 George Feinstein, "Mark Twain's Idea of Story Structure," *American Literature,* XVIII, 162 (May, 1946).

ment, results in one main narrative: the development of a boy from adolescence toward maturity, a theme including the four threads of plot. As the plot moves forward, Blair reminds us, "wholly boylike actions become more infrequent while adult actions increase."[204] Actually the Tom-Becky story progresses from the childishly fickle desertion of Becky by Tom to his chivalrously taking her punishment for her, and finally to his helping her in the cave. With the narrative of Tom and Muff Potter, which begins with a superstitious trip to the graveyard, there is progression to Tom's defiance of boyish superstition and his courageous testimony for Potter. The Jackson Island episode, beginning with the childish revolt of the boy against Aunt Polly, also progresses toward maturity as Tom finally reveals concern over his aunt's uneasiness about him. And the series of happenings involving Injun Joe begins with the boyish search for buried treasure, but terminates with Tom's manfully protecting Becky in the cave and Huck's conquering fear to save the widow. Moreover, as Blair states, "Every subplot in the book eventuates in an expression of adult approval."[205] We have moved from the world of childhood values found at the beginning of all four stories, through a process of development, into the realm of adult actions present at the end of each.

Mark Twain had in mind, then, the normal history of boyhood, and he worked out a "way of characterizing and a patterning of action which showed a boy developing toward manhood."[206] Perhaps the simplest explanation of the arrangement of the strands of narrative is, as Blair suggests, "a fictional working-out of the author's antipathy to the conventional plot structure of juvenile tales."[207] In a

204 Walter Blair, "On the Structure of *Tom Sawyer*," *Modern Philology*, XXXVII, 85 (August, 1939).

205 *Idem.*

206 *Ibid.*, p. 84.

207 *Ibid.*, p. 83.

word, Mark Twain, who had always disliked the unreal stories of moral boys who prospered while the wicked perished, probably decided that he would write a book about boys neither angelic nor wicked—real boys possessing both virtues and flaws. Disdaining burlesque, he turned to fictional representation of boys who were real in their thoughts and actions, and thus came naturally upon the unifying theme for his story: natural development opposed to the melodramatic sermonizing of the good- versus bad-boy tracts. With the four narratives bound together into one plot, Twain takes his children through a series of happenings from the complete world of childhood at the opening into the world of maturity which they enter at the close.

It has so long been the fashion to regard *Tom Sawyer* as structurally superior to *Huckleberry Finn* that many readers were surprised when Lionel Trilling declared, "In form and style *Huckleberry Finn* is an almost perfect work."[208] Even the elaborate game of Jim's escape, which concludes the book, is defended by Trilling as an apt way of allowing "Huck to return to his anonymity, to give up the role of hero," for Huck, modest as he is, would prefer to drop into the background, allowing Tom Sawyer to take the spotlight. As nearly everyone must know, the form of *Huckleberry Finn* is the picaresque novel, its incidents depending on the hero's travels; yet here, as Trilling illuminates, "the road itself is the greatest character in this novel of the road," for the road is the great, moving, mighty river. Indeed, Trilling sees in Huck's departures and returns to the river "a subtle and significant pattern."[209] The river is a place of delight, yet one, also, of danger, and there is no elevation of nature over human nature, for what Huck en-

208 Introduction to *The Adventures of Huckleberry Finn* (New York: Rinehart & Company, 1948), p. xv.

209 *Ibid.*, p. xvi.

joys most is being on the raft with Jim.[210] Nevertheless, the Mississippi assumes the qualities of a god, adored by Huck for its power, charm, and beauty:

> After every sally into the social life of the shore, he returns to the river with relief and thanksgiving; and at each return, regular and explicit as a chorus in a Greek tragedy, there is a hymn of praise of the god's beauty, mystery, and strength, and of his noble grandeur in contrast with the pettiness of men.[211]

In this way, river and narrative flow simultaneously, the whole structure being built around the Mississippi, which furnishes the continuity and movement of the plot. And the absolute freedom of the river-god in contrast to that of Huck and Jim integrates it further with what Edgar M. Branch calls the theme of the story—"the conflict between individual freedom and the restraints imposed by convention and force; or, within Huck's consciousness, the struggle between his intuitive morality and his conventional conscience."[212] There is further integration between Trilling's concept of the river in our story and Branch's statement that the fundamental contrast is "between spontaneous human feeling and the inhumanity of conventional or violent action—a re-embodiment of Huck's ethical problem."[213] Trilling, pointing out one of the great aspects of *Huckleberry Finn,* says that the Mississippi represents "a power which seems to have a mind and will of its own, and which, to men of moral imagination, appears to embody a great moral idea."[214] And Branch states that "the novel's subject matter, episodic and sometimes improvised, is in

210 Trilling quotes from T. S. Eliot's "The Dry Salvages" in *Four Quartets,* which begins with a meditation upon the Mississippi, which Eliot calls, "a strong brown god." *Ibid.,* p. vii.

211 *Ibid.,* p. viii.

212 Edgar M. Branch, "The Two Providences: Thematic Form in "Huckleberry Finn," *College English,* XI, 188 (January, 1950). See also Branch's *The Literary Apprenticeship of Mark Twain* (Urbana: University of Illinois Press, 1950), pp. 195–216.

213 *Ibid.,* p. 190.

214 *Op. cit.,* p. vii.

the main thematically coherent: quickened and made whole by the governing idea."[215] Both Trilling and Branch have seen the two unifying threads: the river and the moral conflict, the latter interwoven in the moral nature suggested by the former. This is further emphasized by an "ethical duality" in Huck's actions, arising from moral intuition and conventional code, which leads to his conflict "anchored in the duality of nature and dramatized through scenic analogues."[216] Branch, also like Trilling, views the final scene of the book as an integral part of the theme, significant because it is the converse of Huck's internal struggle; the difference between Twain's two boys is explained: "Tom is the romantic, working within the accepted social and moral framework; Huck is the moral realist and individualist who goes beyond it."[217] And T. S. Eliot agrees that the ending is right: "It is Huck who gives the book style. The River gives the book its form."[218] Eliot sees the end as bringing us back to the mood at the beginning, and adds that it is as impossible for Huck as for the Mississippi itself to be confined within conventional limitations. In fact, Eliot's praise for the way in which Mark concludes Huck's saga is as high as his praise for the book as a whole, which he declares a great masterpiece.

In *Huckleberry Finn,* Twain achieved organic form in a narrative that suited his ideas of story telling, being alike the most perfect expression for the thematic idea, and also a mature expression of Mark's own personality. In a word, then, the form found in Mark Twain's books is that found in life. At least that is true of his successful ones. At times, however, as E. S. Fussell suggests, Twain's heart and his feelings for the individual were in disharmony with his

215 Branch, *op. cit.,* p. 190.

216 *Ibid.,* p. 189.

217 *Ibid.,* pp. 192–3.

218 Introduction to *The Adventures of Huckleberry Finn.* (New York: Chanticleer Press, 1950), p. xii.

philosophy. Mark's humanity sometimes prevented a complete artistic integration, because he could never really feel as he said he believed about mankind. Fussell says that *The Mysterious Stranger* is an example of Twain's failure to reconcile these conflicting emotions and philosophizings.[219] But when heart and head were as one, as in the books deriving from the Mississippi Valley and the West, the artistic pattern was successful.

Origin of Humor

The origin of Mark Twain's humor is chiefly the humor of the Old Southwest amid which he ripened and matured. But a parallel source was the Negro slave, whose humor was made known to the world by the creator of Uncle Remus. From the Negroes Twain must have first heard the narratives which later went into such fabrications as the bluejay yarn of *A Tramp Abroad*.[220] The actual material is, of course, that of the bestiary, stretching back before Chaucer in point of time, but preserved in Clemens' youth by the Negro slaves, from whom he orally derived this literary type. Into this story, as related by Twain, however, comes the element of the tall tale, for the narrator, Jim Baker, is present, alive and real, to convey fantasy through an idiom, vivid and strong. Thus a narrative of utter fancy is conveyed through a medium of complete reality.[221]

Later, when a celebrity, Mark became a commentator on political and social problems, again in the tradition of frontier humor, best exemplified by Abraham Lincoln. The backwoods philosopher in a leisurely but pragmatic manner took a realistic approach to the problem, which was

219 "The Structural Problem of *The Mysterious Stranger*," *Studies in Philology*, XLIX, 95–104 (January, 1952).

220 Jim Gillis, as DeLancey Ferguson observes, gave Mark "a postgraduate course in the fine art of oral humor." Ferguson, p. 102. The fundamentals were learned from the Negroes in Missouri.

221 See Bernard De Voto's discussion, *Mark Twain's America*, pp. 251–3.

sure to impress his audience as horse sense. As we have seen, this began in the Snodgrass letters, developed steadily through Virginia City correspondence, to flower in San Francisco, with only the consummation of an art needed to lift it into the realm of literature.[222]

So much of Twain's humor derives from the folk that in retelling "The Burning Shame," for instance, or the story of Dick Baker and Tom Quartz, he was actually the folk bard in operation, taking the story by word of mouth and passing it on in print, often in prose of poetic quality. Though reality is modified by imagination—thereby lifting it into literature—the humorous tall tale also has historical value; for it reveals a heterogeneous people, so well known to Mark, engaged in the characteristic activities of everyday life. In fact, these anecdotes preserved by Clemens are a rich source of stock characterizations and incidents set against a real background. One of the origins of Twain's humor, then, is his realistic, truthful approach to life, seeing the gap between life as it is and as it should be. As Pellowe states, "Humor is sanity, a sense of perspective and proportion; it cannot be misled in this valley of illusions. It sees things as they are and keeps everything in its place—including the humorist himself."[223]

Fantasy and realism exist side by side in the humor of Mark Twain; burlesque and extravaganza derive from the former, while the latter often produces satire. Burlesque and caricature in frontier humor arose from exuberance, but as De Voto observes, "The desire to produce laughter is the motive that begets the anecdote."[224] Mark Twain as a son of the frontier came naturally by his desire to create

222 Franklin J. Meine points out that Mark at twenty-six, when the war opened, was rooted in the "kind of story-telling that had its home and earlier vogue in the genial South before the War." *Tall Tales of the Southwest,* p. xv.

223 *Mark Twain: Pilgrim from Hannibal,* p. 4.

224 *Mark Twain's America,* p. 242.

laughter, for it was part of his tradition. In addition to the word of mouth anecdote told by a narrator who skilfully constructed a tall tale of impossible fancy, there was the printed storehouse of native humor in newspapers, occasionally even in books. And Samuel Clemens was heir to it all.

Going West, Twain became even more saturated with a comic spirit of American origin; from the literary comedians came an abundance of devices for producing laughter, such as the description of the dragon in Chapter XVII of *A Tramp Abroad*,[225] or the doctor ("inspired idiot") of *Innocents Abroad.* Part of Western humor, and a very popular part, was shrewdness veiled by an assumption of simplicity.[226] This was the lecture-platform manner of Mark in his younger days, just as it had been the manner of Artemus Ward before him.

There was still another link with the past, not frontier humor or fun of the literary comedians, but the tradition of Down East humor, which furnished him, though probably unconsciously, with Mrs. Partington as a model for Aunt Polly.[227] There was also the stream of humor in the genteel tradition, which included the witty verse of Oliver Wendell Holmes, known to Clemens from formative years. Yet, after all, the actual origins of Samuel Clemens' humor seem to be in the kind of boy he was born and in the environments in which he spent his adolescence and young manhood, the Mississippi Valley and the far West.

A Study of Changing Style

Mark Twain's style is a study in evolution, beginning with his first recorded appearance in print, "The Dandy

225 The dragon passage contains comic similes, exaggeration, anticlimax and understatement. Walter Blair, *Native American Humor,* p. 148.

226 This also lies behind the humor in one of Bret Harte's better stories *An Ingenue of the Sierras.*

227 Blair, *op. cit.,* p. 152.

Frightening the Squatter," published in one of the lesser humorous journals, *The Carpet-Bag,* May 1, 1852.[228] He may have written humorous verses about two marriage announcements in Joseph P. Ament's *Courier* in 1849, while serving as printer's devil, and he may have written humorously on the excellence of a wedding cake for Orion's first Hannibal newspaper in 1850, but no definite proof has yet been established. And two anecdotes said by Paine to have been published in 1851 have to date not been located.[229] Hence "The Dandy" remains his first published writing.

There is nothing impressive about this account of an Eastern dandy who tried to frighten a squatter for the amusement of the steamboat passengers and got the daylights knocked out of him, but it shows young Sam Clemens retelling for a Boston journal a rough, comic yarn, popular along the river. The style is simple and direct with no more dialect than is necessary for conversation.

When Orion left Sam in charge of the *Journal* during the summer of 1852, however, his career of newspaper writing actually commenced. In July a mad dog conveniently caused enough excitement in Hannibal to involve young Clemens in controversy with a rival editor; Sam signd himself "A Dog-be-deviled Citizen" and wrote flippantly in colloquialisms peppered with an occasional pun.[230] Then as "W. Epaminondas Adrastus Blab" he engaged in humor more indicative of the future; such sentences as "The first Blab lived in Adam's time," and "honorable mention was made of one of them in a book that was never published," show an advance over mere physical humor.[231] And though colloquial, the style is free of dialect.

A poem, *Love Concealed: To Miss Katie of H——l,* is a

228 Franklin J. Meine, *Tall Tales of the Southwest,* 446–8.

229 Branch, "Chronological Bibliography," *American Literature,* XVIII, 113–4 (May, 1946).

230 Brashear, *Mark Twain, Son of Missouri,* p. 113.

231 "Blabbing Government Secrets," *Ibid.,* pp. 117–8.

conventional bit of versifying, written by Clemens to provide a series of exchanges purportedly by correspondents, though actually by himself.[232] The opportunities of "H——l" for humorous incongruities were worked to the fullest. Upon being dignified by Orion with the title of assistant editor, Sam next turned out three columns of miscellaneous squibs on current events in which humor mingles with moralizing.[233] Again the style is simple, direct, and free of dialect, though highly colloquial.

Following the sub-editor period in Hannibal, *Mark Twain's Letters in the Muscatine Journal* were written intermittently during 1853 through 1855.[234] Newsy with travel talk of Philadelphia, Washington, and St. Louis, they furnish Clemens' reactions to current events and a record of his leisure hours. Though only five in number they reveal a growing interest in economic, political, and social problems; and even if mainly biographical, these letters for the Muscatine *Journal* reveal a tendency to write succinctly. Professor Lorch points out Clemens' debt to R. A. Smith's *Philadelphia As It Is in 1852* for both description and comments, especially in the letter of December 24, 1853.[235] It was a debt, however, revealing a superiority of style, for Clemens improved the diction of his source. For instance, General Braddock "died" instead of "breathed his last," and was carried to the "grave" rather than his "long home," where he was "buried" and not "interred."[236] More vigorous also than the original, Clemens said that DeKalb "fell fighting for American Independence" while Smith had

232 Reprinted by Brashear, p. 121.

233 "Our Assistant's Column" is ascribed to Clemens by Miss Brashear. The other Hannibal writings can be identified by the story "My First Literary Venture," *Sketches New and Old,* p. 95.

234 Edgar M. Branch, *Mark Twain's Letters in the Muscatine Journal* (Chicago: Mark Twain Association of America, 1942).

235 Fred W. Lorch, "Mark Twain's Philadelphia Letters in the Muscatine *Journal,*" *American Literature,* XVII, 348–52 (January, 1946).

236 *Ibid.*, p. 352.

stated "fell in the cause of American Independence." From these letters we see that the young journalist possessed simplicity and directness of style.

Sam Clemens next wrote three letters for the Keokuk (Iowa) *Saturday Post* which show gusto and robust humor. They are an advance over the Muscatine correspondence, for here we have a humorous character depicted and a narrative of his exploits. These adventures, too, mark Clemens' sole excursion into the realm of dialect spelling. Told through the mouth of Thomas Jefferson Snodgrass, the yarns are narrated in the dialect of a countryman, though the mixed spelling so disastrous to the fame of George W. Harris is held to a minimum. It was a kind of humor then in vogue, conveyed by peculiarities of spelling and grammar. The first letter has the so-often-used scene of the country bumpkin at the theatre. The second letter, however, indicates that Clemens had a travel book in mind:

> You know arter going down there to St. Louis, and seein so many wonderful things, I wanted to see more—so I took a notion to go a travelin, so as to see the world, and then write a book about it—a kind o daily journal like—and have all in gold on the back of it, "Snodgrass' Dierrea," or something of that kind, like other authors that visits forren parts.[237]

In fact, Snodgrass is well equipped with travel guides "and all kinds of sich books, not excepting a 'guide to heaven,' which last ain't much use to a fellar in Chicago."[238]

These letters reveal some of the same delight in coarseness that poured forth later in Washoe. Snodgrass meets an "indigent Irish woman—a widow with nineteen children and several at the breast, accordin to custom"; and when he decides to relate an unpleasant adventure of the previous evening he confides, "but drat if it don't work me worse'n

[237] *The Adventures of Thomas Jefferson Snodgrass,* ed. by Charles Honce (Chicago: Pascal Covici, 1928), pp. 19–20.

[238] *Ibid.,* p. 21.

castor oil just to think of it."[239] Left with a stranger's baby on his hands Snodgrass, "walked it, and tossed it, and cussed it, till the sweat run off my carcass to the amount of a barl at least."[240] And the brutality that has been present in all primitive humor from Beowulf to Minsky's burlesque appears here with the falsely-accused "onnateral father" seeking to extricate himself by "trying to poke the dang thing through a hole in the ice."[241]

Clemens' style is both vigorous and crude in these letters, direct and realistic in detail, however fantastic the situations being narrated. By now he had advanced over the guidebook imitation of the *Muscatine Letters,* had created a character through whom he could give free expression to crudities—a device he was to continue—, and had embarked upon the journey motif, which furnished the framework of his more mature efforts. When next he turned to Snodgrass, however, Clemens changed the given name to Quintus Curtius and eschewed dialect spellings. As befitted the more classical name, the style became more formal; perhaps Sam suspected that what might delight Keokuk would be less acceptable for the more cosmopolitan readers of the New Orleans *Daily Crescent.*[242]

Here Clemens wrote satire, describing first in mock-heroic style the discomforts en route to capture the Federal garrison at Baton Rouge. But he soon turned to parody—something Mark was always inclined to do in his satire—making fun of the Confederate *Manual of Arms* in a way to suggest personal familiarity. The letters are presented to the reader "by the kind permission of our friend Brown" to

239 *Ibid.,* p. 41.
240 *Ibid.,* p. 46.
241 *Ibid.,* p. 47.
242 This second series of Snodgrass letters was first discovered by Miss Brashear, who reprinted one and described three others, *Mark Twain, Son of Missouri,* pp. 180–92. Six additional letters were later discovered by Professor Leisy, who edited the entire series, *The Letters of Quintus Curtius Snodgrass* (Dallas: Southern Methodist University, 1946).

whom they were written by Snodgrass. Physical crudities are absent, yet physical discomfort and lack of dignity are present; five soldiers sleep on one mattress, Snodgrass complaining how he awoke and "found myself vigorously clinging to the nose of one of my comrades, while the foot of another was across the place where my cravat would have been had I been wearing such an article."[243] And there are references to "turpentinery whisky and tobacco largely sprinkled with pine shavings."[244] Horseplay enters with the description of young ladies enthusiastically showering fruit upon the ranks of departing soldiers and bringing about confusion, ended only by "a maliciously inclined party chucking a pippin through the dining-room window."[245] Humor is reached, also, by descriptions of over-eating and too much drinking, but handled in a manner that is humorous without being offensive to the senses. Unlike the humor of the earlier Thomas Jefferson Snodgrass, who was in the tradition of the frontier, that of his successor Quintus Curtius is more urbane and less boisterous, while there is the ring of the future Twain in this advice to volunteers:

> In attacking a fortress, it is well to hang back a little (you can be examining the lock of your musket or taking an imaginary stone out of your shoe) and let the eager ones get in first and draw the enemy's fire, after which you may enter with comparative impunity and take your full share of the glory.[246]

In the evolution of Mark Twain's style, the second series of Snodgrass letters is more literary and mature than the earlier one. But the substitution of satire for exuberance, in view of future developments, seems due to the medium rather than to any fundamental change in Twain's character.

The next work of Samuel Clemens was for the Virginia

243 *The Letters of Quintus Curtius Snodgrass*, p. 7.
244 *Ibid.*, p. 8.
245 *Ibid.*, p. 28.
246 *Ibid.*, p. 59.

City *Territorial Enterprise,* the kind of writing the author of *The Dandy* and the creator of Thomas Jefferson Snodgrass would take to naturally—enthusiastic, spirited, and exuberantly masculine. His audience, rough, energetic, frequently crude, was also realistic, generous, and scornful of pretense. Humor here was elemental, generally physical, often depending on horseplay. An example of his Nevada style is the bloody massacre hoax, coarse and gory in details, fantastic in exaggerations, its satire and social reproof embedded in a native joke.[247] As a piece of literary craftsmanship it has no value whatever; the subsequent account of his own hoax given by Mark later in the East is far more effective, both as humor and narrative, yet the original is stark and vivid. "The scalpless corpse of Mrs. Hopkins lay across the threshold, with her head split open and her right hand almost severed from the wrist," leaves no flights to the imagination, while the description of her husband bearing "a reeking scalp from which the warm, smoking blood was still dripping" seems unusually raw for a hoax of any sort.[248] And the predicament in which Mark found himself and the *Enterprise,* causing him to admit publicly, "I take it all back," shows that at times he might go it too strong even for Washoe.[249]

Still amusing, nevertheless, is the petrified man hoax about the figure found petrified in a position, making it necessary to blast him for burial, a course, however, forbidden as sacrilege by the presiding judge. The position of the right hand thumbing the nose to posterity shows that Mark

[247] The version copied from the *Enterprise* by the San Francisco *Bulletin,* October 31, 1863, is probably verbatim. Reprinted in Benson, pp. 176–7. The later one given by Paine shows emendations, Appendix C, IV, 1597–9. Mark in "My Bloody Massacre," *Sketches New and Old,* adds some touches not found in the original.

[248] Benson, *Mark Twain's Western Years,* p. 176.

[249] *Ibid.,* p. 177.

liked his jokes crude, even as Washoe.[250] In short, the style of Twain's writings from Nevada was such as his readers relished. An invitation to drink brings the reply, "D——n it, old Vermin-ranch, I'll do it."[251] Sentimentality fades before realism; Mark turned drama critic devastated the melodramatic *Ingomar,* remarking upon the abduction of the heroine's father, "It will cost thirty ounces of silver to get him out of soak."[252] Breezy, colloquial, realistic in manner, it was calculated to please an audience possessing similar characteristics.

When shortly thereafter the "wild humorist of the Sage Brush Hills" journeyed to San Francisco to become the "Washoe Giant," we find much the same style persisting, for many readers of the *Golden Era* were themselves lately come from the Stanislaus. Humor revolting to sensitive ears poured forth in the diatribe against "Those Blasted Children" with advice to cure a child of fits by soaking it in a barrel of rain water, and if necessary, "soak it a week. You can't soak a child too much when it has fits."[253] "The Great Prize Fight" bristles with humor based upon the combatants tearing each other apart, until at the end of the fracas "baskets were procured, and Bill Stewart and Judge Field proceeded to gather up the fragments of their late principals."[254]

And recounting an excursion into spiritualism Mark says, "I saw a good-looking, earnest-faced, pale-red-haired, neatly dressed, young woman standing on a little stage behind a small deal table with slender legs and no drawers—the table understand me."[255]

On an early morning excursion to the Cliff House, how-

250 Reprinted in the San Francisco *Bulletin* as "A Washoe Joke," October 15, 1862. Now available in Benson, p. 175.

251 Benson, p. 179.

252 *Ibid.,* p. 182.

253 *The Washoe Giant in San Francisco,* p. 22.

254 *Ibid.,* p. 30.

255 *Ibid.,* p. 122.

ever, he revels in describing the "fragrant, sweaty horse-blankets" and the cold that numbed all senses save smell.[256] Twain apparently enjoyed equally the account of the Kearny Street Ghost with its bloody kittens left on a pillow. "What would you think," he writes, "of a ghost that came to your bedside at dead of night and had kittens."[257] If we recall Thomas Jefferson Snodgrass, we must admit that the West only gave Twain freedom, the coarse inclinations, though dormant in the Muscatine and New Orleans letters, now reappearing.

Though Clemens believed at one time that it was Bret Harte who had trained and schooled him, what he wrote in San Francisco justifies no such statement. What Sam Clemens penned for the *Californian* differs little from what he wrote for the *Enterprise*; his first contribution to the *Californian,* October, 1864, combined a love letter with a soap boiler's advertisement. A week later he had a wonderful time describing a stranded whale which "smells more like a thousand pole-cats."[258] Opening the story with references to sea-sickness and bilious fever, Mark was soon happily describing the long row of bottles behind the bar and the drunken attempts of his comrade at speech. In this same sketch the law of compensation is thus expounded, "Behold, the same gust of wind that blows a lady's dress aside, and exposes her ankle, fills your eyes so full of sand that you can't see it."[259]

All are in the vein of Washoe: "Daniel in the Lion's Den—and Out Again All Right" describes drinking and swapping lies with stock-jobbing brokers, introduces momentarily a "Snodgrass," and ends with the fantasy of St. Peter's admitting those Bulls and Bears into Paradise.[260] Later on Mark, still practicing mining camp puns, called

256 *Ibid.*, p. 85.

257 *Ibid.*, p. 121.

258 *Sketches of the Sixties,* p. 128.

259 *Ibid.*, pp. 127–8.

260 Published November 5, 1864, *Ibid.*, pp. 143–150.

the Great Bear the Great Menken—a reference to the actress who appeared nearly nude; pictured a drunk with a "wine-bred cauliflower" on his nose "spitting on his shirt bosom and slurring it off with his hand";[261] and wrote a jingle about a sow whose "swill is mine, and all my slops her gain." Truly the mature style of Mark Twain seems little influenced by the journalists of San Francisco's literary frontier, for any refining influence Harte may have exerted is unapparent. Indeed, the pieces collected in *Sketches of the Sixties* and *The Washoe Giant in San Francisco* might well have been written in Virginia City; the style is rough, physical, and boisterous.

Shortly thereafter when the Sandwich Island correspondence appeared in the Sacramento *Union* Mark decided to express his coarser humor through a character called Brown, thus using crudity while absolving himself from censure. The primitive delight in physical discomfort persists here in the seasick passengers' vomiting while Brown comforted, "it'll clean you out like a jug, and then you won't feel ornery and smell so ridiculous."[262] Irreverence appears, too, when Balboa becomes "like any other Greaser" and a "shameless old foreign humbug," deserving a blast to make his "old dry bones rattle" for misnaming this violent ocean "Pacific." Yet Twain seemed aware that his subject called for more dignity than his former pieces for the *Golden Era* and the *Californian* because the style is free of puns and illiteracies, and generally less colloquial. At times there are references to smells and indelicacies, while the humor of impropriety—so dear to Mark—appears through the talk of a lady gathering up old bones on a battlefield:

> Mr. Smith, you have got some of my bones; and you have got one, too, Mr. Jones; and you have got my spine, Mr. Twain.

261 *Ibid.*, p. 192.
262 *Letters from the Sandwich Islands*, p. 3.

Now don't any of you gentlemen get my bones all mixed up with yours so that you can't tell them apart.[263]

Nevertheless, three *Union* letters entirely devoid of humor were concerned with statistics, one dealing with Hawaiian trade generally, one with the whaling trade, and one with the sugar industry.[264] Another letter told the tragedy of the *Hornet,* burned at sea, her survivors suffering starvation and exposure. This last, the high-water mark in Twain's achievements to that date, appeared in the *Union,* and again in a fuller account in *Harper's Magazine.*[265]

When the subject demanded, or his audience expected it, Twain could be formal and proper; but if occasion permitted, he lapsed into the unsophisticated, realistic observer, commenting after a fashion to delight Keokuk or Washoe. For this he introduced the fictitious traveling companion, Brown, already used tentatively earlier, who served two functions: primarily to voice crudities Mark wished to utter but preferred to say through another, and secondarily to present the reverse—the realistic in contrast to the romantic, the repugnant and offensive as against the beautiful. That Mark felt it necessary to create Brown shows not alone his duality of romanticist and realist, but also an improvement in taste, a transition from unrestrained crudity to a more refined treatment of subject matter.

These letters from the Sandwich Islands are Twain's first sustained writing, an advance over the burlesque and satire of previous unrelated sketches. Treating his subject comprehensively and informatively, Mark was entertaining, serious, or light as the material demanded. Here he combined

263 *Ibid.,* p. 47.

264 These letters, numbers 3, 10, and 23 respectively in the series of twenty-five, are found in Walter F. Frear, *Mark Twain and Hawaii,* and in Thomas Nickerson, *Letters from Honolulu.*

265 December, 1866, "Forty-three Days in an Open Boat." This letter, number 15, is available in both Frear and Nickerson.

factual statements with passages of beautiful description, filled with sense perceptions that conveyed vividly the sights and sounds of nature; here, too, abundant humor bubbled forth in satire, burlesque, and anecdote, while a propensity to moralize appeared in the ridicule directed at petty politicians. It was his first important reportorial assignment, and Mark worked hard to make it a success. Though he was obligated to cover only the sugar and whaling industries and the transportation problems, the artist in Twain pictured scenic beauty, while the potential novelist described social, political, and religious conditions. An interest in legends, personalities, and history of the islands, an acute foresight of their future importance, a delight in scenic grandeur—all spiced with abundant humor—enlivened what might have been merely trade correspondence. The *Union* letters mark the transition from the rough humor of the Western mining camp to the mature style of the future. Not the cessation, however, for Mark's delight in such humor was not to be so quickly stifled, remaining in abeyance often to break forth in such unexpected places as *Joan of Arc*.

In this transition Mr. Brown figures prominently, for Mark was writing for the West, and the realistic humor and unromantic scepticism, often vulgar or irreverent, were to diminish slowly as Twain found the East less inclined to approve. Brown accompanied him through the letters for the San Francisco *Alta California* in 1866 and 1867, describing adventures in Nicaragua, Hannibal, and New York just prior to departure for Europe. Irrepressible as the humor he expressed, Brown's cynicism and anti-romantic nature intrude upon Mark's descriptions of the voyage from San Francisco, the crossing of Nicaragua, the cholera-stricken passage up the Atlantic, and arrival in New York. The people, fashions, customs, and institutions of the Eastern metropolis are described with an eye on his Western audience, one quick to detect in Brown the alter ego of their correspondent. It was Brown en route who repeated gossip from the venomous old hag Miss Slimmens:

> . . . and she says she knew that innocent old fat girl that's always asleep and has to be shovelled out of her room at four-bells for the inspection, and always eats till her eyes bug out like the bolt-heads on a jail door—knew her long ago up on the San Joaquin, and knows the clothes she's got on now she's travelled in eleven weeks without changing—says her stockings are awful—they're eleven weeks gone, too—and when she complained of the weather being so hot, old Slimmens said, 'Why don't she go and scrape herself and then wash—it would be equal to taking off two suits of flannel!'[266]

In these letters, written at the time Mark was abandoning the California scene to embark upon the voyage that would produce the *Innocents Abroad,* the old delight in repulsive humor remained. In fact, it might be said that the letters from Honolulu show more refinement of style, for Clemens, with the trip abroad ahead of him, was in a gay mood, one always leading into exuberant expression. And exuberance for Twain resulted in more than physical action; it generally led to the roughness of humor to which he had become accustomed. Though in New York he was still writing for San Francisco; moreover he had recently journeyed out to Hannibal, Keokuk, and Quincy. A visit to the places of his youth must have refreshed his memory of the humorists of the Old Southwest, who held so much in common with the literary comedians and humorous lecturers of the Coast.

Soon he was to write his third series of travel correspondence for Western readers, some fifty letters sent to the *Alta California* during his excursion to Europe and the Holy Land. But when prospects for a book appeared, Clemens

[266] *Mark Twain's Travels with Mr. Brown,* p. 26.

realized that he would be addressing a different audience; for six months he revised, also converting the separate letters into a unit. To Elisha Bliss, Jr., he wrote of weeding the letters of "their chief faults of construction and inelegancies of expression"[267]—a task that would eliminate some passages and necessitate creating new ones. Mark knew the difference, even this early, between books and the "wind and water" of newspaper matter.[268] It was form, then, as well as audience that demanded revision. And it was not only construction that improved but also style; repetition of words—often in the same sentence—and monotony of expression disappeared. A glance through his material told Twain that he needed variety, something achieved by introducing new passages and revising old ones. But some changes were made in the interest of decorum; Mark had already confided to Mrs. Fairbanks that a lecture delivered successfully before his Western friends probably "would be pretty roughly criticised in an eastern town."[269] In fact, part of his consternation on hearing that the newspaper owners contemplated publication of his letters themselves was over style, for he had also written Mrs. Fairbanks, "If the *Alta's* book were to come out with those wretched, slangy letters unrevised, I should be utterly ruined."[270]

To adapt his writings to the more genteel taste of the East, Clemens, depending less upon the extravagant, grotesque situations so delightful to his former associates, sought a more polite expression. Revising colloquialisms raised the diction to a more literary level; he struck out many words and references that might give offense. He deleted the word *mangy,* substituted "donkey" for "jackass," and euphemized "lies" into "exaggerations." "Bawdy-

267 *Letters,* I, 141.
268 *Autobiography,* I, 245.
269 *Mark Twain to Mrs. Fairbanks,* p. 34.
270 *Ibid.,* p. 24.

house," "slimy cesspool," and "stink"[271] vanished with his Western audience; yet enough frontier irreverence remained to alarm the publishers with fear of fostering a blasphemous enterprise.[272] Mark, however, had toned down his newspaper version, omitting many criticisms of the church, such as the "fat and greasy" Italian priests, who "would yield oil like a whale"; he left out references to gambling like "She [Venice] bets her all on St. Mark's"; and describing the straight-up view during the ascent of Vesuvius he refrained from repeating "The ladies wore no hoops, which was well. They would have looked like so many umbrellas."[273]

Twain, moreover, revised some of the flippances, omitted passages about the religious habits and beliefs of the pilgrims, as well as some questioning of their piety. And he gave up, no doubt reluctantly, the broad humor involving "Mr. Brown," who disappears from the book, his vulgar remarks generally being left out, while his purely ignorant ones are attributed to other pilgrims, usually to Blucher, sometimes to Jack. The *Innocents Abroad,* too, is less highly seasoned with slang than the *Alta* version, and in general the book is a stylistic improvement over the letters. For one thing, it is clearer; there is more continuity in paragraphing and smoother transition. The loose construction is tightened thereby; and when necessary whole scenes, such as the glove-buying episode in Gibraltar,[274] or the Parisian tour conducted by pilgrim-christened Ferguson,[275] were newly contrived. In these, Twain was on the way to becoming a novelist, for he replaced the satirical humor at the narrator's expense—so prevalent in the letters—with

[271] For a full study of Clemens' efforts to achieve a more polite expression see Leon T. Dickinson, "Mark Twain's Revisions in Writing *The Innocents Abroad," American Literature,* XIX, 139–57 (May, 1947).

[272] *Mark Twain in Eruption,* pp. 147–8.

[273] Dickinson, *op. cit.,* p. 147.

[274] *Innocents Abroad,* I, 60–3.

[275] *Ibid.,* I, 111–17.

detailed situations involving several characters who express themselves through dialogue. An air of reality is achieved as episodes are particularized and characters come to life. And in defense of San Francisco, be it said, not all of the passages needed revision; the description of the Parthenon by moonlight—one of the finest Twain ever wrote—was scarcely altered a word.[276] Even if Mark's Western audience had been predominantly masculine, and the newly-sought Eastern one greatly dominated by feminine taste, both could sometimes enjoy the same material.

During the nineteen-twenties the question would arise as to whether or not Twain was a suppressed genius, a vital creative artist ruined by the censorship of his wife and her associates. While Van Wyck Brooks would have it so, Bernard De Voto has issued a flat denial, thereby setting off a debate which probably cannot be settled until all of the unpublished items in the Mark Twain papers have been printed. What does seem certain, however, is that the censorship was more constructive than harmful, and once he realized that he was now writing for a cosmopolitan audience Twain himself refined his taste.

When *Roughing It* appeared in 1872 Mark incorporated about one third of the Sandwich Island correspondence into it. Much of this text remains unchanged; in fact, the best passages in the Sandwich Island sections of *Roughing It* were taken practically verbatim from the originals.[277] Of course, Mr. Brown's crude humor disappears here, just as it did from the *Innocents,* but the descriptive passages and the observations on native character and custom were little changed. Though discarding about two-thirds of the letters, what Mark did carry over remained practically the same. By now Twain had achieved maturity of style, he addressed an audience on both sides of the Atlantic, and there was to

276 *Ibid.,* II, 54–7.
277 *Letters from the Sandwich Islands,* p. x.

be a steady progression until with *The Mysterious Stranger* even the colloquial was forsaken.

Though maturity of style was established with the *Innocents,* Mark frequently submitted manuscripts to Howells and Livy, generally with the result that they were improved. Actually Howells' expurgations, as DeLancey Ferguson illustrates, were often aimed at verisimilitude rather than bowdlerization.[278] It was Mark himself who changed Huck's "They comb me all to hell," to read "thunder"; indeed Howells had perused the manuscript, even as Livy, her mother, and aunt had listened to Mark read it, without notice.[279] Mark was a Victorian, one who might indulge in an Elizabethan freedom of expression in his unpublished manuscripts, but who in print observed the conventions. And it was just as well that he did; no editor would have wished to offend his readers, and one need no more expect Mark Twain to write with the verbal freedom of a Caldwell or Farrell than he might expect Robert Browning to exercise the same realism as Chaucer. Though the unpublished manuscripts of the Mark Twain Estate contain lengthy discussions of sexual intercourse, revealing a very un-Victorian frankness about its physical delight to women, when he published, Mark wrote for his age—just as Chaucer and Shakespeare wrote for theirs.

DeLancey Ferguson in a minute analysis of the manuscript of *Huckleberry Finn* concludes that the revisions, whether made by Mark or Livy—their handwriting was very similar—"are not the dilution of grim realism to make it meat for babies; they are the work of a skilled craftsman removing the unessential, adding vividness to dialogue and description, and smoothing incongruities."[280] Though the manuscript, which is almost three-fourths complete, con-

278 *Mark Twain: Man and Legend,* pp. 180–1.
279 *Letters,* I, 272–4.
280 *Op. cit.,* p. 219.

tains more than nine hundred differences from the book, the overwhelming majority of alterations are improvements in concrete expression or substitutions to make the language right for the character speaking.[281] Bernard De Voto, however, counts thirty-seven "softenings" such as "damn" toned down to "blame" and "drunk" changed to "mellow." But he finally concludes that almost all changes were made voluntarily by Mark "in obedience to his own judgment and his own conception of propriety and public taste."[282]

In a word, Mark wrote in the style best suited to his audience. Yet there remained, always in abeyance, a natural delight in rough humor; for as late as 1896, Mark wrote that Paul Bourget had charged him with preferring "the manure pile to the violets."[283] And two years later "At the Appetite Cure" gave him a chance to revel in menus that would have delighted strong-stomached Washoe but are the despair of the squeamish: "young cat; old cat; scrambled cat," and "sailor-boots, softened with tallow—served raw."[284] That Mark also took pleasure at times—as did Abraham Lincoln—in robust coarseness expressed in Anglo-Saxon terms is well-known through the notoriety achieved by *1601*.[285] The letter to Mr. Rogers, written presumably in September, 1894, though free of verbal vulgarity, derives its humor from the predicament of Mark's being trapped in the women's water closet of a hotel.[286] Then there is the speech on onanism delivered to the Stom-

281 Ferguson has made a full study of these changes, "Huck Finn A-Borning," *Colophon,* new series, Vol. III, No. 2. See also his *Mark Twain: Man and Legend,* Chapter XIII.

282 *Mark Twain at Work.* p. 83–5.

283 "A Little Note to M. Paul Bourget," first included in the English edition of *Tom Sawyer Abroad,* then in *How to Tell a Story and Other Essays* (Harpers, 1897), now printed in *In Defense of Harriet Shelley and Other Essays,* pp. 171–85.

284 Printed in *Cosmopolitan Magazine,* August, 1898. Now in *In Defense of Harriet Shelley,* p. 348.

285 Most easily procured in *1601 and Sketches Old and New* (New York: Golden Hind Press, 1933).

286 *Notebook,* pp. 238–40.

ach Club in Paris.[287] So far as style *per se* is concerned, too much has been made of these excursions into ribaldry. That Mark sometimes enjoyed a vulgar joke cannot be denied, but that he realized the impropriety of bringing smoking-room humor into the drawing room is equally evident. In brief, Twain had the good taste to realize that a time and place exists for everything. It is evidence of the inclusiveness of the man that his appreciation ranged broadly from the fastidious to the bawdy, without, however, lacking the essential good taste to perceive which was which.

Yet for humor merely coarse without being bawdy his taste often wavered. Mark had delighted too long in such revels on the coast, and they had been too enthusiastically greeted by his readers for him ever to realize entirely that such things might give offense. Had not readers of *The Golden Era* roared with delight at his descriptions of the Pioneer Ball:

> Miss C. L. B. had her fine nose elegantly enameled, and the easy grace with which she blew it from time to time, marked her as a cultivated and accomplished woman of the world; its exquisitely modulated tone excited the admiration of all who had the happiness to hear it.[288]

Was it not natural, then, to believe his audience in 1882 might enjoy a story about the confusion of a corpse in its coffin with a box of guns embellished by a sack of Limburger cheese, and the vivid description of the ensuing nausea accompanied by awe?[289]

Many present-day readers find pleasure in these overflowings of the Victorian dikes of propriety; we frankly delight in much that offended past sensibilities, even as our own taste will perhaps amuse posterity.

287 Unpublished papers of the Mark Twain Estate.

288 *The Washoe Giant,* p. 42.

289 First printed as part of "Some Rambling Notes of an Idle Excursion," *The Stolen White Elephant,* (Webster and Co., 1882). Now in *In Defense of Harriet Shelley* as "*The Invalid's Story,*" pp. 178–96.

Mark Twain's mature style is vivid, direct, and accurate, for he disliked pretension in writing, even as he did in human beings. Twain gives us clear and specific detail to convey accurate description of person or place, an accuracy which demanded American colloquial speech and dialect. Yet his prose, simple, lucid, and graceful—if one looks beyond the dialect—is the result of a conscious, literary effort. It was this knowledge of the actual speech of America that influenced Ernest Hemingway to say, "all modern American literature comes from one book by Mark Twain called *Huckleberry Finn*."[290] The quality of Twain's dialogue, no doubt, enabled Professor Quinn to pick out certain lines in *Ah Sin,* the dramatic collaboration of Bret Harte and Clemens, as indubitably Mark's; for instance the malapropisms of Mrs. Plunkett: "Here we stand, two lonely, friendless, dissolute women," or "I cannot think of him without going into ecstasies of sensibility, perfect ruptures of emotion."[291] Mark's accurate feeling for the precise word led him to deplore the prose of Cooper; among other things, an author should, he stated:

> Say what he is proposing to say, not merely come near it.
> Use the right word, not its second cousin.
> Eschew surplusage.[292]

But what lifts Twain's prose to the highest literary level is not alone his vivid accuracy, but passages also of poetic sense perceptions. There is, for instance, the expression of Huck Finn's melancholy:

> I felt so lonesome I most wished I was dead. The stars were shining, and the leaves rustled in the woods ever so mournful; and I heard an owl, away off, who-whooing about somebody

290 *The Green Hills of Africa* (New York: Charles Scribner's Sons, 1935), p. 22.

291 Arthur Hobson Quinn, *A History of the American Drama* (New York: Crofts, rev. ed., 1937), p. 111.

292 "Fenimore Cooper's Literary Offenses," *In Defense of Harriet Shelley,* p. 63.

that was dead, and a whippowill and a dog crying about somebody that was going to die; and the wind was trying to whisper something to me, and I couldn't make out what it was, and so it made the cold shivers run over me.[293]

Huck, like his creator, is quick to perceive beauty: ". . . the stars over us was sparkling ever so fine; and down by the village was the river, a whole mile broad, and awful still and grand."[294] Sense perceptions of sight and sound are keenly alive in the boy: "The sky looks ever so deep when you lay down on your back in the moonshine; I never knowed it before. And how far a body can hear on the water such nights!"[295] The same feeling, intensified, is repeated later on: "It was kind of solemn, drifting down the big, still river, laying on our backs looking up at the stars, and we didn't ever feel like talking loud, and it warn't often that we laughed—only a little kind of a low chuckle."[296] Towns passed in the night, "away up on black hillsides," became "nothing but just a shiny bed of lights."[297] The steamboat that ran over the raft at night appeared first "a black cloud with rows of glow-worms around it," then "bulged out, big and scary, with a long row of wide-open furnace doors shining like red-hot teeth."[298] Huck standing watch on the raft witnesses a terrific storm: "My souls, how the wind did scream along! And every second or two there'd come a glare that lit up the white-caps for a half a mile around, and you'd see the islands looking dusty through the rain, and the trees thrashing around in the wind."[299]

There is, in addition, the earlier description of the upper Mississippi:

And then you have the shining river, winding here and there and yonder, its sweep interrupted at intervals by clusters of wooded islands threaded by silver channels; and you have

293 *The Adventures of Huckleberry Finn*, p. 4.
294 *Ibid.*, p. 9.
295 *Ibid.*, p. 49.
296 *Ibid.*, p. 90.
297 *Loc. cit.*
298 *Ibid.*, p. 131.
299 *Ibid.*, p. 177.

glimpses of distant villages, asleep upon capes; and of stealthy rafts slipping along in the shade of the forest walls; and of white steamers vanishing around remote points. And it is all as tranquil and reposeful as dreamland, and has nothing this-worldly about it—nothing to hang a fret or a worry upon.[300]

Another passage showing Twain's appreciation of nature had appeared even earlier:

The land that has four well-defined seasons cannot lack beauty, or pall with monotony. Each season brings a world of enjoyment and interest in the watching of its unfolding, its gradual, harmonious development, its culminating graces—and just as one begins to tire of it, it passes away and a radical change comes, with new witcheries and new glories in its train. And I think, that to one in sympathy with nature, each season, in its turn, seems the loveliest.[301]

Twain's figurative language may take the form of a pretty simile: "At half-eclipse the moon was like a gilded acorn in its cup."[302] or it may be humorous: "the house was as empty as a beer closet in premises where painters have been at work."[303] But in every instance a clear-cut impression is conveyed to the reader, one imparting perception of beauty or causing the smile of humor—and always precise. The changing style of Mark Twain retained the humor, realism, and accuracy of the humorists of the Old Southwest and the literary comedians of the Pacific coast, but it went beyond them because its creator was an artist of rare perception, sensitive to beauty. When the author desires, there is a harmony between subject matter and manner that is compatible as nature; and when incongruity of manner and matter is introduced for comedy the art of disparity is quite as great. Mark Twain was an artist born, conditioned by environment, but potentially endowed to grow beyond his originals. Style is the man, and the style of Mark Twain

300 *Life on the Mississippi,* pp. 473–4.

301 *Roughing It,* II, 126.

302 *Following the Equator,* I, 44.

303 "The McWilliamses and the Burglar Alarm," *The Mysterious Stranger,* p. 323.

contains those same qualities of truth, beauty, humor, and humanity that made Samuel Clemens great as a man.

SELECTED BIBLIOGRAPHY

MIND AND ART

Andrews, Kenneth R. *Nook Farm: Mark Twain's Hartford Circle.* Cambridge, Massachusetts: Harvard University Press, 1950.
[Detailed study of Twain's Connecticut environment and its influence.]

Bay, J. Christian. "Tom Sawyer Detective: The Origin of the Plot," *Essays Offered to Herbert Putnam by His Colleagues and Friends on His Thirtieth Anniversary as Librarian of Congress.* New Haven: Yale University Press, 1929, pp. 80–88.

Bellamy, Gladys Carmen. *Mark Twain as a Literary Artist.* Norman: University of Oklahoma Press, 1950.
[Especially helpful for the travel books.]

Benson, Ivan. *Mark Twain's Western Years.* Stanford University, California: Stanford University Press, 1938.
[The standard work on Mark's development in the West, where he became a journalist.]

Blair, Walter. *Native American Humor.* New York: American Book Co., 1937.
[Excellent discussion of Twain in relation to our native traditions in frontier humor.]

Branch, Edgar M. *The Literary Apprenticeship of Mark Twain.* Urbana: University of Illinois Press, 1950.
[Definitive study of Mark's apprenticeship development.]

——. editor. *Mark Twain's Letters in the Muscatine Journal.* Chicago: Mark Twain Association of America, 1942.
[Shows development in style.]

Brashear, Minnie M. *Mark Twain, Son of Missouri.* Chapel Hill: University of North Carolina Press, 1934.
[Invaluable for formative influences.]

De Casseres, Benjamin. *When Huck Finn Went Highbrow.* New York: Thomas F. Madigan, 1934.
[Tells of Twain's admiration for Browning's poetry.]

De Voto, Bernard. *Mark Twain's America.* Boston: Little, Brown and Co., revised edition, 1935.
[Traces the frontier influence; important.]

——. *Mark Twain at Work.* Cambridge, Massachusetts: Harvard University Press, 1942.
[Important contribution.]

Eliot, T. S. Introduction, *The Adventures of Huckleberry Finn.* New York: Chanticleer Press, 1950.
[Good discussion of the book's style, structure, and its qualities of greatness by an important critic and poet.]

Emberson, Frances G. "Mark Twain's Vocabulary: A General Survey," *University of Missouri Studies,* X, 1–56 (July, 1935).
[Sound study, supplemented by a bibliography.]

Frear, Walter Francis. *Mark Twain and Hawaii.* Chicago: The Lakeside Press, 1947.
[Shows maturity influence of the island visit.]

Lewis, Oscar. *The Origin of the Celebrated Jumping Frog of Calaveras County.* San Francisco: Book Club of California, 1931.

Mack, Effie Mona. *Mark Twain in Nevada.* New York: Charles Scribner's Sons, 1947.
[Full account of the Washoe environment.]

Meine, Franklin J. *Tall Tales of the Southwest.* New York: Alfred A. Knopf, 1930.
[Covers its field fully; contains Twain's first story.]

Paine, Albert Bigelow. *Mark Twain: A Biography.* 3 vols. New York: Harper & Brothers, 1912. Revised in 2 vols., 1935.
[Despite critical weakness and factual errors, an indispensable work for a study of Twain's development as an artist.]

Rourke, Constance. *American Humor, a Study of the National Character.* New York: Harcourt, Brace and Co., 1931.
[Relates Mark to the native tradition.]

Scott, Harold P. "The Laughable in Literature," *The Fred Newton Scott Anniversary Papers.* Chicago: University of Chicago Press, 1929.
[Brief analysis of Twain's humor.]

Taylor, Coley B. *Mark Twain's Margins on Thackeray's Swift.* New York: Gotham House, 1935.

Trilling, Lionel. Introduction, *The Adventures of Huckleberry Finn.* New York: Rinehart & Co., 1948).
[Best study of the form of this narrative.]

Wagenknecht, Edward. *Mark Twain: The Man and His Work.* New Haven: Yale University Press, 1935.
[Important; examines Twain's mind and work.]

Walker, Franklin. *San Francisco's Literary Frontier.* New York: Alfred Knopf, 1939.
[Sheds light on Twain's literary progress.]

Webster, Samuel Charles. *Mark Twain, Business Man.* Boston: Little, Brown and Company, 1946.
[Adds to our knowledge of Mark's environment.]

West, Victor R. *Folklore in the Works of Mark Twain* (University of Nebraska *Studies in Language and Literature,* X, Lincoln, Nebraska, 1930).
[Best study so far.]

ARTICLES

Bellamy, Gladys Carmen. "Mark Twain's Indebtedness to John Phoenix," *American Literature,* XIII, 29–43 (March, 1941).
[Gives parallel passages from the two humorists.]

Benson, A. B. "Mark Twain's Contacts with Scandinavia," *Scandinavian Studies and Notes,* XIV, 159–167 (August, 1937).
[Scandinavian acquaintances and sources.]

Blair, Walter. "On the Structure of *Tom Sawyer,*" *Modern Philology,* XXXVII, 75–88 (August, 1939).
[One of the most important treatments of Twain's art.]

Blanck, Jacob. "*The Gilded Age: A Collation,*" *Publishers' Weekly,* CXXXVIII, 186–8 (July 20, 1940).

Branch, Edgar M. "The Two Providences: Thematic Form in *Huckleberry Finn,*" *College English,* 188–95 (January, 1950).
[Illuminating study of form and thought.]

Brashear, Minnie M. "Mark Twain Juvenilia," *American Literature,* II, 25–53 (March, 1930).
[Describes earliest journalism of Clemens and shows the cultural importance of Hannibal as a town.]

Brownell, George H. "Twain's Version of Hamlet," *Twainian,* II, 4–6 (June, 1943).
[Twain introduced a comic book salesman into *Hamlet.* Still unpublished in the Twain papers.]

Buxbaum, Katherine. "Mark Twain and American Dialect," *American Speech,* II, 233–6 (February, 1927).

[Reveals vigor of Twain's dialect.]

Chapman, John W. "The Germ of a Book—a Footnote on Mark Twain," *Atlantic Monthly,* CL, 720–1 (December, 1932).

[Possible source for Simon Lathers in *The American Claimant.*]

Clemens, Cyril, "Mark Twain's Washington in 1868," *Mark Twain Quarterly,* V, 1–16 (Summer, 1942).

[Newspaper correspondence, unfortunately not arranged in order.]

Cooper, Lane. "Mark Twain's Lilacs and Laburnums," *Modern Language Notes,* XLVII, 85–7 (February, 1932).

[Reveals that Mark parodied passages in *The Seamy Side, a Story,* by Walter Besant and James Rice for *A Double-Barreled Detective Story.*]

Cowie, Alexander. "Mark Twain Controls Himself," *American Literature,* X, 488–91 (January, 1939).

[Expresses belief that Mark's robust style was censored.]

De Voto, Bernard. "The Mark Twain Papers," *Saturday Review of Literature,* XIX, 3–4, 14–15 (December 10, 1938).

[Describes material still unpublished in the Twain papers.]

——. "The Matrix of Mark Twain's Humor," *Bookman,* LXXIV, 172–8 (October, 1931).

[Shows the importance of frontier newspaper humor of the first half of the nineteenth century in producing Twain's humor.]

Dickinson, Leon T. "Mark Twain's Revisions in Writing *The Innocents Abroad,*" American Literature, XIX, 139–157 (May, 1947).

[Reveals Twain's revisions as he made the *Alta* letters into a book for Eastern readers.]

——. "The Sources of *The Prince and the Pauper,*" *Modern Language Notes,* LXIV, 103–6 (February, 1949).

[Show that Mark used J. Hammond Trumbull's *The True Blue Laws* and Francis Kirkman's *The English Rogue.*]

Dreiser, Theodore. "Mark the Double Twain," *English Journal,* XXIV, 615–27 (October, 1935).

[Dreiser denies that Twain was two people but rather a dissuaded genius who gradually became his natural self.]

Eidson, John Olin. "Innocents Abroad: Then and Now," *Georgia Review,* II, 186–92 (Summer, 1948).
[Shows that the American soldiers of World War II echoed Mark's attitude toward European culture.]

Feinstein, George. "Mark Twain's Idea of Story Structure," *American Literature,* XVIII, 160–3 (May, 1946).
[Shows individualized form of Twain.]

Ferguson, DeLancey. "Huck Finn A-Borning," *Colophon,* n.s., III, 171–180 (Spring, 1938).
[Based on examination of the original manuscript. Rejects Brooks' theory of undue censorship.]

——. "The Uncollected Portions of Mark Twain's Autobiography," *American Literature,* VIII, 37–46 (March, 1936).
[Important study of differences in magazine and book publication of the *Autobiography.*]

Flack, Frank M. "Mark Twain and Music," *Twainian,* II, 1–3 (October, 1942).
[Twain's appreciation of good music.]

Fussell, E. S. "The Structural Problem of *The Mysterious Stranger,*" *Studies in Philology,* XLIX, 95–104 (January, 1952).
[Discusses Twain's attempt to reconcile his humanitarian feelings for the individual with his philosophy.]

Gary, Lorena M. "Mark Twain—Boy and Philosopher," *Overland Monthly,* XCI, 154–5 (November, 1933).
[Sees all Twain's writings arising from youthful spirit.]

Gay, Robert M. "The Two Mark Twains," *Atlantic Monthly,* CLXVI, 724–6 (December, 1940).
[Reveals the poet hidden beneath the jester.]

Goold, Edgar H., Jr. "Mark Twain on the Writing of Fiction," *American Literature,* XXVI, 141–53 (May, 1954).
[Defines Twain's concepts of realism and organic unity.]

Hemminghaus, Edgar H. "Mark Twain's German Provenience," *Modern Language Quarterly,* VI, 459–78 (December, 1945).
[The extent of Twain's opinions of German writers and his acquaintance with them.]

Hoben, J. B. "Mark Twain's *A Connecticut Yankee:* A Genetic Study," *American Literature,* XVIII, 197–218 (November, 1946).
[An important study of how the story developed, and how Matthew Arnold influenced it.]

Hustvedt, S. B. "The Preacher and the Gray Mare," *California Folklore Quarterly,* V, 109–10 (January, 1947).
[Chapter XXV of *Life in the Mississippi* and the Jonah story.]

Jones, Joseph. "The Duke's Tooth Powder Racket: A Note on *Huckleberry Finn,*" *Modern Language Notes,* LXI, 468–9 (November, 1946).
[Shows actual existence of this ruse.]

Klett, Ada M. "Meisterschaft, or the True State of Mark Twain's German," *American-German Review,* VII, No. 2, 10–11 (December, 1940).
[Reveals Twain's slight knowledge of German.]

Leacock, Stephen. "Two Humorists: Charles Dickens and Mark Twain," *Yale Review,* XXIV, 118–29 (September, 1934).
[Interesting comments by one who is a fine humorist himself.]

Leisy, Ernest E. "Mark Twain's Part in *The Gilded Age,*" *American Literature,* VIII, 445–8 (January, 1937).
[Explains the exact part each author had in the work.]

——. "The Quintus Curtius Snodgrass Letters in the New Orleans *Daily Crescent.*" *Twainian,* V, 1–2 (September–October 1946).
[Recounts an interesting discovery.]

Lillard, Richard G. "Contemporary Reaction to the Empire City Massacre," *American Literature,* XVI, 198–203 (November, 1944).

Long, E. Hudson. "Sut Lovingood and Mark Twain's *Joan of Arc,*" *Modern Language Notes,* LXIV, 37–9 (January, 1949).
[Shows that George W. Harris' yarn, "Sicily Burns' Wedding," was used in Volume II, Chapter XXXVI of *Joan of Arc.*]

Lorch, Fred W. "Mark Twain's Early Views on Western Indians," *Twainian,* IV, 1–2 (April, 1945).
[Shows maturity in outlook of *Tom Sawyer* over the early Western sketches.]

——. "Mark Twain's Philadelphia Letters in the Muscatine *Journal,*" *American Literature,* XVII, 348–51 (January, 1946).
[Shows source to be R. A. Smith's *Philadelphia As It Is in 1852.*]

——. "Mark Twain's Trip to Humbolt in 1861," *American Literature,* X, 343–9 (November, 1938).

[Reprints letter from the Keokuk *Gate City,* which tells of the experiences used in Chapters XXVII to XXXIV in *Roughing It.*]

——. "A Note on Tom Blankenship" (Huckleberry Finn), *American Literature,* XII, 351–3 (November, 1940).

[The original of Huck was still unregenerate in 1861.]

Lowell, Charles J. "The Background of Mark Twain's Vocabulary," *American Speech,* 88–9 (April, 1947).

[Influence of frontier usage.]

McKeithan, D. M. "Mark Twain's *Tom Sawyer Abroad* and Jules Verne's *Five Weeks in a Balloon,*" University of Texas *Studies in English,* XXVIII, 257–70 (1949).

[Indicates a number of similarities.]

Moore, Olin H. "Mark Twain and Don Quixote," *Publications of the Modern Language Association,* XXXVII, 324–46 (June, 1922).

[Traces supposed influence of Cervantes.]

Mott, Howard S., Jr. "The Origin of Aunt Polly," *Publishers' Weekly,* CXXXIV, 1821–3 (November 11, 1938).

[Shows similarity between *Tom Sawyer* and *The Life and Sayings of Mrs. Partington.*]

Partridge, H. M. "Did Mark Twain Perpetrate Literary Hoaxes?" *American Book Collector,* V, 351–7 (December, 1934).

[Discussion of early work under pseudonyms.]

Ramsey, Robert L. and Emberson, Frances Gutherie. "A Mark Twain Lexicon," *University of Missouri Studies,* XIII, i–cxix; 1–278 (January, 1938).

[Classification of Twain's vocabulary under Americanisms, New Words, Archaisms, and miscellaneous groups.]

Roberts, Harold. "Sam Clemens: Florida Days," *Twainian,* I, 4–6 (March, 1942).

[The influence of John A. Quarles and his farm.]

Slater, Joseph. "Music at Col. Grangerford's: A Footnote to *Huckleberry Finn,*" *American Literature,* XXI, 108–111 (March, 1949).

[Affirms the musical compositions mentioned were based upon fact.]

Tidwell, James N. "Mark Twain's Representation of Negro Speech," *American Speech,* XVII, 174–6 (October, 1942).

Vogelback, Arthur L. "Mark Twain: Newspaper Contributor," *American Literature,* XX, 111–28 (May, 1948).

[Discusses Twain's press writings in the decade following the *Innocents.*]

——. "The Prince and the Pauper: A Study in Critical Standards," *American Literature,* XIV, 48–54 (March, 1942).

[Shows how this book fitted genteel tradition.]

Walker, Franklin. "An Influence from San Francisco on Mark Twain's *The Gilded Age,*" *American Literature,* VIII, 63–6 (March, 1936).

[Actual experiences of Laura D. Fair, whose trial was notorious, parallel those of Laura Hawkins in this book.]

Weatherly, E. H. "Beau Tibbs and Colonel Sellers," *Modern Language Notes,* LIX, 310–13 (May, 1944).

[Similarity between Goldsmith's Beau Tibbs in *The Citizen of the World* and Colonel Sellers in *The Gilded Age.*]

Webster, Samuel C. "Ghost Life on the Mississippi," *Pacific Spectator,* II, 485–90 (Autumn, 1948).

[A Twain manuscript reveals more river-ghost lore.]

Wecter, Dixon. "Mark Twain as Translator from the German," *American Literature* XIII, 257–64 (November, 1941).

[Proves Twain's German more fluent than accurate, yet spirited and original in Struwwelpeter translation.]

Whiting, B. J. "Guyuscutus, Royal Nonesuch and Other Hoaxes," *Southern Folklore Quarterly,* VIII, 251–75 (December, 1944).

Williams, Mentor L. "Mark Twain's Joan of Arc," *Michigan Alumnus Quarterly Review,* LIV, 243–250 (May 8, 1948).

[Important study of the sources and of Joan as a symbol to Clemens of humanity at its best.]

Wilson, Robert H. "Malory in the *Connecticut Yankee,*" *University of Texas Studies in English,* XXVII, 185–205 (June, 1948).

CHAPTER V

FUNDAMENTAL IDEAS

THOUGH MARK TWAIN was fully aware of his deficiencies in formal learning,[1] he nevertheless seems to have taken himself seriously as a "philosopher."[2] An early tendency to moralize appears in his sub-editor writings at Hannibal;[3] before leaving San Francisco he was introduced as "The Moralist of the Main";[4] satire mingles with moralizing as his work matures, until finally we have the expounding of his "Gospel" in *What Is Man?* Lacking any inclination to be the founder of a definitely formalized system of thought, having none of the mystical approach, Twain perhaps does not deserve the title of philosopher at all. Yet if to reason upon the purpose of man in this universe, to ponder the question of his existence, and the meaning of life entitles one to be called *thinker,* then surely Mark Twain was that.

The questions engaging Twain, however, were ethical, moral, and practical rather than mystical, speculative, or dialectical. Growing up in a religious household in a religious community, where the law-abiding were in the ma-

1 Of Theodor Mommsen, the German historian and archeologist, Mark wrote, "Been taken for Mommsen twice. We have the same hair, but upon examination it was found that our brains were different." *Notebook,* p. 222. When Twain saw Mommsen at a celebration in honor of another scientist he said, "I could have touched him with my hand—Mommsen—think of it!" Paine, III, 938.

2 Paine states that he repeatedly emphasized his doctrine of man as an irresponsible machine, saying that it covered everything like the sky; "you can't break through anywhere." Paine, IV, 1322.

3 Brashear, pp. 130–1.

4 Webb's preface to *The Jumping Frog.*

jority, Clemens' early religious beliefs came from a normal, healthy background, which as readers of *Tom Sawyer* may perceive, included fun, play, and amusement.[5] Hannibal valued religion as a guide to life, not as speculative theology, and if one were a true Christian his acts would show it.[6] If Sam's father embraced "village-lawyer agnosticism," bequeathing to his son, the "will to disbelieve,"[7] never at any time did he reject the Christian ethics. On the contrary, his ethical character seems to have been transmitted to the future author, who had in his father an example of high ideals and morality. It was not the ethics of Christianity, then, nor the purpose of Christ that Twain was later to assail, but actually the superstitions and dogmas that may accompany any religion. For the code of Christ Clemens had nothing save reverence, and for those who lived by it nought but admiration and respect.[8] But he reserved the privilege to determine his own personal habits and tastes. In other words, the code by which Samuel Clemens lived partook of the philosophy of John Stuart Mill: "The only freedom which deserves the name, is that of pursuing our own good in our own way, so long as we do not attempt to deprive others of theirs, or impede their efforts to obtain it."[9] When people sought to interfere with Mark's personal

[5] The mistaken thesis about the frontier found in Brooks and in Lewis Mumford's *The Golden Day* need no longer detain us.

[6] The attitude is expressed in John Hay's poem *Jim Bludso of the Prairie Belle.*

[7] Dixon Wecter, "Mark Twain," *Literary History of the United States,* II, 918.

[8] In *Captain Stormfield's Visit to Heaven,* where the traditional concept of pearly-gate symbols is burlesqued, the following dialogue occurs:

"Well, sir, I says, pretty humble, "I don't seem to make out which world it is I'm from. But you may know it from this—it's the one the Saviour saved."

He bent his head at the Name. Then he says, gently—

"The worlds He has saved are like to the gates of heaven in number—none can count them."

"Captain Stormfield's Visit to Heaven," *The Mysterious Stranger,* p. 231.

[9] *On Liberty* (Oxford University Press, 1933), p. 18.

habits, simply because they did not approve, his reaction was like Huck Finn's when the widow stopped his smoking:

> Pretty soon I wanted to smoke, and asked the widow to let me. But she wouldn't. She said it was a mean practice and wasn't clean, and I must try to not do it any more. That is just the way with some people. They get down on a thing when they don't know nothing about it. Here she was a-bothering about Moses, which was no kin to her, and no use to anybody, being gone, you see, yet finding a power of fault with me for doing a thing that had some good in it. And she took snuff, too; of course, that was all right, because she done it herself.[10]

Yet for those who admired Christian ethics and who held their high standard in life Twain felt comradeship. The many clergymen who were his friends understood his nature and furnished him spiritual and intellectual companionship. As Pellowe states: "For fundamentally in the weightier things of justice, good government, intelligent living and progressive thought, Mark Twain and these clergymen were kindred spirits."[11] Though reared in the Sunday School, Sam Clemens with the example of his father before him was too sceptical to accept a fundamentalist interpretation of the scriptures. There was, moreover, the subsequent influence of the Scotchman named Macfarlane, who had anticipated the Darwin theory, and whose conclusions left their impress upon Clemens for life.[12] At the fundamentalist then, at the God of the Old Testament, Twain uttered impieties. Mark inherited, also, the spontaneous irreverence of the frontier, an irreverence so natural it could become all embracing.

The frontier, deep down under, had an immature dislike of authority and restraint; ministers and school teachers, as

[10] *Huckleberry Finn,* pp. 2–3.

[11] William C. S. Pellowe, *Mark Twain: Pilgrim from Hannibal* (New York: Hobson Book Press, 1945), p. 117. Clemens once wrote to a friend, "I am glad you are in the ministry. It is the highest dignity to which a man may aspire in this life." Dixon Wecter, *Sam Clemens of Hannibal,* p. 231.

[12] Paine, I, 115.

well as law enforcement officers, fell into this category. Not Sut Lovingood and Simon Suggs alone indulged in acts toward the clergy of prodigious disrespect, for the humor of the Old Southwest abounds with examples of this attitude.[13] Along with the scepticism of his father Samuel Clemens inherited, then, this impious attitude as part of his regional environment, acquiring it by a kind of frontier osmosis. And he never outgrew it. But his disregard was not really for the cloth, for Joseph Twichell remained as valued a friend as Mark ever had.[14]

As already indicated, Twain's dislike was not for the ethics of the Christian faith, but for what he regarded as ignorance and superstition. He had once wondered if God were actually aware of man's existence at all. And, moreover, he could not countenance man's reducing the greatness of God to the level of triviality by talking about "special providence" for himself, a belief he felt gave man a position of too extreme importance:

> In my opinion these myriads of globes are merely the blood corpuscles ebbing and flowing through the arteries of God and we but animalculae that infest them, disease them, pollute them; and God does not know we are there and would not care if He did.[15]

Indeed, he had never accepted the Bible as a guide to spiritual salvation, for large portions of it seemed nothing more than fables and mythology. To Livy, who insisted upon Bible readings during the early days of their marriage he declared that much of it contradicted his reason.[16] It was not the idea of God that he resisted, but the Old Testament

13 An especially good example is "A Tight Race Considerin'" by an author calling himself Madison Tensas in Walter Blair's *Native American Humor,* pp. 299–307.

14 Twichell appealed to Twain from the first, Mark describing him on brief acquaintance as "a bully boy with a glass eye." *Love Letters,* p. 10.

15 *Notebook,* p. 190.

16 Paine, II, 411.

account, which he felt distorted a grand and noble concept. In retaliation he wrote:

To trust the God of the Bible is to trust an irascible, vindictive, fierce and ever fickle and changeful master; to trust the true God is to trust a Being who has uttered no promises, but whose beneficent, exact, and changeless ordering of the machinery of his colossal universe is proof that he is at least steadfast to his purposes; whose unwritten laws, so far as they affect man, being equal and impartial, show that he is just and fair; these things, taken together, suggest that if he shall ordain us to live hereafter, he will still be steadfast, just, and fair toward us. We shall not need to require anything more.[17]

But his belief in a God, "just and fair" was not constant; for the "hell" that man lives in "from the cradle to the grave" assumed larger proportions in Mark's thinking as his personal adversities increased. Twain stated his convictions about Christ in a letter to Orion: "Neither Howells nor I believe in hell or the divinity of the Savior, but no matter, the Savior is none the less a sacred Personage, and a man should have no desire or disposition to refer to him lightly, profanely, or otherwise than with the profoundest reverence."[18] Neither did he desire to mock at any sincere expression of religious faith, such for instance as prayer. Yet his honesty precluded any pretense on his part, leading him once to confess to Twichell that he did not believe the Bible to be inspired by God. And he added, "The problem of life and death and eternity and the true concept of God is a bigger thing than is contained in that book."[19]

It was the fundamentalist attitude toward a personalized devil which led Mark to joke:

A person (Satan) who for untold centuries has maintained the imposing position of spiritual head of 4/5 of the human race, and political head of the whole of it, must be granted the possession of executive abilities of the highest order. In his large

17 *Ibid.*, II, 412. 18 *Letters*, I, 323.
19 Paine, II, 631.

presence the other popes and politicians shrink to midgets for the microscope.

He hasn't a single salaried helper; the Opposition employ a million.[20]

So profound was Clemens' belief in a larger God than the one of the Old Testament, in a greater mind governing the immutable laws of time and change, that eventually he converted his wife. In his philosophy the individual became merely a unit in the larger scheme of life—if at all times he remained even that—a belief which destroyed all illusions of a personal God. Nevertheless, Twain insisted upon a divine spirit. "No one who thinks can imagine the universe made by chance," he once observed. "It is too nicely assembled and regulated. There is, of course, a great Master Mind, but it cares nothing for our happiness or our unhappiness."[21] Declaring the Old Testament portrait of a wrathful God to be merely "a portrait of a man, if one can imagine a man with evil impulses far beyond the human limit," Clemens found it "the most damnatory biography that ever found its way into print."[22]

As Mark grew older he became increasingly preoccupied with evil in the universe; of that he was as acutely conscious as Hawthorne or Melville. And in his gropings for an answer he came, more and more, to disparage whatever Creative Force might be blamed; he declared at the same time that regret filled his mind over the lip-service which alone was so often paid to the teachings of Christ: "There has been only one Christian. They caught Him and crucified Him early."[23] Yet he often talked with his biographer about the unseen forces of creation, those immutable laws hold-

[20] *Notebook,* p. 343. This passage was used in "Concerning the Jews," Mark adding, "I would like to see him. I would rather see him and shake him by the tail than any other member of the European Concert." *In Defense of Harriet Shelley,* p. 265.

[21] Paine, IV, 1353.

[22] *Ibid.,* IV, 1354.

[23] *Notebook,* p. 344.

ing the planets to their courses and bringing the seasons with their miracles of diversity and beauty. Such Twain designated "The Great Law," whose principle seemed to be unity, and whose outward expression was revealed in the beauties of nature.[24] In these conversations Paine failed to find "any suggestion of pessimism, but only justice." However, there is a distinct lack of any optimism in Mark's own statement written on a card at the time:

> From everlasting to everlasting, this is the law: the *sum* of wrong and misery shall always keep exact step with the *sum* of human blessedness.
>
> No "civilization," no "advance," has ever modified these proportions by even the shadow of a shade, nor ever can, while our race endures.[25]

To Livy he wrote, on the other hand, that since man contains a "preponderance of goodness" we may conclude that "what we call God" must possess the same as "his own principal feature."[26] And once Clemens made the following deliberate attempt to formalize his concept of the Deity:

> The Being who to me is the real God is the One who created this majestic universe and rules it. He is the only Originator, the only originator of thoughts; thoughts suggested from within not from without; the originator of colors and of all their possible combinations; of forces and the laws that govern them; of forms and shapes of *all* forms.[27]

And as he continued, Mark came close to Wordsworth and Whitman in this passage:

> He is the perfect artisan, the perfect artist. Everything which he has made is fine, everything which he has made is beautiful;

24 Mark seems close to Whitman here, as well as the Emerson of *The American Scholar*.

25 Paine, IV, 1469. In this chapter "Stormfield Philosophies" there are amusing passages on Satan, Herod, and superstitions in general. Mark burlesqued the Second Advent, laid in Arkansas, in a forthcoming volume, *Letters from the Earth,* now in Twain Mss.

26 *Love Letters,* p. 253.

27 *Notebook,* pp. 360–1.

nothing coarse, nothing ugly has ever come from His hand. Even His materials are all delicate, none of them is coarse. The materials of the leaf, the flower, the fruit; of the insect, the elephant, the man; of the earth, the crags and the ocean; of the snow, the hoar-frost and the ice—may be reduced to infinitesimal particles and they are still delicate, still faultless; whether He makes a gnat, a bird, a horse, a plain, a forest, a mountain range, a planet, a constellation, or a diatom whose form the keenest eye in the world cannot perceive, it is all one —He makes it utterly and minutely perfect in form, and construction.[28]

In this mood, Mark even resorts to a Whitman-like catalogue of wonders, while the Wordsworthian lament for what man has made of man is more explicit in the following praise of the Creator:

His real character is written in plain words in His real Bible, which is Nature and her history; we read it every day, and we could understand it and trust in it if we would burn the spurious one and dig the remains of our insignificant reasoning faculties out of the grave where that and other man-made Bibles have buried them for 2000 years and more.[29]

Yet even here Twain confides that "God cares not a rap for us—nor for any living creature." What purpose evil serves, or the infliction of pain, Mark frankly confesses he does not know, but he does affirm that it is not due to any evil nature of God.[30]

At some time, not definite—Paine thinks during the early eighties—Twain set down a lengthy statement of his religious beliefs, beginning:

I believe in God the Almighty

I do not believe He has ever sent a message to man by anybody, or delivered one to him by word of mouth, or made Himself visible to mortal eyes at any time in any place.

28 *Loc. cit.*

29 *Ibid.*, p. 362. This is similar to Tom Paine in *The Age of Reason*.

30 *Idem.*

I believe that the Old and New Testaments were imagined and written by man, and that no line in them was authorized by God, much less inspired by Him.

I think the goodness, the justice, and the mercy of God are manifested in His works: I perceive that they are manifested toward me in this life; the logical conclusion is that they will be manifested toward me in the life to come, if there should be one.[31]

He dismissed the idea of special providences as a figment arising from man's conceit, and eternal punishment as illogical. As to the moral laws from which the legal laws governing man's conduct are devised, Clemens expressed belief that they came in no manner from the Deity but were "the outcome of the world's experience."[32]

His final statement on immortality, however, is revealed indirectly at the time of Livy's fatal illness. With remorse at having destroyed her own faith, Clemens wrote his wife, "Dear, dear sweetheart, I have been thinking & examining, & searching & analyzing, for many days, & am vexed to find that I more believe in the immortality of the soul than misbelieve in it."[33] As expected her reply was one of pleasure. The clue to his actual convictions, however, appears penciled on the back of the envelope containing Livy's letter: "In the bitterness of death it was G. W.'s chiefest solace that he had never told a lie except this one."[34]

As Mark aged, however, and as the human race continued its course toward two destructive world catastrophes, blasphemous convictions grew that God was not good but wicked. Indeed, he came to blame God for all disease, pestilence, crime, and war. For instance, Twain took the house fly, disease-carrier of filth, to charge that the Creator of the universe was not kind or good, but really man's

[31] Paine, IV, 1582. Save for a changed attitude about God's mercy to man, Twain did not deviate materially from this statement in later years.

[32] *Idem.*

[33] *Love Letters,* p. 344.

[34] *Ibid.,* p. 345.

enemy, devising this affliction to bring upon the human race ill health and death. Thus in the darkness of despair we find him actually going back to the wrathful, vengeful God of the Old Testament he had so oft repudiated as a myth.[35]

One of Twain's most profound statements on prayer occurs when Huck Finn, torn between his loyalty to contemporary customs and the humane promptings of the heart, tries to pray:

But the words wouldn't come. Why wouldn't they? It warn't no use to try and hide it from Him. Nor from *me,* neither. I knowed very well why they wouldn't come. It was because my heart warn't right; it was because I warn't square; it was because I was playing double. I was letting *on* to give up sin, but away inside of me I was holding on to the biggest one of all. I was trying to make my mouth *say* I would do the right thing and the clean thing, and go and write to that nigger's owner and tell where he was; but deep down in me I knowed it was a lie, and He knowed it. You can't pray a lie—I found that out.[36]

Thus did Twain's immortal boy stand alone before his God.

Yet it would seem that Mark Twain rejected the divine inspiration of the scriptures and the divinity of Christ; he rejected all belief in special providences; he rejected as fables or myths the ideas of hell, Satan, and a heaven of harp-playing angels. But he did believe in God as a "Larger Law" governing the universe and all that is in it. Ethically he was a Christian; for in his life, truth, honor, and lofty ideals are the fabric of his character. No one ever held a greater admiration for the ideals of Christianity than Mark, nor ever felt more remorse when those principles were degraded.

[35] Mark Twain Mss. Clemens made a more somber and persistent attack in these unpublished papers than in his books, where the same ideas are presented, sometimes humorously, and less frequently. The manuscript materials reveal how much of Twain's thought was spent upon God in relation to the human race.

[36] *Huckleberry Finn,* p. 295.

Mark Twain's political views were closely allied with his concept of Christian ethics. Though frequently active on behalf of good government, Clemens was himself entirely without political ambition. And when an editorial writer suggested that Twain "the greatest man of his day in private life" merited consideration as a presidential candidate, Mark did not even offer the encouragement of a jest.[37] Yet since the days when he had attacked municipal corruption on the Coast, Twain had worked for good government. It was the good of the nation that he sought, not the intrenchment of any political faction. To Howells he wrote in 1884, "It is not *parties* that make or save countries or that build them to greatness—it is clean men, clean ordinary citizens, rank and file, the masses."[38] Clemens, moreover, practiced his own preaching in politics. And the man who told Howells, "Clean masses are not made by individuals standing back till the rest become clean" was the same speaker who threw his heart and soul into defeating "Boss" Croker.[39]

With a firm belief that the duty of every citizen was first of all to "his own honor," loyalty to his country coming second, and the party last, Twain outlined a plan for a "Casting-Vote party"; it would nominate no candidates but support the better man nominated by either the Democrats or Republicans, thereby forcing the two major parties to select men of honest purpose.[40] For those who felt that their loyalty was to a party, first and last, Mark stated, "I prefer to be a citizen of the United States."[41] He felt that independence of mind was a personal privilege, and Clemens echoed the sentiments of Thoreau that he alone could determine what was patriotic for himself. Once he answered some Republican friends who questioned his desertion to Cleveland:

37 Paine, III, 1201.
38 *Letters,* II, 445.
39 "Mark Twain in Politics," Paine, III, 1145–1148.
40 *Ibid.,* III, 1147.
41 *Notebook,* p. 203.

I said that no party held the privilege of dictating to me how I should vote. That if party loyalty was a form of patriotism, I was no patriot, and that I didn't think I was much of a patriot, anyway, for oftener than otherwise what the general body of Americans regarded as the patriotic course was not in accordance with my views; that if there was any valuable difference between being an American and a monarchist it lay in the theory that the American could decide for himself what is patriotic and what isn't; whereas the king could dictate the monarchist's patriotism for him—a decision which was final and must be accepted by the victim; that in my belief I was the only person in the sixty millions—with Congress and the Administration back of the sixty millions—who was privileged to construct my patriotism for me.[42]

Clemens, in fact, was to become an ardent Cleveland admirer, regarding him as "one of our two or three real Presidents."[43]

It is no surprise, then, to find Mark's Yankee at the court of King Arthur expressing similar sentiments:

You see my kind of loyalty was loyalty to one's country, not to its institutions or its office-holders. The country is the real thing, the substantial thing, the eternal thing; it is the thing to watch over, and care for, and be loyal to; institutions are extraneous, they are its mere clothing, and clothing can wear out, become ragged, cease to be comfortable, cease to protect the body from winter, disease, and death.[44]

The Yankee, in fact, repeats the identical note Twain had struck, so like Thoreau:

Under that gospel, the citizen who thinks he sees that the commonwealth's political clothes are worn out, and yet holds his peace and does not agitate for a new suit, is disloyal; he is a traitor. That he may be the only one who thinks he sees this decay, does not excuse him; it is his duty to agitate anyway.[45]

42 *Autobiography,* II, 17.

43 Paine, IV, 1454. On June 19, 1908, Clemens wrote of Cleveland, "He is high-minded; all his impulses are great and pure and fine. I wish we had another of this sort." *Love Letters,* p. 218.

44 *A Connecticut Yankee in King Arthur's Court,* p. 107.

45 *Idem.*

And it was the Yankee, realizing that about six people alone from each thousand in the land determined its government, who said, "It seemed to me that what the nine hundred and ninety-four dupes needed was a new deal."[46] Here was born the most famous slogan of our times, taken into the political arena by Franklin D. Roosevelt.[47]

The intimate relationship between Twain's politics and his devotion to Christian ethics is made clear in the following passage:

> A man can be a Christian *or* a patriot, but he can't legally be a Christian *and* a patriot—except in the usual way: one of the two with the mouth, the other with the heart. The spirit of Christianity proclaims the brotherhood of the race and the meaning of that strong word has not been left to guesswork, but made tremendously definite. . . .
>
> The spirit of patriotism being in its nature jealous and selfish, is just in man's line, it comes natural to him—he can live up to all its requirements to the letter; but the spirit of Christianity is not in its entirety possible to him.[48]

Mark's international outlook, implicit in the foregoing, shows clearly in these lines from the same passage:

> Word it as softly as you please, the spirit of patriotism is the spirit of the dog and the wolf. The moment there is a misunderstanding about a boundary line or a hamper of fish or some other squalid matter, see patriotism rise, and hear him split the universe with his war-whoop.[49]

Twain was opposed to violence, a believer in law and order in contrast to unreason and emotion, and he thought all cruelty should be punished. Believing that right should appropriate might, that the weak need protection against the strong, Mark looked upon the rising labor unions, such as the Knights of Labor, as equalizing power between the forces of capital and the workers. To Howells he sent an essay extolling the unionized workman as "the greatest

46 *Ibid.*, p. 108.

47 Edward Wagenknecht, *Mark Twain: The Man and His Work*, p. 265.

48 *Notebook*, pp. 332–3.

49 *Idem.*

birth of the greatest age the nations of the world have known," one who "has before him the most righteous work that was ever given into the hands of man to do; and he will do it."[50] In this opinion Twain did not change, for in the year of his death he defended unions as "the only means by which the workman could obtain recognition of his rights."[51]

And the Connecticut Yankee conversing in the realm of Arthur told the working men that the laborer should have something to say about his wages, for a day will come, he foretold, when "all of a sudden the wage-earner will consider that a couple of thousand years or so is enough of this one-sided sort of thing; and he will rise up and take a hand in fixing his wages himself. Ah, he will have a long and bitter account of wrong and humiliation to settle."[52] Then with the boot upon the other leg, "how these fine people's posterity will fume and fret and grit their teeth over the insolent tyranny of trade-unions!"[53]

In his autobiographical papers Twain spoke of what he termed "constitutional monarchy, with the Republican party sitting on the throne." Of this "monarchy" Clemens stated:

It can concentrate and augment power at the Capital by despoiling the States of their reserved rights, and by the voice of a Secretary of State it has indicated its purpose to do this. It can pack the Supreme Court with judges friendly to its ambitions, and it has threatened—by the voice of a Secretary of State—to do this. In many and admirably conceived ways it has so formidably intrenched itself and so tightened its grip upon the throne that I think it is there for good.[54]

50 Paine, III, 850.

51 *Ibid.*, IV, 1557.

52 *A Connecticut Yankee in King Arthur's Court*, p. 332.

53 *Idem.* A careful reading of the *Yankee* shows how much sociology and awareness of the problems of Mark's own age the book contains, being in itself a refutation of the general charges made by Brooks in his chapter "Let Somebody Else Begin," *The Ordeal of Mark Twain*, pp. 269–98.

54 *Mark Twain in Eruption*, p. 3.

The Republican party's tariffs, moreover, engaged the interest of Mark, who possessed at times a penetrating eye:

By a system of extraordinary tariffs it has created a number of giant corporations in the interest of a few rich men, and by most ingenious and persuasive reasoning has convinced the multitudinous and grateful unrich that the tariffs were instituted in *their* interest![55]

About the perpetuation of the Republican "monarchy," on the other hand, Clemens was less the seer. Feeling that a vote for Bryan was a vote lost, he wrote, "The monarchy is here to stay. Nothing can ever unseat it."[56] Yet later in a more optimistic mood he said:

I suppose we must expect that unavoidable and irresistible Circumstances will gradually take away the powers of the States and concentrate them in the central government, and that the republic will then repeat the history of all time and become a monarchy; but I believe that if we obstruct these encroachments and steadily resist them the monarchy can be postponed for a good while yet.[57]

It is clear that Mark Twain abhorred "monarchy," as he styled "dictatorship," and though he does not seem to have considered the idea of any absolute rule by the proletariat —only that of an oligarchy or plutocracy—he does have this to say on the economics of communism:

Communism is idiocy. They want to divide up the property. Suppose they did it. It requires brains to keep money as well as to make it. In a precious little while the money would be back in the former owner's hands and the communist would be poor again. The division would have to be remade every three years or it would do the communist no good.[58]

Twain's politics thus takes human nature into account; and while Mark was concerned with economic betterment for the masses, he was also passionately devoted to the ideal

55 *Idem.*
56 *Ibid.*, p. 34.
57 *Ibid.*, p. 66.
58 Paine, II, 644.

of freedom. When the Spanish-American War opened, Clemens wrote to Joe Twichell:

> I have never enjoyed a war—even in written history—as I am enjoying this one. For this is the worthiest one that was ever fought, so far as my knowledge goes. It is a worthy thing to fight for one's freedom; it is another sight finer to fight for another man's. And I think this is the first time it has been done.[59]

But jubilation was to change quickly to despair as he watched the war for freedom appear in its true guise of imperialism and exploitation. Like Emerson, Twain was never frightened by the hobgoblin of foolish consistency, and he now denounced this "wanton war and a robbing expedition."[60] His particular bitterness over the manner in which the war was waged appeared in the scathingly ironical "Defense of General Funston."[61] Now that freedom had been betrayed, Mark's love of liberty turned to hatred for deceit practiced in the interest of greed. Both Twain and Howells made speeches and wrote pamphlets against imperialistic expansion and its proponents."[62] We know that Mark entered vigorously into battle against municipal corruption in New York, that he defied public opinion in castigating General Funston, and that he turned his pitiless sarcasm against those who exploited the helpless under the hypocrisy of bestowing "Blessings of Civilization."[63]

Indeed, as the new century dawned Twain looked about

59 *Letters,* II, 663.

60 Paine, III, 1165.

61 Printed in the *North American Review,* CLXXIV, 613–24 (May, 1902).

62 See William M. Gibson, "Mark Twain and Howells: Anti-Imperialists," *New England Quarterly,* XX, 435–470 (December, 1947). Gibson here gives evidence that Mark courageously took stands on public issues.

63 When Mark attacked "The Blessings of Civilization Trust," which pretended to bring religion and enlightenment to the heathen, while actually conducting "a private raid for cash," Edward S. Martin wrote him: "How gratifying it is to feel that we have a man among us who understands the rarity of plain truth, and who delights to utter it, and has the gift of doing so without cant, and with not too much seriousness." A. B. Paine's introduction to *Europe and Elsewhere,* p. xxxiv.

with bitterness. All about him in New York was municipal corruption, war raged in South Africa, American troops were conquering the Philippines, Leopold of Belgium was coercing natives in the Congo, and most of the Christian powers were fighting the Chinese for trade-rights. With this in mind Mark composed "A Greeting from the Nineteenth to the Twentieth Century":

> I bring you the stately nation named Christendom, returning, bedraggled, besmirched, and dishonored, from pirate raids in Kiao-Chou, Manchuria, South Africa, and the Philippines, with her soul full of meanness, her pocket full of boodle, and her mouth full of pious hypocrisies. Give her soap and towel, but hide the looking-glass.[64]

And in "To the Person Sitting in Darkness"[65] Clemens publicly stated his attitude on the Philippines:

> . . . we have robbed a trusting friend of his land and his liberty; we have invited our clean young men to shoulder a discredited musket and do bandits' work under a flag which bandits have been accustomed to fear, not to follow; we have debauched America's honor and blackened her face before the world. . . .[66]

For Mark was angered, disappointed, and embittered by betrayal in so many ways of all Christian principles. The fact that bad as our imperialism was, that of Russia and Germany was even worse, furnished small consolation. Mark, who actually regarded the Czar as "this granite-hearted, bloody-jawed maniac of Russia," believing the monarchy alone responsible for brutalities practiced there, declared:

> Of course, I know that the properest way to demolish the

64 Paine, III, 1127. Though Twain did not print this greeting, his *North American Review* article "To the Person Sitting in Darkness" is equally caustic and frank.

65 Published in the *North American Review,* February, 1901, now included in *Europe and Elsewhere,* pp. 250–72.

66 *Supra,* p. 270.

Russian throne would be by revolution. But it is not possible to get up a revolution there; so the only thing left to do, apparently, is to keep the throne vacant by dynamite until a day when candidates shall decline with thanks. Then organize the Republic.[67]

It was monarchy, or as we say, "dictatorship" that Twain detested; to remove that, to set up a truly democratic republic, he felt the remedy for political woes. And he so frequently particularized the evils of a system in an individual. Just as it was the Czar who drew his wrath, so was it "Boss" Croker that he denounced,[68] and Cecil Rhodes of whom he wrote, "I admire him, I frankly confess it; and when his time comes I shall buy a piece of the rope for a keepsake."[69]

With interest in the individual went an insistence upon personal independence; regretting the misuse so often made of the idea of "loyalty" Twain stated in a note made while writing *A Connecticut Yankee:*

> The first thing I want to teach is *disloyalty,* till they get used to disusing that word *loyalty* as representing a virtue. This will beget independence—which is loyalty to one's best self and principles, and this is often disloyalty to the general idols and fetishes.[70]

Yet Mark knew the price that one must pay for insisting upon freedom of thought for himself in any age and any clime, for he records:

> And what a paltry poor lie is that one which teaches that independence of action and opinion is prized in men, admired, honored, rewarded. When a man leaves a political party, he is treated as if the party owned him—as if he were its bond slave, as most party men plainly are—and had stolen himself, gone off with what was not his own. And he is traduced, derided, despised, held up to public obloquy and loathing. His

67 *Letters,* II, 537.
68 Paine, III, 1145.
69 *Following the Equator,* II, 378.
70 *Notebook,* p. 199.

character is remorselessly assassinated; no means, however vile, are spared to injure his property and his business.[71]

Clemens, as his own actions show, valued this independence greatly, placing it above purely physical benefits, though he realized the importance of the latter. We find him saying, "That government is not best which best secures mere life and property—there is a more valuable thing—manhood."[72] And in another place Twain records that only in independence does he find, "spiritual comfort and a peace of mind quite above price."[73] Citing the opprobrium in which the first abolitionists were once held in New England, Mark wrote:

> In any civic crisis of a great and dangerous sort the common herd is not privately anxious about the rights and wrongs of the matter, it is only anxious to be on the winning side. In the North, before the War, the man who opposed slavery was despised and ostracized, and insulted. By the "Patriots." Then, by and by, the "Patriots" went over to his side, and thenceforth his attitude became patriotism.[74]

Like Whitman and Melville, Mark Twain was a democrat; he was not a leveler. Moreover, his conception of democracy embodied a firm insistence on the rights of others, minorities included. Thus indignation mingled with shame for the human race when he once reported, "As I write, news comes that in broad daylight in San Francisco, some boys have stoned an inoffensive Chinaman to death, and that although a large crowd witnessed the shameful deed, no one interfered."[75] When in California Clemens had found the Chinaman to be generally kind and well-intentioned, and in the following passage we see concretely the absence of egalitarianism in Twain's democracy, yet at the same time the presence of an all important humanity:

[71] *Autobiography,* II, 12. Clemens doubtless had in mind the disfavor in which his friend, Rev. Joseph Twichell, found himself with his congregation after voting for Grover Cleveland for president.

[72] *Notebook,* p. 210.

[73] *Autobiography,* II, 15.

[74] *Notebook,* pp. 394–5.

[75] *Roughing It,* II, 105–6.

No Californian *gentleman or lady* ever abuses or oppresses a Chinaman, under any circumstances, an explanation that seems to be much needed in the East. Only the scum of the population do it—they and their children; they, and, naturally and consistently, the policemen and politicians, likewise, for these are the dust-licking pimps and slaves of the scum, there as well as elsewhere in America.[76]

And along with this humanity went an utter contempt for snobbery. During his Buffalo days of writing for the *Galaxy* Twain heard that the Rev. Mr. Talmage, an immensely popular minister, had preached against the right of working-men to attend service at fashionable churches. Mark immediately spoke for human justice, suggesting that the minister in question would have objected to the original twelve disciples because "he could not have stood the fishy smell of some of his comrades who came from around the Sea of Galilee."[77] Moreover, the promptness with which Mark attacked the Rev. Mr. Sabine for refusal to hold burial services over the old actor George Holland attests an equal aversion to prudery and priggishness.[78]

Clemens' democracy like his politics derived largely from Christian ethics. His chief objection to monarchy was the advantage given the fortunate, aversion to an artificial system requiring "the misery of the many for the happiness of the few, the cold and hunger and overworking of the useful that the useless may live in luxury and idleness."[79] And Mark's democracy was more than a matter of theory; it was something to practice, as at the funeral of his coachman, Patrick McAleer, when Clemens asked to serve as pallbearer with his old gardener.[80] Always there is insistence

76 *Ibid.*, II, 111–12.

77 Paine, II, 405. See also "About Smells," *The Curious Republic of Gondour*, pp. 25–9.

78 *Ibid.*, II, 406. From this incident the "Little Church Around the Corner" received its name.

79 *Notebook*, p. 197.

80 *Autobiography*, II, 202.

by Mark Twain upon the worth of the individual, regardless of race, creed, or station, a belief leading him to state:

> The institution of Royalty in any form is an insult to the human race.
>
> The man who believes there is a man in the world who is better than himself merely because he was born royal or noble, is a dog with the soul of a dog—and at bottom is a liar.[81]

There were times when Mark became so incensed over the injustice of unearned privilege that he could declare to Howells:

> When I finished Carlyle's French Revolution in 1871, I was a Girondin; every time I have read it since, I have read it differently—being influenced and changed, little by little, by life and environment (and Taine and St. Simon): and now I lay the book down once more, and recognize that I am a Sansculotte!—And not a pale, characterless Sansculotte, but a Marat.[82]

Yet in essence the democracy of Mark Twain was more that of Shakespeare and Chaucer, the similarity being that each realized he was but human. Like the Whitman who sang the song of mankind as his own, Clemens said, "in myself I find in big or little proportion every quality and every defect that is findable in the mass of the race."[83] So great was his humility in this regard that he even enrolled himself among the cowards and fools.[84]

His democracy, moreover, was essentially that of the natural gentleman. "Good breeding," Twain tells us humorously, "consists in concealing how much we think of ourselves and how little we think of the other person." But circumstances of environment and heredity are not ignored; we even find Huck Finn commenting:

81 *Notebook,* p. 202.

82 *Letters,* II, 490.

83 *Mark Twain in Eruption,* p. xxix.

84 "The human race is a race of cowards; and I am not only marching in that procession but carrying a banner." *Idem.*

"Ah, well, I am a great and sublime fool. But then I am God's fool, and all his work must be contemplated with respect." Paine, II, 609.

Col. Grangerford was a gentleman, you see. He was a gentleman all over; and so was his family. He was well born, as the saying is, and that's worth as much in a man as it is in a horse, so the Widow Douglas said, and nobody ever denied that she was of the first aristocracy in our town; and pap he always said it, too, though he warn't no more quality than a mudcat himself.[85]

Though born without wealth, a self-made man in every detail of the American success story, Samuel Clemens was never an inverted snob of the kind which dislikes wealth, social position, and their holders, *per se.* Rather we find him calmly evaluating each person individually for his spiritual, moral, and intellectual worth. In his masterpiece Nigger Jim through those natural qualities of kindness, generosity, and consideration for others, so evident in his concern for Huck, rises to a natural dignity commanding our respect, even as it elicits Huck's:

En when I wake up en fine you back ag'in, all safe en soun', de tears come, en I could'a'got down on my knees en kiss yo' foot, I's so thankful. En all you wuz thinkin' 'bout wuz how you could make a fool uv ole Jim wid a lie. Dat truck dah is *trash;* en trash is what people is dat puts dirt on de head er dey fren's en makes 'em ashamed."

Then he got up slow and walked to the wigwam, and went in there without saying anything but that. But that was enough. It made me feel so mean I could almost kissed *his* foot to get him to take it back.

It was fifteen minutes before I could work myself up to go and humble myself to a nigger; but I done it, and I warn't ever sorry for it afterward, neither. I didn't do him no more mean tricks, and I wouldn't done that one if I'd 'a' knowed it would make him feel that way.[86]

Here on the raft a Negro slave and a white outcast enacted an everlasting drama of democracy in practice. Like Burns, Mark looked beyond externals to perceive the natural man. In his "Gospel" we find the Old Man saying:

85 *Adventures of Huckleberry Finn,* p. 146.

86 *Ibid.,* pp. 119–20.

There are gold men, and tin men, and copper men, and leaden men, and steel men, and so on—and each has the limitations of his nature, his heredities, his training, and his environment. You can build engines out of each of these metals, and they will all perform, but you must not require the weak ones to do equal work with the strong ones. In each case, to get the best results, you must free the metal from its obstructing prejudicial ores by education—smelting, refining, and so forth.[87]

Here is the English concept of democracy, which has for so long been ours, that the individual by his own worth and his opportunities may rise or fall in the scale. Twain believed, as he has the Old Man add, "Whatsoever a man is, is due to his *make,* and to the *influences* brought to bear upon it by his heredities, his habitat, his associations."[88] Mark by early associations was of the people himself, but he valued the aristocratic tradition, something he never attacked as he did royalty and plutocracy, because it was based upon consideration, enlightenment, and good taste. Naturally, Clemens abhorred any racial oppression or any other unfair discrimination, for Mark judged each individual, regardless of all else, upon his own worth. He was opposed to anything destroying personal liberty or restricting the right to improvement and progress. And he held no prejudices based on the color of a person's skin; yet he seems ever the individualist, endorsing fair play and equal opportunity rather than artificial forcing of equality. Bernard De Voto finds Twain's first importance in American literature to be the "democratizing effect of his work,"[89] reminding us that "Mark Twain was the first great American writer who was also a popular writer,"[90] and pointing out moreover that Mark's democracy was both "implicit and explicit." The books of Samuel Clemens were at once great art and at the same time, as De Voto claims, "the first American

87 *What Is Man?,* p. 4. 88 *Ibid.,* p. 5.
89 *The Portable Mark Twain,* p. 25. 90 *Ibid.,* p. 26.

literature of the highest rank which portrays the ordinary bulk of Americans, expresses them, accepts their values, and delineates their hopes, fears, decencies, and indecencies as from within." In this respect Mark Twain holds kinship with the dramatists who peopled the London stage with characters in plots devised for the amusement of their audience.[91]

Lionel Trilling, also, has pointed out the fundamental democratic quality of Mark Twain's sociological thought, revealing, at the same time, its all embracing aspects:

> The modern sentimental publicist of American democracy is willing to castigate something in American life, capital or management, the South or the State Department. But he insists on holding harmless what he would call the "real America," the mass of little men, by implication his readers and himself. In our notion of democracy someone else is always to blame. But Mark Twain, if he called Jay Gould a source of corruption of American ideals, yet knew that the American people accepted the corruption.

And Professor Trilling adds this explanation of Twain's democratic ideas:

> He could tell us that we were cowards or trucklers or lynchers, actually or potentially—he knew we were because he knew himself. "I am the whole human race without a detail lacking," he said. He believed in the great brotherhood of human depravity. The loafer on the wharf, he knew, was his equal, or Andrew Carnegie's equal, in the important respects of badness and weakness and foolishness. He had not one touch of that inverted condescension of our current democratic piousness—to be seen, for notable example, in the books of John Steinbeck—which assumes that the less a man is established the greater

[91] *Idem.* Alfred Harbage has demonstrated that Shakespeare wrote for the "fundamental convictions of men," *As They Liked It: An Essay on Shakespeare and Morality,* (New York: Macmillan, 1947), p. 55. And Professor Harbage adds, "Those who admire his work but despise the 'generality' to whom it was shaped, are suffering from some kind of social-spiritual maladjustment."

is his personal moral glory. He was too humble, too democratic a man to believe that.[92]

In *Huckleberry Finn* when Pap reforms and takes the pledge, to the ecstasy of the sentimentalists, he soon finds thirst driving him back to accustomed habits; while those who had shed tears over the reclaimed sinner were sadder but wiser: "The judge he felt kind of sore. He said he reckoned a body could reform the old man with a shotgun, maybe, but he didn't know no other way."[93] Huck, also, is lacking in class-antagonism, for he can say frankly, "It was 'baker's bread'—what the quality eat; none of your low-down corn-pone."[94] But his humanity is all embracing, and when the murderers are left on the disintegrating wreck, his thought reveals the basic democracy of all human kinship: "I begun to think how dreadful it was, even for murderers, to be in such a fix. I says to myself, there ain't no telling but I might come to be a murderer myself yet, and then how would I like it?"[95] Later when Jim complains to Huck about those rascals, the King and the Duke, the boy replies, "It's the way I feel, too, Jim. But we've got them on our hands, and we got to remember what they are, and make allowances."[96]

Finally when the two dead beats are caught, Huck is aghast at the inhumanity of people who torture them with tar and feathers: "Well, it made me sick to see it," he tells us with a sense of deep shame for the human race, a feeling that was "kind of ornery, and humble, and to blame, somehow—though *I* hadn't done nothing."[97] Here we find the democracy of Twain at one with that of Whitman, as broad in concept and as deep in feeling as the code of ethics which inspired it.

[92] Lionel Trilling, Review of the *Portable Mark Twain* in the New York *Times Book Review,* p. 4 (July 28, 1946).

[93] *Huckleberry Finn,* p. 31.

[94] *Ibid.,* p. 52.

[95] *Ibid.,* p. 100.

[96] *Ibid.,* pp. 214–15.

[97] *Ibid.,* pp. 320–21.

Naturally Twain was interested in education as a means of improving the human mind. The Yankee in Arthur's realm found that the brightest intellect in the kingdom could not perceive beyond the bounds of its knowledge. We find him saying, "Arguments have no chance against petrified training; they wear it as little as the waves wear a cliff."[98] The only way then to combat ignorance and superstition was through education. One should train in the right direction, which to Mark meant proper morality in one's relationships. In *What Is Man?* we are told, "Inestimably valuable is training, influence, education, in right directions—*training one's self-approbation to elevate its ideals.*"[99] The importance of education in Twain's whole philosophical concept of man is here stated. Since each acts according to his nature, seeking his own self-approval, then it becomes necessary to establish standards on a high ethical plane. Only by education of the common mind can this be accomplished.

Clemens' utopian essay "The Curious Republic of Gondour" contains a voting process which places education as a counterbalance to wealth. His model constitution outlines a unique law:

> Under it every citizen, howsoever poor or ignorant, possessed one vote, so universal suffrage still reigned; but if a man possessed a good common-school education and no money, he had two votes; a high-school education gave him four; if he had property likewise, to the value of three thousand *sacos,* he wielded one more vote; for every fifty thousand *sacos* a man added to his property, he was entitled to another vote; a university education entitled a man to nine votes, even though he owned no property.[100]

While granting that people with property generally have a greater stake in the community than those with no material

98 *A Connecticut Yankee,* p. 143. 99 *What Is Man?,* p. 9.

100 *The Curious Republic of Gondour* (New York: Boni & Liveright, 1919), p. 3.

responsibilities, Mark still tips the scales in the direction of knowledge. "Learning goes usually with uprightness, broad views, and humanity;" he tells us, "so the learned voters, possessing the balance of power, became the vigilant and efficient protectors of the great lower rank of society."[101] The voters with "property, character, and intellect" had a greater voice in government than the ones without; all official positions were filled by educated, intelligent men.

> Competitive examinations were the rule and in all official grades. I remarked that the questions asked the candidates were wild, intricate, and often required a sort of knowledge not needed in the office sought.
>
> "Can a fool or an ignoramus answer them?" asked the person I was talking with.
>
> "Certainly not."
>
> "Well, you will not find any fools or ignoramuses among our officials."[102]

Mark believed his utopia thoroughly democratic, valuing "marked ability, education, and high character"; therefore, "If a hod-carrier possessed these, he could succeed; but the mere fact that he was a hod-carrier could not elect him, as in previous times."[103]

Mark, we may repeat, saw no virtue in mere lack of wealth; in his notebook he records:

> Saturday, January 3, 1903. The offspring of riches: Pride, vanity, ostentation, arrogance, tyranny.
>
> Sunday, January 4, 1903. The offspring of poverty: Greed, sordidness, envy, hate, malice, cruelty, meanness, lying, shirking, cheating, stealing, murder.[104]

Yet he was never a materialist. It was, for instance, his belief that the motto "In God We Trust" should be removed from

[101] *Ibid.*, pp. 3–4. Twain ascribes the "balance of power" to the educated voters by belief that knowledge is "more easily acquired than riches." Consequently there will be more men wise than wealthy.

[102] *Ibid.*, pp. 7–8. [103] *Idem.*

[104] Paine, III, 1194.

our coins because it "stated a lie." And to Andrew Carnegie he said, "If this nation has ever trusted in God, that time has gone by; for nearly half a century almost its entire trust has been in the Republican party and the dollar—mainly the dollar."[105]

Practicality, however, was never absent from his thinking, though never to the exclusion of ethics. "Essentially, nobilities are foolishness," Twain once wrote, "but if I were a citizen where they prevail I would do my best to get a title, for the consideration it furnishes—that is what we want. In Republics we strive for it with the surest means we have—money." In a letter to Twichell (1905) Mark deplored the lack of human advancement in matters of the heart and mind, refusing to take comfort in mankind's colossal material progress:

> Prodigious acquisitions were made in things which add to the comfort of many and make life harder for as many more. But the addition to righteousness? Is that discoverable? I think not. The materialities were not invented in the interest of righteousness; that there is more righteousness in the world because of them than there was before, is hardly demonstrable, I think.[106]

Mark then deprecated the "money-lust" that had always existed, but now had become a craze making the nations of the world "sordid, ungentle, dishonest, oppressive."[107] In *A Connecticut Yankee* the Boss is trying to explain to some of Arthur's subjects that wages must be evaluated in terms of purchasing power. And the manner of his argument leaves no doubt of its contemporary application to Clemens' own age:

> What those people valued was *high wages;* it didn't seem to be a matter of any consequence to them whether the high wages would buy anything or not. They stood for "protection," and

105 *Mark Twain in Eruption,* p. 50. 106 *Letters,* II, 769–70.
107 *Ibid.,* II, 770.

swore by it, which was reasonable enough, because interested parties had gulled them into the notion that it was protection which had created their high wages.[108]

As he grew older Twain gradually developed a philosophy of determinism based upon the concept of an inexorable chain of events. He exists for us, therefore, not alone as a great creative artist, but like Melville and Hawthorne in kinship with serious thinkers who have concerned themselves with the basic problems of man's destiny. Mark's idealism did not deny evil as it did not deny the reality of life, a concept making him alike the romanticist and idealist on one hand, the satirist and pessimist on the other.[109] Thus Clemens could delight naturally in material possessions, while at the same time placing as high a value upon spirituality as the most abstract philosopher. He saw no reason why physical comfort should mean loss of soul. In fact, Twain took a broad view of life, one based upon comprehension of the shrewd and vicious, the stupid and gullible, the helpless and innocent, even as it embraced the wise and noble. If Mark gradually transferred his early distrust of the Creator to his creation, man, he nevertheless continued to approach the problem of evil through introspection Pondering such problems as the ambiguity of good and evil, how man's effort to do good, although well meant, often produces evil, Mark Twain represents a philosophical and ethical maturity.

In seeking truth Clemens felt compelled to account for the fact that man is so often tragically afflicted. The answer of Calvinism, the doctrine of original sin, was one early rejected. Finally, as revealed by the unpublished papers of his estate, Twain dropped the plummet deeper into the well of speculation in search for a final sounding. Yet con-

108 *A Connecticut Yankee,* p. 328.

109 This duality is blatantly present in *Those Extraordinary Twins. Joan of Arc* illustrates the former; *The Mysterious Stranger* the latter.

cern over evil never remained purely philosophical with him, for he held a practical, reforming interest. And because he concentrated on matters agitating him at the moment, he was often led astray from the basic philosophical problem. Clemens, moreover, sensitive by nature, was profoundly shocked because civilization, which should have been a blessing, now appeared an evil. His visit to the Sandwich Islands, like Melville's sojourn in the South Seas, showed civilization bringing degradation, rather than spiritual improvement. In his personal life, there was first-hand knowledge of human suffering and cruelty, derived from his experiences on the river and in the mining camps. Then, too, there were the family misfortunes—loss of loved ones and financial disaster.

Mark speculated on the tragic flow of events; yet like the Greek dramatists he sought the vulnerable crack in the protagonist's armor that allowed fate to set the furies on his track. There could be one's own guilt, his own fatal determination or lack of it, which led Mark at first out of natural humility to blame himself for his woes. Thinking, then, on this problem, he evolved his own concept of evil in the world, facing it with Promethean courage, a good warrior to the end.

For earlier signs of an important aspect of his final "gospel" we need look no further than *Tom Sawyer Abroad* (1894). Here Huck describes the crowd heckling the inventor:

> But, good land! what did he want to sass back for? You see, it couldn't do him no good, and it was just nuts for them. They *had* him, you know. But that was his way. I reckon he couldn't help it; he was made so, I judge. He was a good enough sort of cretur, and hadn't no harm in him, and was just a genius, as the papers said, which wasn't his fault. We can't all be sound: we've got to be the way we're made.[110]

[110] *Tom Sawyer Abroad,* p. 14.

William E. H. Lecky's *History of European Morals* furnished Clemens an echo of another tenet of his own theories; the English historian's conclusion that desire to obtain happiness and to avoid pain provides man his motive for action caused Mark to write in the margin "Sound and true."[111] And in another place, when Lecky states that since we are all dependent upon others, cooperation becomes essential to our happiness, that laws are made to restrain the individual for the good of the community, until it finally becomes to the interest of each to regard the interests of others, Twain comments, "He has proceeded from unreasoned selfishness to reasoned selfishness. All our acts reasoned and unreasoned are selfish."[112]

Once in conversation with Twichell Clemens held that no such thing as an accident existed, since all was forewritten from the day of the beginning. However slight, he contended, each event was embryonic in the first instant of created life and thus timed to appear unalterably in the future web of destiny.[113]

At times there appears in Twain's attitude toward nature something Wordsworthian, a feeling almost pantheistic, as in this response to the magnificence of Switzerland:

> Those mountains had a soul: they thought, they spoke. And what a voice it was! And how real! Deep down in my memory it is sounding yet. Alp calleth unto Alp! That stately old Scriptural wording is the right one for God's Alps and God's ocean. How puny we were in that awful Presence, and how painless it was to be so! How fitting and right it seemed, and how stingless was the sense of our unspeakable insignificance! And Lord, how pervading were the repose and peace and blessedness that poured out of the heart of the invisible Great Spirit of the mountains![114]

In a speech to the Monday Evening Club (1883) Clemens had pointed out that selfishness may be of two kinds:

111 Paine, II, 511. 112 *Ibid.*, II, 512.
113 *Ibid.*, II, 628. 114 *Ibid.*, II, 637.

"brutal and divine; that he who sacrifices others to himself exemplifies the first, whereas he who sacrifices himself for others personifies the second—the divine contenting of his soul by serving the happiness of his fellow-men."[115] Because of misunderstanding of his philosophy, no doubt, Mark made this clarification:

> Diligently train your ideals upward, and still upward toward a summit where you will find your chiefest pleasure, in conduct which, while contenting you, will be sure to confer benefits upon your neighbor and the community.[116]

"The Facts Concerning the Recent Carnival of Crime in Connecticut" (1876) had previously set forth Mark's ideas on conscience, something which was to play so important a part in *Huckleberry Finn*. In this paper, read before the Monday Evening Club, Twain elaborated on the differences in individuals, showing how a good man with a weighty conscience might suffer remorse for an innocent act, while a scoundrel might commit crimes without a twinge. In this imaginary interview between Clemens and his own conscience, the former complains:

> "Smith is the noblest man in all this section, and the purest; and yet is always breaking his heart because he cannot be good! Only a conscience *could* find pleasure in heaping agony upon a spirit like that."[117]

His own conscience, indeed, plagued Samuel Clemens through life. In *Huckleberry Finn* circumstance and temperament in Huck produce a clash between sympathy and will to freedom, on one hand, and custom and law, on the other; for in this book conscience is the agent of law and

115 *Ibid.*, II, 744.

116 *Idem.*

117 "Recent Carnival of Crime in Connecticut," *Tom Sawyer Abroad*, p. 321.

custom, and it is only when Huck rises superior to it that he wins the battle.[118]

One aspect of his final philosophy that developed through the years was that life was a dream. To Mrs. Crane he once wrote (1893):

> I dreamed I was born & grew up & was a pilot on the Mississippi & a miner & a journalist in Nevada & a pilgrim in the *Quaker City* & had a wife & children & went to live in a villa at Florence—& this dream goes on & on & sometimes seems so real that I almost believe it is real. I wonder if it is? But there is no way to tell, for if one applies tests they would be a part of the dream, too, & so would simply aid the deceit. I wish I knew whether it is a dream or real.[119]

Much in life had to be taken on faith, but even there Mark sometimes wondered. "There are those who scoff at the schoolboy, calling him frivolous and shallow," he wrote, "Yet it was a schoolboy who said: 'Faith is believing what you know ain't so.' "[120] Even Livy's beliefs, so firmly rooted in early Christian training, gradually evaporated before his scepticism.[121] Clemens indeed was convinced that few people ever reasoned on such matters:

> Does the human being reason? No; he thinks, muses, reflects, but doesn't reason. Thinks *about* a thing; rehearses its statistics and its parts and applies to them what other people on his side of the question have said about them, but he does not compare the parts himself, and is not capable of doing it.
>
> That is, in the two things which are the peculiar domain of the heart, not the mind—politics and religion. He doesn't want

118 Coleman O. Parsons uses "moral sense" to mean man-made laws, man-evolved conscience, in his study of Twain and conscience. "The Devil and Samuel Clemens," *Virginia Quarterly Review,* XXIII, 582–606 (Autumn, 1947).

119 Paine, III, 964.

120 *Notebook,* p. 237.

121 Paine records that Livy once told him she could not lean on the old faith for comfort, because she no longer held it. II, 651. Livy herself wrote the same thing to Clemens. *Love Letters,* p. 167.

to know the other side. He wants arguments and statistics for his own side, and nothing more.[122]

In a more philosophical mood he phrased it thus:

We are nothing but echoes. We have no thoughts of our own, no opinions of our own, we are but a compost heap made up of the decayed heredities, moral and physical.[123]

As for the fact of existence itself, Twain once stated his belief that nothing can exist for us that is in the past or the future:

There is in life only one moment and in eternity only one. It is so brief that it is represented by the fleeting of a luminous mote through the thin ray of sunlight—and it is visible but a fraction of a second. The moments that preceded it have been lived, are forgotten and are without value; the moments that have not been lived have no existence and will have no value except in the moment that each shall be lived. While you sleep you are dead; and whether you stay dead an hour or a billion years the time to you is the same.[124]

Speculating as he so often did on the nature of truth, Mark said, "Truth is more of a stranger than fiction," and a little later he added, "Truth is mighty and will prevail. There is nothing the matter with this, except that it ain't so."[125]

The interest in man's duality which had led Twain to publish "The Recent Carnival of Crime in Connecticut" continued to influence his thoughts. January 7, 1897, found him attempting to account for the seeming presence of two persons in each individual.[126] This duality meant the presence in each "of *another* person; not a slave of ours, but free and independent, and with a character distinctly its own." At first Mark conceived of this other person as our

122 *Notebook*, p. 307. 123 *Ibid.*, p. 312.
124 *Ibid.*, p. 323. 125 *Ibid.*, p. 345.
126 This theme was used, of course, by Robert Louis Stevenson in *Dr. Jekyll and Mr. Hyde* (1886) and in *Markheim* (1884); by Edgar A. Poe in *William Wilson* (1840).

conscience, but he came to modify this as erroneous. He believed that Stevenson's concept of the duality of man's nature, each with its own conscience was nearer the truth, but he thought Stevenson's plot rang false in having the two separate natures aware of each other's presence. Twain came finally to believe, as he expressed it: "Inborn nature is Character, by itself in the brutes—the tiger, the dove, the fox, etc. Inborn nature *and* the modifying Conscience, working together make Character in man." Conscience then is not another self; yet each person does have duality of character, each character possessing its own conscience.

Clemens came finally to divide his own character into the physical self and the "spiritualized self." It was common memory that made him aware of the oneness of his spiritual and physical selves, which he explains:

> Now, as I take it, my other self, my dream self, is merely my ordinary body and mind freed from clogging flesh and become a spiritualized body and mind and with the ordinary powers of both enlarged in all particulars a little, and in some particulars prodigiously.[127]

For once, here, Mark becomes the utter mystic, saying: "Waking I move slowly; but in my dreams my unhampered spiritualized body flies to the ends of the earth in a millionth of a second· Seems to—and I believe, *does*."[128] And the most definite expression that Twain has made upon spiritual immortality occurs in this philosophy of duality: "When my physical body dies my dream body will doubtless continue its excursion and activities without change, forever."[129]

Three years earlier (1894) he had written to Mrs. Fairbanks on her husband's death: "I am sorry for you—very, very sorry—but not for him nor for any body who is granted

127 *Notebook,* p. 350. Twain had been reading French psychologists on somnambulism and hypnotism.

128 *Idem.*

129 *Ibid.,* p. 351.

the privilege of prying behind the curtain to see if there is any contrivance there that is half so shabby & poor & foolish as the invention of mortal life."[130] And generally Clemens saw no hope beyond. "One of the proofs of the immortality of the soul is that myriads have believed it," he says, only to add, "They also believed the world was flat."[131]

No doubt, it was the attempt of each person to win his own self-respect in a material world that caused Twain to state the same thought expressed by his admired poet Robert Browning, that the failure is in having too-easily-achieved ideals, not striving ever upward for the unattainable. And there is far more than humor in Mark's aphorism, "Let us so live that when we come to die even the undertaker will be sorry."[132]

Inherited traits engrossed him at times, leading him to declare, "We don't create any of our traits; we inherit all of them. They have come down to us from what we impudently call the lower animals. Man is the last expression, and combines every attribute of the animal tribes that preceded him."[133] In other words, the timidity of the rabbit, the murderousness of the tiger, the gentleness of the lamb are all present in each of us: "We describe a man by his vicious traits and condemn him; or by his fine traits and gifts, and praise him and accord him high merit for their possession. It is comical. He did not invent these things; he did not stock himself with them. God conferred them upon him in the first instant of creation."[134]

Another facet of his thought was that the moral idea is constantly undergoing change; that what was in earlier days considered highly immoral may no longer be so. This was to Clemens further evidence of the general scheme of things, arising from some primal cause and developing up-

130 *Mark Twain to Mrs. Fairbanks,* pp. 274–5.

131 *Notebook,* p. 379.

132 *Ibid.,* p. 392.

133 Paine, IV, 1296.

134 *Ibid.,* IV, 1297.

ward. DeLancey Ferguson has called our attention to the conversation between Clemens and Kipling at the full-tide of Mark's powers to show that it was not personal misfortune but life itself that caused his pessimism.[135] Surely his philosophy seems at times to embrace the whole scheme of things, for it was the *temperament* of Adam and Eve that allowed them to be tempted. And Mark once wished that Joan of Arc and Martin Luther had been in their places: "There would have been results! Indeed, yes. The apple would be intact to-day; there would be no human race; there would be no *you*; there would be no *me*."[136]

Far indeed from being unduly impressed by the material progress of his age, Clemens looked beneath the surface to observe:

> Whenever man makes a large stride in material prosperity and progress he is sure to think that *he* has progressed, whereas he has not advanced an inch; nothing has progressed but his circumstances. *He* stands where he stood before. He knows more than his forebears knew but his intellect is no better than theirs and never will be. He is richer than his forbears but his character is no improvement upon theirs. Riches and education are not a permanent possession; they will pass away, as in the case of Rome and Greece and Egypt and Babylon; and a moral and mental midnight will follow—with a dull long sleep and a slow reawakening.[137]

In a note made probably for *The Mysterious Stranger* Clemens indicated the lack of spiritual progress he found so distressing: "the little stinking human race, with its little stinking kings and popes and bishops and prostitutes and peddlers."[138] Pellowe is no doubt partially right in saying that Twain's pessimism arose from his perfectionist

[135] Clemens talked with Kipling about ideas later expressed in his "Gospel." *Mark Twain: Man and Legend,* p. 242.

[136] "The Turning-Point of My Life," *What Is Man?,* p. 140.

[137] *Mark Twain in Eruption,* p. 67.

[138] *Notebook, p.* 337.

ideals,[139] while Richard Altick seems on equally sound ground, seeking an explanation in Clemens' humanity.[140] Yet we must, at the same time, bear in mind his philosophy of determinism and belief in an inexorable chain of events.

Mark's explosions against the human race finally drew this remonstrance from Livy, "Does it help the world to always rail at it? There is great and noble work being done, why not sometimes recognize that? Why always dwell on the evil until those who live beside you are crushed to the earth & you seem almost like a monomaniac."[141] The nobility of human nature was recognized at times by Twain. Once when a particularly brutal act of imperial despotism had occurred in Russia, he declared that all over that vast Empire "a myriad of eyes filled with tears"; and he concluded, "If I am a Swinburnian—and clear to the marrow I am—I hold human nature in sufficient honor to believe there are eighty million mute Russians that are of the same stripe, and only one Russian family that isn't."[142] Another time, while discussing the Deity, Twain made this statement about man:

> Next I am privileged to infer that there is *far* more goodness than ungoodness in man, for if it were not so man would have exterminated himself before this; & I may also infer this supremacy (in quality) of goodness over ungoodness in man by calling up in my mind the various servants whom I know; the various mechanics whom I know; the various merchants, military men, the various Tom-Dick & Harrys of *all* walks, whom I know—in this long list I find goodness the rule & ungoodness the exception. I should still find this the case among all tribes of

139 "And it was because he matched his vision of possible perfection against the actualities that with advancing years a bitterness gnawed at his heart." *Mark Twain: Pilgrim from Hannibal,* p. 215.

140 "Mark Twain's Despair: An Explanation in Terms of His Humanity," *South Atlantic Quarterly,* XXXIV, 354–367 (October, 1935).

141 *Love Letters,* p. 333.

142 *Letters,* II, 538.

savages in all parts of the earth & in all the centuries of history. I detest Man, but nevertheless this is true of him.[143]

This attitude was essentially expressed in the opening lines of *Huckleberry Finn,* when Huck tells us, "I never seen anybody but lied one time or another, without it was Aunt Polly, or the widow, or maybe Mary."[144] We are not only told here that lying is infrequent, but that a few individuals never prevaricate.

We may seek an explanation of Twain's pessimism, then, from a number of causes. Mark like his predecessors, Hawthorne and Melville, was profoundly aware of evil in the world. Moreover, while growing to maturity on the river and as a young man in Washoe he saw life at its worst, which never makes for optimism. His personal life, though ultimately one of worldly success, was actually filled with sickness, loss of loved ones, and temporary disaster. And as he watched the trend of world affairs, at home and abroad, doubts increased for the future, doubts now justified by a world of strife, uncertainty, and wars. An idealist who saw ideals betrayed, one sensitive to suffering, a Christian in the best sense of ethical conduct, Mark often felt cause for pessimism.

Mark had an intense sense of justice, hatred of wrong, and admiration for nobility of action. It was the ignorance, cowardice, and stupidity of the human race in contrast to the noble actions of individuals that he deplored. A world-traveler, he advocated knowing others as a means to universal peace and understanding: "Travel is fatal to prejudice, bigotry, and narrow-mindedness, and many of our people need it sorely on these accounts. Broad, wholesome, charitable views of men and things cannot be acquired by vegetating in one little corner of the earth all one's lifetime."[145]

143 *Love Letters,* p. 253. 144 *Adventures of Huckleberry Finn,* p. 1.
145 *Innocents Abroad,* II, 407.

In *Huckleberry Finn* the failings of mankind are pictured by one who understands and sympathizes, even as he regrets. Professor Trilling seems eminently correct in his dictum that the greatness of this masterpiece lies "Primarily in its power of telling the truth,"[146] adding, "it takes the risk of dealing directly with the virtue and depravity of man's heart."[147] When Huck fools Pap in order to escape, leaving the impression that he has been murdered, suspicion centers first on Old Man Finn, then on Nigger Jim; says a woman to Huck, now disguised as a girl:

"Some think old Finn done it himself."

"No—is that so?"

"Most everybody thought it at first. He'll never know how nigh he come to getting lynched. But before night they changed around and judged it was done by a runaway nigger named Jim."[148]

There is no need here for explicit didacticism; the implicit moral strikes home like a right to the jaw.

And when Huck's trying to keep two men from discovering Jim on the raft leads them to suppose his parents are sick with small-pox, we see the human race, kind and generous, yet at once, also, selfish and stupid; one of them tells Huck:

You float along down about twenty miles, and you'll come to a town on the left-hand side of the river. It will be long after sun-up then, and when you ask for help you tell them your folks are all down with chills and fever. Don't be a fool again, and let people guess what is the matter. Now we're trying to do you a kindness; so you just put twenty miles between us, that's a good boy.[149]

And they actually give Huck two twenty-dollar gold pieces, out of sympathy. In such passages Twain the artist leaves each of us to perceive the action in the light of his own morality.

146 Introduction to *Huckleberry Finn,* p. vi.
147 *Ibid.,* p. vii.
148 *Huckleberry Finn,* p. 78.
149 *Ibid.,* pp. 126–7.

Later in the narrative, during the Shepherdson-Grangerford feud, Huck sees how human beings can turn into unreasoning beasts:

> The boys jumped for the river—both of them hurt—and as they swum down the current the men run along the bank shooting at them and singing out, "Kill them, kill them!" It made me so sick I most fell out of the tree. I ain't a-going to tell *all* that happened—it would make me sick again if I was to do that. I wished I hadn't ever come ashore that night to see such things. I ain't ever going to get shut of them—lots of times I dream about them.[150]

There is brutality enough in this book, even as there is some brutality in *Tom Sawyer*; and also hypocrisy. It is in the guise of mistreated innocence that the King and the Duke become passengers on the raft. They appealed to Huck—"sung out and begged me to save their lives—said they hadn't been doing nothing, and was being chased for it—said there was men and dogs a-coming."[151]

There is the description of loafers in the Arkansas village setting the dogs on a sow with her litter of pigs;[152] there is the cold-blooded shooting of Boggs;[153] followed by the attempted lynching of the murderer, Sherburn, who with double-barreled gun in hand, says scornfully:

> "The idea of *you* lynching anybody! It's amusing. The idea of you thinking you had pluck enough to lynch a *man!* Because you're brave enough to tar and feather poor friendless cast-out women that come along here, did that make you think you had grit enough to lay your hands on a *man?* Why, a *man's* safe in the hands of ten thousand of your kind—as long as it's daytime and you're not behind him.[154]

Yet all those in the story are not wicked, for the girls whom the Duke and King seek to defraud are so kind, gentle, and generous that Huck comes to their rescue, saying,

150 *Ibid.*, p. 160.
151 *Ibid.*, p. 167.
152 *Ibid.*, p. 194.
153 *Ibid.*, p. 198.
154 *Ibid.*, p. 202.

"I felt so ornery and low down and mean that I says to myself, my mind's made up; I'll hive that money for them or bust."[155] And when the King advises the Duke, who fears the one well-informed man of the community, "Cuss the doctor! What do we k'yer for *him?* Hain't we got all the fools in town on our side? And ain't that a big enough majority in any town?"[156] we have a damning indictment of the human race succinctly stated. Just as the conversation between Huck and Mrs. Phelps leaves nothing more to be said on the inhumanity of slavery:

"It warn't the grounding—that didn't keep us back but a little. We blowed out a cylinder-head."

"Good gracious! anybody hurt?"

"No'm. Killed a nigger."

"Well, it's lucky; because sometimes people do get hurt."[157]

Mark Twain's strong sense of justice made him sensitive to any deviation, large or small. In his books we see humanity in the mass struggling through ignorance, stupidity, and cowardice, sometimes accompanied by crime, but we see, also, the noble actions of individuals: perchance a Huck or Jim, perhaps a Joan of Arc. And it is upon these great in soul that hopes for the future must rest.

SELECTED BIBLIOGRAPHY

AUTOBIOGRAPHICAL SOURCES

Mark Twain's Letters, arranged with comment by Albert Bigelow Paine. 2 vols. New York: Harper & Brothers, 1917.

[By no means complete, but important.]

Mark Twain's Speeches, with an Introduction by Albert Bigelow Paine, and an Appreciation by William Dean Howells. New York: Harper & Brothers, 1923.

[A selection of Twain's speeches, not complete.]

155 *Ibid.,* p. 243.
156 *Ibid.,* p. 246.
157 *Ibid.,* p. 306.

Mark Twain's Autobiography, with an Introduction by Albert Bigelow Paine. 2 vols. New York: Harper & Brothers, 1924.
[Indispensable.]

Mark Twain's Notebook, prepared for publication by Albert Bigelow Paine. New York: Harper & Brothers, 1935.
[Selections from Twain's journals, brief and sketchy but important.]

Mark Twain in Eruption, edited by Bernard De Voto. New York: Harper & Brothers, 1940.
[Autobiographical papers from the Clemens Literary Estate, a valuable contribution to our knowledge of Twain's mind and thought.]

Mark Twain to Mrs. Fairbanks, edited by Dixon Wecter. San Marino, California: Huntington Library, 1949.
[Interesting correspondence adding to our knowledge of Twain's mind.]

The Love Letters of Mark Twain, edited by Dixon Wecter. New York: Harper & Brothers, 1949.
[Valuable addition to our knowledge of Twain's ideas, especially on religion and politics.]

STUDIES OF TWAIN'S IDEAS

Bellamy, Gladys Carmen. *Mark Twain as a Literary Artist.* Norman: University of Oklahoma Press, 1950.
[Useful and stimulating.]

Brooks, Van Wyck. *The Ordeal of Mark Twain.* New York: E. P. Dutton & Company, revised edition, 1933.
[More perceptive of Twain's feelings than of his thought or action.]

——. *The Times of Melville and Whitman.* New York: E. P. Dutton & Company, 1947.
[Twain is pictured as the victim of the Gilded Age, though admitted to be a great folk-artist.]

Cowie, Alexander. *The Rise of the American Novel.* New York: American Book Co., 1948.
[Treats Twain's ideas as expressed in his novels; a sound study.]

De Voto, Bernard. *Mark Twain at Work.* Cambridge, Massachusetts: Harvard University Press, 1942.
[Penetrating study of Twain's final philosophy.]

Ferguson, DeLancey. *Mark Twain: Man and Legend.* Indianapolis: Bobbs-Merrill, 1943.
[Sound conclusions on Twain's thought.]

Grattan, C. Hartley. "Mark Twain" in *American Writers on American Literature.* New York: Horace Liveright, Inc., 1931.

[Reveals Twain as critic and idealist.]

Harnsberger, Caroline Thomas. *Mark Twain at Your Fingertips.* New York: Beechhurst Press, 1948.

[A useful reference guide to Mark's comments and ideas on many subjects, alphabetically arranged.]

Henderson, Archibald. *Mark Twain.* New York: Frederick A. Stokes Company, 1911.

[Discusses Twain as sociologist and philosopher.]

Hemminghaus, Edgar H. *Mark Twain in Germany.* New York: Columbia University Press, 1939.

[Discusses Twain's ideas which appealed to the German mind.]

Howells, William Dean. *My Mark Twain.* New York: Harper & Brothers, 1910.

[Twain's mind as revealed to an intimate friend.]

Lemonnier, Léon. *Mark Twain: L'Homme et Son Oeuvre.* Paris: Librairie Artheme Fayard, 1946.

[Briefly treats Twain's thought.]

Liljegren, S. B. *The Revolt Against Romanticism in American Literature as Evidenced in the Works of S. L. Clemens.* Upsala: Lundequistska Bokhandeln, 1945.

[Relates Clemens to the stream of European realism.]

Paine, Albert Bigelow. *Mark Twain: A Biography.* 3 vols. New York: Harper & Brothers, 1912. Revised in 2 vols., 1935.

[Important for Twain's philosophy, especially his religious thought.]

Parrington, Vernon L. "The Culture of the Seventies" in *Main Currents in American Thought.* New York: Harcourt, Brace & Co. 1930. III, 86–101.

[Still an interesting appraisal of Twain's mind.]

Pellowe, William C. S. *Mark Twain: Pilgrim from Hannibal.* New York: Hobson Book Press, 1945.

[Fullest discussion of Twain's religion.]

Schönemann, Friedrich. *Mark Twain als literarische Persönlichkeit.* Jena: Verlag der Frommanschen Buchhandlung, Walter Biedermann, 1925.

[The most important German study of Twain's ideas as expressed in his writings.]

Taylor, Walter Fuller. *The Economic Novel in America.* Chapel Hill: University of North Carolina Press, 1942.

[Fullest discussion of Twain's economic thought; refutes charge of not expressing his opinions.]

Wagenknecht, Edward. *Mark Twain: The Man and His Work.* New Haven: Yale University Press, 1935.

[Brief but sound examination of Mark's thought.]

ARTICLES

Adams, Sir John. "Mark Twain, Psychologist," *Dalhousie Review,* XIII, 417–26 (January, 1934).

[An attempt to analyze the psychology of *What Is Man?*]

Altick, Richard D. "Mark Twain's Despair; An Explanation in Terms of His Humanity," *South Atlantic Quarterly,* XXXIV, 359–68 (October, 1935).

[Twain's despair is credited to circumstances of his life and lack of formal education.]

Branch, Edgar M. "The Two Providences: Thematic Form in 'Huckleberry Finn,'" *College English,* XI, 188–95 (January, 1950).

[One of the best studies of the moral conflict in Twain's masterpiece.]

Brownell, George H. "Mark Twain's Tribute to Francis Lightfoot Lee," *Twainian,* III, 1–3 (November, 1943).

[A serious article written for the *Pennsylvania Magazine* in 1877.]

Carter, Paul. "Mark Twain and War," *Twainian,* I, 1–3, 7 (March, 1942).

[Twain's advanced and civilized views.]

Davidson, William E. "Mark Twain and Conscience," *Twainian,* I, 1–3 (April, 1942).

[Sound Study.]

Feinstein, George W. "Twain as Forerunner of Tooth-and-Claw Criticism," *Modern Language Notes,* LXIII, 49–50 (January, 1948).

Gibson, William M. "Mark Twain and Howells: Anti-Imperialists," *New England Quarterly,* XX, 435–70 (December, 1947).

[Important study of Twain's dislike of imperialism.]

Gilder, Rodman. "Mark Twain Detested the Theatre," *Theatre Arts,* XXVIII, 109–116 (February, 1944).

[Actually Twain was greatly interested in the theatre.]

Hamada, Masajiro. "Mark Twain's Conception of Social Justice," [Japanese] *Studies in English Literature,* XVI, 593–616 (October, 1936).

[Twain had no metaphysical interests, but applied the evolutionary theory to human actions.]

McKeithan, D. M. "More About Mark Twain's War with English Critics of America," *Modern Language Notes,* LXIII, 221–8 (April, 1948).

[Shows that Mark's quarrel was with individual critics and that he remained fond of England.]

Masters, Edgar Lee. "Mark Twain: Son of the Frontier," *American Mercury,* XXXVI, 67–74 (September, 1935).

[Twain's Western realism prevented escapism from problems of his later years.]

Parsons, Coleman O. "The Devil and Samuel Clemens," *Virginia Quarterly Review,* XXIII, 582–606 (Autumn, 1947).

[A penetrating study of Twain and conscience.]

Stewart, Herbert L. "Mark Twain on the Jewish Problem," *Dalhousie Review,* XIV, 455–8 (January, 1935).

[Evaluation critically of "Concerning the Jews."]

Taylor, Walter Fuller. "Mark Twain and the Machine Age," *South Atlantic Quarterly,* XXXVII, 384–96 (October, 1938).

[Penetrating analysis of Clemens' economic thought.]

Waggoner. H. H. "Science in the Thought of Mark Twain," *American Literature,* VIII, 357–70 (January, 1937).

[Reveals Mark's interest in scientific thought through his reading and natural scepticism.]

CHAPTER VI

MARK TWAIN'S PLACE IN LITERATURE

THE EARLY literary reputation of Samuel Clemens, one in fact continuing into his maturity, was that of literary comedian. As Dixon Wecter says, "his reputation throughout life kept returning to that of "a 'phunny phellow' turning cartwheels to captivate the groundlings."[1] Mark Twain, we must remember, grew up amid the flowering of the Old Southwestern humor; his first book featured a comic story picked up from a miner on Jackass Hill, while his first bestseller mingled irreverent Washoe guffaws with brash contemplation of European culture. No wonder nineteenth century criticism, accustomed to the genteel tradition, failed readily to perceive the greatness of Twain's stature, even as academicians of that period failed to evaluate Whitman fairly, and in America at least Melville went his way unnoticed.

When *Innocents Abroad* (1869) appeared, it was reviewed in the *Nation* as typical of "our peculiar school of humorists,"[2] the unsigned critic failing, however, to accord the book literary status, even though enjoying its fun. William Dean Howells, who acclaimed the *Innocents* for its humor, limited his praise to saying that Mark was now worthy to rank among the best of "the humorists California has given us."[3] With the reading public, notwithstanding,

1 "Mark Twain," *Literary History of the United States,* II, 922.
2 *Nation,* IX, 194 (September 2, 1869).
3 *Atlantic Monthly,* XXIV, 766 (December, 1869).

it suddenly brought what Carl Van Doren called "explosive fame,"[4] and Oliver Wendell Holmes wrote the author a complimentary acknowledgment.[5] But it was humor and fun that brought responsive sales; readers did not dream that Twain was a serious artist.

When *Roughing It* (1872) was published, though in general the leading journals took no notice of what seemed another funny, journalistic effort, Howells remarked upon its verisimilitude expressed through "grotesque exaggeration and broad irony."[6] It was still the fun-maker, nevertheless, that Mark remained, not social historian, or literary artist. Many readers continued to echo J. G. Holland's comment on the *Innocents* that its author was a "mere fun-maker of ephemeral popularity."[7] As more books continued to appear, critical evaluation altered slightly. Richard Watson Gilder paid his respects to Mark as a "humorous story-teller and ingenious homely philosopher," even saying, "it is because Mark Twain is a satirist, and in a measure a true philosopher, that his broadly humorous books and speeches have met with wide and permanent popular favor."[8] Yet Gilder felt, as he said of *The Prince and the Pauper* (1882), that Clemens could not successfully produce a work after the older models. Critics who did like *The Prince and the Pauper*—and it appears to have been liked better than Mark's earlier books— approved because it complied with conventional ideas of literature. Here was less originality and more of those qualities of the genteel tradition, which if less vigorous, at least could be evaluated on critical scales adjusted for historical romance in Old England.[9]

Across the Atlantic, John Nichol, professor of English literature in the University of Glasgow, found Twain mas-

[4] *The American Novel* (New York: Macmillan, revised ed., 1940), p. 141.

[5] *Letters,* I, 166.

[6] *Atlantic Monthly,* XXIX, 754–5 (June, 1872).

[7] Paine, I, 382.

[8] *Century,* I, n.s., 783–4 (March, 1882).

[9] See Authur L. Vogelback, "*The Prince and the Pauper:* A Study in Critical Standards," *American Literature,* XIV, 48–54 (March, 1942).

ter of a "degenerate style," one who has "done perhaps more than any other living writer to lower the literary tone of English speaking people."[10] Nichol declared Mark a joker, who could not be a fine writer, because he turned everything into jest. But the succeeding year another English writer, Haweis, dealt more kindly: "Mark Twain's strong points are his facile but minute observation, his power of description, a certain justness and right proportion, and withal a great firmness of touch and peculiar—I had almost said personal—vein of humor."[11] And in America *Harper's* finally decided to recognize Clemens' existence with a review of *Life on the Mississippi* (1883), though even then it was historical and regional interest which drew the reviewer rather than literary quality.[12]

With the appearance of *Huckleberry Finn* (1885) there was slight critical acclaim. T. S. Perry, reviewing it in the *Century* did little more than praise the plot;[13] Charles F. Richardson placed its creator in a chapter headed "Borderlands of American Literature,"[14] while writing of Charles D. Warner and Oliver Wendell Holmes as having "actually contributed to literature." Arthur L. Vogelback finds that Twain's masterpiece "received at the time practically no critical attention in America," despite the fact that "Of all Clemens' books published up to 1885, *Huckleberry Finn* received the greatest pre- and post-publication notice."[15] In spite of this, however, it appears that Mark's work in general continued to be widely popular with the general pub-

[10] *American Literature: an Historical Sketch 1620–1880* (Edinburgh: Adam and Charles Black, 1882), p. 426.

[11] H. R. Haweis, *American Humorists* (London: Chatto and Windus, 1883), p. 167. The author lectured on American humor at the Royal Institute.

[12] "Editor's Literary Record," *Harper's Magazine,* LXVII, 799 (October, 1883).

[13] *Century,* VIII, n.s., 171 (May, 1885).

[14] *American Literature 1607–1885* (New York: G. P. Putnam, 1886; student's edition, 1904), p. 396.

[15] "The Publication and Reception of *Huckleberry Finn* in America," *American Literature,* XI, 260–272 (November, 1939).

lic; and French translations appeared in 1883 and during 1884–6.[16] In 1890 William Dean Howells praised Clemens for "the delicious satire, the marvellous wit, the wild, free, fantastic humor" found in his writings.[17] Comparing Twain with Cervantes, he said, "the two writers are of the same humorous largeness."[18] Howells then lauded Clemens' writings for being "true to human nature"[19] and declared that "his fun is unrivalled" because of the "right feeling and clear thinking"[20] that it contains.

One year later, however, Professor Henry A. Beers found Mark nothing more than an able jokester, below the literary level of Lowell and Holmes, one destined to last only through his humor.[21] However, in England, Andrew Lang perceived that *Huckleberry Finn* was "a nearly flawless gem of romance and humor," though even he qualified his praise by assertion that "Mark Twain often sins against good taste."[22]

As time went on, Twain's importance as social historian impinged even more on critical consciousness. Charles M. Thompson said he had "recorded the life of certain southwestern portions of our country, at one fleeting stage in their development, better than it is possible it will ever be done again."[23] To this Henry C. Vedder added an appreciation of Mark's "broad humanity, his gift of seeing far below the surface of life, his subtle comprehension of human nature, and his realistic method."[24]

16 H. Houston Peckham, "The Literary Status of Mark Twain, 1877–1890," *South Atlantic Quarterly,* XIX, 332–40 (October, 1920).

17 *Harper's Monthly,* LXXX, 318–23 (January, 1890). Reprinted in *My Mark Twain,* p. 145.

18 *Ibid.,* p. 147.

19 *Ibid.,* p. 149.

20 *Idem.*

21 *Initial Studies in American Letters* (New York: Chautauqua Press, 1891), p. 188.

22 "The Art of S. L. Clemens," *Critic,* XIX, o.s., 45 (July 25, 1891).

23 "Mark Twain as an Interpreter of American Character," *Atlantic,* LXXIX, 448 (April, 1897).

24 *American Writers of Today* (New York: Silver, Burdett & Co., 1898), p. 138.

Just one year later, Brander Matthews, writing a preface to a collected edition of Clemens' works, declared:

At how long an interval Mark Twain shall be rated after Molière and Cervantes it is for the future to declare. All that we can see clearly now is that it is with them that he is to be classed—with Molière and Cervantes, with Chaucer and Fielding, humorists all of them, and all of them manly men.[25]

Higher praise was to come shortly, and from whence least expected, Professor Barrett Wendell of Harvard, who designated *Huckleberry Finn* "a book which in certain moods one is disposed for all its eccentricity to call the most admirable work of literary art as yet produced on this continent."[26]

Two other historians of the same year failed to see Clemens with Wendell's perception; Henry S. Pancoast grouped Mark with the literary comedians, dismissing the *Innocents* with this comment: "but to some of us even shallow raptures are better than a cynical levity";[27] at the same time, Walter C. Bronson briefly placed Clemens with Harte and Miller, and while complimenting the originality and imagination of this "greatest writer of the West,"[28] treated him in less than a page.

William P. Trent, only three years later, though designating Twain a "socio-political humorist," nevertheless rated him below Holmes and Lowell,[29] while George E. Woodberry said that Clemens missed being a national au-

25 Reprinted as "An Appreciation," *Europe and Elsewhere,* (New York: Harpers, 1923), p. xxx.

26 *A Literary History of America* (New York: Charles Scribner's, 1900), p. 503.

27 Henry S. Pancoast, *An Introduction to American Literature* (New York: Henry Holt & Co., 1900), p. 329.

28 Walter C. Bronson, *A Short History of American Literature* (New York: D. C. Heath & Co., 1900), p. 286.

29 William P. Trent, *A History of American Literature, 1607–1865* (New York: D. Appleton & Co., 1903), p. 518.

thor because he belonged to a "provincial caste"—that is, the West.[30]

In 1904 Professor Richard Burton stated that we possessed "One living writer of indisputable genius . . . Mark Twain."[31] Thus by the last years of his life the literary reputation of Samuel Clemens had risen from the lowly status of a mere "funny man" to that of a major figure in the eyes of some initiated critics. Such, for instance, was the opinion of Professor Phelps of Yale, who wrote: "Indeed, it seems to me that Mark Twain is our foremost living American writer."[32]

John Macy, a few years after Clemens' death, spoke of *Huckleberry Finn* as our "greatest piece of American fiction."[33] Macy praised Mark's wide appeal, his abundant humor, importance to social history, realism, true chivalry, breadth of knowledge; then he said: "Mark Twain's mind was of universal proportions; he meditated on all the deep problems, and somewhere in his work he touches upon most of the vital things that men commonly think about and wonder about."[34] And Macy concludes by calling Mark's portrait of Mankind "the greatest canvas that any American has painted."[35]

Yet there were those who still voiced an adverse attitude; "the verdict of time," said Walter C. Bronson, "will be that he could see and describe far better than he could think."[36] Waldo Frank, however, that same year called Huck Finn

[30] George E. Woodberry, *America in Literature* (New York: Harper and Brothers, 1903), p. 206.

[31] *Literary Leaders of America* (New York: Scribners, 1904), p. 312.

[32] William Lyon Phelps, "Mark Twain: Humorist and Philosopher," *North American Review,* CLXXXV, 542 (July 5, 1907).

[33] *The Spirit of American Literature* (New York: Doubleday, Page, 1913), p. 249.

[34] *Ibid.,* p. 274.

[35] *Ibid.,* p. 275.

[36] *A Short History of American Literature* (New York: Heath, 1919), p. 290.

"the American epic hero" and acclaimed, "the soul of Mark Twain was great."[37] Official academic sanction was placed upon his literary reputation when the *Cambridge History of American Literature* (1921) appeared; it represented something in the nature of a final court of scholarly judgment. Here Stuart P. Sherman praised Mark for "his exhibition of a masterpiece or so not unworthy of Le Sage or Cervantes." And added, "He is a fulfilled promise of American life."[38] Brander Matthews in a reissue of an earlier appraisal affirmed that Twain's "place in the English literature of the nineteenth century is with its leaders."[39] But even as a position of security seemed to have been reached, a damaging frontal attack occurred; Van Wyck Brooks decided upon a Freudian analysis of Mark's writings to prove that he had failed to become a serious, mature artist. Briefly the thesis ran: Mark Twain was born with potentialities which were not realized, because of his environment and his lack of courage. "Mark Twain's attack upon the failure of human life was merely a rationalization of the failure in himself." Brooks concludes, "And this failure was the failure of the artist in him."[40] Then he dismisses Clemens' books by calling their appeal "largely an appeal to rudimentary minds."[41]

Thus the general line was established for a school of criticism which misunderstood the frontier, deplored humor, and demanded that all literature devote itself to political and sociological problems. Though students of the frontier, such as Lucy Lockwood Hazard, saw the complete mis-

37 *Our America* (New York: Boni & Liveright, 1919), p. 38.

38 "Mark Twain," *The Cambridge History of American Literature* (New York: Macmillan, 1921), III, 1.

39 *Introduction to American Literature* (New York: American Book Co., 1896, revised 1923), p. 226.

40 *The Ordeal of Mark Twain* (New York: E. P. Dutton, 1920, revised 1933), p. 313.

41 *Ibid.*, p. 28.

understanding in all this, the idea swept across critical ranks like prairie fire.[42]

A leading exponent was Lewis Mumford, who saw Mark Twain "caught as deeply in the net of the industrialist and the pioneer as any of his contemporaries."[43] Believing with Brooks that Clemens as a pilot most fully realized his capabilities, Mumford found him unaware of the "black squalor of the new immigrant workers."[44] In a word, the Twain pictured here liked industrialism because it brought him personal comfort and accepted unthinkingly the values of the Gilded Age.

To Vernon L. Parrington, Mark Twain was the answer to Walt Whitman's query about the absence of a fresh, courageous, Western writer: "Here at last was an authentic American—a native writer thinking his own thoughts, using his own eyes, speaking his own dialect—everything European fallen away, the last shred of feudal culture gone, local and western yet continental,"[45] To Parrington, Clemens was "an embodiment of three centuries of American experience,"[46] born and reared on the frontier, inheriting all its vigor, exuberance, and folk-ways. Yet because of his frontier origin Mark suffered from a lack of spiritual, intellectual, and cultural background, never achieving an "untroubled, conscious integrity" as did Emerson and Whitman. And Brooks is termed partly right about Twain's bitter pessimism arising from surrender to the ideals of the Gilded Age;[47] however, Parrington credits the "inevitable toll exacted by the passing years" with exerting an equal

42 Miss Hazard in *The Frontier in American Literature* (New York: Crowell, 1927) credits Mark with writing of the Gilded Age with a "fierce undercurrent of savage criticism." p. 220. She also says that he exposed "the relation of Big Business to the government." p. 228.

43 *The Golden Day* (New York: Boni and Liveright, 1927), p. 170.

44 *Ibid.*, p. 172.

45 Vernon L. Parrington, *Main Currents in American Thought* (New York: Harcourt, Brace & Co., 1930), III, 86.

46 *Ibid.*, p. 87.

47 *Ibid.*, p. 89.

influence, until we have a slow change from the gaiety of youth to the "fierce satire of disillusion."[48] Parrington believed that Clemens wished to be a satirist, but refrained because "the wares of the satirist were not in demand at the barbecue,"[49] yet Parrington sees at the heart of Mark Twain's philosophy "the individual will in opposition to society."[50] Thus he finds Mark turning within and escaping reality:

> And when in the end the fool's gold turned to ashes in his mouth, as a frontiersman still he pursued his way alone, a solitary pioneer exploring the universe, seeking a homestead in an ironical cosmos, until overwhelmed by the intolerable solitude he made mock at all the gods. What a commentary on the Gilded Age![51]

Soon, however, Constance Rourke in a penetrating analysis of American humor as a revelation of national ideals and character also showed the talent of Twain to be "consistently a pioneer talent." Mark Twain, Miss Rourke stated, was not a failure as an artist; rather he was a "great repository" for all the national moods, attitudes, and legends; for Clemens had "achieved scale, with the gusty breadth astir in the country as the Pacific was reached."[52] The difference here in critical attitudes arose, it might be said, from what the critic expected, or valued, in Twain's subject matter. At the same time, a balanced, penetrating essay on Twain appeared by C. Hartley Grattan, in which Mark's ability to gather up into himself "more elements of the life of his day than any other writing man of the time"[53] was stressed. In contradiction of the Brooks-Mumford thesis, Grattan found Mark "an idealist of a most uncom-

[48] *Ibid.*, p. 91.
[49] *Ibid.*, p. 94.
[50] *Ibid.*, p. 95.
[51] *Ibid.*, p. 101.
[52] *American Humor* (New York: Harcourt, Brace, 1931), pp. 218–219.
[53] "Mark Twain" in *American Writers on American Literature* (New York: Horace Liveright, 1931), p. 274.

promising sort."[54] Declaring that *The Gilded Age, Huckleberry Finn* and *Pudd'nhead Wilson* reveal Mark's true attitude toward the America of his day, Grattan found no cause for wonder over the bitter books of later years.

Another important estimate was that of Ludwig Lewisohn, who saw Twain as the "bardic type of artist" speaking with understanding to the people, one who did possess an awareness of the "dark and desperate problems of humanity."[55] Lewisohn doubted the "ordeal" or frustration, for he found instead the artist, whose material was that "inimitable American civilization which Mark Twain not only recorded as in its living character it was, but which he raised, by the heightening and isolation of art, into a permanent realm of the human imagination."[56]

Also refuting the failure of Twain, V. F. Calverton, declared that perhaps the *Innocents* might be justly termed our first American book because Mark's democracy was more than political; it was economic, and here it even carried into art.[57] And Calverton met the Brooks attack squarely with the denial, "at no time did he 'sell out' his philosophy to the upper bourgeoisie of the East."[58] Yet Granville Hicks kept the frustration theory current. "The frontier humorist and realist might have become a great social novelist," he said, adding, "In minor ways Mark Twain made progress, but he never transcended the limitations of his tradition."[59] And Hicks dismissed Mark from literature: "He was and knew he was, merely an entertainer."[60]

Then Newton Arvin, adapting social, class attitudes to literature, criticized Clemens: "He should have remained

[54] *Ibid.*, p. 276.

[55] *Expression in America* (New York and London: Harpers, 1932), p. 225.

[56] *Ibid.*, p. 232.

[57] *The Liberation of American Literature* (New York: Scribners, 1932), p. 324.

[58] *Ibid.*, p. 327.

[59] *The Great Tradition* (New York: Macmillan, 1933), p. 46.

[60] *Idem.*

true to the best traditions of his family and his class, or have gone beyond them. He did neither."[61] Clemens wrote for the vast majority with whom he was popular, and Arvin, following in part the Brooks thesis, seemed to believe such books could not really be good. Yet "the stultification was never complete" and Twain, however much edited by Howells and Livy, retained enough "original freedom of spirit"[62] at times to write literature, though Arvin even dismisses much of *Huckleberry Finn* from that realm.

Gradually, however, through the efforts of DeVoto, Ferguson, Wecter, and Trilling, informed opinion has come to agree with James T. Farrell that "too much of the critical writing on Mark Twain has stressed his failure and his limitations."[63] And Farrell frankly issues a challenge:

> Tom and Huck are symbols of the possibilities in human beings. Today they stand as a test not only of ourselves but of the whole of American society. They are, with all their charm, like two accusing figures, with their fingers pointing down the decades of American history. Their very characters seem to ask why—why has this promise not been realized? Why is it so rarely that the man becomes what the boy gave promise of becoming? This is part of their significance as enduring characters in American literature.[64]

England

In *Tom Sawyer Abroad,* Mark Twain has Tom say, "Why, look at England. It's the most important country in the world; and yet you could put it in China's vest pocket."[65] And in *What Is Man?,* there is this explanation of Shakespeare: "In England he rose to the highest limit attainable through the *outside helps afforded by that land's ideals, in-*

[61] "Mark Twain: 1835–1935," *New Republic,* LXXXIII, 126 (June 12, 1935).

[62] *Ibid.,* pp. 125–6.

[63] *The League of Frightened Philistines* (New York: Vanguard Press, 1945), p. 25.

[64] *Ibid.,* p. 30.

[65] P. 80.

fluences, and training."[66] Mark himself wrote to Howells in 1897, "This has been a bitter year for English pride, and I don't like to see England humbled—that is, not too much. We are sprung from her loins, and it hurts me. I am for republics, and she is the only comrade we've got, in that."[67] Another time he wrote to Twichell that poor as our civilization is "it is better than *real* savagery," adding, "And so we must not utter any hurtful word about England in these days, nor fail to hope that she will win in this war, for her defeat and fall would be an irremediable disaster for the mangy human race."[68]

Just before Mark Twain received an honorary degree from Oxford he wrote:

> I have received since I have been here, in this one week, hundreds of letters from all conditions of people in England, men, women, and children, and there is compliment, praise, and, above all, and better than all, there is in them a note of affection.[69]

Such was Clemens' fame in the eyes of the English people and his place in their hearts. At the Lotos Club, when attending his last great banquet, Mark said of his Oxford robe, "I like its splendid color. I would dress that way all the time if I dared."[70] There was a mutual bond, as it were, between Mark and his English readers, one uniting them in a common love of both pageantry and democracy.

Before 1880 Twain's work had appeared in England, along with other American authors, in a "Select Library of Fiction,"[71] one of the titles, *Funny Stories and Humourous Poems* by Mark Twain and O. W. Holmes, indicating British delight in different aspects of American humor. When Chatto and Windus took over many of the items pirated by

66 P. 9.
67 *Letters,* II, 643.
68 Paine, III, 1096.
69 *Ibid.,* IV, 1391.
70 *Ibid.,* IV, 1433.
71 Clarence Gohdes, *American Literature in Nineteenth Century England* (New York: Columbia University Press, 1944), p. 23.

John C. Hotten, they soon issued a "Popular Novels" series at two shillings each; three were by Mark Twain.[72] The earlier writings of both Twain and Harte appeared regularly in these cheap editions, a popularity never granted either Howells or James. During the last two decades of the century at least sixty editions or issues of books by Clemens appeared, stimulated in part by the large number of subscribers to Mudie's circulating library.[73]

The English *Review of Reviews,* started as a monthly in January, 1890, ran a condensed version of *A Connecticut Yankee* in the February number.[74] Indeed, Clemens' popularity had long been so great that prior to the copyright act of 1891 he had protected himself with previous publication in London. Though *The Jumping Frog* appeared first in America, an authorized version was published by Routledge in England only a few months later. Such were the possibilities following the reception of *The Jumping Frog* that John C. Hotten, the literary pirate, not only reprinted it, but with an eagle eye on the cash drawer, had an unauthorized edition of *Innocents Abroad* on the market before the legitimate publisher, Routledge, could issue his. This literary buccaneering was so lucrative that the greedy Hotten, intent upon turning more ink into gold, reached for the "Memoranda" from the *Galaxy*.[75] By the time Twain visited England in 1872 he was fully aware of his financial loss from inability to collect royalties on his increasing sales; it was then that the idea of pre-publication in England was adopted as a solution. Indeed, Routledge and Hotten, between them, had published twelve separate books by Twain during 1871–2, and several other items appearing

72 *Ibid.,* p. 24.

73 See Clarence Gohdes, "British Interest in American Literature During the Latter Part of the Nineteenth Century as Reflected by Mudie's Select Library," *American Literature* XIII, 356–62 (January, 1942).

74 Gohdes, *American Literature in Nineteenth-Century England,* p. 63.

75 Johnson, *Bibliography,* p. vii.

at the same time represented combinations of some of those titles.[76]

By 1883 Thomas Hardy asked Howells why people did not realize Twain was more than a great humorist, indicating how critical appreciation in England was keeping step with general popularity.[77] And this popularity increased as his books continued to appear there; Andrew Lang received *Huckleberry Finn* as "a nearly flawless gem of romance and humor,"[78] a critical dictum more concretely expressed by the large numbers who read it.

When Rudyard Kipling called on Clemens during the summer of 1889, he found no disillusion with "this man I had learned to love and admire fourteen thousand miles away."[79] More than a decade later Kipling wrote to his publisher, Frank Doubleday:

> I love to think of the great and godlike Clemens. He is the biggest man you have on your side of the water by a damn sight, and don't you forget it. Cervantes was a relation of his.[80]

No higher praise, nor from a more acceptable source, could have come to Twain than William Archer's dictum on *Huckleberry Finn:* "If any work of incontestable genius, and plainly predestined to immortality, has been issued in the English language during the past quarter of a century, it is that brilliant romance of the Great Rivers."[81] Yet Clarence Gohdes finds such appreciation scant among run of the mill critics in England, who continued to regard Clemens as "too vulgar, irreverent, and eccentric" for ad-

76 Gohdes, *op. cit.*, pp. 89–90.

77 *Life in Letters of William Dean Howells* (Garden City: Doubleday, Doran & Co., 1928), I, 349.

78 "The Art of S. L. Clemens," *Critic,* o.s., XIX, 45 (July 25, 1891).

79 Rudyard Kipling, *From Sea to Sea* (New York: Doubleday and McClure, 1899), II, 171.

80 Paine, III, 1208.

81 William Archer, *America To-Day* (London: W. Heinemann, 1900), pp. 178–9.

mission into the front rank of authors.[82] Despite this, however, Mark Twain probably had more articles written about him for the British journals than were devoted to any other of his American contemporaries.[83] Mark was entertaining; moreover, he represented the United States—so well that George Bernard Shaw wrote him: "I am persuaded that the future historian of America will find your works as indispensable to him as a French historian finds the political tracts of Voltaire."[84] Always popular in England, at the time of his death Clemens was honored by a Mark Twain number of the London *Bookman* (June, 1910), to which several distinguished literary men contributed.[85]

More recently, English criticism has divided somewhat on Twain's place in literature—perhaps the influence of Brooks across the Atlantic. D. H. Lawrence in his *Studies in Classic American Literature* (1923), for instance, does not even mention Mark Twain, although he includes both Melville and Whitman. A. C. Ward in a treatment of American letters, which becomes at times rather supercilious, deplores Twain's lack of taste and insight, especially in the *Innocents* and the *Yankee:* "at his worst," says Ward, "he was a rhinoceros among porcelain."[86] Ward follows Brooks in believing Mark was "chafed" and restrained, though he does perceive the "complexity and subtlety" of his work, realizing, also, that "Tom Sawyer and Huckleberry Finn are among the few humorous masterpieces in world literature."[87] Indeed, Ward finally praises Twain for his independent vision and for dealing freely with human experience.

82 Gohdes, *op. cit.,* p. 129. 83 *Ibid.,* p. 139.

84 Paine, IV, 1398.

85 A list of contributors is conveniently found in Archibald Henderson, *op. cit.,* pp. 228–9.

86 A. C. Ward, *American Literature 1880–1930* (London: Methuen & Co., Ltd., 1932), p. 55.

87 *Ibid.,* p. 61.

George Stuart Gordon, Merton Professor of English Literature, later President of Magdalen College, writing of Clemens in *Anglo-American Literary Relations* (1942), calmly declared him an "authentic man of genius" and *Huckleberry Finn* "among the great books of the world."[88] And this dictum would seem justified by the continuing numbers of its readers in Great Britain. More recently, Marcus Cunliffe, lecturer in American Studies at Manchester University, has commented on the "warmth and accuracy" of Clemens' best works, saying, "But *Huckleberry Finn,* apart from the Tom-Sawyerish rescue of Jim, is perfect, the unforgettable portrait of a frontier boy."[89] And Cunliffe calls Mark Twain "a great artist whose touch is sure."[90]

France

In France recognition came first from Marie Thérèse Blanc (Th. Bentzon), whose significant estimate of Twain appeared in the *Revue des Deux Mondes* (1872).[91] Mme. Blanc, wishing to popularize American literature in her native country, translated *The Jumping Frog,* which Mark later playfully retranslated into English.[92] Misunderstanding much of Twain's humor, such as his pretended naive astonishment, she did see the extravaganza therein and also his democratic qualities, even if not granting them entire critical approval. Three years later, this same critic wrote an elaborate review of *The Gilded Age* including lengthy

88 George Stuart Gordon, *Anglo-American Literary Relations* (Oxford: University Press, 1942), p. 109.

89 *The Literature of the United States* (London: Penguin Books, 1954), p. 167.

90 *Idem.*

91 Th. Bentzon, "Les Humoristes américans: I, Mark Twain," *Revue des Deux Mondes,* C, 313–35 (July, 1872).

92 See "Private History of the Jumping Frog Story," *In Defense of Harriet Shelley,* pp. 100–10.

quotations from it.[93] Though failing to appreciate the character of Colonel Sellers, Mme. Blanc did praise Mark's accuracy as a reporter; and her strictures upon the collaboration from the standpoint of art are just. It was through her quotations of long passages from *Innocents Abroad,* and *The Gilded Age,* together with the whole of the *Jumping Frog,* that Mark Twain was first introduced to the French people, an introduction, it must be admitted, which presented him more as a wild and untamed funster than a civilized man of letters.

Émile Blémont next continued the introduction of Mark's work to French readers with *Esquisses Américaines de Mark Twain* (1881), a volume of translations of some of Mark's lighter sketches. More important, Eugène Forgues contributed a summation of French critical attitudes toward Twain in "Les Caravanes d'un humoriste" published in *Revue des Deux Mondes* (1886), to which was added several full quotations from *Life on the Mississippi*. Forgues, however, was unfriendly in his estimates; the Frenchman with his admiration for form could see little to praise in Twain's writings, abounding, so they seemed, with brutal wit and lack of taste.[94] Yet Forgues says,

> Ce qu'il y a donc de meilleur jusqu'à présent dans l'oeuvre de Mark Twain, en dehors de son exquise idylle, les Aventures de Tom Sawyer, ce sont ses voyages et ses fortunes de terre et de mer.[95]

While *Life on the Mississippi* drew this comment: "Il a donné dans son livre une partie de lui-même, ce qui en fait une oeuvre attrayante et vivante."[96]

The attempts made, up to then, to popularize Clemens' work in France had failed because the French did not like

[93] L'Age doré en Amérique, *Revue des Deux Mondes,* (March 15, 1875). XLV, 319–43.

[94] *Revue des Deux Mondes,* LVI, 874–918 (February 15, 1886).

[95] *Ibid.,* p. 882.

[96] *Ibid.,* p. 883.

the roughness and blatancy of his humor; however, the success that had been achieved—and there had been some—came through the penetrating observation with which Twain looked at life, together with his art for evoking scenes and situations.

Archibald Henderson tells us, notwithstanding, that eventually Mark's comedy "won its way with the *blasé* Parisians" who gradually began to purchase the copies of *Roughing It* appearing in the bookstalls.[97] And by the time the authoritative edition of Twain's work appeared in English, Gabriel de Lautrec in the *Mercure de France* paid him surprising tribute as probably the greatest humorist then living.[98] Yet even so, at the time of Clemens' death, *Le Figaro* pointed out that Twain's popularity in France would probably remain restricted, even as that of La Fontaine in America, for there is a difference between wit and humor, though both are based upon good sense.[99]

And so it seems, for four years later, H. Houston Peckham could find only the following translations: Emile Blémont (Paris, 1881), Paul Largillière (Paris, 1883), W. Hugues (Paris, 1884, 1886).[100] In 1920 the Professor of American Literature and Civilization at the Sorbonne overlooked Mark Twain entirely in a survey of our literature which treated Whitman adequately and mentioned Bret Harte favorably.[101] And in a summary of French studies from 1923 through 1933, Jean Simon though finding critical works on major figures and even some American authors of second rank, cites no material whatever on Clemens.[102]

97 *Mark Twain,* p. 137.

98 Vol. XXXV. September, 1900.

99 "Mark Twain, Intime" *Le Figaro,* May 7, 1910.

100 "Is American Literature Read and Respected in Europe " *South Atlantic Quarterly,* XIII, 382–388 (October, 1914).

101 Charles Cestre, "American Literature Through French Eyes," *Yale Review,* n.s., X, 85–9 (October, 1920).

102 "French Studies in American Literature and Civilization," *American Literature,* VI, 176–90 (May, 1934).

In June, 1935, Maurice le Breton stated that Mark Twain was hardly known in France and never read since the greater part of his writings remained untranslated, the great public judging him entirely on certain extracts which did not reveal him at his best.[103] Adding that Twain had never excited in France the same interest as had Fenimore Cooper and Bret Harte, who were more respectful of conventions, Le Breton then said, however, that Twain's book represented America no less than the lyric work of Whitman: "Mieux que quiconque aussi, il a su peindre les aspects familiers et exprimer l'âme profonde de son pays."[104]

Commenting briefly on the Van Wyck Brooks thesis, which he rejects, Le Breton says in contradiction that the American West of 1840 to 1870 remained the source of Mark's inspiration. And he sees the individualism in his work, the idealism joined to an awareness of reality, while the whole Brooks following is dismissed, "Comme écrivain, il [Clemens] est parfaitement sincère."[105]

After discussing the two veins in Clemens' humor, pure fantasy arising spontaneously, and the serious side based upon reflection, Maurice le Breton praises him: "Mark Twain demeure une des grandes figures de la littérature américaine et sa gloire ne semble pas menacée."[106] Le Breton finds Mark to be the poet of a phase unique in the experience of America and his books to be original and lasting.[107]

Léon Lemonnier contributed a biographical sketch of Samuel Clemens' youth to *La Grande Revue* (1935) in which he followed Paine's account. At times sentimental in tone and somewhat distorted, as when Poe and Dickens

[103] Maurice le Breton, "Un Centenaire: Mark Twain," *Revue Anglo-Américaine,* XII, 401 (June, 1935).

[104] *Ibid.,* p. 403.

[105] *Ibid.,* p. 414.

[106] *Ibid.,* p. 417.

[107] *Ibid.,* p. 418.

are presented as Sam's favorite authors, the sketch is otherwise a good, flowing narrative.[108]

Also, in this centenary year, Gabriel de Lautrec, who a quarter of a century earlier had praised Twain in the *Mercure de France,* now wrote a further appreciation for that same journal. De Lautrec praised Mark's courage which led him to attack any and all persons and things he thought deserved it. De Lautrec retells *Une Interview* (An Encounter with an Interviewer) with the simple comment, "There you have Samuel Langhorne Clemens," yet he also perceives "La vision des choses, chez Mark Twain, est en réalité, sérieuse."[109] Moreover, De Lautrec like Le Breton sees Mark as the supreme literary example of the prodigious development of the American continent and declares, "Mark Twain est Américain."[110] A sensitive humorist who resents cruelty and has compassion, Samuel Clemens the man appeals to De Lautrec equally as much as Twain the author. It seems strange, nevertheless, that in this article filled with praise for both the man and author none of Twain's great books are mentioned.

Another critic, John Charpentier, returned almost full cycle to the first French impressions of Clemens; for Charpentier, Mark is the "enfant sauvage de l'Ouest,"[111] one so natural, energetic, so representative of the American people it was fitting that President Roosevelt in Washington should touch the button to open the centennial celebration at Hannibal. In brief, too, Charpentier views Mark as the "incarnation of an art where the muscle participates equally

108 Léon Lemonnier, "Les débuts d'un humoriste," *La Grande Revue,* CXLIX, 76–88 (November, 1935).

109 Gabriel de Lautrec, "Mark Twain," *Mercure de France,* CCIXIV, 76 (November, 1935).

110 *Ibid.,* p. 80.

111 John Charpentier, "Humour anglais et humour américain. A propos du centenaire de Mark Twain," *Mercure de France,* CCLXIV, 490 (December 15, 1935).

with the intelligence."[112] Little indeed is said about any of Mark's great works, rather his popularity with the masses in America is dwelt upon.

It remained for Léon Lemonnier to write an adequate appreciation of Clemens, *Mark Twain: L'Homme et Son Oeuvre* (1946). Lemonnier understands the personalized, organic nature of Twain's literary expression: "Son oeuvre et sa vie sont deux expressions à peine différentes de sa personnalité, qui apparaît alors comme le seul sujet d'études qui puisse vraiment être attachant."[113] And Twain's humor receives sympathetic appreciation, even Colonel Sellers, of whom Lemonnier says, "Le Colonel Sellers appartient à la grande famille des personnages excentriques que les auteurs anglais ont toujours décrits avec une bienveillance amusée."[114] Lemonnier also shows sound critical judgment; while calling *Tom Sawyer* one of Twain's major works, he says of *Huck Finn,* "C'est sans doute le meilleur roman de Mark Twain."[115] Indeed, Lemonnier's discussion of Twain's pessimism is one of the most logical, taking into account his temperament, inheritance, and the tragic happenings of his life calculated to produce such an outlook. Then, too, the observation is here made that "L'humour de Mark Twain est aussi lié à son pessimisme,"[116] the final comment on Twain being: "Alors, son humour construit un monde de rêve, d'où la douleur est absente, où la vie n'a plus ni monotonie ni contrainte, où l'esprit se meut dans l'imprévu avec une liberté parfaite."[117]

Roger Asselineau has written a perceptive appreciation of Clemens' work in *The Literary Reputation of Mark Twain from 1910 to 1950* (1954), which contains a very useful bibliography of books and articles from European and

112 *Ibid.,* p. 500.

113 *Mark Twain: L'Homme et Son Oeuvre* (Paris: Librairie Arthème Fayard, 1946), pp. 7–8.

114 *Ibid.,* p. 78.

115 *Ibid.,* p. 114.

116 *Ibid.,* p. 230.

117 *Ibid.,* p. 259.

American sources. Asselineau, however, limits his study to American criticism of Twain's books because he believes that no major critical contribution has come from any other country. Though never so popular in France as in England and Germany, Twain has gained readers there, even as he has received more attention from the critics. Asselineau concludes, "This gradual discovery of the merits of Mark Twain's works, this constantly deeper and better-motivated appreciation of his books is the best guarantee that his literary reputation will suffer no eclipse in the coming years."[118]

Germany

It was due to the success of Bret Harte in German translation that Mark Twain first appeared in that language; the steady sale of *The Tales of the Argonauts* caused the publishers to expect a similar interest in other Western stories. Within a brief four years Wilhelm Grunow in Leipsic brought forth *The Jumping Frog, Roughing It and Other Sketches* (1874), *The Innocents Abroad* (1875), *The Gilded Age* (1876), *The Adventures of Tom Sawyer* (1876), and *Sketches New and Old* (1877), all translated by Moritz Busch, who was a strong exponent of republicanism.[119] These translations were so popular that Tauchnitz at once issued *Tom Sawyer* in 1876, following it with other Mark Twain volumes as they appeared, these, of course, being in English. Though Tauchnitz made Twain available to those who could read English, it was, naturally, through translations that the bulk of the reading public came to know him. *Life on the Mississippi* appeared in 1888, soon followed by *Huckleberry Finn,* translated by a capable short story writer, Henny Koch.[120]

118 *The Literary Reputation of Mark Twain from 1910 to 1950* (Paris: Librairie Marcel Didier, 1954), p. 65.

119 Edgar H. Hemminghaus, *Mark Twain in Germany* (New York: Columbia University Press, 1939), pp. 9–10.

120 *Ibid.*, p. 13.

Archibald Henderson tells us of the unprecedented manner of Clemens' reception in Vienna,[121] and it was an Austrian critic and literary historian, Anton Emanuel Schönbach, who first accorded Twain full critical treatment, an appraisal more favorable than otherwise, but one placing him below Bret Harte.[122] Some of the journalists, on the other hand, failed completely to appreciate Twain's humor. Yet the extensive publications of his writings in Germany at least impressed the critics, so that gradually informed opinion began to view Clemens as a literary personality worth serious attention.[123]

The years 1892–1904 witnessed numerous reprints of Twain's books, publication of new works, and a steady growth of public interest; the resulting literary prestige led Robert Lutz in 1892 to undertake a six-volume edition of selected writings.[124] During these years German critical opinion divided on Clemens, many seeing him as a mere buffoon, working without any moral or artistic purpose, while others began to view him, in the words of an anonymous critic, as one who "instructs and educates as well as amuses and cheers."[125]

During the closing years of Clemens' life some German critics pointed out the "glorious unconstraint and wholesomeness of the era in which he lived"[126] as one reason for the unique quality of his output. Another element in his art, later recognized, was "the strongly human appeal of his colorful career,"[127] one so closely interwoven into the web of his fiction as to become at times indistinguishable. Finally the "heroic honesty and iron diligence" of Clemens' personal dealings in business contributed to his general popularity.[128] The reading public, as repeated publica-

121 *Mark Twain,* p. 142.
122 Hemminghaus, *op. cit.,* p. 16.
123 *Ibid.,* p. 30.
124 *Ibid.,* p. 31.
125 *Ibid.,* p. 49.
126 *Ibid.,* p. 57.
127 *Ibid.,* p. 58.
128 *Idem.*

tions demonstrated, admired most the *Sketches, Tom Sawyer,* and *Huck Finn.*[129] During the years immediately following Clemens' death and through the first world conflict, no German critic of note had anything much to say about him, although there were a few magazine articles now and then, with an occasional review in an educational journal. The *Deutsche Revue* in 1911 carried an important article on Mark Twain by Archibald Henderson of the University of North Carolina, whose books on Ibsen, Shaw, and other contemporary dramatists were well known abroad. Henderson, pointing out that the fame of no single international figure in literature rests on humor alone, emphasized the basic seriousness and moral conviction in Twain's writings, notably in *Huckleberry Finn.*[130] This recognition of Twain as a philosopher and sociologist, though not entirely new to the Germans, suggested a fresh appraisal of this aspect of his work. But of even more importance were the lectures delivered in German at the University of Berlin by C. Alphonso Smith, serving there as Roosevelt Professor of American History and Institutions while on leave from the University of Virginia, where he was the first Edgar Allan Poe Professor of English. Smith, observing that Mark had enjoyed more numerous opportunities for viewing human life in all aspects than any other American author, advanced the opinion that Twain's ultimate purpose was to express the truth as he found it.[131] Meanwhile popular demand had caused the issuing of *Tom Sawyer* and *Huck Finn* together in a single volume, while *The Prince and the Pauper* and *Tom Sawyer* were published in textbooks for school instruction.[132] In 1914, Grace I. Colbron found *Tom Sawyer* and *Huckleberry Finn* to be especially popular with Ger-

129 *Ibid.,* p. 64.

130 *Deutsche Revue,* XXXVI, 189–205 (February, 1911).

131 Smith's lectures on American literature were published in *Die Amerikanische Literatur* (Berlin, 1912).

132 Hemminghaus, *op. cit.,* p. 69.

man novel readers, so much so that among American writers Twain's popularity was second to none save Bret Harte.[133]

During the summer of 1921 *The Adventures of Tom Sawyer* reappeared, this time in a new jacket designed to catch the imagination of spring buyers at the Leipsic Fair, where advance orders for Christmas quickly demonstrated its popularity for juveniles. This led six months later to a new edition of *Huckleberry Finn,* which soon proved popular with adults as well as children. A demand for other works brought *A Tramp Abroad, Roughing It,* and a selection of *Sketches* in cheap editions, a revival due, it should be said, to Georg Steindorff, who made modernized translations of *Tom Sawyer* and *Huckleberry Finn* designed for popular appeal.[134] Success of the Steindorff translations caused others, a new volume of selections from *The Innocents Abroad* coming from the press in 1924, followed by several other Twain items during 1925. And this latter year, also, saw the appearance of the most important German book on Mark Twain, Friedrich Schönemann's *Mark Twain als literarische Persönlichkeit.*[135] Schönemann began his study with a refutation of Van Wyck Brooks' *Ordeal of Mark Twain* before proceeding to an analysis of Twain's nature, which he found a "combination of barbaric force and intense sweetness," leading to inner conflict, a duality of romantic and anti-romantic tendencies.[136] Schönemann's constructive contribution to an understanding of Twain's literary personality apparently helped to intensify German interest. Yet by the end of the twenties, the vogue enjoyed

133 Grace I. Colbron, "The American Novel in Germany," *Bookman*, XXXIX, 45–9, (March, 1914).

134 Hemminghaus, *op. cit.*, p. 85–6.

135 Published as Volume VIII in the Jenaer Germanistische Forschungen, 1925.

136 *Mark Twain als literarische Persönlichkeit* (Jena: Verlag der Frommanschen Buchhandlung, Walter Biedermann, 1925), pp. 61–72.

by Twain in Germany was drawing to a close; Hemminghaus concluded on the basis of published criticism that Mark's popularity there was "gradually on the decline."[137] Though the one hundredth anniversary of Clemens' birth was commemorated in Germany, the scale was much smaller than elsewhere. For the more penetrating German readers, Hemminghaus believes Twain is valued most as a "realistic chronicler of an important era of original American life."[138] Largely, we may assume, because of the Hitler regime the market for Twain's books dwindled, and it is now too early to hazard a guess as to his fate, critical or popular in the future.

Other Countries

The Latin countries, other than France, seem to have paid little or no critical attention to Clemens, but his books have been translated into Spanish and Italian.[139] On the other hand, in Scandinavia, where a general interest in American letters exists, Twain enjoyed an individual popularity. The chief librarian of the Royal Swedish Library records learning *Huckleberry Finn* almost by heart after receiving it for a birthday present.[140] Before Clemens' death a Danish critic and novelist, Johannes von Jensen, demanded a more serious consideration of Twain as an author, his own evaluation being translated into German.[141] Ivan Benson has found that the copies of Twain on the shelves of the Stockholm City Library today are numerous, and although generally in English, are read enough to demand frequent rebinding.[142] *Tom Sawyer* and *Huckleberry*

137 *Op. cit.,* p. 131.

138 *Ibid.,* p. 137.

139 The Mark Twain Museum in Hannibal has copies. *Twainian,* VII, 6 (Jan.–Feb., 1948).

140 Malcolm Cowley, "American Books Abroad," *Literary History of the United States,* II, 1383.

141 Hemminghaus, *op. cit.,* p. 61.

142 *Twainian,* II, 4 (May, 1940).

Finn, however, were early translated into Swedish.[143] *Pudd'nhead Wilson,* too, made its way into that language, where it appears titled *En Droppe Negerblod.*[144] An interesting study of Mark Twain is S. B. Liljegren's *The Revolt Against Romanticism in American Literature as Evidenced in the Works of S. L. Clemens,* an essay which places Mark in the cultural tradition of Europe, one altered by American environment, but nevertheless basically the same.[145] Liljegren claims that Clemens' literary roots go back to Beowulf rather than Franklin, his revolt against the romanticism of Scott and the others being but the transatlantic aspect of the same attitude in Thackeray.[146] The Scandinavian scholar disagrees with Parrington and others who find the Western influence strongest in Twain's literary development, pointing out Mark's "essential mental refinement, culture, and poetic sense of values."[147] While Liljegren undervalues the Western influences, both social and literary, in the development of Twain's art, he does remind us once more of the European tradition which, as Miss Brashear proved earlier, played an important part in the shaping of Samuel Clemens as a man of letters.[148]

In the year of Twain's centenary a Swiss scholar issued a small study designed to show Clemens interest in Switzerland as the cradle of liberty. Telling of Mark's first visit there in 1878, and the later ones of 1891 and 1897, August Hüppy called him "Dem grossen freund und Bewunderer."[149] The book contributes nothing to Twain criticism,

143 *Idem.*

144 *Twainian,* VII, 6 (January, 1948).

145 One of the studies on American language and literature of the American Institute in the University of Upsala (Upsala: Lundequistska Bokhandeln, 1945).

146 *Ibid.,* pp. 50–1.

147 *Ibid.,* p. 51.

148 Liljegren is particularly interested in Twain's burlesque poetry, which reveals that he had literary ideals of his own.

149 August Hüppy, *Mark Twain und die Schweiz* (Zürich: Reutimann Co., 1935).

nor does it add any new biographical facts, its interest being only in its appreciation of Clemens as a glorifier of the Alps.

Of importance is Mark Twain's reception in Russia which began there prior to 1910, for Clemens followed Cooper, Harriet Beecher Stowe, and Bret Harte in winning favor with Russian readers.[150] First of his stories to appear was *The Jumping Frog,* published in the St. Petersburg *Stock Exchange News* (1872), accompanied by an article praising Mark for "a highly original gift molded under the influence of the completely new life now springing up in the deserts of California and the mountains of Sierra Nevada." Though warning readers not to expect literary finesse, Twain's "inexhaustible supply of humor, vivid imagination, powerful fantasy, and unaffected gaiety"[151] received praise. From then on Mark appeared in newspapers and magazines, his first magazine appearance being in *Homeland Notes* (1877).[152]

Before the revolution the Czar's subjects apparently liked American books that were "realistic or humorous or heroic in treatment, if they were democratic in sentiment, if they dealt with life in a great city or, still better, with adventures on the frontier, and if the characters were representative of the American masses."[153] Mark Twain, like O. Henry, another favorite in Russia, easily fitted into this pattern for popularity. Twain was widely enough read to make his own way into Ukrainian or Little Russian dialect.[154] Among his books *The Prince and the Pauper* seems to have been read more often even than *Tom* and *Huck,* and the

150 Cowley, *op. cit.*, II, 1385.

151 Quoted by Robert Magidoff, "American Literature in Russia," *Saturday Review of Literature,* XXIX, 11 (November 2, 1946).

152 *Idem.*

153 Cowley, *op. cit.*, II, 1384–5.

154 A. Yarmolinsky, "The Russian View on American Literature," *Bookman,* XLIV, 47 (September, 1916).

purely humorous sketches, issued sometimes in "cheap yellow-covered brochures," enjoyed a good sale.[155]

When control of the publishing industry in Russia passed into the hands of the Soviet there was apparently no great change in the reading taste of the people, although many books were kept out of the country for political reasons. Of all American authors in the Soviet Union only Jack London is more widely read than Clemens, whose books sold 3,100,000 copies between 1918 and 1943.[156] This popularity has led to a multitude of translations of Twain into Russian, each one of which, naturally enough, reflects the political and nationalistic leanings of the translator. For instance, a version of *Innocents Abroad* published during the Czarist regime expounded the beneficence of the upper classes, whereas a later version prepared by the Leninites satirizes the former Russian nobility.[157] A fine edition of Mark Twain's complete works has been issued, along with nineteen separate printings of his most popular books. During the Second World War Soviet publishing houses printed several editions for the Red Army and Red Navy publishing branches.[158] Soviet criticism has since followed an underlying theme of patriotism, a nationalistic attitude the disillusioned Twain could never hold.[159] What the future of Mark Twain's reputation in Russia will be, we must wait and see; perhaps it will suffer as it did in Germany under the Nazis.

That Clemens should still find a wide audience abroad, even as at home, is not surprising, for he was an interna-

155 *Idem.*

156 Cowley, *op. cit.*, II, 1386.

157 Albert Parry, "Mark Twain in Russia," *Twainian*, I, 1 (April, 1939).

158 Magidoff, *op. cit.*, p. 11. Some volumes have been illustrated. Magidoff reproduces an interesting illustration by Feodor Konstantin for "Journalism in Tennessee," *Ibid.*, p. 10.

159 Clarence Manning, "Socialist Realism and the American Success Novel," *South Atlantic Quarterly*, XLVIII, 218 (April, 1949).

tionally minded thinker, one who had resided in, or visited, all the great countries of Europe. Travel in foreign lands, residence abroad, contact with the most intellectual and cultured society on both sides of the Atlantic gave him a cosmopolitan vision. Even his Americanism was continental in scope rather than sectional. The native Southwesterner, born in a Missouri slave-holding community, of Virginia and Kentucky parentage, soon transformed himself into the Westerner, then into the resident of New England—finally to become the complete cosmopolitan of New York, London, and the Continent. Yet, withal, he remained the typical American—indeed, the boy from Hannibal—until the end of his days. So substantial and strong was the base of Twain's character that the superstructure of later experience only added to his intellectual height and breadth; the soundness of heart and mind were native. Mark Twain was an artist of great human spirit, devoted to honor and truth, whose concern for his fellow man was profound and universal.

SELECTED BIBLIOGRAPHY

MARK TWAIN'S PLACE IN LITERATURE

United States

Arvin, Newton. "Mark Twain: 1835–1935," *New Republic* LXXXIII, 125–7 (June 12, 1935).

[Sees Clemens surviving more as a legendary figure than as a literary man.]

Bellamy, Gladys Carmen. *Mark Twain as a Literary Artist.* Norman: University of Oklahoma Press, 1950.

[Useful criticism of Twain's creative art.]

Boynton, Percy H. "The West and Mark Twain" in *American Literature.* Boston: Ginn and Company, 1919, pp. 380–95.

[Sees Twain as a serious artist of importance.]

Brooks, Van Wyck. *The Ordeal of Mark Twain.* New York: E. P. Dutton & Company, revised edition, 1933.

[The critic here failed to see Twain's greatness.]

——. *The Times of Melville and Whitman.* New York: E. P. Dutton & Company, 1947.
[Interesting, sometimes stimulating.]

Cowie, Alexander. *The Rise of the American Novel.* New York: American Book Co., 1948.
[Chapter XIV contains a sound critical evaluation of Twain as a novelist.]

De Voto, Bernard. *Mark Twain's America.* Boston: Little, Brown and Company, revised edition, 1935.
[Indispensable as an evaluation of Twain's contribution to literature.]

Ferguson, DeLancey. *Mark Twain: Man and Legend.* Indianapolis: Bobbs-Merrill Company, 1943.
[This excellent study is equally as valuable for criticism as for biography.]

Gohdes, Clarence. "Mirth for the Million," *The Literature of the American People,* edited by Arthur H. Quinn. New York: Appleton-Century-Crofts, 1951, pp. 708–20.
[Sees Clemens chiefly as our supreme contribution to world humor.]

Grattan, C. Hartley. "Mark Twain" in *American Writers on American Literature.* New York: Horace Liveright, Inc., 1931.
[Valuable estimate, still of interest.]

Henderson, Archibald. *Mark Twain.* New York: Frederick A. Stokes, 1911.
[A perceptive evaluation of Twain as a world author.]

Howells, William Dean. *My Mark Twain.* New York: Harper & Brothers, 1910.
[Laudatory, but in keeping with recent evaluations.]

Matthews, Brander. *Introduction to American Literature.* New York: American Book Co., revised edition, 1923.
[Chapter XVII is an excellent appreciation of Twain's place in literature.]

Parrington, Vernon L. "The Culture of the Seventies" in *Main Currents in American Thought.* New York: Harcourt, Brace & Co. III, 86–101.
[Still an interesting appraisal.]

Pattee, Fred Lewis, editor. *Mark Twain: Representative Selections.* New York: American Book Company, 1935.
[Sees Clemens as an author more popular than great.]

Quinn, Arthur Hobson. "Mark Twain and the Romance of Youth" in *American Fiction: An Historical and Critical Survey*. New York: D. Appleton-Century Company, 1936, pp. 243–256.

[Views Clemens in the light of the Genteel Tradition.]

Rascoe, Burton. "Mark Twain: the First American" in *The Story of the World's Great Writers*. New York: Blue Ribbon Books, 1932.

[Sees Twain as the first native American writer of world stature.]

Sherman, Stuart P. "Mark Twain" in *The Cambridge History of American Literature*. New York: Macmillan Company, 1921, III, 3–20.

[Sound comments, still of value.]

Van Doren, Carl. "Mark Twain," in *The American Novel,* revised edition. New York: Macmillan, 1940.

[Sketchy, but good, general estimate.]

Van Doren, Mark. "A Century of Mark Twain," *Nation* CXLI, 472–4 (October 23, 1935).

[Credits Twain's popularity to the ease and naturalness of his stories.]

Wagenknecht, Edward. *Mark Twain: The Man and His Work.* New Haven, Connecticut: Yale University Press, 1935.

[Good, general evaluation.]

Wecter, Dixon. "Mark Twain" in *Literary History of the United States.* New York: Macmillan & Company, 1948, II, 917–39.

[Sound, critical estimate.]

West, Ray B., Jr. "Mark Twain's Idyl of Frontier America," *University of Kansas City Review,* XV, 92–104 (Winter, 1948).

[Views *Huckleberry Finn* as the nearest thing we have to a national epic.]

Wister, Owen. "In Homage to Mark Twain," *Harpers,* CLXXI, 547–56 (October, 1935).

[Sees Twain as representative of the "Lincoln era."]

England

Archer, William. *America To-Day*. London: W. Heinemann, 1900.

[Affirmation of Twain's genius.]

Cunliffe, Marcus. *The Literature of the United States.* London: Penguin Books, 1954.

[Interesting criticism of Twain as a classic.]

Gohdes, Clarence. *American Literature in Nineteenth Century England.* New York: Columbia University Press, 1944.

[The best study of Twain's popularity in England.]

Gordon, George Stuart. *Anglo-American Literary Relations.* Oxford: University Press, 1942.

[Sees Twain as a genius who wrote one of the world's great books.]

Haweis, H. R. *American Humorists.* London: Chatto and Windus, 1883.

[Perceived Twain's artistry.]

Henderson, Archibald. *Mark Twain.* New York: Frederick A. Stokes Company, 1911.

[Contains some early English comments on Twain's work, and a bibliography.]

Kipling, Rudyard. *From Sea to Sea.* New York: Doubleday and McClure, 1899.

[High praise from England's most popular writer of the day.]

Nichol, John. *American Literature: an Historical Sketch,* 1620–1880. Edinburgh: Adam and Charles Black, 1882.

[Sees Twain only as the jester.]

Roberts, R. E. "Mark Twain," *Fortnightly Review,* n.s. DCCCXXVII, 583–92 (November, 1935).

[Critical estimate based on *Huckleberry Finn.*]

Ward, A. C. *American Literature 1880–1930.* London: Methuen & Co., Ltd., 1932.

[Inclines toward the Brooks theory.]

France

Arnavon, Cyrille. *Les Lettres américaines devant la Critique française* (1887–1917). Paris: Société D'Edition les Belles Lettres, 1951.

[Contains information about French translations of Twain.]

Asselineau, Roger. *The Literary Reputation of Mark Twain from 1910 to 1950.* Paris: Librairie Marcel Didier, 1954.

[Sound critical essay with useful bibliography.]

Bentzon, Th. "Les Humoristes américains: I. Mark Twain," *Revue des Deux Mondes,* C, 313–335 (July, 1872).

[The article introducing Twain to the French.]

——. "L'Age doré en Amérique," *Revue des Deux Mondes,* XLV, 319–43 (March 15, 1875).

[Reviews and quotes from *The Gilded Age.*]

Charpentier, John. "Humour anglais et humour américain. A propos du centenaire de Mark Twain," *Mercure de France,* CCLXIV, 475–500 (December 15, 1935).

[Sees Twain as the Western savage.]

De Lautrec, Gabriel. "Mark Twain," *Mercure de France,* CCLXIV, 69–82 (November, 1935).

[Praise of Twain which cites none of his great work.]

Forgues, Eugène. "Les Caravanes d'un humoriste," *Revue des Deux Mondes,* LVI, 875–918 (February 15, 1886).

[An adverse estimate.]

Henderson, Archibald. *Mark Twain.* New York: Frederick A. Stokes Company, 1911.

[Quotes a number of early French criticisms; contains a bibliography.]

Le Breton, Maurice. "Un Centenaire: Mark Twain," *Revue Anglo-Américaine,* XII, 401–19 (June, 1935).

[Affirms Mark little known in France, but a sound critical evaluation.]

Lemonnier, Leon. "Les debuts d'un humoriste," *La Grande Revue,* CXLIX, 76–88 (November, 1935).

[Biographical rather than critical.]

——. *Mark Twain: L'Homme et Son Oeuvre,* Paris: Librairie Arthème Fayard, 1946.

[A full length study, sound in judgment.]

Peckham, H. Houston. "Is American Literature Read and Respected in Europe?" *South Atlantic Quarterly,* XIII, 382–8 (October, 1914).

[Found Twain little read in France.]

Germany

Colbron, Grace I. "The American Novel in Germany," *Bookman,* XXXIX, 45–9 (March, 1914).

[Found Twain second only to Bret Harte in popularity of American writers.]

Hemminghaus, Edgar H. *Mark Twain in Germany.* New York: Columbia University Press, 1939.

[A definitive study; contains bibliography.]

Henderson, Archibald. *Mark Twain.* New York: Frederick A. Stokes Company, 1911.

[Records Clemens reception in Germany and Austria.]

Möhle, Günter. *Das Europabild Mark Twain.* Berlin: Junker und Dunnhaupt Verlag, 1940.

[Stresses racial rather than Democratic aspects of *The Innocents Abroad* and *A Connecticut Yankee.*]

Schönemann, Friedrich. *Mark Twain als literarische Persönlichkeit.* Jena: Verlag der Frommanschen Buchhandlung, Walter Biedermann, 1925.

[The most important German study of Twain; refutes the Brooks theory.]

——. "Neue Mark-Twain-Studien," *Neueren Sprachen,* XLIV, 260–72 (1936).

[Critical evaluation of DeVoto, Brashear, Wagenknecht and others' contributions.]

Smith, C. Alphonso. *Die Amerikanische Literatur.* Berlin: Weidmann, 1912.

[Lectures at the University of Berlin, helping to introduce Clemens to the students.]

Scandinavia

Benson, Adolph B. "Mark Twain's Contacts with Scandinavia," *Scandinavian Studies and Notes,* XIV, 159–67 August, 1937).

[Chiefly biographical.]

Benson, Ivan. "Mark Twain in Swedish," *Twainian,* II, 4 (May, 1940).

[Notes several translations.]

Brownell, George H. "En Droppe Negerblod," *Twainian,* VII, 6 (January, 1948).

[*Pudd'nhead Wilson* in Swedish.]

Cowley, Malcolm. "American Books Abroad," *Literary History of the United States.* New York: Macmillan Company, 1948, Vol. II, pp. 1374–91.

[Comments on Twain in Sweden.]

Liljegren, S. B. *The Revolt Against Romanticism in American Literature as Evidenced in the Works of S. L. Clemens.* Upsala: Lundequistska Bokhandeln, 1945.

[Relates Clemens to the stream of European realism.]

Russia

Cowley, Malcolm. "American Books Abroad," *Literary History of the United States*. New York: Macmillan Company, 1948, II, 1374–91.

[Notes Twain's introduction and popularity in Russia.]

Magidoff, Robert. "American Literature in Russia," *Saturday Review of Literature,* XXIX, 9–11 (November 2, 1946).

[Interesting and informative.]

Mendelson, M. *Mark Twain.* Moscow: Fskblksm Molodaya Gvardiya (Young Guard, 1939).

[Follows the frustration theory of Brooks and attempts to fit Mark into the Soviet pattern, blaming his failure on his environment and lack of courage.]

Parry, Albert. "Mark Twain in Russia," *Twainian,* I, 1 (April, 1939).

[Notes differences in translations before and after the revolution.]

Yarmolinsky, A. "The Russian View on American Literature," *Bookman,* XLIV, 44–8 (September, 1916).

[Contains interesting facts to that date.]

Other Countries

Hüppy, August. *Mark Twain und die Schweiz.* Zürich: Reutimann Co., 1935.

[A Swiss compliment to Twain.]

Leacock, Stephen. "Two Humorists: Charles Dickens and Mark Twain," *Yale Review,* XXIV, 118–29 (September, 1934).

[An appreciation by a Canadian humorist.]

Templin, E. H. "On Re-reading Mark Twain," *Hispania,* XXIV, 269–76 (October, 1941).

[Sees Clemens as "a sort of adolescent Cervantes."]

Verdaguer, Mario. "Humorismo inglés e ironía yanqui," *La Razón* (Panama), V, 2 (July 3, 1937).

[Stresses English appreciation of Clemens.]

INDEX

Abbreviations: *n* indicates footnote; *b*, bibliography

G